Respect for the Elderly

Implications for Human Service Providers

Edited by
Kyu-taik Sung and Bum Jung Kim

University Press of America,® Inc.
Lanham · Boulder · New York · Toronto · Plymouth, UK

Copyright © 2009 by
University Press of America,® Inc.
4501 Forbes Boulevard
Suite 200
Lanham, Maryland 20706
UPA Acquisitions Department (301) 459-3366

Estover Road
Plymouth PL6 7PY
United Kingdom

Library of Congress Control Number: 2008942617
ISBN-13: 978-0-7618-4530-0 (paperback : alk. paper)
eISBN-13: 978-0-7618-4531-7

For the reillustration of

the values of humanity and propriety

in treating our elderly

Contents

Foreword   ix
Contributors   xi
Preface   xiii
Acknowledgments   xvii

Part I—Respect for Persons

1. Respect For Persons As Ends   3
R. S. Downie and Elizabeth Telfer

2. Respect and Care: Toward Moral Integration   23
Robin S. Dillon

3. Roots of Elder Respect: Ideals and Practices in East Asia   45
Kyu-taik Sung

Part II—Perspectives on Care and Service

4. The Principles of the Belmont Report Revisited   65
Eric J. Cassell

5. Respectful Treatment Values Inherent in Medical Education   81
Martin R. Lipp

6. Respect for Persons: Nursing Ethics   91
Rose Mary Volbrecht

7. Respect and Caring: Ethics and Essence of Nursing   101
Brighid Kelly

8. Respecting Ethnic Elders: A Perspective for Care Providers   117
  Jo Ann Damron-Rodriguez

9. Social Workers Demonstrate Respect for Elderly Clients   133
  Kyu-taik Sung

Part III—Expressions and Practices

10. Elder Respect Among American College Students: Exploration of   149
Behavioral Forms
  Kyu-taik Sung

11. How Do I Respect Thee? Let Me Count the Ways: Deference   167
Towards Elderly Men and Women
  Philip Silverman and Robert J. Maxwell

12. Chinese Young Adults and Elder Respect Expressions in Modern   179
Times
  Kyu-taik Sung

13. Respect for the Elders in Japan   217
  Erdman B. Palmore and Daisaku Maeda

14. Elder Respect Among Young Adults: Exploration of Behavioral   225
Forms in Korea
  Kyu-taik Sung and Han Sung Kim

15. Respect Redefined: Focus Group Insights From Singapore   241
  Kalyani Mehta

Part IV—Comparative Study

16. Culture: The Conspicuous Missing Link to Understand Ethical   259
and Moral Dimensions of Human Care
  Madeleine Leininger

17. Elder Respect Among Young Adults: A Cross-Cultural Study of   271
Americans and Koreans
   Kyu-taik Sung

18. A Longitudinal Analysis of Perceived Respect Among Elders: 287
Changing Perceptions for Some Ethnic Groups
   Judith G. Chipperfield and Betty Havens

19. Respect for the Elderly in Asia: Stability and Change   301
   Berit Ingersoll-Dayton and Chanpen Saengtienchai

20. Filial Piety in Asian Chinese Communities   319
   Nelson Chow

Part V—Religious Perspectives

21. Filial Morality in an Aging Society   327
   Stephen G. Post

22. Respectful Service and Reverent Obedience: A Jewish View on   339
Making Decisions for Incompetent Parents
   Benjamin Freedman

23. Repayment for Parents' Kindness: Buddhist Way   353
   Kyu-taik Sung

24. Islamic Teachings and Elder Respect   367
   Ahmad H. Sakr, Hammudah Abdalati, and Maulana Qazi Dyed
Shah Ali Soofi

Index   375
About the Editors   379

Foreword

One main objective of this volume is to introduce papers and book chapters describing the way in which elder respect is practiced in various cultural and human service settings. Writings on elder respect are scarce in our culture, but Dr. Sung and Mr. Kim have obtained a number of rare writings published in the East as well as in the West.

In this impressive volume, the editors present to us the challenge of treating elderly persons with respect. Human service providers, wherever they may be located, should benefit from its comprehensive coverage of academic and practice aspects of elder respect. However, for the providers in the United States, it will have special value. In this country, the number of aged persons is steadily increasing. In the development of programmatic efforts for senior Americans, the greatest stress has been on tangible services. But a more qualitative aspect of care, such as respect—a value which Americans traditionally cherished—has not received due attention. Also, studies have reported recently on tendencies of some adults to disrespect older persons by neglecting and disregarding their problems, and by mistreating frail and sick elderly persons. The publication of this volume could not have come at a better time.

Dr. Sung's research on elder respect spans decades. Elder respect is the most stressed expression of filial piety—the value that has most influenced the way in which East Asian people treated their elders with respect for generations. Dr. Sung has developed a typology of elder respect. Based on empirical data obtained from his national and cross-cultural studies, he has identified comprehensive sets of expressions and categories of elder respect being practiced in different nations and cultures, and published these results in prominent journals and books in the United States.

Based on Dr. Sung's extensive academic knowledge and practical experience in the subject, the editors have carefully selected those writings which are relevant to services for elderly persons, and incorporated them into a comprehensive presentation of various dimensions of elder respect.

Papers and book chapters in this volume are based on quantitative as well as qualitative data obtained from empirical studies conducted in the West and the

East. Despite the fact that elder respect has influenced people for generations, the concept of it remains too general and abstract to provide clear guidelines for practice and research. Yet, elder respect remains as an essential element in up-lifting elders' statuses, in integrating them more fully into family and society, and in providing them with proper human care and services. The chapters in this volume explore significant issues and specific categories and measures focusing on such care and services.

The increasing need of older people for humane and proper treatment will remain to be an important issue in our aging society. Readers in both the West and the East will find that this volume provides insight and guidance as to what ways elder respect needs to be expressed and demonstrated in services and caring for older people in a variety of human interactions and service settings.

Against that background, the publication of this comprehensive and scholarly presentation of respect for the elderly with regard to timely issues—moral and ethical aspects of elder respect, needs for elder respect in practice settings, ways in which elder respect are demonstrated in different cultures, similarities and differences in the practice of elder respect, and religious aspects of respecting elderly persons—is an event to be celebrated.

Readers in the West and the East who are interested in care and services for the elderly and cultural differences between ethnic groups and nations will find this volume very useful in understanding the critical but overlooked issues of respect for the old.

Fernando Torres-Gil, Ph.D.
Acting Dean
School of Public Affairs
Director
Center of Policy Research on Aging
University of California, Los Angeles

Contributors

Hammudah Abdalati
Eric J. Cassell
Judith G. Chipperfield
Nelson Chow
Jo Ann Damron-Rodriguez
Robin D. Dillon
R. S. Downie
Benjamin Freedman
Betty Havens
Berit Ingersoll-Dayton
Brighid Kelly
Han Sung Kim
Madeleine M. Leininger
Martin R. Lipp
Daisaku Maeda
Robert J. Maxwell
Kalyani Mehta
Erdman B. Palmore
Stephen G. Post
Chanpen Saengtienchai
Ahmad H. Sakr
Philip Silverman
Ali Soofi
Kyu-taik Sung
Elizabeth Telfer
Rose Mary Volbrecht

Preface

We happened to come across only a small number of papers about how to respect the elderly (hereafter called "elder respect"). In our libraries, there were only a limited number of writings which took up the issue of elder respect and explored the meanings and expressions of it. This book introduces those writings.

Aged persons are those who have contributed to their families, communities and nations. Many of them have reared, cared for and educated children and youth. For these elderly, food, shelter and health care are all necessities. But they have another cardinal need: that is the need to be treated with respect. Without respect, society is less likely to treat and care for elderly persons as dignified members of society.

Many elderly persons have a variety of problems. To resolve these problems, they most often depend on human service providers outside of their home. When they are dependent upon these providers, respectful care has very significant implications. The elderly who are respected tend to have greater life satisfaction, which in turn enhances their sense of usefulness and involvement in their family, community, and with significant others.

Forms of elder respect—such as providing care and services using proper language and greetings, complying with elders' wishes, asking for their counsel and advice, giving precedential treatment, furnishing honorable seats, serving foods and drinks of their choice, etc. (Sung, 2004)—are all actions for conveying elder respect. These behavioral expressions reflect values of caring for and serving elderly persons with benevolence imbued with the sense of humaneness and propriety.

When receiving human services, elderly persons treated with respect are likely to involve themselves in a cooperative effort to achieve desired treatment outcomes whereby treatment benefit can be increased. Significantly, elder respect remains a crucial factor in delivering proper care and services and in improving elders' well being. Therefore, respect for persons has very important implications for human services.

It remains puzzling, however, that the theme of respect is so noticeably absent from most discourses concerning aging, with little discussion of respect in the relationship between the caregiver and the elderly care recipient.

In this book, we have tried to place the subject of elder respect in a broader context of human services as it is perceived and practiced in various service settings. We have put forward normative or value claims of various sorts with regard to elder respect. In addition, conceptual analyses and empirical findings on the theme of respect are presented. Respect is described in a more explanative and practicable way. The chapters in this book explain the reasons why elderly persons need to be treated with respect, and present specific ways in which respect can be demonstrated. We tried to introduce these ways in hope that the readers might consider that the term respect is in fact a variable that can be expressed in various forms of concrete and visible actions or behaviors.

Thus, the largest part of this book is devoted to discussions of the values of elder respect and actual practices of them. Some chapters come from the senior author's own writings done at the University of Southern California School of Social Work, where he benefited greatly from the support given to him by the dean Marilyn Flynn and the Wu Chair professorship.

In Part I of this book, we take up the subject of respect with the aim of pursuing the fundamental issues of respect for persons and the importance of the resolution of accompanying issues. The first two chapters critically discuss why respect for persons matters; this discussion extends to the Kantian critique of utilitarianism and how an impartial moral theory can accommodate the preferential treatment of persons. These chapters include the conceptual analysis of the fundamental reason why persons are to be respected and the connectedness between care and respect. The third chapter discusses the ideal and practice of elder respect prescribed in Confucian teachings which still influence the attitudes and behaviors of East Asian people toward the elderly. The root meanings of respect are explored and the forms and expressions by which respect is to be demonstrated are presented. Also in this chapter, the readers will find that care is part of respect. Thus, Part I combines a theoretical discourse on respect for persons with the discussion of the practical way in which respect is to be expressed.

In Part II, six chapters are presented. The perspectives and practices of elder respect by physician, nurses and social workers serving in the health care and social service settings are introduced. There are two chapters each discussing respect for patients by physicians, nurses, and social workers. Readers will find commonalities as well as certain differences in the perspectives and practices between the professions, service settings and subcultures in which the providers practice.

In Part III, we take up specific ways in which elder respect is expressed by young and old adults. A systematic exploration of the various ways of client respect is a challenging area in human services. Certain similarities and differences of behavioral expressions in which the sense of respect is conveyed are distinguished and categorized where possible based on empirical research in different nations.

Part IV presents four chapters on the practice of elder respect in different ethnic groups and cultures. Nowadays, transcultural knowledge of Western and non-Western cultures is needed to help human service providers deliver ethically proper care and services to clients of different cultural backgrounds. The papers included introduce findings from rare studies on elder respect from cross-cultural, cross-national and cross-ethnic comparisons of behavioral expressions of elder respect.

In Part V, four chapters introduce how respect for aged persons are perceived of and practiced in different religious communities—Christian, Jewish, Buddhist and Islamic. These chapters provide insights into religious ethics with which an aging society can sustain the morality of elder respect and mitigate any trend toward disrespectful treatment of aged persons.

As the world becomes more multicultural, elderly clients with various cultural and ethnic backgrounds will expect that their values and ways of relating with others be respected and acted upon properly by their care and service providers. Therefore, knowledge about how service providers and caregivers in different cultures and nations treat aged persons becomes important.

The writings presented in this book describe issues of elder respect in a variety of ways depending on the individual authors' beliefs and cultural and social characteristics. We are well aware that some of the writings do not fit together into a neat whole. However, the introduction of the various writings should situate our editorial project within a larger context of contemporary interpretation of elder respect and give the reader some scheme as to how we think the chapters of this admittedly loosely constructed book hang together.

We hope that, through this book, the meaning and practices of elder respect in different cultures and service settings will be better understood by readers in human services as well as by those who are caring for elderly relatives in the West and the East.

The editors are grateful to Elder-Respect International for its aid in bringing our work to completion.

Kyu-taik Sung, M.S.W., Ph.D.
The University of Michigan

Bum Jung Kim, M.S.W., Ph.D. Candidate
University of California at Los Angeles

Acknowledgments

We gratefully acknowledge the publishers of the following writings who permitted the authors to use these articles, chapters and excerpts from their journals and books. The order of these acknowledgements and the lists within them is the same as the order in which the extracts appear in the book.

Schocken Books (Random House Publisher Services): R. S. Downie and E. Telfer. 1970. Respect for persons as ends. In R. S. Downie and E. Telfer, Respect for Persons. 13-37.

University of Calgary Press: Robin S. Dillon. 1992. Respect and care toward moral integration. Canadian Journal of Philosophy, 22(1). Univ. of Calgary Press.

The Hastings Center: Eric J. Cassell. 2000. The principles of the Belmont Report Revisited. Hastings Center Report, 30 (12-21).

Elsvier: Martin R. Lipp. 1986. Respectful treatment: A practical handbook of patient care. 2nd ed.

Prentice-Hall: Rose Mary Volbrecht. 2002. Nursing ethnics: Communities in dialogue. "Rule ethics: Moral rules relevant nursing practice" (47-56).

Wayne State University Press: Brighid Kelly. 1990. Respect and caring: Ethics and essence of nursing. In M. M. Leininger (Ed.). Ethical and Moral Dimensions of Care.

The Haworth Press: Jo Ann Damron-Rodriguez. 1998. Respecting ethnic elders: A perspective for care providers, Journal of Gerontological Social Work, 29(2/3).

Baywood Publishing Co.: Kyu-taik Sung. 2002. Elder respect among American college students: Exploration of Behavioral forms. International Journal of Aging and Human Development, 55(4).

Philip Silverman and Robert J. Maxwell. 1977. How do I respect thee? Let me count the ways: Deference towards elderly men and women. Behavior Science Research, 13(91-108).

Duke University Press: Eldmore B. Palmore and Daisaku Maeda. 1985. Respect for the Elders. In The Honorable Elders Revisited (81-89).

Transaction Periodicals Consortium, Rutgers-The State University of New Jersey: Kyu-taik Sung and Han Sung Kim. 2003. Elder Respect among young adults: Exploration of behavioral forms in Korea. Ageing International, 28 (279-294).

Baywood Publishing Co.: Kalyani Mehta. 1997. Respect redefined: Focus group insights from Singapore. International Journal of Aging and Human Development, 44 (205-219).

Wayne State University Press: Madeleine M. Leininger. 1990. Culture: The conspicuous missing link to understand ethical and moral dimensions of human care. In M. M. Leininger (Ed.), Ethical and Moral Dimensions of Care.

Elsvier: Kyu-taik Sung. 2004. Elder respect among young adults: A cross-cultural study of Americans and Koreans. Journal of Aging Studies, 18(215-230).

University of Toronto Press: Judith G. Chipperfield. 1992. A longitudinal analysis of perceived respect among elders: Changing perceptions for some ethic groups. Canadian Journal on Aging, 11(15-30).

Baywood Publishing Co.: Berit Ingersoll-Dayton and Chanpen Saengtienchai. 1999. Respect for the elderly in Asia: Stability and change. International Journal of Aging and Human Development, 48(113-130).

5th Asia/Oceania Regional Congress of Gerontology: Nelson Chow. 1995. Filial piety in Asian Chinese communities.

The Haworth Press: Stephen G. Post. 1989. Filial Morality in an Aging Society. Journal of Religion & Aging, 5(4)(15-29).

The Hastings Center: Benjamin Freedman. 1996. Respectful service and referent obedience: A Jewish view on making decisions for incompetent parents. Hastings Center Reports, 26(31-37).

The Haworth Press: Kyu-taik Sung. 2003. Journal of Religious Gerontology. Repayment for parents' kindness: Buddhist way.

The Islamic Education Center, Walnut, CA: Ahmad H. Sak, Hamrnudah Abdalati, and Ali Soofi . 2007. Respecting parents: The Muslim Way. Writings of others on Islamic teachings on support for parents and elders.

PART I

Respect for Persons

Part I consists of three chapters that introduce the central ideal of respect for persons that has influenced peoples in the West and the East. These three chapters set the stage for the rest of the book with an extensive discussion of the principles of respect for persons and the ways in which respect is to be practiced. The critical discussions presented in Part I will place this effort in context. The first chapter, *Respect for Persons as End* by R. S. Downie and E. Telfer, presents a discussion on 'respect for persons' as the regulative principle of morality. The authors argue that the expression 'respect for persons' is used to indicate both an attitude which is morally fundamental and an action to be explained in terms of an attitude. The attitude involves the evaluative concept of a person who is worthy of respect, an account in term of rational will which is exercised by our abilities to be self-determining and rule-following. Chapter 2 presents *Respect and Care: Toward Moral Integration* by R. S. Dillons. The author argues that the conception of respect incorporates many of the most characteristic elements of the care perspective, and subsequently defines that care is one kind of respect. Hence, the moral orientation of respect and care involves the same perception of their objects and regards the same dimensions of human beings as worthy of attention—the same moral concern under two different labels. Care respect involves a commitment to attend and determination to care for with tender and gentle emotions by impartial love for all. She argues that this conception of care respect is different from Kantian respect that is dispassionate and detached valuing of others. Care respect joins individuals together in a community of mutual concern and mutual aid through appreciation of individuality and interdependence. In Chapter 3, we examine Confucian conception of respect which has greatly influenced the attitudes and behaviors of East Asian peoples toward parents and elderly persons. The paper introduces a study which explored the root meanings of respect for parents and elders by an extensive review of passages excerpted from Confucian classics. It distinguishes the forms of respect ranging from care respect to ancestor respect. In Confucian teachings, respect is also closely tied to care. Communality between East Asian peoples in practicing the forms and changing expressions of respect among the young are discussed. The inventory of traditional forms from this study provides specific forms against which the practice of respect might be assessed in the East Asian cultural context.

Chapter 1

Respect For Persons As Ends

R. S. Downie and Elizabeth Telfer

1. Ends

There is something odd about speaking of *persons* as ends, although this oddity does not strike one at first because the Kantian formula is so familiar. One begins to see it as odd, however, if one considers what is meant by an 'end'. The term is ambiguous, but it is used to mean, in the first place, a purpose, aim or objective. It is therefore something which can (logically) be desired and brought about. But can one speak of 'desiring and bringing about persons'? This does not seem to be intelligible (in any relevant sense), and the reason is that a category mistake is involved. To bring this out let us consider the category of that which can be desired or brought about.

The category of what can be desired or brought about seems to be that of a situation or state of affairs. It may be objected that we can speak of desiring a *thing* ('I want an apple') or *to do* something ('I want to sing and skip about'). But this difficulty is only apparent. For when a man wants a thing, he wants some state of affairs to begin in which this activity is taking place, or that he wants the present state of activity on his part or another's to continue. We can therefore characterize the category of the object as a situation or state of affairs which is to be brought about or maintained; and when one talks of 'desiring an x' it is usually clear from the context and the sense of 'x' what state of affairs is in question in any given case. A *person* cannot therefore be an end in this sense because it is not clear how he is linked with a situation which can be desired or brought about. It is true that his continued existence might be so described. But there is more to treating a person as an end that desiring his continued existence.

An 'end' can mean, in the second place, that which is desirable in itself. This sense of 'end' seems to be closer to what we are seeking, for it can be used to distinguish that which is desirable as a means from that which is desirable as an end; and this distinction seems to have connections with treating people as means and treating them as ends. It is true that there can be chains of means and ends, so that what in one context is desirable as an end may in another be desirable only as a means to a further end. For example, the winning of the battle may be desirable as a means to the desirable end of winning the way; but the winning of the war can itself be viewed as a means to the further desirable end of a political settlement. Yet chains of means and ends must stop somewhere, and where they stop we have an end-in-itself. Can we say that persons are ends desirable in themselves?

We cannot, for once again we are in the wrong category: that which is desirable can necessarily be desired and, as we have argued, all that logically can be desired are situations or states of affairs; but persons are not situations or states of affairs. Thus, while the sense of 'end' which means that 'that which is desirable' enables us to introduce the distinction, certainly relevant to our purposes, of means and ends, it does not enable us to identify the sense in which we can speak of persons as ends.

There is, however, a third sense in which 'end' can be used: an 'end' can mean 'that which is valuable in itself'. It may be thought that the distinction between the desirable and the valuable is merely one of linguistic style. But this is not so, for in discussing the valuable we are not restricted to situations or states of affairs; a thing or an activity can be said to be valuable in itself. Moreover, the distinction between means and ends is still relevant to this sense of 'end'; we can speak of something being valuable as a means or being valuable as an end. Now to regard something as being valuable merely as a means is to regard it as valuable merely for what one can get out of it—it is no more than useful. A valuable thing which is not merely a means is valuable in itself. It should be noted that to say that a thing is valuable in itself is not to exclude the possibility that it is valuable *also* as a means and can be regarded or treated as a means; it is to say only that it is not *merely* a means. Applying this to persons, we can say that the meaning of the injunction to treat and regard people not merely as means but also as ends is that we ought to treat them as valuable in themselves and not only as useful instruments. Certainly, the postman is used to deliver our letters, but it is wrong to regard him solely under that description.

So far we have tried to show that respecting a person as an end means regarding him and treating him as something which is not merely useful but also valuable in itself. The task which remains is that of trying to explain what is meant by a thing's or a person's being valuable in itself in those cases which cannot be explained by equating this description with 'desirable in itself'.

Roughly, a situation which is desirable in itself is one which should be *brought about* because of what it is, while a thing which is valuable in itself is one which should be *cherished* because of what it is. The expression 'because of what it is' suggests not only why it is valuable but also what cherishing it amounts to; to cherish a thing is to care about its essential features—those which, as we say, 'make it what it is'—and to consider important not only that it should continue to exist but also that it should flourish. Hence, to respect a person as an end is to respect hi for those features which make him what he is as a person and which, when developed, constitute his flourishing.

2. Rules, Principles and Attitudes

There is sometimes ambiguity, when 'respect for persons' is spoken of as a moral *principle*, as to whether it is *one* of our basic principles, on a par, say, with principles dealing with truth-telling or promise-keeping (if we assume for the moment that they are on a par with each other) or whether it is the basic moral principle. If the first interpretation is adopted, then to respect persons as ends will be one of the many specific requirements of the moral life; if the second, the principle will sum up or characterize what all the other specific requirements have in common—they will all be ways or modes of respecting persons. If we adopt the second interpretation we can regard the many specific requirements of morality as reflecting the existence of moral *rules*, while 'respect for persons as ends' will express their supreme regulative *principle*. The second interpretation is the one adopted and defended in this essay.

Now to regard 'respect for persons' as the supreme regulative principle of morality still leaves unresolved an ambiguity as to its category. For sometimes philosophers speak of it as a *principle*, but sometimes as an *attitude*. What is the relationship between a principle and an attitude?

The term 'attitude' is used a good deal in recent moral philosophy, but the frequency of its occurrence is probably connected with its convenient lack of precision. For example, Professor P. Nowell-Smith is explicit that he has chosen the term 'attitude' in his expressions 'pro-' and 'con-attitude' precisely because it is vague, and he is not even bothered by the fact that some of the items in his lists of pro- and con-attitudes are not really attitudes at all.[1] Professor R. M. Hare is more definite in the meaning he attaches to the term.[2] He writes that if the term 'attitude' means anything, it means a principle of action. But while it is certainly correct to say that an attitude will necessarily have connections with principles of action, the connection cannot be one of identity, for the notion of an attitude is wider than that of a principle of action to have a cold bath in the mornings we still cannot tell from this knowledge alone even such basic things as whether his attitude towards cold baths is *pro* or *con*; he may like them, or he may dislike them but have a pro-attitude towards health or towards a reputation for endurance. What, then, is the connection between an attitude and a principle of action?

There are two connections, one logical and one causal. There is a logical connection in that if a person has a certain attitude towards something he will necessarily adopt certain principles of action towards it *other things being equal*, and the general nature of the principles can be inferred from knowledge of the attitude. We need to add the qualification in order to allow for conflicting attitudes. Thus, if a man has an attitude of fear towards cows, he will (other things being equal) adopt a principle of avoiding cows; but if he has another attitude which is one of humiliation and self-loathing towards the first attitude, he may well make it a principle to walk through fields of cows as often as he can, hoping to cure himself. We can make this point in another way by saying that certain principles of action are logically connected with certain attitudes in so far as these attitudes can be regarded as working in isolation.

As can be seen in the example of the man's attitude towards cows, the connection between an attitude and a principle can also be causal. For, even although a person does not have a certain attitude, if he consistently acts on a certain principle he may find he has acquired the attitude; to act *as if* one had a certain attitude may be the first step, and a necessary one, in acquiring the attitude.

If we apply this analysis to 'respect for persons as ends' we find that the expression can refer both to an attitude and to a principle of action. The attitude is *logically* basic in that the principle has to be explained in terms of it; it is the principle which logically must be adopted 'other things being equal' by someone who has the attitude of respect. But it is also *morally* basic in that it includes in its scope modes of feeling and thinking as well as of acting; and that which is morally fundamental is a total quality of life rather than a principle of action in the narrow sense. Our primary task is therefore to attempt to characterize the attitude of respect for persons. This will be the main concern of the present chapter, and in the next two we shall go on to consider in more detail the principles or rules of action to which this attitude may give rise. It should also be noted that the causal connection between the principle of action and the attitude is important, for it will enable us at a later stage to meet the objection that sometimes a person may not be able to act with a certain attitude: he can always act on a principle and thus take the first step towards acquiring or revitalizing the attitude. In the meantime, as a necessary preliminary to investigating the attitude of respect, let us consider further what it is to have an attitude.

3. Attitudes

The most important point about an attitude (for our purposes) may be brought out if we say that an attitude is two-sided. In the first place, it must be an attitude *of* something, where 'something' is always a disposition of some sort, such as hope, fear, distrust, forbearance or the like. In the second place, attitudes must be *to* something; it is conceptually impossible for an attitude to lack an object. It will be possible to describe this object in various ways, but for any particular attitude there will be one description under which the object of the attitude must be definition fall. For example, an attitude cannot logically be one of hope unless it is to an object which is believed to be in some sense a good to the hoper. The connection between hope and an imagined good is thus a necessary one, and we might go as far as to say that a person could not understand the meaning of 'hope' unless he knew what it was to imagine a good, and that to imagine a good is lay the foundation for acquiring the concept of hope. A similar analysis applies to all attitudes; they can be identified by means of the characteristics which their object is believed to possess, and thus a belief is at the root of all attitudes. The object under the description which is implied by the attitude-name may be called the *formal object* of that attitude. For example, the formal object of hope is an imagined good, which, it is believed, may come about, and the formal object of fear is a believed danger, and so on. Of course, this specification of the formal object of an attitude leaves quite open the answers to two further totally separate questions: what can (empirically) fall under a formal-object description—in the case of fear, for example, what can in fact be regarded by human beings as dangerous; and what should fall under it—what can truly or appropriately be regarded as dangerous. The first of these questions will be empirical; the second will be partly empirical but also partly evaluative, since the answer to it will depend in the last resort on our view of good and evil. They are thus quite different from any question as to the nature of the formal object of an attitude, which is really a conceptual question about the attitude itself.

What is the formal object of the attitude of respect? Of the several relevant senses of 'to respect' the one basic to 'respect for persons' was that of 'to value' or 'to esteem'; to respect persons is to value them as persons. It seems, then, that the formal object of the attitude we are investigating is something like 'that which is thought valuable or estimable. Thus, to understand in more detail what it means to respect persons we must find out why persons are regarded as valuable. Why, then, do we respect or value persons?

4. Persons

It may be said that we value people because of their merits; and merits vary a good deal. For example, we may respect, in the sense of 'value', one man for his courage while we may value another for his integrity. Now, if it is the case that we value people because of their merits, then, since people's merits vary, there seems to be a problem about understanding what it is about persons as such that we value; for it does not seem easy to compile a list of merits characterizing people as such in virtue of which they are objects of esteem or respect. A possible answer to the problem is to e found if we try to compile a list of those features which constitute the 'generic' human 'self' or are the 'distinctive endowment of a human being' (to use Mill's phrase).[3] Now the items on such a list would not exactly be merits in the sense in which integrity, say, is a merit; but they might nevertheless be the qualities which human beings value in themselves, for they would make up the 'distinctive endowment of a human being'. Moreover, there is a connection between valuing the 'distinctive endowment' of a human being (his 'generic' self) and valuing his specific merits or individuality (his 'idiosyncratic' self); for the development of the distinctive endowment will, granted the existence of idio-

syncratic variations in human beings, lead to the production of specific merits. Let
us at any rate assume the validity of this approach and enquire what is the distinctive endowment of a human being, or what constitutes the 'generic' human
self.

Before we try to answer this question, however, we should become clear
about what kind of question it is. It is not merely an investigation into what distinguishes humans from other animals. This can be seen by considering whether
we would call such things as differences in the number and type of teeth, or in the
way hair is distributed on the body, part of the 'distinctive endowment' of a human being. Rather we are looking for the most important difference between
humans and other animals, where 'important' indicates an *evaluative judgement*
which picks out certain features rather than others (as the evaluative word 'endowment' suggests). It may seem that we are simply *analyzing* the concept of a
person in an evaluatively neutral manner. But the concept of a *person* is already
an evaluative concept with something of the force of 'that which makes a human
being valuable' implied in it, and this is even more true of the more abstract
concept 'personality'. Thus, our original question, 'Why do we respect or value
persons?' can be put in another way: 'What makes a human being a *person* (with
all that that implies)?'

An objection may be raised here to the emphasis we have placed on the
evaluative nature of the concept of a person: namely, that it makes the dictum
'Persons ought to be respected' trivial, if not indeed analytic. But this would be a
mistaken objection. The concept of a person retains a connection with the less
evaluative concept of a human being. Thus, to say 'Persons ought to be respected'
is not merely to say 'What is valuable ought to be respected,' but rather, 'Humans
ought to be respected for what is valuable in them'. And this is not a trivial claim,
for it asserts that there is something worthy of respect about a human being. We
can now return to our enquiry into the distinctive nature of a human being, having
tried to clarify the nature of this enquiry.

Traditionally it has been assumed that basic to the distinctive endowment of a
human being is his ability to reason, and it may be helpful to discuss this view in
terms of the Kantian thesis that what gives a person absolute worth is his possession of a rational will. An initial objection to this claim might be that there is
surely more to human nature than an ability to reason. Such an objection would
misconceive what is meant by a 'rational will', for to have a rational will is to be
capable not simply of thinking rationally but also of acting rationally; to accept
the concept of 'rational will', for to have a rational will is to be capable not simply
of thinking rationally but also of acting rationally; to accept the concept of 'rational will' is to commit oneself to the view that reason can be practical as well as
theoretical. What is involved in the practical exercise of reason?

It involves, in the first place, the ability to choose for oneself, and, more
extensively, to formulate purposes, plans and policies of one's own. A second and
closely connected element is the ability to carry out decisions, plans or policies
without undue reliance on the help of others. These two abilities are connected by
a kind of pragmatic necessity, in that the ability to decide requires for its devel-

opment the concurrent development of the ability to execute. The importance we attach to these manifestations of the rational will is reflected in our firm approval of such traits of character as 'being able to stand on one's own feet', 'being relatively independent of others', 'sticking to one's guns', 'knowing what one wants, or what one ought to do', 'having aims in one's life (as distinct from being aimless)', 'knowing one's own mind' and 'being able to decide for oneself'. The necessary connection between developing such traits of character and being a person is reflected in theories of education which stress the importance of cultivating such dispositions in children. Conversely, to impair a person's abilities to formulate and carry out aims and policies of his own devising is to that extent to destroy him as a person. For example, if a person is injured physically or mentally there is often a tendency for friends to help too much; it is often easier to do something for people than to wait patiently and encourage while they do it for themselves, and this ease and convenience can assume the guise of kindness. But this may well be a subtle way of eroding an individual's nature as a person. The development of personality can also be blocked on a grander scale by political arrangements which restrict the range of images which people can form of themselves, as (perhaps) in Communist China. The exercise of the rational will involved in the foregoing examples are expressions of the first feature which makes up the distinctive endowment of a human being. Let us call it the ability to be self-determining. It is clearly important in any analysis of what is valuable in human personality. But there is a second feature—much stressed by Kant—involved in the possession of a rational will: the ability to govern one's conduct by rules, and indeed, more grandly, to adopt rules which one holds to be binding on oneself and all rational beings. This feature of the exercise of rational will is the one which most clearly distinguishes man from animals, for whereas some animals may possess to a slight extent the ability to carry out plans of their own devising (Köhler's apes)—or at least to act in ways which invite the use of such language—it is not plausible to suggest that they can have a conception of a rule, far less adopt rules for themselves. The ability to shape one's conduct in terms of rules, and to adopt (or even create) rules valid for all men, is called by Kant the autonomy of the will, and in the autonomy of the will Kant sees the very essence of personality. In Chapter V we shall cast doubt on one aspect of this Kantian conception—the notion of self-validating moral legislation—but meanwhile we can take from Kant the weaker thesis that human beings are not only self-determining but also formulate and follow rules, some of which (such as moral rules) they hold to be binding on others besides themselves.

It might be objected that the analysis has not yet mentioned emotions, feelings or desires. Yet they surely contribute something of distinctive value to human personality. Now it would be unfair to Kant to say that he saw no value at all in sentience, but he certainly did not see it as contributing anything to the intrinsic worth of a person; this he restricted to the exercise of reason in a narrower sense. But it may be that the sharp distinction between reason and sentience accepted by Kant and other philosophers is artificial. Sentience in the form in which it is characteristic of a person does not involve reason. It is true that some animals may be able to experience certain emotions, but the ability to feel and express a wide range of sustained emotions is characteristically human, and it involves the perception and discrimination which only reason can supply. Hence, to see the value of the human person as lying in the ability to experience emotion is not to see anything which is inconsistent with the exercise of rational will; for in so far as emotions are characteristically human they necessarily involve rational will. In a similar way, the experience of complex desires involves rational will. The exercise of rational will is to be seen, then, as something at once (in old-fashioned terminology) cognitive, conative and affective, and it is the ability to exercise such a will in self-determination and rule-following which gives human personality its intrinsic value.

It should be noted that Kant sees the rational will as being necessarily free. Now it is certainly the case that if the concept is being used to indicate that a person is a center of purposive activity in terms of rules, the rational will must be free in some sense. But whether it must be free in Kant's sense is a question which may be postponed. Let us rather consider what objections may be made against the view that the value of the human person is to be seen in his distinctive endowment—the possession of a rational will.

The main objection to putting the concept of rational will at the center of our analysis of human personality is that it seems to beg a number of questions about the nature of human action and purposiveness. We have been interpreting the characteristic endowment of a human being in terms of factors such a the ability to pursue ends, to create and adopt rules, to cultivate and sustain complex emotions. Now it may be said that to regard all these factors as necessarily involving or expressing rational will is to beg questions about the respective places of reason, feeling and desire in human life by giving the pride of place to reason without providing arguments to support this. There is a good deal of force in this objection, but, in mitigation, two points at least may be made. The first is that, as we have already stressed, to see the activity of reason in all these factors is by no means to imply that reason is the only thing operative in determining their nature; it is to stress only that without the activity of reason they could not have the nature hey do in fact have. The second point is that some of the gaps in the detailed argument required to establish the practical force of reason will be supplied later in the discussion [See Chapter V]. We shall therefore assume for the present that what is of value in persons can be characterized roughly as the exercise of rational will, taking that concept in a broad sense which does not exclude the concomitant presence of feeling and desire.[4]

5. Respecting Persons

It is now possible to make an attempt to explicate the concept of respect as it occurs in 'respect for persons'. We argued that the expression 'respect for persons' is used to indicate both an attitude which is commonly thought to be morally fundamental and a principle of action to be explained in terms of the attitude. The task of spelling out in detail the modes of conduct and of social organization which follow from the principle is reserved for the next two chapters and we shall be concerned here with analyzing the nature of the attitude conveyed by the concept of respect. We can see what this attitude involves in the light of our account of the evaluative concept of a *person* (the concept which picks out those features of human nature which make it worthy of respect); this account was in terms of rational will. In the exercise of rational will there are two main features, which we have called 'self-determination', and 'rule-following', and allowance must be made for the different nature of each in our shaping of the concept of respect. Let us first consider self-determination.

Kant provides an example in the *Groundwork* which hints at what is required as a morally fitting attitude towards self-determination. He takes the case of a man for whom things are going well but who sees others, whom he could help, struggling with hardships. Kant supposes that this man says to himself, 'What does it matter to me? Let everyone be as happy as Heaven wills or as he can make himself; I won't deprive him of anything; I won't even envy him; only I have no wish to contribute anything to his well-being or to his support in distress'.[5] Now Kant holds that such an attitude is the worst possible, but he also holds that a will which decided to act in such a manner 'would be in conflict with itself, since this situation might arise in which the man needed love and sympathy from others, and in which he would rob himself of all hope of the help he wants'. The point emerges more clearly when Kant discusses the same example again another context.[6] He writes that 'the natural end which all men seek is their own happiness. Now humanity could no doubt subsist if everybody contributed nothing to the happiness of others but at the same time refrained from deliberately impairing their happiness. This is, however, merely to agree negatively and not positively with humanity as an end in itself unless everyone endeavors also, so far as in him lies, to further the ends of others. For the ends of a subject who is an end in himself must, if this conception is to have its *full* effect in me, be also, as far as possible, *my* ends.' Kant is here suggesting that we should treat the ends of others, their ends of inclination, or what they pursue in the exercise of their self-determination, as if they were our own.

Now if respecting persons as self-determining agents involves positive concern for them of this nature it will involve what is best characterized by the concept of sympathy. But 'sympathy' can mean various things, and we shall have to qualify it to distinguish the relevant sense.

Professor W. G. Maclagan distinguishes three meanings of 'sympathy' (while admitting that other meanings may be possible).[7] The first he calls 'animal sympathy', by which he means a sort of 'psychological infection of one creature by another, as when panic fear spreads in a herd', and even in a human context there is 'in the operation of such animal sympathy, little or no sense of others as independent individual centers of experience. What we have is rather a sense of an indeterminate psychological atmosphere." In the second place, there is what Maclagan terms 'passive sympathy' or 'empathy'. This is sympathy in a distinctively human mode because, while there may be no clear line between it and animal sympathy, passive sympathy does involve consciousness of others as experiencing subjects. It is a matter of 'feeling oneself into the experience of the other' or of an emotional 'identification of ourself with the other'. The third form of sympathy, which Maclagan distinguishes as 'active sympathy', is the 'sympathy of practical *concern for* others as distinguished from simply *feeling with* them'. Now sympathy in the third of Maclagan's senses is the concept we require to analyze the example which Kant provided of a man who did not help others in pursuing their ends of inclination. Such a man did not show respect for persons as ends, and he did not do so because his conduct lacked the concern for others expressed in the concept of 'active sympathy'. We must therefore make room for this concept in our account of what it is to respect persons as rational wills.

It should be noted by way of qualification that in showing active sympathy for people—in making their ends our own—we must be careful not to help too much, as we argued in discussing the concept of self-determination. It is possible to secure a man's ends for him at the price of impairing his ability to pursue ends for himself, and so a morally fitting attitude towards self-determination must temper the giving of assistance to others with due regard for their ability to execute their own purposes.

Now at this point an objection may be lodged against our claim that active sympathy is a necessary ingredient in the concept of respect as we are using it. For we are proposing 'respect for persons' as a characterization of the ideal moral attitude, but it may be said that all the components in a moral attitude must be under the control of the will. What has been called 'active sympathy', however, seems to be a gift of nature—some may have it, others not—and it is a mistake to make a gift of nature a necessary ingredient in a moral attitude, especially the supreme one. Indeed, the argument may go on, Kant himself in an earlier passage seems to admit the possibility that a man may have by nature little or no sympathy with the sufferings of others, but he stresses that such a man, however cold or indifferent by temperament, could none the less help others not from inclination but from a sense of duty. (And he seems to have an admiration for such a person.) The objection, then, is that we cannot make sympathy a necessary ingredient of the supreme attitude of morality (however it may add grace to the moral life) because not everyone has been given a sympathetic nature. Moreover, we can do without it, for, if we are to believe Kant, it is possible to do one's duty without sympathy.

In replying to the objection we may first of all deny that it is in fact possible to do all that is implied in the attitude of respect for persons without active sympathy. It may be possible to go through the outward motions of actions which conform to duty without such sympathy, but the creative and imaginative exercise of the moral life is not possible without active sympathy. What, then, are we to say of the point that sympathy is a gift unevenly distributed by nature, and as such is unsuitable as an ingredient in a *moral* attitude? The answer is to insist that the relevant form of sympathy is not so unevenly distributed that it cannot form the basis of the supreme attitude of morality. And here again we may borrow an argument from Maclagan.[8]

Maclagan argues that what he has called 'passive sympathy' or 'empathy' is a natural capacity, 'natural not only as contrasted with moral but also as opposed to unnatural'. It may be inhibited in some cases, like other natural capacities, and what inhibits the growth of passive sympathy is an extreme of self-concern. 'If and so far as we can escape from obsession with ourselves, passive empathetic sympathy, I suggest, flowers in our experience quite naturally.' Now it may be argued that, even if we concede that passive human sympathy is a capacity in every normal human make-up, we have not shown that this is true of active sympathy, and is active sympathy which is required if we are to see in the attitude of respect a practical concern for other persons as such. The answer suggested by Maclagan is that it is psychologically impossible to sympathize with someone in the passive mode without at the same time having some measure of active concern for him. In fact, Maclagan goes as far as to doubt whether there are even *pathological* instances to the contrary in this matter.

We might indeed wonder whether there is not a *conceptual* connection between active and passive sympathy. For if passive sympathy involves sharing to some extent the feelings of others, must this not also mean sharing to some extent in the actions which are the expression of those feelings? If someone has a certain aim and e share with him his feelings about this aim, then, just as the existence of his own feelings implies the existence of a motivation to appropriate action, so we too will be motivated to take steps to fulfil the aim (to make his ends out own). In fact, the difficulty my be to prevent the identification of our feelings and his, and therefore of our policies, from becoming too complete; we may need to remind ourselves that the other man's aim is often not merely that he should in the end have something, but also that he should acquire it by his own efforts. The argument, then, is that active sympathy is necessarily connected with passive sympathy, and passive sympathy is a capacity which is the possession of all normal beings. It is therefore permissible to make active sympathy an ingredient in the attitude of respect, when that attitude is directed towards persons conceived as exercising self-determination in the pursuit of objects of inclination.

Support for the view that a natural capacity, such as that for sympathetic feeling, can be a permissible element in a moral attitude is to be obtained from a paper by Professor Bernard Williams.[9] Williams points out that the emotions are passively experienced, but he does not regard this fact as counting against their moral importance. On the contrary, he argues that the element of passivity 'may itself make a vital contribution to the notion of moral; sincerity'. There are, of course, as Williams admits, important distinctions to be drawn between various kinds of natural capacity—some will be more relevant to a moral attitude than others—but 'among the relevant sorts of characteristic, the capacity for creative emotional response has the advantage of being, if not equally, at least broadly, distributed'. Our claim is that active sympathy is one form of 'creative emotional response', and that it is a response to the conception of persons as self-determining agents pursuing ends of inclination. As such it is a necessary component in the attitude of respect.

It may be added here that those who object to our making the natural capacity for sympathy an ingredient in the moral attitude of respect may have failed to grasp the distinction between an attitude and a principle. We said at the beginning of the chapter that acting on a principle was causally connected with the possession of an attitude, in that a man can always act on a principle and hence develop in himself the connected attitude. In the light of the present discussion we can supplement this by saying that if a man possesses the raw material of an attitude, in the form of some measure of the appropriate feelings, he can develop it by acting appropriately; and whereas the strength of an attitude may not always be under the direct control of a man's will, it is always possible for him to adopt the principle of action which will develop the germs of active sympathy which (we hold) everyone possesses, and thus strengthen his moral attitude.

It was argued that people are not only self-determining but also rule-following. This feature of persons also moulds the attitude of respect. The nature of the modification it requires in the attitude of respect may be seen if we draw a specific distinction which brings out one of the most important aspects of rule-following. The distinction is between forgiving and condoning.[10] Let us suppose that A has been injured by B. A may condone the injury in the sense of treating it lightly. Now there may be contexts in which this attitude of condonation is morally appropriate—especially where the injury is trivial—but it may not always be morally appropriate. To play down an injury may be morally inappropriate in that it represents an attempt to minimize the fact that rules which both parties accept have been violated. In other words, an attitude of condonation may be an inappropriate one to adopt towards a person in that it ignores the fact that he is able to satisfy rules as well as pursue certain purposes. To condone is to fail to respect persons in that it is to ignore one of the features essential to being a person—the ability to adopt and satisfy rules.

But a second point emerges from the distinction between forgiving and condoning. For B may reject A's rules, and so deny the need for forgiveness. Now sometimes of course B's position may be justified. But in establishing this B ought to take into account the possibility that A's rules apply to him also. This is the point which Kant expresses in terms of his often-parodied thesis of universal legislation. Kant assumes that all men, in so far as they are rational, will legislate in the same way in the same way. Such a conception can be only an ideal, but the truth it exaggerates is that in dealing with others we ought to reveal in our attitudes a realization that the rules in term of which they act may also be valid for us. In so far as we are in moral disagreement with other persons our attitude towards them ought to display a realization that we could be mistaken, and that their rules could be the valid ones.

The same point can e made in terms of reasons. For in seeing persons as essentially rule-following we are conceiving of them as rational agents who are able to act or forbear because they can see good reasons for their actions. We ought therefore to consider how far their reasoning may apply to us.

Let us now try to tie together the various components in our attitude of respect. In so far as persons are thought of as self-determining agents who pursue objects of interest to themselves we respect them by showing active sympathy with them; in Kant's language, we make their ends out own. In so far as persons are thought of as rule-following we respect them by taking seriously the fact that the rules by which they guide their conduct constitute reasons which may apply both to them and to ourselves. In the attitude of respect we have, then, two necessary components: an attitude of active sympathy and a readiness at least to consider the applicability of other men's rules both to them and to ourselves. These two components are independently necessary and jointly sufficient to constitute the attitude of respect which it is fitting to direct at persons, conceived as rational wills.

It is arguable that an attitude so constituted may best be described as one of love. Now many different kinds of attitude may be called 'love', but the relevant kind seems to be what in the language of the Gospels is called *agape*. The term *agape* is not without its own obscurities but it seems the most suitable for characterizing an attitude which combines a regard for others as rule-following with an active sympathy with them in their pursuit of ends. It is an attitude illustrated in the story of the Good Samaritan, and again in the well-known passage from St. John's Gospel: 'Greater love hath no man than this, that a man lay down his life for his friends'. To lay down one's life for one's friends may be a supreme example of making the ends of others one's own, but it should also be noted that to *accept* such sacrifice may also be to show respect or *agape* because such acceptance may be an expression of the recognition that others too are moral agents who can follow rules and display the attitude of *agape* in their lives.

We argued earlier that attitudes necessarily have formal objects, and that understanding what is meant by the name of an attitude involves knowing what its formal object is. We said that the formal object of respect is 'that which is thought valuable', and that those aspects of human beings in virtue of which they fall under this description—those aspects which are thought valuable—are summed up by the expressions 'a person' and 'personality'. Our ability to arrive at some notion of what constitutes personality was thus dependent on a prior idea, however vague, of what 'respect' means. Having arrived at this notion of personality, we were then able to show more precisely what is involved in valuing and esteeming personality, and have in effect tailored the attitude to fit its object, trimming off what does not apply to an attitude directed towards persons as we have defined them. This attitude we have called *agape*, and since it has been defined to fit the concept of a person, it can be said that 'a person' is the formal object of *agape*. Thus, just as 'Hope is always for an imagined good' is an analytic judgement, so '*Agape* is always felt towards those regarded as persons' is an analytic judgement. But, as we shall see in the next section, this fact leaves open the possibility of debate as to who or what is properly or truly to be regarded as a person, as there can be debate about whether something hoped for is really good or not.

Now a difficulty arises if we regard persons as the formal object of *agape*. The difficulty can best be seen if we consider first the analogy we have already used—that of hope and its formal object, viz something which may come about and which is thought to be good. It seems to be the case that if something which may come about is *in fact* good then it logically follows that it ought to be hoped for. In the same way, if something is in fact dangerous it logically follows that it ought to be feared. This logical feature of the relationship between hope or fear and their formal objects does not hold of all verbs and their formal objects. For example, the formal object of 'divorce' is 'a spouse', but it does not follow from this that if someone really is my spouse I ought to divorce him or her. What distinguishes hope and fear is that they and their formal objects are *evaluative*, and in this they resemble *agape* and its formal object, a person. But if *agape* is like hope and fear in this way, it may be argued that 'Persons ought to be respected' becomes analytic, in the same way that 'The dangerous ought to be feared' is analytic. If this were so, the respect-for-persons principle could no longer be regarded as a basic moral principle, because it would be empty of content.

This difficulty can however be met if we recall the argument of Section 5. As we saw there, the notion of a person has a good deal of descriptive content—far more than the notions of the good or the dangerous. It retains its connection with the non-evaluative concept of a human being, even though it may be appropriate to extend the notion of 'person' to include the non-human also. Because of the high descriptive content of the notion of a person, we can say 'Persons ought to be respected' without triviality. For to say 'Persons ought to be respected' or 'Persons ought to be regarded with *agape*' is to say not merely 'What is valuable ought to be respected' but rather 'Human beings (and other creatures like them in the relevant respects) ought to be respected for what is valuable in them'.

6. Objections

A number of objections may be raised to this account of what it is to respect persons. A radical objection may be that there is something unrealistic about the whole idea of respecting persons, for a 'person' is an abstraction; we in fact encounter *personae* or persons in various social roles. Now the truth in this objection is that the idea of the pure individual isolated from social influence is an abstraction. Indeed, it is not just that we are in some external way moulded by the social roles we adopt, but rather that our very identity as persons is constituted by the relationships in which we are placed by our social roles. Consider, for example, not only the occupational roles of lawyer, teacher or postman but also roles which enter into the depths of personal life such as those of husband, daughter or friend. It is therefore true to say that there is no such thing as the pure ego uncontaminated by social influences; and to that extend the idea of a 'role' as a *mere* part one can play while remaining essentially unaffected by it is misleading. But it does not follow from this that the idea of 'respect for persons' is an abstraction.

In the first place, it may be doubted whether all that we do is done in a role. There are many simple, spontaneous acts of kindness, malice or high spirits which do not proceed from one's conception of a role. A much more important point, however, is that even when we act in roles it is as *persons* that we are acting. 'Role' is a concept of social description and it is a useful tool for grouping duties, revealing structure in apparently unconnected activities and identifying various forms of social pressure. But this must not lead us to ignore the fact that it is *people* who perform the duties, pursue the activities and experience the pressures. If the idea of a pure ego is an abstraction, so is that of a role which is enacted without leaving the imprint of the person who is in the role. Hence, even if it is conceded that we never meet a person who is not in a role, this in no way suggests that it is not really a person whom we meet. Indeed, a common moral failing is to attend too much to a person's social role and not enough to the fact of his personality; to have contempt for him because he is a dustman or over-deference towards him because he is a television actor. Along these lines lies the sort of 'respect for persons' which is a vice, corrected, or corrected, by being 'no respecter of persons'.

The objections to regarding a person as simply a set of roles are developed by Professor Bernard Williams in his analysis of what it is to respect a person.[11] Williams points out that, in the first place, there is a distinction 'between regarding a man's life and character from an aesthetic or technical point of view, and regarding them from a point of view which is concerned primarily with what is *for him* to live that life and do those actions in that character. . . . The technical or professional attitude is that which regards the man solely under that title as "miner" or "agricultural labourer" or "junior executive", the human approach that which regards him as *a man who has* that title (among others) willingly, unwillingly.' As a development of this distinction, Williams argues, in the second place, that involved in the notion of treating each man as an end is the point that 'each man is owed an effort of identification: that he should not be regarded as the surface to which a certain label can be applied, but one should try to see the world (including the label) from his point of view'. Now a man can be so exploited the he will be unable to see himself as other than one who has a certain role, and this leads Williams to make the third point that respecting a person involves the avoidance of any policy that will suppress or destroy a man's consciousness of himself as one who has purposes and policies other than those given him by a certain role. And one might add here (extending Williams' argument) that a man can *himself* inhibit or even destroy his own consciousness of himself as a *person* who happens to occupy a given role and who may have purposes other than those of the role: the student who plays all the time at being a student, the over-officious civil servant and the too-charming salesman are examples of this. The phenomenon has indeed been explored by Sartre in his literary and philosophical writings. The three points made by Williams (with this extension) help to clarify the claim that, however much a person may be moulded by his social roles, we feel that he ought not to be regarded, or to regard himself, wholly in terms of the roles he occupies.

It might be objected that the concept of a person is itself a role-concept. In a discussion of this claim Professor Dorothy Emmet draws attention to the history which lies behind it.[12] She points out that one strand in Greek ethics sees the significance of a doctor as lying in his function (*ergon*) of being a doctor, and his 'virtue' in being a good doctor. This notion is extended by Aristotle and others to apply to a man as such, and we find bequeathed to the later Natural Law theorists the idea that 'human beings are not just members of the biological species *homo sapiens*, but can be seen as having a *social role* in the universe. So "natural" and "human" become role concepts with a normative overtone, calling attention to the obligation to live according to this social role.' There is a good deal of substance in this point. Certainly, as Professor Emmet points out, the concept of a social role is (perhaps unhelpfully) extended when one begins speaking of the role of a person as such. But this terminological point should not obscure the fact that the concept of a person is evaluative and has built into it conceptions, however un-defined, of what a human being ought to be like. Still, to stress that the concept of person is thus evaluative is not to admit that personality can be analyzed in terms of the *specific* roles in which a person may find himself in his daily life.

A central contention of the chapter has been that the attitude of respect for persons is *morally basic*. But a query may be raised as to whether, and if so, in what sense, this is the case; for the term 'basic' is ambiguous. It may mean that the attitude is paramount in the sense that in any conflict between it or a principle derived from it, and another attitude of principle, priority ought always to go to whatever policy seems to be required by *agape*. To interpret 'morally basic' in this way would allow for the possibility that some moral principles and attitudes have a basis other than that of the attitude of respect for persons. We wish to assert, however, that the attitude of respect for persons is morally basic in a stronger sense—that not only is it the paramount moral attitude but also that all other moral principles and attitudes are to be explained in terms of it. It is not easy to be sure that we can meet all the objections which may be raised to this thesis, but let us consider some of the more obvious ones.

In the first place, how is our admitted duty to seek the truth to be explained in terms of the attitude of respect for persons as ends it should be noted that this question is not the same as the question how the duty to *tell* a person the truth is to be explained. The latter question can be answered by the reminder that to respect a person is take into account in one's dealings with him that he is a rational creature able to shape his life in accordance with reasons, and that to tell him lies is to fail to take such factors into account. The former question concerns our duty to seek the truth or to seek knowledge (and a similar difficulty can be raised over the duty to pursue art). The answer to this questing cannot be fully developed until Chapter III, but it can be outlined at this stage. It is natural to assume that 'respect for persons' means respect for *other* persons, the attitude being interpreted as a social attitude and the principle as one of social morality. But, as we shall show, the attitude is also one of respect for humanity in one's own person—so much was stressed by Kant. Now we have argued that essential to being a person is the possession of a rational will; but such a feature, but is very nature, will lead a person to seek the truth. Hence, the duty to seek the truth is in fact derivative from the duty to act as a person.

But even if we grant that the duties to seek the truth and tell it can be explained in terms of respect for the humanity in one's own person, we are still left with some cases which are difficult to explain in terms of respect for persons. (And that they present difficulties to any theory of morality is not really an excuse for failing to make an attempt to account for them.) These are the cases of children, the senile, lunatics and animals. They present difficulties, for, while we do not regard it as a matter of moral indifference how we treat children, the senile, lunatics and animals, it is not clear that the attitude of respect for *persons* is appropriate because personality seems to be lacking, to a greater or lesser extent, in these cases. If respect and persons-as-rational-will are necessarily related, as we have been maintaining, can it be fitting to show *agape* towards the cases mentioned, and, if not, how can we account for our duties towards them?

The first step in meeting this difficulty is to point out that the relationship between *agape* and persons givers us the central cases of the concepts of *agape* and of persons—we would not properly know what *agape* meant unless we knew what it was to direct the attitude towards a person in the full sense—but that once we have the concept of *agape* it becomes possible to extend it to objects which are persons in the full sense. Thus, children are potentially persons, and to some extent already persons although still children; and the senile are lapsed persons, although they may remain persons to some extent. It may be objected here that children and the senile are obviously persons in the full sense, and that speaking of them as 'potential persons' or 'lapsed persons' is misconceived. But this objection misses the point of our analysis of 'person'. Certainly, children and the senile are human beings in the full sense, but the word 'person' in our usage is a more precise term, implying the possession of capacities (to be self-determining and rule-following) which are not fully developed in children and may have decayed in the senile. It may further be objected, however, that congenital idiots have never been and will never be persons in the full sense. The answer is that there are still sufficient resemblances between them persons to justify extending the language of *agape* to them, although it would not be possible to adopt such an attitude to them unless we first knew that it was to adopt it towards normal persons.

The second step in meeting the difficulty is to stress that there are other possible attitudes which are helpful in dealing with persons in this minimal sense. Affection, for instance, is perhaps the dominant attitude in a normal family atmosphere and as such it is what motivates parents and others in their dealings with children. Pity, again, is a powerful motive force which lean people to care for the senile or congenital idiots, and if it is objected that not everyone can experience pity to a sufficient degree to lead them to care for the senile or congenital idiots, the answer is that not everyone *is* suitable for that job. Affection, pity and the like are not themselves moral attitudes, but they are consistent with *agape* and can reinforce it, while it in turn controls them when their natural springs are funning dry, or are flowing too freely or becoming poisoned.

Can similar arguments be used to account for our moral duties to animals? There are, of course, views to the effect that we have no moral duties at all to animals as such; it is wrong to ill-treat animals only in so far as this is bad for the character of the ill-treater. (What lies behind this view is the claim that persons are to be respected in virtue of their possession of a soul, and since animals lack a soul they themselves can have no real claim on our respect.) But most people hold that we do have duties towards animals—or at least that we have the duty to avoid causing them unnecessary suffering. If then we are to succeed in explaining how all other moral principles and attitudes can be explained in terms of respect for persons, we shall need to show that animals have personality in some minimal sense. This can be done by suggesting that our duty to avoid causing them unnecessary suffering arises out of a respect for animals as, to a greater or lesser extent, *sentient* beings; and possession of sentience is not only a feature common to animals and human beings, but also the basis in the human being of the defining characteristics of personality—self-determination and the ability to follow rules.

In answering the foregoing objections we spoke of a person in the *full* sense as being the proper object of the attitude of *agape*, and argued that, once understood, such an attitude can be directed towards those who are not persons in this strict sense. But it may be objected to this that if we apply the word 'person' only to human beings we do not here have personality in the fullest sense. It may be said that to understand the nature of personality in the fullest sense we must consider the nature of God, and that hence God is the only proper object of respect or *agape*. We can therefore view human beings with respect only because they are made in the image of God.

Now if we consider the objection as a matter of psychology of acquiring attitudes it cannot stand; we must first learn what it is to respect a person in the give-and-take of real life situations before we can direct the same attitude to an object we have not seen. So much indeed is no more than Scriptural.[13] It may be replied here that once we have acquired a grasp of the concept of *agape* and of 'person' in a human context we required to apply them to the relationship between God and man to deepen our understanding of their proper meaning. But it is possible to deepen our understanding of their proper meaning. But it is possible to deepen our understanding of *agape* and of personality by *imagining* a being called God who has the attributes and the attitude in a developed form, without presupposing the real existence of such a being. Hence, as a psychological thesis the objection is not damaging to our position.

The objection may be restated, however, in the form of a theological or philosophical thesis—that it is only so far as God loves us that we become proper objects of love for each other, or, in different words, that our value as human persons derives from the love which God has for us. Now this form of the objection, unlike the previous one, does require us to presuppose the existence of God. But let us, for the sake of argument, presuppose the nonexistence of God. We arc surely not forced to conclude (although some theologians have concluded) that personality thereby loses its value. And if we can see human personality as having value without presupposing the existence of God, *a fortiori* we are not obliged to see the value of personality as dependent on the prior love of God.

7. Conclusion

At this point we can tie together the conclusions so far reached. Basically, 'respect for persons as ends' refers to an attitude—a way of *regarding* persons—although the attitude will necessarily give rise to certain characteristic principles of action—ways of *treating* persons. To respect a person as an end is to value or cherish him for what he is—and that is a possessor of a rational will, where 'rational will' refers to the abilities to be self-determining and rule-following with all that these imply. To *respect* such a person is to make his ends one's own (show sympathy with him) and to take into account in all one's dealings with him that he too is self-determining and rule-following. In a word, to respect a person (so understood) is to have an attitude of *agape* towards him; and we can say that a person as a rational will is the formal object of the attitude of *agape*. To assert this is not to deny the influence of special roles and other social influences in moulding personality and giving content to duties. Such an attitude is morally basic not only in that it is paramount but also in that all other moral attitudes and principles can be explained in terms of it. This is not to exclude from moral attitudes creatures which have personality only in a minimal sense, for once we understand what it is to have respect for a person in the full sense (and a belief in God, while not essential to this understanding, may well aid it) we can then extend the attitude in a suitably modified form to whatever is thought to have traces of personality.

Notes

1. Bernard Williams, 'The Idea of Equality', pp. 114-20, in Philosophy Politics and Society, Second Series, edited by P. Laslett and W. G. Runciman (Oxford, Blackwell, 1964).

2. Bernard Williams, 'Morality and the Emotions', pp. 22-4, An Inaugural Lecture (London, 1965).

3. Dorothy Emmet, Rules, Roles and Relations, Chap. 8 (London, Maclagan, 1966).

4. For other objections to the 'rational will' analysis see W. G. Maclagan, 'Respect for Persons as a Moral Principle', Part I, Section 3, Philosophy, July 1960.

5. J. S. Mill, On Liberty, Chap. 3, p. 187 (London, Collins, The Fontana Library, edited by Mary Warnock, 1962).

6. Kant, The Fundamental Principles of the Metaphysic of Morals, translated by H.J. Patton as The Moral Law, pp. 90-91 (London, Hutchinson's University Library, 1948).

7. Kant, op. cit., p. 98.

8. Maclagan, op. cit., Section 8.

9. Maclagan, op. cit., Section 8.

10. P. Nowell-Smith, Ethics, p. 112 (London, Pelican Books, 1954).

11. R. M. Hare, The Language of Morals, p. 70 (Oxford University Press, 1952).

12. R. S. Downie, 'Forgiveness', Philosophical quarterly, April 1964.

13. The First Epistle of John, iv. 20.

Chapter 2

Respect and Care: Toward Moral Integration[1]

Robin S. Dillon

In her provocative discussion of the challenge posed to the traditional impartialist, justice-focused conception of morality by the new-wave care perspective in ethics, Annette Baier calls for 'a "marriage" of the old male and newly articulated female ... more wisdom,' to produce a new 'cooperative' moral theory that 'harmonize[s] justice and care.'[2] I want in this paper to play matchmaker, proposing one possible conjugal bonding: a union of two apparently dissimilar modes of what Nel Noddings calls 'meeting the other morally,'[3] a wedding of respect and care.

It may seem obvious, however, that respecting a person and caring for her are quite different and distinctly ill-suited to such a match. Indeed, if we recall what Kant says about love and respect, the two might seem in tension, even at odds with one another: 'The principle of *mutual love* admonishes men constantly to *come nearer* to each other; that of the *respect* which they owe each other, to keep themselves at a distance from one another.'[4] The now-familiar contrast that Carol Gilligan has drawn between two distinct conceptions of morality seems to reinforce the idea of a divergence of respect from care, since impartial respect for persons and for their rights as autonomous moral equals is central to the 'justice perspective' conception of morality, while compassionate, responsive caring for particular I don't interdependent individuals is the heart of the 'care perspective.'[5]

Recognizing the value of care and respect, we might wonder about the place of each in moral theory and moral life. One approach is to deny the moral significance of one or the other: care is nice but not distinctively moral; the ethic of impersonal and distancing respect should be replaced with a more personally responsive ethic of care. Kant takes another approach. He regards both respect and love (that is, *practical* love) as morally important, maintaining that we have both duties of respect and duties of love. Yet the latter seem morally more important in the Kantian scheme, for they are strictly owed to every person, while 'no one is wronged when we neglect duties of love.'[6] And while both love and respect are essential between friends, Kant argues that friendship is insecure unless respect constrains and limits love, suggesting that even in intimate contexts respect has moral priority.[7] The standard interpretation of the end-in-itself formulation of the categorical imperative as the principle of respect for persons further underscores the idea of respect as the more fundamental basis for all interactions among persons.

A third approach is to regard respect and care as especially suited to different moral contexts. Care, it might be thought, belongs to the domain of intimate personal relationships—now recognized as a fully moral sphere—but cannot easily, if at all, be universalized or applied to our moral relationships with those whom we will never meet; while respect, although important in intimate contexts, is particularly appropriate to interactions among strangers and within large-scale or institutional contexts.[8]

However, while respect and care may appear to be very different and to occupy different places in the moral scheme, I want to propose an alternative view, one which has its roots in an intriguing similarity between some discussions of respect and various accounts of care. I will argue that there is a conception of respect for persons which incorporates many of the most characteristic elements of the care perspective. This conception, which differs significantly from the familiar view of respect for persons that finds its inspiration in Kant, views caring for a person as a way of respecting her. Care, on this conception, is one kind of respect rather than a disparate rival for our moral allegiance. And it is a kind of respect we owe to all persons, not just to our loved ones and friends. So, while the present distinction between the ethic of justice and the ethic of care seems to require us to choose sides, prioritize, or segregate, I believe we may find in a union of respect and care resources for a more integrative approach to moral theory and moral life.

I. Respect

Central to the integration is the recognition that there are different varieties of respect. Care considerations, I will argue, overlap wit one of these varieties. To make this clearer, let me begin with a general account of respect. Respect has affective, conative, active, and cognitive dimensions; it is an attitude, a way of treating something, a kind of valuing. But most centrally, it is a particular mode of apprehending something, which is the basis of the attitude, conduct, and valuing. The person who respects something perceived it quite differently from one who does not respect it and responds to it in light of that perception.

The idea that perception is the core of respect should come as no surprise to those who attend to etymological cues. 'Respect' comes from the Latin 'respi-

cere,' which means 'to look back at' or 'to look again.' The idea of looking belongs also to many words used synonymously with 'respect': for example, 'regard' (from 'to watch out for') and 'consideration' ('examine (the stars) carefully'). This suggests that respect is not merely *about* its object but is *focused* on
it. So *attention* is a central aspect of respect: we respect something by paying
careful attention to it and taking it seriously. To ignore, neglect, or disregard
something, or to dismiss it lightly, thoughtlessly, or carelessly is to not respect it.

This attention is, moreover, a kind of response to an object: we re-spect
things that are worth looking at again, that deserve our attention, that demand to
be taken seriously. Respect is, we might say, object-generated rather than sub-
ject-generated; it is something we *render*, something that is called for, commanded, elicited, due, claimed from us. Thus it differs from liking or loving, and
from fearing, to take another emotion with which respect is sometimes confused,
all of which have their source in the agent's own desires and interests. When we
respect something, we heed its call, accord it its due, acknowledge its claim to our
attention. Thus there is, so to speak, a dialogic dimension to respect as well as a
perceptual one. At the same time, respect is deliberate; it is a matter of directed
rather than grabbed attention, of reflective consideration. In this way it differs
from immediate attraction and fascination, for we can refuse to heed the call.

Of course, attention can be inconsiderate, and looks disrespectful. So respect
cannot simply be a matter of staring long and hard at something; rather, it involves
a certain way of perceiving the object, namely, regarding it as worthy. To respect
something is to appreciate it, to recognize its value, or at the very least, to regard it
as important and so as something worth paying attention to, worth taking seriously.[9] And insofar as it is a valuing, respect involves having and acting from
certain positive attitudes towards the object: esteeming or admiring it, for example, or cherishing or venerating it, or thinking it is good that there are such things.

Finally, respect has a behavioral component. To respect something is to treat
it in a certain manner or to act in particular ways in connection with it. Respect
involves regarding the object as calling for more than our attention, as making
claims on our subsequent behavior; so we consider certain actions or forms of
conduct to be deserved by the object, to be warranted, due, owed, fitting, appropriate. And there are many ways to respect things: by showing consideration for
them or taking them into account; by keeping our distance from them and giving
them room; by praising, honoring, or worshiping them; by obeying or abiding by
them; by avoiding them; by protecting and being careful with them. When we
violate, interfere with, or encroach upon something, or despise, scorn, or condemn
it, or act high-handedly, or arrogantly, or carelessly in connection with it, we are
not respecting it.

Exactly how we should act with respect to any particular thing and what sort
of attitude is appropriate depend on the nature of that object. That is, respect
involves believing that there is something about the object, some feature of it or
fact about it, that makes it worthy of this kind of attention and treatment.[10] This
fact or feature is the ground of respect: that in virtue of which it is worthy of
respect. So, while it is possible to like something for no reason, we cannot respect

something for no reason nor for any old reason. Rather, our reason for respecting the object must be that it has, in our judgment, that respect-warranting characteristic; our reason for respecting it in the way we do must be that it is, in our view, the kind of object that calls for that kind of response. A person's respect for some object can thus be inappropriate or undeserved, for the object may not, after all, have the features she takes it to have, or, if it does have those features, they may not be features that make something worthy of respect. But if it does and if they do, if the person's attitude and actions are directed toward a worthy object, then her respect is appropriate and well-grounded.

To put this another way, the logic of respect is the logic of objectivity and universality. To respect this particular object is to have a sense of what is appropriate not only here and now between this object and me, but in the nature of the object itself. In respecting some object we perceive it as having value in its own right and not only in terms of its relationship to us, and we act as we do toward it because of (what we take to be) a fact that is external to us rather than from some taste or preference of our own. We experience the value of the object as giving direction to our actions and constraining our attitudes, independently of what we might happen to desire. To return to an earlier point, one views the object as *worthy* of respect, which is to say, worthy of and calling for others' respect as well as one's one. Thus one takes one's reasons for respecting an object to be reasons for other people (perhaps, for anyone) to respect it. In this way, respect differs from admiration, perhaps, and liking, certainly, which have much more to do with one's own aesthetic sense and preferences. A person need not think others are blind or are doing something they should not if they do not like the things she does, but other things being equal she would view them thus if they failed to respect the things she does.

Further, since it is some fact about or feature of an object which makes it worthy of respect, then respecting some object because it has feature F commits us, other things being equal, to respecting to other objects which also have feature F. So respect is universalizing in a way that love, for instance, is not. Myra's love for her friend Joan does not involve any requirement of logical consistency that she also love any woman sufficiently similar to Joan. But the respect which is due Ann as a Superior Court judge is also due Maggie in virtue of the fact that she, too, is a Superior Court judge; and if Diana respects Joanne as a person of integrity, then other things being equal, she ought to respect Heather in virtue of her integrity.

The nature of the object, then, determines it respect-worthiness, and there are different kinds of objects calling for correspondingly different kinds of attention and different attitudes and treatment. Consider the differences among the following sets of example: (a) a mountain climber's respect for the elements and a tennis player's respect for her opponent's strong backhand; (b) respecting the terms of an agreement and respecting a person's rights; (c) showing respect for a judge by rising when she enters the courtroom and treating a nation's flag with respect; (d) an environmentalist's profound respect for nature and an art lover's deep respect for the *Mona Lisa*; and (e) having a great deal of respect for a colleague, either as a person or as a scholar.

Attention to such cases suggests, I think rightly, that there are different varieties of respect. For example, the mountain climber's respect, which is grounded in prudence and is a matter of acting in ways that take account of the power and danger of the elements, differs from the respect one has for a colleague's honesty or philosophical acumen, which involves admiration and perhaps a desire to emulate her. I propose to take advantage of Stephen Hudson's helpful terminology here and label the varieties thus: (a) obstacle respect, (b) directive respect, (c) institutional respect, and (e) evaluative respect.[11] (I'll return to [d] shortly.)

That there are different varieties is not yet the end of the story of respect, for these varieties can be further sorted into two groups. The variety in (e) differs from the others insofar as it is a comparative appraisal of a person's merits or an evaluation of her relative quality in light of some standards of excellence, whereas varieties (a)-(d) do not consist in an appraising look at the object. One can show institutional respect for a judge without thinking that she is a particularly good judge, or directive-respect the terms of an agreement without regard to its merits or demerits; but to have evaluative respect for a person for her honesty is both to think that honesty is an excellence of persons and to evaluate her as more honest that most.[12] This grouping corresponds to a useful distinction Stephen Darwall has drawn between two kinds of respect, one ('appraisal respect') that involves a positive appraisal of persons or the traits of persons that manifest their excellence, and another ('recognition respect') that consists in giving appropriate recognition or consideration to something in deciding how to act. Institutional, directive, and obstacle respect are all varieties of what Darwall calls 'recognition respect.'[13]

What of (d)? The environmentalist, whose deep respect for nature comes close to a kind of love, regards the environment as in need of care and protection and so works to preserve it. A cosmetic company's advertisement urges women who care about their skin to respect it after sunbathing by applying a special soothing cream. Art-lovers decry the manifest disrespect for a Renoir shown by the thieves who cut the painting from the frame, thus threatening its value. These cases of respect all involve cherishing some object, regarding it as having great value and as fragile or calling for special care. When we respect things that are regarded this way, we act or forbear to act out of benevolent concern for them. The distinctive perception of an attitude toward the object that these cases involve serve to distinguish yet another variety of recognition respect. This variety, which has been neglected by other discussions and parsings of respect, has obvious affinities to the notion of care that informs discussions of the care perspective in ethics; and I want in the rest of the paper to pursue some implications of this affinity. It is important to recognize, however, that this is a notion of *respect*, as the general account of respect reveals. It is also, I will argue, a variety of recognition respect that can constitute an alternative conception of respect for persons as such.

II. Respect for Persons

An individual person, as we've seen, can be the object of different varieties of respect. A person can earn evaluative respect for her moral merit or excellence; she can be entitled to institutional respect in virtue of occupying a certain role in an institution whose rules and procedures prescribe certain conduct in connection with such role-occupants; she can warrant obstacle respect because of her power to harm one. Not every person will, as a matter of fact, deserve all varieties of respect; some individuals may not deserve any of most varieties. But there is a respect which we are said to owe to all persons equally, regardless of personal merit, role, or power. Such respect is a matter of taking appropriate account of the fact that someone is a person. Following Darwall, we can call this 'recognition respect for persons.' It involved (a) recognizing that a being is a person; (b) appreciating that persons as such have intrinsic moral value; (c) understanding that the fact that someone is a person constrains us to act only in certain ways in connection with her; and (d) acting or being disposed to act in those ways out of that recognition, appreciation, and understanding. When we respect a person in this sense, we view her, think about her, feel towards her and treat her in a manner due all persons simply because they are persons.

Now, as respect in general is grounded in those features of an object that make it worthy of attention and appropriate response, so recognition respect for persons is grounded in what we might call 'the morally significant features of persons': those features which make something a person and make persons matter morally. What constitutes an appropriate response to a person as such, then, depends on what the morally significant features of persons are.

Of course, how persons ought to be treated simply because they are persons is a matter of dispute among moral theories, but the idea of *respect* for persons is most commonly associated with Kant's conception of treating persons as ends in themselves. Indeed, the end-in-itself formulation of the categorical imperative is widely regarded as the preeminent statement of the principle of respect for persons. On the Kantian account, the morally significant feature of persons is the capacity for rationally autonomous moral agency: it is possession of this capacity which makes a being a person and grounds our intrinsic value as persons. The fundamental moral task of each person is to develop and exercise this capacity; our primary moral task with regard to others is to let them do this. Thus, recognition respect for persons on the Kantian conception most centrally involves, to recall Kant's metaphor, keeping our distance from others: giving them room to realize and exercise their capacity to be rationally self-determining and responsible moral agents, as well as 'constraining myself within certain limits in order to detract nothing from the worth that the other, as a man, is entitled to posit in himself' (Kant, 117).

Though Kant's own account of respect is rather complex, the notion of respect for persons which finds its inspiration in Kant has come to be understood primarily in terms of respecting each individual's basic human rights. These are the rights that protect the defining capacity of persons' rational autonomy, and include the fundamental right of each person to live her own life as she sees fit (so long as she doesn't interfere with others' right to do likewise).

However, as personhood is an essentially contestable, ideologically malleable concept, so is the concept of recognition respect. That is, the concept of recognition respect treats personhood as a variable: the concept itself cannot settle substantive questions of what a person is, but rather requires some antecedent specification of the conception of a person. The Kantian view is, of course, not the only way of conceiving of persons; it is certainly possible to identify others features of human beings as the morally significant features of persons. And although the notion of respect for persons is most often identified with Kantianism, Kantians have no privileged claim on the concept of respect. Rather, since how one should value and take appropriate account of an object depends on the nature of its morally significant features, or more to the point, on how it is conceptualized, then a different conception of personhood, of what matters for and about being a person, will call for a different conception of recognition respect for persons.[14] This opens the possibility of there being ways of respecting persons distinctly different from respecting their moral rights.[15]

As it happens, the philosophical literature contains a number of interconnected themes about persons and respect that are not captured by the Kantian conception of recognition respect for persons.[16] This family of ideas strikes a surprising but familiar chord, for it is structured by motifs that are central to various accounts of the care perspective, motifs such as the fundamental particularity and interdependence of persons, loving attention and understanding as primary modes of moral response, and insistence on active sympathetic concern for another's good.[17] When woven together, these themes form a pattern according to which re respect persons by caring for them as the particular individuals they are. That is to say, these themes suggest that care (or at least, certain characteristic elements of the care perspective) constitutes a kind of recognition respect for persons. The themes include the following.

1. What matters about each of us is not (only) some abstract capacity but the fact that we are the specific concrete individuals that we are. So, respecting persons involves valuing and responding to others in their concrete particularity.

2. It is a morally significant fact about us that we each have our own perspective from which we try to make sense of the world and ourselves, and we each have a self-conception that is a significant dimension of who we are. So, respecting persons involves coming to understand them in light of their own self-conceptions and trying to see the world from their point of view.

3. Another of our morally significant features is that we are not as independent and self-sufficient as philosophical characterizations of au-

tonomy might suggest. We must depend on others for help in satisfying our needs and wants and for the sustenance and realization of our projects and interests. But more importantly, we depend on others for our very existence and development both as persons and as the particular persons we are. We are not wholly self-making but are shaped and influenced by others, whom we also shape and influence; and what and who we are depends in deep and important ways on how others perceive and treat us. At the same time, however, and no less importantly, each of us is a separate individual, always engaged in living our own lives and in self-construction and self-interpretation. So respect for persons involves taking account of both our connectedness and interdependence and our distinctness. In particular, respect requires not so much refraining from interference as respecting our power to make and unmake each other as persons and exercising this power wisely and carefully. Respecting others also involves, more positively, caring for others by responding to their needs, promoting their well-being, and participating in the realization of their selves and their ends.

What emerges from these themes is a conception of recognition respect for persons that fits into the account of variety (d) discussed above and contrasts significantly with the way of understanding respect for persons that derives from Kant. I think it is appropriate to call variety (d) 'care respect,' and I propose that the conception of 'care respect for persons' is a suitable anchor for a more integrative, 'cooperative' moral theory. In the rest of this paper, I want to explore some of the dimensions of care respect for persons.

III. Care Respect for Persons in their Particularity

A striking feature of the Kantian conception is that in viewing us as worthy of respect it abstracts from all particularities, regarding the details of our selves as contingencies irrelevant to our intrinsic moral worth. The morally significant feature of persons on this view is something abstract and generic, not what distinguishes one individual from another but what makes us all indistinguishably equal. An individual human being is an object of respect only insofar as she is an instance of the universal type 'being with the capacity for rationally autonomous moral agency.' It is, in the words of the categorical imperative, the 'humanity in us' that matters morally and so calls for respect. That is, although morality may require us to treat others in light of the details of their individual selves, what is due *respect* is this abstract capacity and not our concrete and richly particular selves.

This aspect of Kantianism has drawn fire from a number of critics who contend that we are *essentially* fully specific and concretely particular individuals, each with our unique blend of needs, desires, and abilities, our own peculiar history, emotional constitution, concerns, and projects, each with our own way of viewing the world and our relationship to it.[18] These critics decry what one vividly describes as 'flens[ing], the individual down to the bare bones of abstract personhood' (Johnson, 93), for they maintain that persons have intrinsic value *as* concretely specific individuals. Rather than disregarding particularity, they insist, what we ought morally to value and take account of are precisely the details that make each person the unique person she is. We ought to respect, that is, the reality of our human individuality. Thus, as one writer claims, 'respect for a person includes respect for this core of individuality . . . [and] appreciation of . . . the individual and human *me*.'[19] To respect a person, on this account, involves valuing and treating her not as a case of generic personhood but as the whole and concretely particular person she is.

This view of respect compares interestingly with Carol Gilligan's description of the ethic of care as 'grounded in the specific context of others';[20] with Nel Noddings' account of caring as 'special regard for the particular person in a concrete situation' (24); with Seyla Benhabib's identification of the morality of care and responsibility with 'the standpoint of the concrete other,' which requires us to recognize and confirm the other as a concrete individual (164); with Marilyn Friedman's observation that 'responsiveness to other persons in their wholeness and their particularity is of singular importance' to the care standpoint (105).

These accounts of the fundamental moral orientation of respect and of care involve the same perception of their objects, regard the same dimensions of human beings as worthy of attention. We have here, that is, the same moral concern under two different labels. This intersection of accounts locates the conception of care respect for persons.

Diana Meyers has suggested that while the ethic of rights and justice tells us how to respect people's fundamental humanity and human dignity, 'it is let to the ethic of care (or some other ethical theory) to tell us how we must act to respect people's individuality.'[21]. It is, I maintain, the conception of care respect, anchoring an integrative ethical theory, which tells us how to respect persons as the persons they are. And it begins by grounding our intrinsic moral worth in what we might call our individual and human 'me-ness.'[22]

Any account of recognition respect for persons must ground that respect in something which all, or nearly all, human beings have, in virtue of which we have intrinsic moral worth, and which each has in a way that would justify our belief in the fundamental moral equality of persons. The Kantian conception posits one capacity which nearly all humans are claimed to have (excepting cases of serious defect) and which is a morally valuable capacity (Kant maintains that it is the ground of the possibility of morality). Moreover, because it is a capacity, all humans who have it can be thought to have it equally, so to have equal worth and hence to be worthy of equal respect. The problem with Kantian conception is that it does not have the resources to enable us in respecting persons (as opposed to dealing with them in other moral modes) to transcend the abstractness of *person as such* in order to focus on and respect the individual human being as herself.

Care respect does, however, have these resources. For it grounds respect for persons in something which, considered in the abstract, nearly all human beings have and can be said to have equally—the characteristic of being an individual human 'me'—a characteristic which each of us values and thinks is both morally important and profoundly morally problematic not only in others but in ourselves as well, and which pulls our attention to the concrete particularities of each human individual. We are, on the care respect approach, to pay attention not only to the fact that someone is a 'me' but also to which particular 'me' she is. Care respect thus involves viewing persons simultaneously in the abstract and in the particular, valuing this person as *the* fully specific concrete individual 'me' she is because she is *a* particular individual and human 'me.' Care respect, we might say, sees at the same time both the person in the individual and the individual in the person.

In the abstract, the notion of individual human 'me-ness' encompasses characteristics such as being reflectively self-conscious, having an historical experiential unity, continuity, and trajectory, having a plan of life and a conception of one's own good, being always engaged (though never single-handedly) in the tasks of self-construction and self-interpretation as well as world-construction and world-interpretation and so having one's own peculiar perspective on oneself and the world: characteristics which various accounts have posited as definitive of personhood. However, care respect values these characteristics only insofar as they are dimensions of or conditions for each person's being the particular person she is. Autonomy, while one path to becoming a 'me,' is not on this account viewed as either necessary or as especially important for being a person deserving of respect. This has the satisfactory consequence that even a manifestly and profoundly non-autonomous human being has intrinsic value and dignity, and has it as she is now rather than in virtue of her potential to be a very different kind of being. This is not, of course, to deny the moral and personal value of autonomy; it is rather to say that autonomy is neither all that matters nor what matters most.

The notion of 'me-ness' considered in the abstract establishes commonality among all persons. Considered in the particular, it involves the richly complex plethora of details that yields yet more specific similarities, connections, and relationships among individuals, as well as the multitudinous differences, distinctive concatenations of characteristics, and idiosyncratic perspectives which identify and differentiate each person. Care respect responds to persons both in the richness of this distinguishing detail and in the shared humanity that encompasses and is encompassed in it.

IV. Attention and Valuing

The object of care respect is the whole, specific, individual human 'me' as such. But precisely what constitutes respect for persons so conceived? In accordance with the general account of respect, the core of an appropriate response is paying attention to and valuing the person in her particularity. Significantly, a number of writers within the care perspective have also emphasized attention to and appreciation of concretely specific others, often invoking Iris Murdoch's notion of attention as the condition of an adequate moral response to others.[23]

Attention, 'the characteristic and proper mark of the active moral agent,' according to Iris Murdoch, is the 'just and loving gaze directed upon an individual reality,' the 'patient and just discernment and exploration' of another person that involves 'seeing the other as she really is' (34;34;40). The moral activity of attention is to be understood not simply in terms of its usefulness in providing the information about others that we need in order to care for them properly, although it does indeed serve this purpose. Rather, attention is, as we saw earlier, a dimension of respect itself, what Iris Murdoch calls 'respect for the real' (91). And because this 'endless' and 'infinitely difficult' task requires continual struggle to achieve clear vision against the impediments and distortions of selfishness, personal desires and fears, fantasy, an consoling self-pity, the effort which attention requires is itself an indication of our valuing of the other for her own sake (Ibid.).

Another characterization of care respect's alternative orientation toward others may be drawn from Martha Craven Nussbaum's eloquent description of the Jamesian moral ideal of attention.[24] First, care respect involves a commitment to attend, with 'intensely focused perception,' to all aspects of the irreducible particularity of individual human persons in their concrete contexts. Care respecters thus 'strain to be people on whom none of their subtleties are lost.' The change in focus from the abstractive Kantian conception of respect is matched by a change in attitude. For care respect also entails 'a determination to care for (this particular) as a whole . . . [and] to be guided by the tender and gentle emotions . . . by impartial love for them all.'

The change in attitude is a dramatic one. For Kantian respect is a dispassionate and detached valuing of others which is compatible with supreme indifference toward and even hatred of the other person. But while this has been viewed as a strength of the Kantian conception, the care conception regards its indifference and attenuation of concern as a significant threat to our ability to care for ourselves and to have a robust sense of our own worth as persons. The core attitude in care respect, by contrast, is cherishing, a form of respect that involves profoundness of feeling, treasuring, warm regard, solicitous concern. This affectively rich responsiveness to others provides the basis for the active engagement with them that care respect also involves.

To return to the perceptual aspect, the finely focused attention of care respect reveals much about persons which Kantian respect ignores but which care respect regards as valuable and worth taking seriously in its own right. Indeed, this focus on the details of each individual human 'me' insists that there is nothing about human beings and human lives that is irrelevant to respect. So, for example, care respect embraces the individual not despite what she is but *as* she is—ordinary, imperfect, limited, incomplete, and always under construction; and it values us in this light. Thus, it regards our very human selves as having worth in our everyday ordinariness—in the monotony, dinginess, inadequacy, and despair of banal existence as well as in the shining moments of achievement and the flashes of profundity—worthy as such of attention, our own as well as others', and worthy also of care. In acknowledging human limitedness, imperfection, and continual construction, care respect also comprises acceptance of frailty, patience, and lenience (thus constraining perfectionist tendencies of evaluative respect), as well as responsiveness to each other's needs.

The principle theme of care respect, however, is that each person has intrinsic moral worth as the particular person she is. Care respect thus involves valuing another not just for being a self but for being herself: appreciating and cherishing each person as an unrepeatable individual, as 'irreplaceably himself or herself' (Elizabeth Maclaren, 41). By contrast, although the Kantian formula of persons as ends in themselves is claimed to regard persons as irreplaceable,[25] there is a sense in which Kantian respect does in fact view persons as intersubstitutable, for it is blind to everything about an individual except her rational nature, leaving each of us indistinguishable from every other. Thus, in Kantian-respecting someone, there is a real sense in which we are not paying attention to *her*, for it makes no difference to how we respect her that she is who she is and not some other individual. Kantian respect is thus not a 'respecter of persons,' in the sense that it does not discriminate or distinguish among persons. By contrast, care respect is a respecter of individual persons.

This is not to say that care respect loses sight of the commonality of persons or that it cannot value persons equally. Some philosophers have expressed concern that an emphasis in ethics on particularity might preclude recognition of common humanity and equality of value among persons.[26] For valuing each person in her particularity has to do with grasping the unique specificity of each; but unique specificity is what makes us different from each other, not what makes us the same or equal. Moreover, responding to persons as the particular concrete individuals they are would seem also to involve attending to their character and behavior, in virtue of which individuals have, as a matter of fact, differential moral value: some are virtuous and admirable, others vicious and despicable. In terms of our specificity as such and our particular characters, then, it would seem we are not all equal in value.

However, while particularity does indeed have to do with differences among individuals, it also encompasses the multitude of similarities among us as well as our innumerable connections to and relationships with other individuals. In attending to our particularity, care respect acknowledges us as both distinct from one another and alike, as separate consciousnesses each making our own way in the world, replete with both admirable and despicable traits, formed of longings, fears, joys, concerns, values, hopes, and impulses which are, many of them, resoundingly familiar to other individuals, and many also inscrutable to them. Care respect also recognizes us simultaneously as separate and self-synthesizing and as embedded in innumerable networks of personal, social, and institutional relationships with others in ways that mark our very being as relational and interdependent. Thus, care respect values persons not only in our distinctness but also in our commonality, which is seen to reside as such in the profuse details of our individual selves and in our mutuality as in the congruence of abstract 'me-ness.'

Further, because care respect begins with a recognition of the intrinsic value of persons insofar as they are individual and human 'me's,' it has no difficulty with the idea of equality of worth. Indeed, care respect sees institution as equally worthy of attention, consideration, and concern, equally worthy of understanding and care. This equality is not grounded (as it is in Kantian respect) in being identical, nor does it entail equal treatment or equality of outcome. Indeed, in responding to particularity, care respect makes room for the appropriateness of treating different persons differently. But the aim of care respect is to keep in sight both the fact that this person is the unique individual she is and that she is but one among innumerable fully specific and unique individuals. The most powerful aspect of care respect is, I believe, its ability to maintain a constructive tension between regarding each person as *just as valuable* as every other and regarding this individual as *special.* Nor should this ability be unfamiliar: that gracefully maintaining this tension is indeed possible is manifest in the way some friends and some parents of more than one child manage to see each of their friends or children at the same time both as special and as equally valuable to them as the others.

There is power, too, in care respect's treatment of the differences among persons, which traditionally have been viewed as stumbling blocks to harmonious moral relationships among persons. Respect for persons is not simply a matter of recognizing similarity ('We are both persons') but has also to do with how we respond to difference; indeed, it might well seem that it is precisely in the face of difference that respect is called for. Kantian respect is one approach: overcoming differences. The Kantian conception seeks to secure moral relationships through a mutual respect disregards differences, or where that is not possible, adopts an attitude of toleration (an attitude, compatible with hatred, which implies a reluctant acceptance). Care respect, by contrast, tries to achieve harmonious moral relationships by acknowledging differences, calling us to affirm others in their differences, to embrace, perhaps even to celebrate human differences. Care respect demands that we take seriously, stay open to, and appreciate differences in perspectives and values, for example, by considering the possibility of their validity or their applicability to us. It thus enables us to value difference rather than seeing it as something that must separate us or as an obstacle that must be overcome.

In its response to difference, care respect contrasts also with evaluative respect, which is also responsive to the specific details of individuals, particularly their character and conduct. But whereas evaluative respect involves judging and appraising persons, care respect involves an acceptance of the differences of another that goes beyond toleration, even when her distinctive qualities are not intrinsically good or admirable. Care respect thus provides a kind of constraint on evaluative respect: it calls us to be slow to judge and generous in our evaluation, recognizing the reality of deep disagreement among morally sincere persons, our own limitations in understanding, and the profound impact of our evaluations. Care respect does not, however, require us to be uncritical, to tolerate the intolerable, to admire the despicable or the inane; rather, it seeks a kind of acknowledgement and acceptance that does not extend to endorsement but instead provides the framework for questions of endorsement.

A conception of respect for persons that is responsive to the fullness of human reality must acknowledge persons as both the same and different. Care respect, in doing this, contains the possibility for more fluent and supple ethical behavior in relation to what is foreign, strange, distant. It enables us to appreciate another individual person as one of an endless number of variations on a theme which itself consists of many more notes than one. And where, because of geographical, cultural, emotional, or ideological distance, we can see the other only fuzzily, only generally, care respect constantly reminds us that there is more of great moral significance to that person than what we presently perceive.

V. Respect and Understanding

The core of care respect, then, is attention to and appreciation of individual persons in the richness of their concrete particularity. What more might care respect involve? What modes of conduct or manner of treatment of others manifests care respect for them? In the intersection of discussions of care and of respect we find two suggestions: first, care respect for another involves trying to understand her in her own terms; and second, it includes seeking to promote the other's well-being.

An important theme within the care perspective is the way in which caring for another person involves a certain understanding of her. For example, Carol Gilligan calls care 'a way of knowing,' and not simply a way of feeling or acting; the care perspective, she maintains, involves 'the ability to perceive others on their own terms' ('Moral Orientation,' 29; and 'Conquistador,' 77). For Nel Noddings, the fundamental aspect of caring is 'engrossment': the receptive apprehension of another's reality 'from the inside' (14f.). Sara Ruddick reminds us of the centrality to personal relationships of Murdoch's 'loving attention,' which requires one to set aside one's own needs, fears, and fantasies in order to understand, in concrete and contextual detail, 'how it is' for the other and so to understand and meet her particular needs (347-8). I hear echoes of this concern with understanding the other in certain discussions of respect.

Bernard Williams, for example, has argued that respecting a person involves what he calls 'identification' ('The Idea of Equality,' 158-61). He explains the connection by distinguishing two ways of viewing someone. There is, on the one hand, regarding a person, or her life, actions, or character from an aesthetic, technical, or professional point of view, which 'regards the man solely under [some] title.' This contrasts with 'the human approach' of respect, which considers someone from 'a point of view which is concerned primarily with what it is *for him* to live that life,' which 'regards him as *a man who has* that title (among others), willingly, unwillingly, through lack of alternatives, with pride, etc.' Williams maintains that people 'should be regarded from the human point of view.' Each person, he claims 'is owed an effort at identification: that he should not be regarded as the surface to which a certain label can be applied, but one should try to see the world (including the label) from his point of view.' Each person, he claims 'is owed an effort at identification: that he should not be regarded as the surface to which a certain label can be applied, but one should try to see the world (including the label) from his point of view.' Each person, he claims 'is owed an effort at identification: that he should not be regarded as the surface to which a certain label can be applied, but one should try to see the world (including the label) from his point of view.'

Lorraine Code has also argued for a conception of respect for persons at the heart of which is the demand that we 'attempt to *know* other people responsibly and well,' that we try 'to know their situation empathetically' ('Persons and Others,' 143; 154). Such respect, she maintains, eschews dealing with others through stereotyped ways of 'knowing,' and so requires the cultivating of moral sensitivity and imagination in order to be able to respond to others as the persons they are. Similarly, Elizabeth Spelman has suggested that respecting a person involves responding to her on the basis of her self-conception: 'I treat you as the person you are just insofar as I recognize and respond to those features of you which, in your view, are necessary to who you are. We treat others as the persons they are just insofar as we try to respond to the way in which they choose to be seen, and not through our favored ways of seeing them' (151).

The conception of care respect captures these characterizations of respect as the Kantian conception cannot. Indeed, in keeping with its abstractive approach to persons, Kantian respect is compatible with complete ignorance of the other; it may even encourage a reliance on stereotyping and pigeonholing. By contrast, care respect obliges us to make an effort to discover how the other views herself and the world, to try to understand what it is like to be her living her life from her point of view. The attention that care respect calls for is thus neither the coolly detached and emotionless stare that objectifies and depersonalizes, nor the coolly appraising look that can be invasive, presumptive, and diminishing even when it is admiring. Rather, the attention of care respect expresses sympathetic, concerned, involved engagement with an participation in the other.

We might wonder, however, why care respect calls for this kind of understanding of another. For in the everyday sense of care, caring for someone and knowing her well do not necessarily entail one another. On the one hand, I can identify with another in order to discover her weakness and so destroy or exploit her; and on the other, we are often content to let those we love remain enigmas to us. But care respect's insistence on understanding makes it clear that the latter is as much as moral failure as the former. Let me suggest two reasons why.

First, there is a practical point. Since care respect involves, as I will claim, promoting the other's good, then grasping her good in as much detail as possible would seem to be a prerequisite for performing that task well. Hence, careful attention and clear-eyed perception of the other's particular needs, desires, projects, and so on are instrumentally valuable. But there is more her. If there is to be care *respect* and not just paternalistic taking care of, then we have to promote what the other person regards as important; or where that is not possible or where we cannot bring ourselves to do that, then we at least have to take account of her conception of her own good. And that, too, requires informed understanding.

But this suggests a more important connection between care respect and understanding. For sometimes a person's own perception of what she needs and even of what she desires is mistaken, sometimes deeply so. Understanding things from her point of view thus does not automatically give us access to what we would need in order to promote her good. Nevertheless, we still owe it to her to take account of her sense of herself, to acknowledge her self-conception, not necessarily accepting it as true, but taking seriously the possibility of truth in it, and recognizing the relevance of her self-conception to who she is.

But why should we owe her that? We can call on a familiar idea here. Barring certain cases of mental defectiveness, a person is, from the perspective of care respect, an individual and human 'me': a being who is reflectively conscious of herself and her situation. She lives her life and has certain purposes in living it; and she has a certain understanding of what she does which informs and structures her living. Moreover, she sees some of her characteristics and the characteristics of her situation as more crucial to her identity than others. She has, then, a particular life of her own that she is interested in living, and she sees herself, her situation, and the world from the point of view of living that life. This is not to say that a person and her life are nothing other than or different from what she takes them to be; but it does mean that her self-conception and her conception of her world are an integral part of who she is, even when those conceptions are not complete or wholly accurate. And to take such a being seriously requires trying to understand her own consciousness of her herself, her activities, and her purposes, trying to understand her and her world in her own terms. In this way, understanding is integral to care respect and not simply a precondition for it.

Respect for the reality, including the self-defined reality, of another person requires, in particular, resisting the temptation to project my own reality onto her or to impose a reality-structure onto her that neatly pigeonholes her and so makes the task of comprehending her seem easy: 'I know *just* what you are going through; I went through the same thing myself when I—'; My cousin had the same experience and *she felt*—' Such responses to others, while seeking to make connection and perhaps to reassure, also ignore and diminish the other and her construction of her experience and are thus incompatible with respect. There is also a need to make an effort to be aware of and to try to avoid the tendency to project my own anxieties, needs and fantasies onto the other and to then act out of concern for my own self while thinking I am really helping the other person. Care respect would also seem to demand that we try to avoid making assumptions, or make them only cautiously and as a last resort when access to others t too difficult remaining always cognizant of their evasiveness and of the risks attendant on making them, and cognizant, too, of the arrogance and danger of assuming, in particular, that we've got the other person right.

Taking appropriate account of a person, then, involves focusing on *her* as the whole specific individual she is and takes herself to be. Nor is this limited to close personal interactions; there are, for example, political implications; think of the misery and peril which have arisen from the failure of both the leaders and the citizens of this country to try to appreciate the perspectives of people in other parts of the world, and vice versa.

The understanding that care respect calls for takes great effort; and there are surely limitations on our abilities to fully understand others, some arising from our own ineliminable epistemological incapacities, others from the instability of selves and self-conceptions and the tendency of persons to be opaque even to themselves. Thus, what we owe others is our sincerest *efforts* to understand them; and as care respecters we also need an appropriate sense of humility about our access to others and about our own abilities to understand, in order to avoid depersonalizing assumptions. At the same time, however, difficulty does not entail impossibility; and our responsibility to try to understand entails a responsibility to develop skills of communication, imagination, sensitivity, and emotional responsiveness, to cultivate a flexible repertoire of techniques and strategies, to train ourselves and others to be able to approach that understanding more closely than we can now.

VI. Respect and Responsibility

The active and concerned engagement with others that understanding involves is one mode of respectful behavior, but there are still other ways of treating persons that manifest care respect for them. The discussions of respect to which I am attending suggest two additional forms of conduct.

The first flows from the discussion of understanding. Williams rightly acknowledges that understanding another through her self-conception, though an important part of respect, cannot be sufficient for respecting her (160). For an individual's sense of herself and indeed her very ability to have her own self-conception can be warped or destroyed through various forms of manipulation, exploitation, or degradation. But it would be a grossly perverted view of respect which maintained that respecting a person meant merely viewing the world through the lenses of exploitation or degradation; respect surely must prohibit exploiting and degrading persons in the first place. And the appreciation and cherishing of individual 'me's' which care respect involves concurs in this prohibition. Insofar as it demands that we take seriously and value the self-conceptions which partially define individuals as the persons they are, then (following Williams' proposal) care respect must insist at the very least that we not suppress or destroy an individual's reflective consciousness of herself and her situation. But more than this, the treasuring of self-constructed and self-constructing individuality would

VII. Care Respect, Kantian Respect, and Care

Many discussions of care emphasize its home in the domain of close personal relationships and its essential connection with the emotional responses of affection and bonding love that are appropriate to such relationships. Care is thus not something we could or probably even should extend to those who stand outside our networks of personal relationships. Although care and personal relationships, I would argue, clearly have moral significance, nevertheless since care is not universalizable, we would be hard pressed to regard it as the whole of morality or as by itself a fully adequate basis for morality. Impartiality and universality are also essential for morality; and the question then becomes how to integrate the demands of emotional connection and detached impartiality.

One important consequence of the notion of care respect is that it provides a route to achieving that integration. For care respect, unlike care, is not restricted to the domain of personal relationships, and it is not essentially connected with the emotions of love and affection, though it may involve sympathy and compassion. Not only can it be extended to the stranger, but care respect is properly extended to all human beings; it is what the person as a human 'me' demands of us. Each of us is a fully particular and concrete individual, and that fact about us calls for recognition and response from each of us. But all of us also share a common humanity and warrant respect on that ground as well. Care respect enables us to keep both of these facts in sight, as it calls our attention to the moral significance both of the particularity of persons and of this richly specific and contextualized individual. Care respect might thus be thought of as care universalizing itself, though reshaped by the demands of the universal context.

It might be objected, however, that care respect as I have described it cannot be universalized in the way Kantian respect is. For it just does not seem humanly possible to meet everyone with the attention to detail, the effort to understand, the active promotion of their good, and so on, that care respect requires. Indeed, many of us barely manage to achieve this even with those we love. It is hard enough to try to understand my daughter in a full and sensitive way, even though we share a deeply intimate relationship and the incentive that love provides to make the effort that understanding requires. How, then, can I rightly be expected to approach the supermarket clerk in the same fashion as I try to hurry through the check-out line to get home to make dinner for my daughter?

We need to recognize here, however, that attention, understanding, responsiveness, promoting the other's good, and so on, are all activities that admit of degrees; moreover, pulling out all the stops for every individual one comes across is not only not humanly possible but may also be inappropriate for many individuals in many situations. For instance, trying to apprehend the reality of another can be, with regard to certain individuals in certain circumstances, neither caring nor respectful but threatening insofar as it opens up possibilities for exploitation of revealed vulnerabilities. But the inappropriateness of always pulling out all the stops for everyone does not mean that it would be either inappropriate or impossible to approach others generally with more constrained, context-sensitive expressions of care respect. One advantage of the idea of care respect is that it calls us to recognize that human responsiveness cannot be restricted to the relative ease and safety of personal relationships, and it engages us in the task of trying to find ways to make our encounters with others and the institutions within which we encounter them more fully and flexibly responsive.

Finally, recognizing a connection between care and respect invites us to see care, care respect, and Kantian respect as arranged on a continuum of responsive stances toward others, rather than as competing and mutually exclusive stances. So we might then see Kantian respect as the minimal level of respect that care itself requires: I may not care about an individual; I may be altogether unable to identify with her or to forge and sustain a relationship with her; I may never even encounter her in any non-metaphorical sense. But somebody might care for her: she is someone's daughter, friend, or sister; and so she constrains my actions.[31] And where I cannot help, I can at least refrain from harming. But we would do well, I believe, to maintain an attitude of regret about such situations. We ought, I want to suggest, to regard Kantian respect as a morally incomplete and evasive response and try to resist its facile depersonalization and distancing detachment. We ought, that is, to shift care respect to the heart of our responsive repertoire. We may in this way open up possibilities not only for the integration of seemingly distinct moral theories but also for the transformation of human society and individual human lives.

Notes

1. This is a revised and expanded version of my 'Care and Respect,' in Susan Coultrap-McQuin and Even Browning Cole, eds., *Explorations in Feminist Ethics: Theory and Practice* (Bloomington: Indiana University Press forthcoming). Ancestral versions of this paper were presented at the University of Minnesota-Duluth's Conference 'Explorations in Feminist Ethics'; at the 1989 meeting of the Society for Philosophy and Public Affairs; at the 1989 Central Division meetings of the American Philosophical Association; and at the Lehigh Valley Feminist Research Group. I have benefited greatly from the discussions in these sessions. I am especially grateful to Marilyn Friedman, my respondent at the APA Central Division session, for her insightful criticisms and suggestions. I have also benefited from comments by Edmund Abegg, Kurt Baier, Gordon Bearn, Aaron Ben-Zeev, Ann Cudd, Janet Fleetwood, John Hare, Ralph Lindgren, and Jean Rumsey, and from discussions with Annette Baier, David Gauthier, and Geoffrey Sayre-McCord.

2. Annette C. Baier, 'The Need For More Than Justice,' in Marsha Hanen and Kai Nielsen, eds., *Science, Morality, and Feminist Theory* (Calgary: University of Calgary Press 1987) 56.

3. Nel Noddings, *Caring: A Feminine Approach to Ethics and Moral Education* (Berkeley, CA: University of California Press 1984) 4.

42   Respect and Care: Toward Moral Integration

4. Immanual Kant, *The Doctrine of Virtue*, Mary Gregor, trans. (Philadelphia: University of Pennsylvania Press 1964) 116.

5. Carol Gilligan, *In a Different Voice: Psychological Theory and Women's Development* (Cambridge, MA: Harvard University Press 1982), and 'Moral Orientation and Moral Development,' in Eva Feder Kittay and Diana T. Meyers, eds., *Women and Moral Theory* (Totowa, JN: Rowman and Littlefield 1987) 19-33. Seyla Benhabib explicitly contrasts care and respect in 'The Generalized and The Concrete Other: The Kohlberg-Gilligan Controversy and Moral Theory,' in *Women and Moral Theory* 164.

6. Kant 134. A few sentences earlier Kant refers to them as '*mere* duties of love.'

7. See 'Conclusion of the Doctrine of Elements: The Union of Love and Respect in Friendship,' in *The Doctrine of Virtue*, 140-5.

8. Such a view is suggested by, for example, Virginia Held, 'Feminism and Moral Theory,' in *Women and Moral Theory* 111-28; Marilyn Friedman, 'Beyond Caring: The De-Moralization of Gender,' in *Science, Morality, and Feminist Theory* 109; Claudia Card, 'Caring and Evil,' *Hypatia 5* (1990) 101-8; Lawrence Kohlberg, Charles Levine, and Alexandra Hewer, *Moral Stages: A Current Formulation and a Response to Critics* (Basel: S. Karger 1983), 220-1. For a discussion of Carol Gilligan's views on this issue, see Lawrence A. Blum, 'Gilligan and Kohlberg: Implications for Moral Theory,' *Ethics 98* (1988) 472-91.

9. It might seem that not everything worth attending to has its own worth, not everything we respect is something we value. For we respect dangerous and fearsome things: the prudent sailor has a healthy respect for the sea, the tennis player has a healthy respect for her opponent's backhand, the lion tamer has a healthy respect for his animals. In each case, it is the dangerousness of the object that seems to callus to respect it, making respect akin to fear. However, this is not an adequate understanding of such cases, as David Gauthier pointed out to me. For in such cases the fearsome element of the object is part of what makes the object valuable to us. Thus the sailor respects the sea in part because of its power not only to give but also to take away; it is her powerful backhand that makes the tennis opponent a great player and a worthy opponent; and part of what attracts the lion tamer to her profession is the excitement of facing the danger her animals pose. Moreover, wile there may be an element of fear in some forms of respect, we do not respect those fearsome things that we view as having no worth at all in virtue of their dangerousness, such as the AIDS virus or nuclear waste.

10. I draw here on Carl Cranor, 'Toward a Theory of Respect for Persons,' *American Philosophical Quarterly 12* (1975) 309-19.

11. Stephen D. Hudson, 'The Nature of Respect,' *Social Theory and Practice 6* (1980) 69-90.

12. There may, however, be an appraisal *behind* the other varieties of respect. For example, institutional respect for a country's flag may involve viewing it as the symbol of a great country. Moreover, disrespect for such institutional symbols as flags, presidents, and judges is often an expression of our lack of evaluative respect for the institutions they represent. Similarly, directive-respecting a person's advice may involve having evaluative respect for her as an advice-giver. However, the institutional or directive respect itself does

not consist in an appraisal of the relative quality of the flag or the advice; and we can respect the flag of a country we despise and respect advice we think is poor.

13. Stephen L. Darwall, 'Two Kinds of Respect,' *Ethics 88* (1977) 36-49. Darwall does not distinguish varieties of his two kinds.

14. One complaint that has been raised against the notion of a principle of respect for persons is that such a principle ought to tell us precisely how to treat persons, but it cannot do this. (See, for example, Carl Cranor, 'On Respecting Human Beings as Persons,' *Journal of Value Inquiry 17* (1983) 103-17, and Allan Gibbard, *Wise Choices, Apt Feelings* (Cambridge, MA: Harvard University Press 1990), 264-9.) One of the implications of my argument is that this view misconceives the function of the notion of respect for persons. The concept of respect does not contain the resources for telling us *how* to treat persons; its function is rather to keep in the forefront of moral consciousness the attitude of valuing persons for their own sake and so to remind s of the reasons *why* we should treat persons as morality obliges us to treat them. To place a principle of respect for persons at the heart of morality is to say that our moral attention ought in the first instance to be focused on *persons* in virtue of their fundamental worth, rather than, for example, on actions, consequences, rules, duties, or social cooperation.

15. It is worth noting that although we don't usually think of utilitarianism as dealing in respect for persons, my account entails that utilitarians can in a sense rightly claim to respect persons by taking each into account in determining the overall good. That is to say, utilitarian respect for persons is yet another conception of recognition respect for persons. However, it is a conception of respect which may be seen to focus on treatment rather than attitude insofar as utilitarian reasons for moral conduct have to do with the intrinsic value of states of affairs rather than the intrinsic moral value of persons. That the worth of persons is not in the forefront of utilitarian concern my be what underlies the belief that utilitarianism does not have a respect-for-persons principle. For a discussion of utilitarian respect, see Bart Gruzalski, 'Two Accounts of Our Obligations to Respect Persons,' in O.H. Green, ed., *Respect for Persons (Tulane Studies in Philosophy 31* [New Orleans: Tulane University Press 1982] 77-89).

16. I draw these elements primarily from the following: Bernard Williams, 'The Idea of Equality,' in Joel Feinberg, ed., *Moral Concepts* (Oxford: Oxford University Press 1969) 153-71; Elizabeth Spelman, 'On Treating Persons as Persons,' *Ethics 88* (1977) 150-61; R.S. Downie and Elizabeth Telfer, *Respect of Persons* (London: Allen and Unwin 1969); Elizabeth Maclaren, 'Dignity,' *Journal of Medical Ethics 3* (1977) 40-1; and Lorraine Code, 'Persons and Others,' in Judith Genova, ed., *Power, Gender, and Values* (Edmonton: Academic Printing and Publishing 1987) 143-61.

17. I have relied primarily on the following: Carol Gilligan, *In a Different Voice* and 'Moral Orientation'; Seyla Benhabib, 'The Generalized and the Concrete Other'; Nel Noddings, *Caring*; Virginia Held, 'Feminism and Moral Theory,'; Marilyn Friedman, 'Beyond Caring'; Sara Ruddick, 'Maternal Thinking,' in Marilyn Pearsall, ed., *Women and Values* (Belmont, CA: Wadsworth 1986) 340-51; Margaret Urban Walker, 'Moral Understandings: An Alternative "Epistemology" for a Feminist Ethics,' *Hypatia 4* (1989) 15-28; and Lorraine Code, 'Second Persons,' in *Science, Morality, and Feminist Theory* 357-82.

18. In addition to those mentioned in not 16, above, see Bernard Williams, 'Persons, Character, and Morality,' in Amelie Oksenberg Roty, ed., *The Identities of Persons* (Berkeley, CA: University of California Press 1976) 197-216; Alasdair MacIntyre, *After Virtue* (Notre Dame: Notre Dame University Press 1981); Robert Paul Wolff, 'There's Nobody Here But Us Persons,' in Carol C. Gould and Marx Wartofsky, eds., *Women and Philosophy: Toward a Theory of Liberation* (New York: Perigee/Putnam 197) 128-44; Edward Johnson, 'Ignoring Persons,' in *Respect for Persons* 91-105; Michael Sandel, *Liberalism and the Limits of Justice* (Cambridge, MA: Cambridge University Press 1982).

19. Melvin Rader, *Ethics and the Human Community* (New York: Holt, Rinehart, and Winston 1964), 157; quoted in John E. Atwell, 'Kant's Notion of Respect for Persons,' in *Respect for Persons*, 22.

20. Carol Gilligan, 'The Conquistador and the Dark Continent: Reflections on the Psychology of Love,' *Daedalus 113* (1984) 77.

21. Diana T. Meyers, 'The Socialized Individual and Individual Autonomy: An Intersection between Philosophy and Psychology,' in *Women and Moral Theory 146*.

22. In what follows, I draw on Robert Nozick, *Philosophical Explanations* (Cambridge, MA: Belkap Press of Harvard University Press 1981), 452-7.

23. Iris Murdoch, *The Sovereignty of Good* (London: Routledge & Kegan Paul 1970). See also Lawrence A. Blum, 'Iris Murdoch and the Domain of the Moral,' *Philosophical Studies 50* (1986) 343-67.

24. Martha Craven Nussbaum, "Finely Aware and Richly Responsible": Literature and the Moral Imagination," in Stanley G. Clarke and Evan Simpson, eds., *Anti-Theory in Ethics and Moral Conservatism* (Albany, NY: State University of New York Press 1989) 128-9.

25. See Kant's discussion of dignity and irreplaceability in *Groundwork of the Metaphysic of Morals*, H.J. Paton, trans. (New York: Harper and Row 1964), 102-3.

26. Marilyn Friedman raised this objection in her commentary on an earlier version of this paper. Alison Jaggar has also articulated this concern in 'Feminist Ethics: Some Issues for the Nineties,' *Journal of Social Philosophy 20* (1989) 91-107.

Chapter 3

Roots of Elder Respect:
Ideals and Practices in East Asia

Kyu-taik Sung

Respect for the elderly is practiced in diverse cultural contexts. Although various cultures share the values of respect for the elderly, the extent to which elders are respected and specific forms of respect most often practiced seem to vary by culture (Silverman & Maxwell, 1978; Streib, 1987; Leininger, 1990; Mehta, 1997; Sung, 2004). This is because cultural difference has a significant effect on how people treat the elderly (Nydegger, 1983; Sokolovsky, 1990; Simic, 1990; Holmes & Holmes, 1995; Siverstein, Burholt, Wenger, & Bengtson, 1998; Palmore, 1999; Liu & Kendig, 2000). Hereafter, "respect for the elderly" is termed "elder respect." The term "elder" here denotes parent, other elderly relative, elderly teacher, and elders in general.

The peoples of East Asia have a notable tradition of elder respect rooted in Confucian teachings of filial piety (Lang, 1946; Silberman, 1962; Lew, 1995). Filial piety essentially directs the young to recognize the care and aid received from elderly relatives and, in return, respect and care for them (Kong, 1995; Lew, 1995). The Chinese, the Japanese, Koreans, and other ethnic groups in that region—comprising roughly one third of the world's population—have shared this tradition for many generations.

In the teachings, elder respect is of central concern (Teachings of Filial Piety, Ch. 7 & Ch. 9). Expectations regarding respecting elders and providing care for elders in China strongly resemble those found in Japan and Korea, as all three of these East Asian cultures have been greatly influenced by Confucian ethical conception of filial piety (Elliot & Campbell, 1993; Chow, 1995). The values of filial piety are reflected in their rituals, propriety, and manners of daily living.

Until recently these values have served elders well as family readily provided care needed. However, changes have occurred; more elderly people are living longer and fewer children are being born throughout East Asia (Liang, Tu, & Chen, 1986; Ogawa & Rutherford, 1994; Kim, Liang, Rhee, & Kim, 1996). As these demographic changes continue, eldercare responsibilities will be placed on the shoulders of fewer younger people. Along with these changes, East Asian nations are undergoing social changes, including the growth in the number of adult children living at a distance from their aging parents, the movement toward smaller families, and the emerging tendency among the young to have individualistic lifestyles. Heavier burdens of smaller families needing to provide the eldercare combined with these other changes have tempted some of the young to unravel the traditional values affirming elder respect (Choi, 2001; Maeda, 1997; Chow, 1995).

In recent years, concern over declining consensus on filial morality has increased. Studies have reported on the tendencies of some adults to mistreat and abandon frail and sick elders, to disrespect older persons in general by neglecting and disregarding their problems, and to be prejudiced against them as manifested in negative attitudes and discriminatory practices (Koyano, Inoue & Shibata, 1987; Tomita, 1994; Levy, 1999; Han, 2000; Park, 2001; Kim, 2003; Lee, 2004).

Old people are vulnerable to the shifts of moral consciousness of young people. As history tells us, treatment given for old and burdensome family members was not respectful and humane in some bygone eras. There have been tales of immorality, e.g., "Chilaukuo" in China, a country wherein old parents were taken to a prairie outside the village and discarded there, "Koryojang" in Korea where aged parents were put into a cave with some food and sealed off, and "Obasute" in Japan, where old parents were taken to a hilltop and abandoned there. In modern civilized societies, under no circumstances, would younger people have recourse to such antiquated and inhumane practice of senicide.

Without respect, society is less likely to have positive attitudes toward its elders or treat and care for them as dignified members of society. Many elderly persons have a variety of problems (Dunkle, Robert, & Haug, 2001). To resolve these problems, they most often depend on care providers. When they are dependent on the providers, respectful care has even more significant implications as one of psychosocial sources of the quality of their later life (Noelker & Harel, 2000; Applegate & Morse, 1994; Downie & Telfer, 1969).

It remains puzzling, however, that the theme of respect is so noticeably absent from most discussions concerning aging. Gerontologists have concentrated their attention on instrumental roles of caregivers, with little discussion of respect in the relationship between the young and the old, and the caregiver and the old care recipient. One explanation for this regrettable oversight is that the concept of respect is classified as a sheer qualitative dimension which is hard to quantify or to be accounted for.

The general view is that elder respect is "being courteous and obedient to elderly persons" (Lew, 1995; Kong, 1995). Elder respect as colloquially described has often been characterized by emphasis on these principles. However, such a simplistic conceptualization is not enough for a true understanding of this complex and extensive ideal in the East Asian cultural context. Confucian writers prescribed how elders should be respected in a variety of forms, depending on their beliefs and the context of the discussion. Thus, the complete distinction of how elders should be respected is still unresolved.

The purpose of this paper is to review the original teachings of elder respect prescribed in Confucian literature and identify traditional forms of elder respect that have influenced the way East Asian peoples treat their elderly. For this purpose, this paper reviews passages excerpted from Confucian literature to find the root meanings of elder respect and distinguishes specific forms of elder respect prescribed therein. Communality of the way these forms are practiced among East Asian people, cross-cultural differences in the use of the forms, and changing expressions of elder respect are discussed.

Exploration of Forms of Respect: Approach

The following are Confucian classics which laid down a number of rules and prescripts that adults were to follow in order to fulfill their filial duties, which included respect for parents, ancestors, and elders: *The Book of Rites* (Li Chi, Confucian teachings on rites or propriety), *Teachings of Filial Piety* (Hsiao Ching, guidelines for the practice of filial piety), *Analects of Confucius* (Lun Yu, sayings and deeds of Confucius and his disciples on a scope of subjects including education and moral cultivation), and *Works of Mencius* (Meng Tzu, a collection of opinions and conversations of Mencius, a principal disciple of Confucius). To identify expressions of respect, the texts of the above classics were explored. Each of these Chinese classics met the following criteria for inclusion in the present study: (1) being most frequently quoted in discussions of the meanings and practices of filial piety that includes respect for elders; (2) contains multiple discourses that prescribe specific behavioral expressions of respect for elders; (3) translated into English.

Passages in the above classics were explored to identify the forms and expressions of respect for elders. Initially, the seven cross-cultural forms distinguished by Silverman and Maxwell (1978) were chosen as reference forms, which are "service respect" (providing housekeeping service), victual respect (serving drinks and foods), gift respect (bestowing gifts), linguistic respect (using respectful language), presentational respect (showing courteous appearances), spatial respect (furnishing honorable seats or places), and celebratory respect (celebrating birthdays). These forms were identified based on data from 186 distinctive world areas which included areas in which Chinese, Korean, and Japanese peoples resided.

For the present study, the authors collaborated with two scholars with a doctoral degree in the study of Neo-Confucianism to explore specific forms of elder respect. Relevant passages in the classics describing forms and expressions of elder respect that fit into the reference forms were located and compared to delineate specific forms of elder respect. While the seven forms guided the analysis, other forms were allowed to emerge in the process of the exploration. For instance, the form of care respect was distinguished by one or more expressions and behaviors directed to provide care and services for parents. In the case of Teachings of Filial Piety, all but one of its chapters were dedicated to the prescriptions of various types of care and services for parents. All these chapters combined were categorized as the form of care respect, which includes service respect that Silverman and Maxwell distinguished. Excerpts of some of these chapters are presented in the following section. In other instances, an entire paragraph or a whole chapter described how to connote a single form of respect. For instance, in The Book of Rites, Chapters 20, 21, and 22 dealt with respect for parents after their death. These chapters were transformed into ancestor respect. In contrast, the following single passage was considered to reflect two different ways of elder respect—salutatory respect and presentational respect: "When a son is called by parents, he should answer `Yes' politely and greet them in a courteous manner. In entering and exiting their room, the child should keep sincere and respectful posture" (Book of Rites, Bk. 2, Ch. 12). An inference was made based on the meanings of two or more sentences or passages. For instance, the statements "A child should use proper language" (Teachings of Filial Piety, Ch. 4) and "A gentleman should speak the proper words in the proper tone of voice" (Analect, Bk. 8, Ch. 4) were interpreted as expressions of linguistic respect. Similarly, precedential respect was inferred from "Allowing visitors to enter a room first" (Book of Rites, Bk. 1, Ch. 1) and "Not leaving a drinking table before the elderly had done so" (Analect, Bk. 10, Ch. 13). Passages prescribing the same form and expression of elder respect were found in two or more of the four classics. In this case, only one of those passages was quoted.

The interpretation and categorization of the forms and expressions of elder respect were cross-checked by independent testimonies of the authors and the two analysts who conducted the exploration separately. Any form cited by two or more of the analysts was counted for. Forms and expressions of elder respect were subsequently defined.

The following are passages and excerpts denoting various expressions of elder respect discovered in Chinese and English versions of the four classics (Legge, 1960).

Passages and Excerpts of Elder Respect in The Classics

To Confucius (also known as `the Master') (551-478 B.C.), being filial to parents meant treating parents with propriety, 'li' (Analects, Bk. 2, Ch. 7; de Bary, 1995). (The Chinese `li' means propriety or rites: rules of proper conduct). The nexus of propriety in Confucian teachings is caring for parents with respect.

Mencius (the principal disciple of Confucius) said,

"Of all human conducts, none is greater than filial piety. In filial piety nothing is greater than to respect one's parents" (Teachings of Filial Piety, Ch. 10).

For Mencius, elder respect was the proper conduct or righteousness of human being (Works of Mencius, Bk. 7, Pt. 1, Ch. 15).

When a disciple asked about being filial, the Master said,

"Filial piety today is taken to mean providing nourishment for parents, but even dogs and horses are provided with nourishment. If it is not done with respect for parents, what is the difference between men and animals?" (Analects, Bk. 2, Ch. 7; de Bary, 1995).

For the Master, mere material support without respect would not be sufficiently proper to be considered as parent care. Thus, his priority refers not only to formal ritual prescriptions for parent care but also to an inner disposition of the mind and heart for respectful care (de Bary, 1997: 58-59).

The teachings on respect invariably prescribed ways of taking good care of aged parents. *[Italics in a parenthesis denote forms of respect attributable to the quotation.]*

The Master outlined specific ways of providing respectful care:

"In the morning, the couple should pay a call on parents in their room. When they arrive at their room, they should keep themselves at ease. Then, they should ask the parents in gentle voices if their clothes are warm enough and if they have any pain or discomfort. If they do, they should be given proper care and relieved from discomfort. They should be served foods of their choice and the foods should be tasty, fresh, soft, and fragrant." (Book of Rites, Bk. 2, Ch. 12). *[Care respect, Victual respect, Privacy respect]*

Nourishment for parents or serving meals was recurrently prescribed.

"When parents are alive, a daughter-in-law should make every effort to serve them enough meals . . . when only a mother is alive after father's death, the eldest son should serve her meals, while his wife and other grown children urge the mother to enjoy hearty meals." (Book of Rites, Bk. 2, Ch. 12). *[Victual respect]*

Besides, the couple should regularly help the parents wash their faces, hair, and bodies (Book of Rites, Bk. 2, Ch. 1). *[Care respect]*

"When a parent's nose is running, a son or his wife should wipe the parent's nose. One should not show this happening to others. (Book of Rites, Bk. 2, Ch. 2). [Care respect, Privacy respect]

The Master prescribed how the parents' room should be maintained.

"In the morning, when a housekeeper makes the parents' bed and arranges their sitting places, younger family members should help the housekeeper and assist the parents in occupying their seats." (Book of Rites, Bk. 2, Ch. 2). [*Care respect*]

These services and works for elders are mostly '*instrumental forms*' of parent care.

The Master prescribed the affective forms of parent care as well.

"In caring for parents, filial children should make them feel happy, not act against their will, let them see and hear pleasurable things and provide them with comfortable places to sleep." (Book of Rites, Bk. 1, Ch. 1; Bk. 2, Ch. 12). [*Care respect, Privacy respect*]

Not encouraging anxiety is an important way of caring for parents. The Master said,

"When one's parents are alive, one should not go far away. If one goes, one should tell them where one is going" (Analects, Bk. 4, Ch. 19). [*Care respect*]

Thus, in order to relieve their parents of anxiety, children should keep themselves near their home at all possible times and try to refrain from traveling in distant places.

When a disciple asked about being filial, Confucius replied,

"A child should show special concern for the health of his parents" (Analects, Bk. 2, Ch.6). [*Care respect*]

Making elders happy, letting them see and hear pleasurable things, relieving them of anxiety, having concern for their health, etc. are all '*affective forms*' of parent care.

And, the couple have obligation to consult with their elders and ask their advice on family matters and customs and rituals to be observed (Book of Rites, Bk. 2, Ch. 12). The Master said,

"Open your ears to all kinds of advice and opinions" (Analects, Bk. 1, Ch. 18). [*Consulting respect*]

Respect is concerned also with a child's proper manner. The Master said,

"When a son is called by parents, he should answer `Yes' politely and greet them in a courteous manner. In entering and exiting their room, the child should keep sincere and respectful posture" (Book of Rites, Bk. 2, Ch. 12). [*Salutatory respect, Presentational respect*]

The Master stressed the importance of complying with parents' wishes and directives (Book of Rites, Bk. 2, Ch. 12). He said,

"Observe his aspirations when his father is alive. . . . He will be called filial if he sticks to his father's way." (Analects, Bk. 1, Ch. 11). [*Acquiescent respect, Identifying respect*]

In speaking and addressing parents, a child should use proper language (Teaching of Filial Piety, Ch. 4):

"A gentleman should take care to speak the proper words in the proper tone of voice so as to avoid coarseness" (Analects, Bk. 8, Ch. 4). [*Linguistic respect*]

The Master advised on the celebration of parents' birthdays:

"One must always keep in mind parents' birthdays; on the one hand, one is glad to offer birthday congratulations; on the other hand, one is worried to see they grow one year older" (Analects, Bk. 4, Ch. 21). [*Celebrative respect*]

This saying implies that children ought to celebrate festivities for parents but at the same time they should have concern and sympathy for parents who are getting older.
Children should offer elders seats or places that are tied to respect.

"In a room, one must leave center seats for parents and the direction of parents' seats should be arranged according to their wish"(Book of Rites, Bk. 1, Ch. 1; Bk. 2, Ch.12). [*Spatial respect*]

The Master gave precedence to elders out of courtesy (Analects, Bk. 12, Ch. 20). He allowed elderly visitors to enter rooms first (Book of Rites, Bk. 1, Ch. 1). And, he did not leave a drinking table before the elderly had done so (Analects, Bk. 10, Ch. 13). [*Precedential respect*]
Exhibiting proper manners and postures was an important way of connoting respect. The Master held good manners and wore neat and appropriate dresses (Analects, Bk. 10, Ch. 3 & Ch 6) when he received guests and elders. And, when he expressed regards to others, he bowed deeply toward them (Analects, Bk. 10, Ch. 15). [*Presentational respect*]
Dedicating gifts is a valued expression of respect frequently prescribed (Book of Rites, Bk. 2, Ch. 12; Twenty-Four Stories of Filial Piety). But mere material support without reverence could not be called elder respect. Mencius said,

"Honoring and respecting are what exist before any offering of gifts" (Works of Mencius, Bk. 7, Pt. II, Ch. 37). [*Gift respect*]

As is evident, to the Master, the innermost feelings of respect was most important. Mencius' story demonstrates such sentiment:

"Ts'eng-tz'u's father was fond of sheep-dates, a sweet fruit. When his father was alive, Ts'eng-tz'u often offered him this fruit. After his death, Ts'eng-tz'u could not bear to eat the fruit, because he was reminded of his father whenever he saw it" (Works of Mencius, Bk. 7, Pt. II, Ch. 36). [*Ancestor respect*]

This unlimited compassion and affection for the father was a genuine expression of respect. In this way, parents should be respected even when they are no longer in sight and their voices are not heard (Book of Rites, Bk. 1, Ch. 1). [*Ancestor respect*]

It would seem that the Master in the foregoing passages authorized no blind conformity to formalities; material support without a showing of propriety consisting of inner reverence was not considered to be a true way of respect.

The greatest regret a child could have is an eternally lost opportunity of serving his parents with medicine and soup on their deathbed or not being present when they die (Lin, 1982). Mencius said,

"The nourishment of parents when living is not sufficient to be accounted as the great thing. It is only in the performance of funeral rites when dead that we have what can be considered a great thing" (Works of Mencius, Bk. 4, Pt. 2, Ch. 12). [*Funeral respect*]

"In discharging funeral duties to parents, men indeed are constrained to do their utmost . . . by wearing coarse cloth . . . with deep dejection of countenance and the mournfulness of wailing." (Works of Mencius, Bk. 3, Pt. 1, Ch. 2). [*Funeral respect*]

The Master was particular about what he wears in the period of mourning (Analects, Bk. 10, Ch. 6). He even detailed the use of the inner and outer coffins for the burial of parents (Works of Mencius, Bk. 2, Pt. 2, Ch. 7). The choice of mourning attire and quality coffins is an expression of filial respect and affection toward the departed parents. [*Funeral respect*] However, the Master said,

"In ceremonies of mourning, it is better that there be deep sorrow than a minute attention to observances. For mourning, inner grief is more important than formalities" (Analects, Bk. 3, Ch. 4). [*Funeral respect*]

He stressed the importance of continuous mourning (Analects, Bk. 17, Ch. 21).

Thus, respect for parents—whether they are alive or deceased—is concerned with our external behavior as well as our inner disposition. The Master said,

"One should offer sacrifices to one's ancestors as if they were present." (Analects, Bk. 3, Ch. 12). [*Ancestor respect*]

"They served the dead as they would have served them alive; they served the departed as they would have served them had they continued among them. This was the highest evidence of filial piety" (Teachings of Filial Piety, Ch. 22). [*Ancestor respect*]

Confucius envisioned respectful relations between all members of the family and society. The Master said,

> "Treat with reverence the elders in your own family, so that elders in other families shall be similarly treated" (Teachings of Filial Piety, Ch. 2). [*Public respect*]

> "At home, a young man should be dutiful towards his parents; going outside, he should be respectful towards other elders" (Analects, Bk. 1, Ch. 6). [*Public respect*]

Thus, propriety extends beyond the boundary of the family to respecting elders in the neighborhood and larger society.

The above 39 passages and excerpts (Analects of Confucius 17, The Book of Rites 12, Mencius 6, The Teachings of Filial Piety 4) reflect the traditional ideal of elder respect which has influenced East Asian people and exemplify the ways in which they should convey elder respect. In the exploration of these classics, which started with the seven reference forms, nine other forms (consulting, acquiescent, precedential, salutatory, identifying, privacy, ancestor, funeral, and public) subsequently emerged, bringing the total number to 16. The following are these forms and expressions thereof.

List of Traditional Forms

FORMS AND EXPRESSIONS OF ELDER RESPECT

Form 1 Care respect (Providing care and services)
      Sample key expressions:
        1. Providing affective care
          * Speaking in gentle voice
          * Making happy and comfortable
          * Relieving of anxiety
          * Having concern over health
          * Extending efforts to help
          * Having innermost feeling of caring
        2. Providing instrumental services
          * Providing with nutrition
          * Providing with warm clothes
          * Housekeeping
          * Assisting with personal hygiene
          * Providing with comfortable resting place
            * Relieving from physical discomfort

       * Maintaining contact

Form 2 Consulting respect (Asking for consent and advice)
       Sample key expressions:
          1. Consulting with parents
          2. Asking parents for advice

Form 3 Victual respect (Serving foods)
       Sample key expressions:
          1. Serving foods of parents' choice

Form 4 Acquiescent respect (Complying with parents' wishes)
       Sample key expressions:
          1. Being obedient to parents' wishes
          2. Not acting against the will of parents
          3. Listening to parents words

Form 5 Gift respect (Bestowing gifts on parents)
       Sample key expressions:
          1. Providing parents with material things

Form 6 Celebrative respect (Celebrating birthdays in honor of parents)
       Sample key expressions:
          1. Celebrating parents' birthday

Form 7 Linguistic respect (Using proper language to convey a sense of respect)
       Sample key expressions:
          1. Using respectful language
             * Using honorifics
             * Using proper words that connote respect

Form 8 Precedential respect (Giving precedential treatment to parents)
       Sample key expressions:
          1. Bestowing benefits or convenience first

Form 9 Presentational respect (Holding courteous manners to convey respect)
       Sample key expressions:
          1. Holding respectful postures
          2. Showing proper physical appearance

Form 10 Salutatory respect (Greeting parents with respect)
        Sample key expressions:
          1. Greeting
            * By bowing (bending body)

Form 11 Spatial respect (Furnishing parents with honorable seats)
        Sample key expressions:
          1.   Furnishing with a scat of honor

Form 12 Identifying respect (Identifying with elders)
        Sample key expression
          1.   Identifying with elder's values
          2.   Identifying with elder's lifestyles

Form 13 Privacy respect (Respecting privacy of elders)
        Sample key expression
          1. Respecting elders' personal privacy

Form 14 Ancestor respect (Worshipping ancestors)
        Sample key expressions:
          1. Paying respect to ancestors
            * Commemorating ancestors' death anniversaries
          2. Maintaining family continuity
            * Attaining wishes of ancestors

Form 15 Funeral respect (Holding funeral rites for deceased elderly kin)
        Sample key expressions:
          1.   Mourning for departed elderly kin
            * Mourning with inner grief
            * Expressing mournfulness by wailing
          2.   Holding solemn funeral ceremony
          3.   Conducting a respectful burial

Form 16 Public respect (Respecting elders of larger society)
        Samples key expressions:
          1.   Respecting elders of other families
          2.   Serving neighborhood elders

Communality of Forms Practiced in East Asia

The above forms (hereafter called 'traditional forms') were compared with the forms of elder respect reported by three empirical studies conducted in recent decades in East Asia. The three studies met the following criteria: (1) analyzed expressions and forms of elder respect, (2) used a sample of East Asian people, and (3) met commonly accepted canons of methodological adequacy for qualitative or quantitative research.

Palmore and Maeda (1985) studied the Japanese based on data from a survey of the aged, trend data showing the extent of change in the situations of the aged, observations of public and voluntary programs for the aged, interviews with gerontologists, and reviews of literary works. Ingersoll-Dayton and Saengtienchai (1999) studied in four Asian countries based on 79 focus group discussions (14 in Taiwan, 21 in Singapore, 18 in the Philippines, and 26 in Thailand) focused on the same topic of elder respect. Meanwhile, Sung and Kim's study (2003) was based on response from 401 young South Korean adults to a single question designed to identify various forms of respect which was partially open by adding an "'Other'—Please specify" category.

Although all of the three studies addressed the same topic—ways of respecting elders—their research methods varied. Yet, they yielded parallel results for identification of a set of similar, if not identical, forms of elder respect. This result would seem to justify considering them in terms of a single summary of the ways of respecting elders among the East Asian people (Larson, 1978).

Palmore and Maeda (1985) cited 13 forms: care, victual, gift, linguistic, presentational, consulting, spatial, celebrative, acquiescent, salutatory, precedential, ancestor, and public. Except funeral respect, identifying respect, and privacy respect which they did not cite, all other forms are nearly identical to the traditional forms in terms of the meanings and expressions. Ingersoll-Dayton and Saengtienchai (1999) examined gestures and manners, customs, rituals, and tokens associated with elder respect and distinguished 12 forms, one form (ancestor) short of the 13 forms that Palmore and Maeda prescribed. Their 12 forms are nearly identical to the corresponding traditional forms. Sung and Kim (2003) identified a comprehensive set of 14 forms in South Korea, which are also nearly identical to all the traditional forms.

Thus, the above three studies combined distinguished 14 different forms which are important corollaries of elder respect(hereafter called 'modern form') in modern East Asia. Of the 14 modern forms, 12 are cited by all three studies. This finding denotes that almost all of these forms are commonly practiced by the East Asians. The meanings and expressions of these modern forms are consonant with those of the traditional forms. This presumably indicates that the modern forms of elder respect are embedded in the ideal reflected in the traditional teachings and that the influence of the traditional ideal persists. One of the less frequently cited forms is ancestor respect. Ancestor respect was cited by Palmore and Maeda, and Sung and Kim. In fact, this form is still widely practiced not only in Japan and Korea but also in China and other Chinese communities including

Hong Kong, Taiwan and Singapore. Thus, the three studies yielded parallel results for identification of a set of similar, if not identical, forms of elder respect, enlarging the power of the interpretation of elder respect in East Asia.

Modifying Expressions among The Young

As Chow (1995), and Elliott and Campbell (1993) reported, the traditional values associated with elder respect and family care for elders persist in East Asia. However, certain ways in which elder respect is expressed are changing. As yet, few studies have systematically assessed how much, how fast, and in what way the ways are shifting.

While the traditional forms of elder respect are still used in East Asia, the meanings and expressions of elder respect appear to be changing, if not being modified. Mehta (1997) found that in Singapore the meaning of respect is shifting from obedience and subservience (acquiescent) to courtesy and kindness. Ingersoll-Dayton and Saengtienchai (1999) report that consulting elders (con-sultative), which involves open communication and mutual aid between genera-tions, has become a prevalent form of elder respect in Taiwan, Singapore, Thailand, and the Philippines. Meanwhile, Sung and Kim (2003) found in South Korea that listening to parents when they talk (acquiescent), though not always following their instructions, is taken by many young people as a way of being obedient. Also notable in East Asia is the visible trend of shaking hands instead of bowing (salutatory). The young in Japan and Korea also tend to prefer simpler and shorter honorific expressions (linguistic). A growing number of adults use the telephone and other means of communication to express respect toward their elderly relatives (care). They may choose paid-for services to care for these relatives. Increasingly money is used by adult children to compensate for the inadequacy of their care and support for elderly parents and to show respect to the parents. As more young people value their time and convenience, these modified expressions are bound to be widely practiced. And, as more people are living longer, many families tend to postpone the traditional celebration of a parent's sixtieth birthday (celebrative). Even ancestor worship—a core of the traditional forms of respect—are being modified: the number of days for worship tend to be reduced and mourning rituals simplified and economized. Meanwhile, public respect—services for elders in the community—is taken more seriously by indi-viduals as well as public organizations. There are other noticeable changes. In response to the challenges from social changes, young East Asians are modifying the traditional ways of respecting elders. Looking ahead, young generations are likely to continue to alter or modify their way of elder respect.

Discussion

In our exploratory study, a set of 16 traditional forms of elder respect emerged. These forms highlight the ways in which elders have been respected by East Asian people. These behavioral forms will be useful in developing a more comprehensive typology of elder respect that includes forms not identified in the present study.

There seem to be two types of elder respect within the traditional forms. First, there is respect involving some action or work, such as caring, housekeeping, serving choice foods and drinks, providing gifts, and so forth. Secondly, there are symbolic displays of respect – those falling into linguistic, presentational, acquiescent, spatial, precedential, and celebrative forms. Both types constitute elder respect according to the precepts in the classics. Besides, the review of the literature evidenced the important association between the two dimensions—the inner feeling of respect and the outer expression of it. That is, elder respect is concerned with our external behaviors as well as our innermost feelings.

The traditional forms distinguished in this exploratory study provide insights into elder respect, a subject that has until now been discussed in the abstract. While they may be interrelated in their meanings and practices, each form appears to reflect a particular facet of elder respect. Hence, discussion of the traditional elder respect in East Asia requires the consideration of all the 16 forms, as it is only together that they provide a holistic portrait of respect for elders.

The tradition is rooted in East Asian family system and social structure. In the family system, respect as a benevolent and altruistic expression is heavily imbued with the sense of filial obligation, repayment of debt, and affection toward parents. In the social structure, consequential interpersonal relations tend to have a vertical structure that demands deference and loyalty to elders. In these relations, symbolic and ritualistic expressions of elder respect—linguistic, salutatory, presentational, precedential, celebratory, gift, and acquiescent—are shown often and widely.

Cultural variation exists in the practice of these forms. Not all of the forms practiced in East Asia seemed to be applicable to other cultures. A typical case is ancestor respect. Throughout East Asia, this form is widely practiced and this culture-rooted practice remains the core of elder respect. In the classics reviewed, a number of chapters and passages elaborately prescribed how to respect deceased parents and ancestors. But,

this form is not practiced in most western countries. The way of expressing other forms appear to be different, as well.

Knowledge of culture-specifics and universals about elder respect remains largely undiscovered. Although all cultures share the values of elder respect, the extent to which elders are respected and the forms of elder respect with which they most often respect seem to vary by culture. In what manner the effect of a certain culture engenders such a variation is an important issue to which researchers need to be sensitive.

In the course of social changes, the way in which elder respect is expressed appears to be changing or being modified. Overall, the expressions seem to be shifting from subservient to egalitarian and from the complex to the simple. These shifts indicate a new trend, a move from authoritarian relationships to reciprocal patterns of mutual respect between generations.

While the traditional expressions are changing, feelings of respect continue to bind generations together in China, Japan, and Korea as well as in other East Asian ethnic communities (Goldstine & Ku, 1993; Chow, 1995; Xie, Defrain, Meredith, & Combs, 1996; Mehta, 1997; Koyano, 1996; Maeda, 1997; Yoon & Cha, 1999; Choi, 2001). Elliott and Campbell (1993) aptly summed up the communalities in this respect between East Asian peoples: "Expectations regarding family care of the elderly and intergenerational reciprocity in Korean and Chinese cultures strongly resemble those found in Japan, as all three of these East Asian cultures have been greatly influenced by Confucian ethical conception of filial piety." The traditional foundation for elder respect in East Asia is the Confucian teachings of filial piety. This tradition continues to influence the way East Asians treat the elderly. In the course of modernization, the cultural characteristics of the East Asians thus persist (Caudill, 1973; Parish & Whyte, 1978; Streib, 1987), although today the young tend to adhere to it less rigorously.

The typology of the traditional forms shed light on the long standing abstract nature of elder respect. From the historical literature and the new material on elder respect, there is empirical evidence to support the distinction of a variety of ways of connoting elder respect. However, these findings have been brought up here not in order to resolve the results of the present study but rather to introduce the kinds of forms of elder respect that have been practiced in the East Asian cultural context and to indicate a need to develop a more comprehensive typology of forms of respect that has cross-cultural applicability.

References

Analects of Confucius (Lun Yu) [English translation] (1996). Beijing: Sinolingua, 2nd ed.

Applgate, M., & Morse, J. M. (1994). Personal privacy and interactional patterns in a nursing home. *Journal of Aging Studies*, 8, 413-434.

De Bary, W. T. (1995). Personal reflections on Confucian filial piety. In: *Filial piety and future society* (pp. 19-36). Kyunggido, Korea: The Academy of Korean Studies.

Book of Rites (Li Chi) [Collection of Confucian Teachings of Rites] (1993). O. S. Kwon (trans.) Seoul: Hongshin Moonwha-Sa.

Caudill, W. (1973). The influence of social structure and culture on human behavior in modern Japan. *Ethos*, 1, 343-382.

Choi, S. J. (2001). *Changing attitudes to filial piety in Asian countries*. Paper presented at 17th World Congress of International Association of Gerontology. Vancouver, Canada, July 1-6.

Chow, N. (1995). *Filial piety in Asian Chinese communities*. Paper presented at Symposium on

Downie, R. S., & Telfer, E. (1969). *Respect for persons*. London: Allen and Unwin.

Dunkle, R., Roberts, B., & Haug, M. (2001), *The oldest old in everyday life: Self perception, coping with change, and stress*. New York: Springer Publishing Co.

Elliott, K. S., & Campbell, R. (1993). Changing ideas about family care for the elderly in Japan. *Journal of Cross-Cultural Gerontology*, 8, 119-135.

Filial Piety, 5th Asia/Oceania Regional Congress of Gerontology, Honk Kong, 20 November.

Goldstein, M. C., & Ku, Y. (1993). Income and family support among rural elderly in Jheziang Province, China. *Journal of Cross-Cultural Gerontology*, 8, 197-223.

Han, J. (2000). Undergraduate students' attitude toward the elderly. *Journal of the Korea Gerontological Society*, 20 (3), 115-127.

Holmes, E. R., & Holmes, L. D. (1995). *Other cultures, elder years*. Thousand Oaks: Sage.

Ingersoll-Dayton, B., & Saengtienchai, C. (1999). Respect for the elderly in Asia: Stability and change. *International Journal of Aging and Human Development*, 48, 113-130.

Kim, I. K., Liang, J., Rhee, K. O., & Kim, C. S. (1996). Population aging in Korea: Changes since the 1960s. *Journal of Cross-Cultural Gerontology*, 11, 369-388.

Kim, W. (2003). An exploratory study on ageism experienced by the elderly and its related factors. *Journal of the Korea Gerontological Society*, 23(3), 21-35.

Kong, D. C. (1995). The essence of filial piety. In: *Filial piety and future society* (pp. 127-137).

Koyano, W. (1996). Filial piety and intergenerational solidarity in Japan. *Australian Journal of Ageing*, 15, 51-56.

Koyano, W., Inoue, K., & Shibata, H. (1987). Negative misconceptions about aging in Japanese adults, *Journal of Cross-Cultural Gerontology*, 2, 131-137.

Kyunggido, Korea: The Academy of Korean Studies.

Lang, O. (1946). *Chinese family and society*. New Haven, CT: Yale University Press.

Larson, R. (1978). Thirty years of research on the subjective well-being of older Americans. *Journal of Gerontology*, 33, 109-125.

Lee, E. H. (2004). A study on the factors affecting the dementia elderly abuse in Kyung-gido. *Journal of the Korea Gerontological Society*, 24(3), 91-110.

Legge, J. (1960). *The Chinese Classics*, 3rd ed. Hong Kong: Hong Kong University Press. Bk. 1.

Leininger, M. (1990). Culture: The conspicuous missing link to understand ethical and moral dimensions of human care. In: M. Leininger (Ed.), *Ethical and moral dimension of care*. Detroit: Wayne State University.

Levy, B. R. (1999). The inner self of the Japanese elderly: Defense against negative stereotypes of aging. *International Journal of Aging and Human Development*, 48, 131-144.

Lew, S. K. (1995). Filial piety and human society. In: *Filial piety and future society* (pp. 19-36). Kyunggido, Korea: The Academy of Korean Studies.

Liang, J., & Jay, G. M. (1990). *Cross-cultural comparative research on aging and health*. Institute of Gerontology and School of Public Health, The University of Michigan.

Liang, J., Tu, E. J., & Chen, X. (1986). Population aging in the People's Republic of China. *Social Science Medicine*, 23, 1353-1362.

Liu, W. T., & Kendig, H. (2000). *Who should care for the elderly? An East-West value divide*. Singapore: Singapore University.

Maeda, D. (1997). *Filial piety and care of aged parents in Japan*. Paper presented at Symposium on myths, stereotypes, and realities of filial piety. The 16th World Congress of Gerontology, Singapore, August 17.

Mehta, K. (1997). Respect redefined: Focus group insights from Singapore. *International Journal of Aging and Human Development*, 44, 205-219.

Noelker, L. S., & Harel, Z. (2000). Humanizing long-term care: Forging a link between quality of care and quality of life. In: L. S. Noelker & Z. Harel (Eds.), *Linking Quality of Long-Term Care and Quality of Life*. New York: Springer.

Nydegger, C. N. (1983). Family ties of the aged in the cross-cultural perspectives. *The Gerontologist*, 213, 26-31.

Ogawa, N., & Rutherford, R. D. (1994). *Care of the elderly in Japan: Changing norms and expectations*. (Tokyo: Nihon University Population Research Institute).

Palmore, E. B. (1999). *Ageism: Negative and positive*. New York: Springer Pub. Co.

Palmore, E. B., & Maeda, D. (1985). *The Honorable elders revisited*. Durham, NC: Duke University Press.

Parish, W. L., & Whyte, M. K. (1978). *Village and family in contemporary China*. Chicago: The University of Chicago Press.

Park, K. R., & Yi, Y. (2001). Streotypes of the elderly held by university students. *Journal of the Korea Gerotological Society*, 21(2), 71-83.

Silberman, B. (1962). *Japanese character and culture*. Tucson, University of Arizona Press.

Silverman, P., & Maxwell, R. (1978). How do I respect thee? Let me count the ways: Deference toward men and women. *Behavior Science Research,* 13, 91-108.

Silverstein, M., Burholt, V., Wenger, G. C., & Bengtson, V. L. (1998). Parent-child relations among very old parents in Wales and the United States: A test of modernization theory, *Journal of Aging Studies*, 12, 387-409.

Simic, A. (1990). Aging, world view, and international relations in America and Yugoslavia. In J. Sokolovsky (Ed.), *The cultural context of aging: Worldwide perspectives* (pp. 17-89). New York: Bergin & Garvey.

Sokolovsky, J. (Ed.) (1990). *The cultural context of aging*. New York: Bergin and Garvey.

Streib, G. F. (1987). Old age in sociocultural context: China and the United States. *Journal of Aging Studies*, 7, 95-112.

Sung, K. T. (2004). Elder respect among young adults: A cross-cultural study of Americans and Koreans. *Journal of Aging Studies,* 18, 215-230.

Sung, K. T., & Kim, H. S. (2003). Elder respect among young adults: Exploration of behavioral forms in Korea. *Ageing International*, 28, 279-294.

Teachings of filial piety [Hsiao Ching]. [Translated by J. Legge.]. (1989). *Sacred books of the east*, Vol. III. London: Oxford. Originally published 1879-1885.

Tomita, S. (1994). The consideration of cultural factors in the research of elder mistreatment with an indepth look at the Japanese. *Journal of Cross-Cultural Gerontology*, 9: 39-52.

Twenty-four stories of filial piety. (1956). Taipei: Chen Ta Press (Bilingual edition).

Works of Mencius. (1932). [Translated by L. Lyall.] London: Murray.

Xie, X., Defrain, J., Meredith, W., & Comb, R. (1996). Family strengths in the People's Republic of China: As perceiv3d by the university students and government. *International Journal of Sociology of the Family*, 26, 17-2.

Yoon, H. S., & Cha, H. B. (1999). Future issues for family care of the elderly in Korea. *Hallym International Journal of Aging,* 1, 78-86.

PART II

Perspectives on Care and Service

Part II of this book consists of six chapters that elaborate and illustrate the ways in which clients are respected in the context of human services. We will look in major human service professions, which have historically been concerned with respect for clients. Chapters 4 through 9 introduce the ideals and practices of respect for patients and clients in medical, nursing, and social service settings. Each chapter describes specific dynamics and skills associated with the practice of respect in a particular service setting. Research findings are cited to provide an empirical basis for the practice.

In Chapter 4, we review the Principles of the Belmont Report, i.e., respect for persons, beneficence and justice. These principles have permeated clinical medicine. They have caused a broad cultural shift that has reworked the relationship between doctors and patients. However, in the practice of these principles, medical practitioners encountered challenges. The chapter elaborates some ways in which the challenges can be overcome.

In Chapter 5, we examine values inherent in medical education; the focus is on the need to place emphasis on patients as persons and as colorful human beings. The central issue in patient-doctor relationships is adjusting physicians' personal style of approaching the patient to the need and wishes of individual patients and their families. The author, based on his experiences and those of his colleagues, presents the values that need to be emphasized in treating patients—the primary value being respect for the patient as an individual.

In Chapter 6, we will consider nursing ethics. Following a discussion on Kant's categorical imperatives—universalization (fairness) and respect for persons (intention to show respect for all persons), the chapter describes principles of universalized respect grouped into four categories—nonmaleficence, respect for autonomy, beneficence and principle of justice, and provides a list of moral rules relevant to nursing practice.

Chapter 7 describes respect and caring as ethics of nursing and the very essence of nursing. This chapter elaborates on the nature of respect and care in the practice of nursing. It ends with a theoretical commentary on the relationship between the concepts of respect, caring and nursing.

Chapter 8 is concerned with the practice of respect for clients by social workers. The chapter develops a perspective for respectful care provision with attention to the diversity of an aged population, and defines key concepts which help social workers to understand ethnic aging. These concepts are then translated into a practice perspective and service relevant considerations for care providers, such as the need to recognize the individual as a person rather than a patient.

Chapter 9 introduces a study of how social workers serving elderly clients demonstrate respect for clients. An increasing number of elderly persons depends on social service providers for care and services. The extent to which the providers treat the elderly with respect becomes a significant factor that affects the quality of their clients' later life. The study explores the way in which social workers express their respect for elderly clients and provides specific forms by which they demonstrate respect for clients. The forms include linguistic respect, care respect, salutatory respect, acquiescent respect, presentational respect, and consultative respect. Respect for clients has previously been discussed in invariably abstract forms. The various forms presented in this chapter could be useful in developing a comprehensive typology of the concrete forms of elder respect that can assess the propriety of the service provider and the quality of the relationship between the client and the provider.

Chapter 4

The Principles of the
Belmont Report Revisited

How Have Respect for Persons, Beneficence, and
Justice Been Applied to Clinical Medicine?

Eric J. Cassell

Although written primarily for medical research, the Belmont principles have permeated clinical medicine as well. In fact, they are part of a broad cultural shift that has dramatically reworked the relationship between doctor and patient. In the early 1950s, medicine was about making the patient better and maintaining optimism when the patient could not get better. By the 1990s, medicine was about the treatment of specific physiological systems, as directed by the patient, but as limited by the society's concern for justice.

In 1954 a man in his fifties was admitted to a teaching hospital with a heart attack of a few hours' duration. He was to be the first subject of an innovative treatment (intravenous streptokinase and streptodornase) to dissolve the thrombosis in his coronary artery.

The patient was chosen because he was a derelict with no living relatives. In the fashion of the day, he was not told what was to be done and no consent was requested or obtained. An attending physician, resident, and medical student were in constant attendance. After a number of hours of receiving the new medication, an irregularity of his heart rhythm developed. The treatment was stopped out of fear for his safety.

In 1997 a thirty-eight-year-old woman with stage IV (metastatic) cancer of the breast received high-dose chemotherapy followed by a bone marrow stem-cell transplant at a major western medical center, after almost three years of continuous disease and multiple treatments. Months later a routine CT scan revealed what appeared to the transplant oncologist to be recurrent cancer in the spine. The implication was that the chemotherapy in the spine. The implication was that the chemotherapy and bone marrow transplant had failed.

The transplant oncologist sent the following letter to the patient, her radiation oncologist, and the chief of the breast service at a major cancer center in the patient's home city:

Dear Olga [the patient], Cheryl, and Jimmy:

Enclosed is the relevant bone window from Olga's 11-12-97 CT Scan (as well as the formal reading) demonstrating the new sclerotic focus in the left pedicle of L2. I have circled it in red. It looks real to me and I would have Cheryl buzz [radiate] that area.

Olga, this is our only copy so will you send that one sheet back to us for our files? Hope all is well with the three of you. Talk to you soon.

Sincerely

[Signed]

Associate Director
Bone Marrow Transplant Program

In the forty-three years between these cases both medicine and the society around it have changed significantly under the influence of complex and intertwining forces. Scientific and technological advance have come to drive medical practice; the organization and financing of medical services have been remodeled in response both to new therapeutic capabilities and to the increasing costs of those therapies; chronic disease has displaced infectious and other acute diseases as the leading reason for seeking medical care and the leading cause of death; and the relationship between the patient and the physician has shifted not only toward "patient-centered" care but equally toward consumerism.

American society, of course, has undergone equally deep changes as government and authority were challenged in the social unrest of the '60s and '70s, rights movements of all kinds (civil rights, women's rights, patients' rights, gay rights, disability rights, and others) have gained prominence, individualism and pride in ethnicity have superseded the metaphor of the American "melting pot," and information technologies and financial and economic forces have captured the social imagination, allowing an ever-widening gap to open between rich and poor.

Like the wider society, neither the profession of medicine nor medical education is what it was a scant four decades ago.

Just about midway through these forty years of transformation, in 1978, the National Commission for the Protection of Human Subjects in Biomedical and Behavioral Research published the *Belmont Report*, introducing the principles of respect for persons, beneficence, and justice into research with human sub-jects—and foreclosing scenarios like the opening case. The Belmont principles have permeated clinical medicine as well. For example, recognition of the im-portance of freedom of choice as an aspect of respect for persons is now instan-tiated in informed consent documents, laws and court ruling. Similarly, the prin-ciples of respect for persons and beneficence are institutionalized in hospital functions that monitor quality of care, such as the tissue committees that insure that surgical procedures are appropriate. Patterns of practice, professional ideals, and the everyday behavior of both doctors and patients also demonstrate the definitions and application of the principles. They show what patients expect or demand and what physicians feel obligated to do. But what the principles mean is closely bound up with the changes in medicine and the social context in which medicine is practiced.

Eric Avery, *As It Is*, 1987, five-color lithograph with woodcut overprint, courtesy of the artist.

Beneficence

I begin with the principle of beneficence because the place of respect for persons and judge in clinical practice is easier to understand when one becomes aware of the changes since the 1950s in what counts as beneficence in medicine. Beneficence (or benevolent) actions or behaviors are those that actively that actively do good or that actively protect from harm. Initially, the idea of doing good and avoiding harm was seen as resulting from both physicians' personal characteristics and medical effectiveness. The former, if ideal, would be devoid of overweening pride, venality, impure motives, untrustworthiness, and careless-ness. The latter was a function of technical knowledge and proficiency. The physicians of the derelict with the heart attack suffered both moral and technical inadequacies of which they were largely unaware. They were, however, unques-tionably aware of the dangers and fearful of harming him.

The intervening period in medicine has seen an explosion of technical ca-pacity and a great increase in moral awareness, but the concept of benevolence has shrunk pari passu. The personal characteristics of physicians that served beneficence and were believed to be of great importance in previous generations now serve nostalgia more than clinical medicine.

In the early 1950's, being made better was often defined as having the bur-dens of disease lifted. Benevolence had to do with making patients better. During my training and early years of moral practice, disease manifestations were treated because they were there. Hernias, hemorrhoids that made any trouble, and most varicose veins of the legs were surgically removed, as were many superficial tumors and abnormalities. By the late 1950s, psychological determinants of illness began to be better known, leading to the attribution of many common complaints to psychological causes. With that awareness, the psychotherapies began to displace the sympathetic ear that had been part of medical benevolence since antiquity.

A FIFTY-YEAR PERSPECTIVE

Alterations in the relationship between patient and physician over the last fifty years have occurred within a set of large transformations in the medical and social parameters that enframe the relationship. The following changes occurred in medicine:

- Chronic diseases became overwhelmingly the most common cause of death and most frequent reason for seeking medical care, displacing infections and other acute diseases.
- Access to health care came to be considered a right. Most western nations (but not the United States) provided universal access to care.
- The "therapeutic revolution" took place, grounded on progressively greater knowledge of medical science. Technological advance became a driving force.
- The cost of medical care rose worldwide. Economic and legal forces became increasingly important, frequently displacing moral determinants.
- The organization and financing of the delivery of medical services changed. Fee-for-service medicine withered and physicians increasingly became employees of medical care organizations, were paid according to predetermined fee schedules, or received a capitated rate. The political and social power of physicians shrank.
- Physicians' performance was increasingly measured by evidence-based, process, or outcome guidelines.
- The bioethics movement arose in the 1960s and became an influential voice.
- The relationship between patient and physician shifted. Consumerism and ideas such as centered medicine became commonplace. The public became knowledgeable about medicine and medical science.
- The form and content of medical education changed little, although the curriculum was updated to reflect advances in medical science.

The surrounding society was also in flux:

- The social unrest and antiwar protests of the 1960s challenged the social structure of the nation and accompanied a decreased respect for government and authority in general.
- Rights movements came to prominence—civil rights, women's rights, patients' rights, disability rights, and gay rights.

- Pride in ethnicity and diversity and a still greater emphasis on individualism made the "melting pot" metaphor of the United States obsolete.
- Computers and, latterly, the Internet widely disseminated information that was previously available only to professionals.
- The power of the law and financial incentives to influence social behavior and professional relationships increased, overwhelming the established moral order. The bottom line became the bottom line.
- The gap between the rich and the poor grew steadily.

Increasingly, the focus of medicine has come to be understanding functional abnormalities and pathophysiology—the chain of bodily events that lead to and define the abnormal state as well as explaining its manifestations. This important conceptual evolution has been supported by a number of trends. In medical science primacy is given to research on mechanisms of disease, including molecular biology: Newer diagnostic technologies facilitate study of the body and its parts in motion, replacing the static view of disease afforded by, for example, plain X-rays, electrocardiograms, and biopsies. Pharmacological innovation has produced legions of drugs that give excellent symptom control for complaints as diverse as migraine headaches, angina pectoris, asthma, and panic attacks. The old belief that one should treat the disease not the symptoms gave way to the understanding that in many conditions the symptoms *are* the disease.

The good of patients that was identified with making them better has changed as a structural understanding of disease has been superseded to a large extent by a pathophysiological perspective that focuses on the function of parts. This encourages measuring benefit by the good done to only a part of the patient. With the rise of scientific medicine, what doctors had long done out of kindness, sympathy, patience, and personal interest—attentions directed solely at the person rather than the disease—were derogated as handholding or bedside manner, were not scientific medicine. As therapeutic effectiveness and scientific medicine came into bloom, the sick person lost standing to the body or disease as the place of clinical interventions and was no longer the primary locus of benevolence. The code of what was called medical ethics in times past was devoted to protecting patients (among other goals). Now termed medical etiquette, it has largely disappeared.

Patients were also gaining power as a result of the rights movements, their increasing knowledge of medicine and science, and of the erosion of respect for authority in general and the authority of physicians specifically. The profession's view of benevolence as the cure of disease or the relief of its manifestations came under public scrutiny, as did the view of physicians as benevolent helpmates in general. For example, the 1973 self-help book *Our Bodies, Our Selves* was published to promote what the authors saw as the need for women to take back their bodies from physicians, whose motives and actions were viewed with increasing suspicion. Doing "what the doctor ordered" without question and out of respect for his or her benevolence and authority had long been the mode when I went into practice in 1961. It was largely gone by the end of the decade and has not returned.

With increasing knowledge about science and medicine, the public bought into medical definitions of treatment, improvement, and cure—largely devoted to parts of the patient rather than to the person of the patient—as evidence of the benevolence of the medical profession. It is, however—if one can imagine such an attribute—a disembodied benevolence. It is not doctors, one might guess from the attitude of the public, but their scientific knowledge and technology that diagnose, treat, and cure diseases. Knowledge of medical science and information about medicine began to pervade the media. With the advent of the Internet, patients have an ever-increasing array of options from which to choose, leading to a kind of evidence-based and guideline-driven "cafeteria medicine." Patients, now at center stage in medicine, define benevolence, while physicians retreat or are forced by managed care to retreat from taking responsibility for the whole patient.

Over the same forty-some years there have been countervailing trends within and outside medicine as well. Response to wounds suffered during WWII started the rehabilitation medicine movement, which brought new understandings of function, thereafter defined not solely by the action of a body part but by the ability of a person to participate in a social role. Rehabilitation may not correct the underlying pathogenic mechanism, but it can restore function by retraining abnormal parts, utilizing other body mechanisms to compensate for lost function, and teaching persons to accommodate to their impairments.

When the goal is removing diseased tissues or restoring a diseased organ to normal—defined structurally—professional standards can define benevolence. But when the idea is to restore function to a part, or actively relieve symptoms, or return the patient to social function, then the sick person is the final arbiter of success. Only the patient knows when he or she is better.

In the care of the dying, the paradoxes of beneficence are easily seen. The goal of keeping people alive first entered medicine in the nineteenth century, well before the necessary technical capability existed. As time went on doctors became better able to support one physiological function after another apart from the state of the whole patient. Kidney dialysis replaced lost renal function, better ventilators replaced failed lungs and supported oxygenation, pacemakers and defibrillators maintained heart rhythm, total intravenous nutrition took over when oral nutrition failed, various methods of blood pressure support and volume replacement maintained circulation. Transfusions of various blood components as well as means for stimulating production of blood elements allowed for continued function of the blood as an organ. By the 1980s intensive care units contained patients on life support even though they had no chance of returning to meaningful life, whatever the outcome of their therapies. The patients lay alongside others with diseases for which resuscitation and life support were appropriate because, if they could be maintained long enough, their return to full function was probable. These excesses led to a reaction among the public and physicians. The importance of a good death, first brought to public awareness by Elisabeth Kubler-Ross in her 1972 book *On Death and Dying,* received increasing support and was the subject of widespread discussion. Advance directives and "do not resuscitate" orders became more common, and the assignment of surrogates for medical purposes became easier and more frequent. The hospice movement provided an alternative for the care of the terminally ill and focused attention on the relief of pain. Nonetheless, as in other aspects of medical care, technical proficiency and scientific knowledge continued to define medical benevolence, again most often as the good done to a part. Patients were constantly told what was wrong and what was happening in considerable technical detail, and then given technical options to choose from, as was the case with Olga, the patient with breast cancer mentioned earlier. She, like others with similar end-stage diseases, chose to accept the physicians' recommendations, because choices were described to her only in terms of technical procedures.

The patient has become increasingly central, but codes, guidelines, laws, and legal actions have pushed the notion of wronging the patient to the fore, while the calculus of benefit and harm has receded as physicians have withdrawn even more from the ideals of the past.

Respect for Persons

The physicians of the derelict with the heart attack probably did not entertain the notion that he had a right to decide whether to participate in the experiment or that he was wronged by not having been asked for his consent. They chose a derelict with no family because ore sophisticated patients were always wary of being "experimented on." By the standards of the time they did the right thing: they protected the patient from harm. He was after all a patient, not a person. When persons became patients, the social status changed. In the late 1960s I admitted a mentally fit corporate president with pneumonia to the hospital. After I explained to him what I thought was wrong and what would take place, his wife and I went out into the corridor for a full discussion of his case—a discussion that would not now take place without his participation. Patienthood had in minutes deprived him of his status as a self-determined person. This was the fashion of the times.

The letter to Olga, the young woman with stage IV breast cancer, suggests that to the physicians Olga is clearly a person; it is the sick patient part of her identity that seems to have diminished. She has gained rights as a person, but no longer commands obligations due a patient.

The idea of respect for persons as described in the *Belmont Report*—or even the concept of persons qua persons—was not present in medicine in 1954. Benevolence and the avoidance of harm were the expressions of respect for the humanity of patients. Patients were to be treated as fully human. Persons, in contrast, are not merely human; hey are social, moral, legal, and political entities with rights, to whom obligations are due. Because of this persons can not only be harmed, they can be wronged. It seems probable that the idea of person as we use it today—derivative as it is from the evolving concept of atomistic individuality—was just beginning to take full form after WWII. In the time period covered in this essay, the nature of persons changed, society changed, and medicine changed, resulting in a change in the meaning of respect for persons and autonomy. In the 1950s and early 1960s, women in public were not persons in their present sense, nor were people with disabilities, nor gay people. The civil rights movement achieved legal rights for blacks and other ethnic minorities but also changed their social status by making them persons in the wider American community in a legal and political sense. The changes were the official beginning of a process that had started well before the civil rights movement and that continues to this day.

In *The Patient as Person: Explorations in Medical Ethics* (published in 1970), Paul Ramsey discusses the bond between physician and patient and how that bond defines both. Before the patient became fully a person, physicians were patients' decision-makers: doctors made decisions about the best thing to do and about what and how to tell patients about their circumstances. It was part of physicians' obligations and part of their patients' obligations and part of their patients' expectations. Good physicians knew that patients had to be informed about what was happening because too much uncertainty was considered bad.

But full disclosure of fatal or dangerous diagnoses or situations was thought to be harmful because it would be followed by hopelessness. When one patient I cared for was back in his room after his surgery for inoperable cancer of the stomach, he asked his surgeon what he had found. The surgeon said, "We did a lot of cuttin' and schnitten and removed a lotta junk and you're gonna be fine." I took care of the patient until he died months later. A few days before he died he said, "Sometimes lately I think maybe I'm not getting better."

Medicine was only a few decades into the beginning of the therapeutic revolution that now is taken for granted. Then, despite great expectations of the bounty to be expected from medical science, there was little optimism about the outcome of diseases such as cancer, strokes, heart attacks, heart failure, advanced diabetes, and emphysema. Only for children had everything improved, as their death rates from now curable infectious diseases dropped precipitously in the Western World.

It is important to understand the relation among the fall in death rates, the improvement in health and well-being, the optimism fed by scientific advances, and the notions of respect for persons and freedom of choice. Previously, if you believed that your cancer inevitably meant a hopeless outcome and a painful death, and if your physicians believed that there was nothing beyond surgery that could be done for you, you might not have been so eager for knowledge or the freedom to choose. Beyond refusing or agreeing to (say) surgery, there was not much choice. One did the mastectomy and waited for the patient to get a recurrence and die, or be lucky. So doctors lied, not because they were morally defective but because, in their eyes, all they had to offer was an attitude of optimism and denial of a bad truth. Especially since at that time personal matters that might arise from these illnesses and the doctors' lies—lost hoes, unhappiness, anxieties, sadness, suffering, death, and grief—were personal matters kept from the view of others, even physicians (unless they looked).

On the other hand, if death rates are falling and the expectation of becoming hopelessly ill is disappearing in the face of new treatments, if persons with disabilities are entering active life in increasing numbers, if optimism pervades medicine, and if the world around is encouraging a further blossoming of individualism, then telling the truth and freedom of choice have new meaning.

The effects of the change in disease burden, the advance of medical science, change in social status, and personal freedom are easily seen in the rise of the women's movement. Would the continuing emergence of women to their present social and political state have been possible without a low birthrate, effective contraception, the virtual disappearance of the complications of childbirth, and the increased survival of children? As recently as 1928 Virginia Woolf, in *A Room of One's Own*, could decry the paucity of women in letters or any other profession. At that time, none of the four benefits mentioned above were available to women. Is widespread freedom of choice possible in their absence? Virginia Woolf did not think so.

Like WWI, WWII had put women in the work force, but I believe it took these medical changes to continue their advance. By the end of the social turmoil of the 1960s, as the women's movement grew, abortion had become legal, common venereal diseases were easily treatable (although new ones were appearing), and the physical constraints on the emergence of women were disappearing. Further, the opinion held by physicians about women were disappearing. Further, the opinion held by physicians about women gradually changed with the changing social milieu so that their climate of choice was also altered—even in advance of the entrance of large numbers of women into medicine. Women seized the locus of choice from physicians prior, I believe, to a similar change in the general population.

The bioethics movement was also a major force in spreading the importance of patient autonomy in clinical medicine. Publications, public discussions, the education of interested physicians and individuals who were making bioethics their academic field, and increased public interest brought power to the idea of patient autonomy.

By 1997 when Olga came to be making decisions about how her breast cancer would be treated, respect for persons in clinical medicine had become identical in many minds with autonomy defined solely as freedom of choice.

As time went on, the emphasis in the meaning of freedom of choice in medical practice shifted from choice from among the reasonable alternatives offered by physicians to whatever the patient (or surrogate) wanted. This was most evident in intensive care units where unconscious patients with no possibility of survival in the absence of support equipment were kept alive because (the physicians said) the family wanted a "full court press." It was not unusual at this time for the family and the medical staff to become adversaries. Influential guidelines in the bioethics literature (such as the Hastings Center Guidelines) supported the right of the family or patient to insist on resuscitation no matter what the clinical situation or the patient's prognosis.

In earlier years, learning to base clinical decisions on prognostication—carefully considered alternative possible outcomes (not merely what a physician wanted to do)—had been an important part of clinical training. With freedom of choice, this element began to disappear from clinical medicine. (Surgeons remained constant in this regard. They remained firmly in control of the decision to operate—if the patient agreed.) Absent concern about the impact of the past and the future on a clinical decision (what prognostication is all about), the exercise of autonomy in medicine came to be marked by immediacy.

Issues such as the nature of the person, the impact of illness on decision-making capacity, the problems of autonomy that were specific to medicine and care of the sick, and the meaning of autonomy in the context of the special relationship between patient and physician were buried under the tide of legal interpretations of these concepts and rise of the language of rights. As required by law, in every hospital in New York State a "Patients' Bill of Rights" was posted prominently next to elevators or other visible sites. The tone of the document was adversarial, as though everything that could be undertaken by physicians was determined by patient rights and medical obligations rather than patient needs and medical responsibilities. The balance of power had clearly shifted to the patient. For many physicians it became easier to acquiesce when patients wanted medications or diagnostic technologies than to assert medical authority or negotiate a middle ground. Patients and the public at large had become so knowledgeable that their choices were often well informed and cogent.

There can be no freedom of choice in the absence of knowledge on which to base choices. As previously noted, until the 1970s physicians commonly withheld the truth from patients who had life-threatening diseases. Earlier, doctors did not tell patients about the facts of their illnesses even when they were not serious. For example, doctors frequently did not reveal blood pressure to patients. Why would they want to know? After all, it was thought, they did not know what a specific blood pressure meant. The reasons for a specific medication might be revealed because it had been shown that explanations increased compliance (otherwise only about half of prescriptions were ever filled), not because it was believed that patients wanted to participate in the decision. Why would they? That was the doctor's job. It was commonly believed that doctors did not tell the truth—that they hid bad news. By the late 1970s patients were increasingly told the truth. By the late 1980s, any reticence on the part of the physician about revealing the truth was gone. The criterion for telling something to a patient became its truth.

From the destructiveness of complete lies to the destructiveness of mediated truth took less than three decades. Attempts to teach the harm that could be done by "truth bombs" and "truth fragments" fell on deaf ears. But the truth of information is only one of its aspects. Of importance also are accuracy, reliability, and completeness, the meaning to the patient of the information, its relevance to the patient's problem, whether it increases or decreases uncertainty, what it indicates about appropriate or possible action, and what impact it has on the relationship between patient and physician. The understanding that information is a tool that can be used for healing or hurting disappeared under the new avalanche of truth revealed to patients in the service of autonomy. Deciding what should be said when, where, and how requires knowledge of not just the medical facts, but the nature of the sick person and his or her needs beyond the simply "medical." Physicians who have distanced themselves from their patients cannot obtain this kind of personal knowledge.

Decisions made in the name of respect for persons and their autonomy can result in different conclusions about the right thing to do. Consider, for example, the following two cases: A terminally ill patient with terminal respiratory disease decided against further treatment and entered a home hospice program. He soon became very sick and was brought to an emergency room in respiratory failure. Severely short of breath, he chose to go on a respirator despite having previously decided against resuscitation. His request was granted, although he could have been made comfortable without a respirator, and ultimately he will again be in the terminal state he was in before entering the emergency room. The second instance is that of a patient who had been on dialysis for a log time and decided to stop treatment. When he was close to death he requested that he be restarted on dialysis. His physicians chose not to do so and he soon died.

In the first instance the decision was justified by saying that the patient wanted to be resuscitated despite his previous refusal of further treatment. In the second instance the decision was justified by saying that the patient's previous decision against dialysis. The first case probably represents the more common contemporary occurrence. Here the patient's choice is atemporal—as though the person of the past does not count in the present and as if there is no future. Choice is exercised as if it were independent of circumstances, as if the panic of respiratory distress had no impact on the choice and the patient in his profoundly sick circumstances is as representative of the person as the less sick voice of the recent past. It is the immediate, individual choice that counts.

In the second case the physicians take responsibility for deciding that the previous decision to stop dialysis is more representative of the person than the current choice to restart dialysis. How do they know that they are correct, that they are not condemning the patient to death based solely on their judgment? They cannot know; it is merely a judgment. Their decision is based on their knowledge of end-stage renal disease, the life of a dialysand, and this patient's previous experience with both. The patient will die of renal disease—no action or decision will change that fact. His previous decision was made over time and was justified over time. No patient is removed from dialysis without a lot of discussion with his or her physicians—it is in the nature of dialysis units. To honor his immediate choice would return him to the situation that he opted to end with death rather than face its continuance. Here the decision acknowledges the effect of illness and, perhaps most important, entwines the acts of the physicians with those of the patient.

In the years since the early 1950s, clinical medicine has moved away from respect for persons expressed primarily be benevolence and the avoidance of harm toward respect for persons defined by autonomous freedom of choice with little regard for other aspects of autonomy. Before the current era, patients were not accorded full status as persons by society—sickness removed them from the community of equals, impaired their autonomy, and required that physicians accept full responsibility for their benevolent treatment. At present, in the absence of obviously diminished mental capacity, the easily demonstrable impairment in the very sick of the ability to make reasoned decisions is essentially denied and they are accorded the full autonomy of normal persons who make decisions in which their physicians no longer share much responsibility.

Justice

In 1981 I was asked to discuss justice as it applied at the patient's bedside. I argued that "love of humanity, compassion, and mercy, not justice, are the appropriate concepts to guide actions at the bedside."[1] But in the years that have followed, society and medicine itself have come to realize that no nation is rich enough to make available all that medicine has to offer. Accordingly, there have been many discussions of the need for some kinds of rationing or the awareness that covert rationing already exists. With that wakening has come concern for fairness in distribution, whether the problem is seen as one of large-scale social institutions such as governments, or of more local institutions such as transplant teams, hospitals, or other medical care organizations.

Inevitably, this involves the belief that individual physicians should play a part in preserving society's medical resources. Simply put, this means that the physician should be thinking not solely about a particular patient, but also about how the resources used in that patient's care affect conservation of the general resource supply. Only a few decades ago, such an idea would have met with strong opposition. The ethos held that physicians' primary obligation is to their patients and all else comes second—including physicians themselves, their institutions, and society.

The rise of managed care in the last decade has highlighted the distributive issues that arise when cost becomes the primary value by which services are measured. Eliminating services from a plan's benefit package, reducing the level of reimbursement for specific services, and reducing the time allotted for services can directly reduce costs. Each of these cost-saving strategies raises the question whether these medical services are not merely commodities that can be allocated fairly or unfairly.

It is not surprising that in this changing climate attention has turned to issues of justice arising from the individual physician's attention to an individual patient. The idea of concepts of justice applying to the physician's acts at the bedside, to which I denied legitimacy in 1981, has now become a focus of attention. In *Local Justice*, published in 1992, Jon Elster explores allocation of resources in situations not usually considered matters of justice, including military draft, admission to colleges, and certain larger medical allocation problems such as organ transplantation, which he discusses at some length.[2] Elster cites previous work by others, including Michael Walzer, that has focused on similar local issues. *Local Justice*, however, allows me to demonstrate the application of these ideas to clinical medicine.

The values underlying Elster's arguments are simple: To meet the standard of justice, the distribution of scarce resources should be both equitable and efficient. The existing norms of clinical medicine appear to conflict with justice as a principle of clinical medicine. The following excerpt from Elster makes the point:

> In many cases, professional norms are self-explanatory. There is no need to ask why colleges want good students, why firms want to retain the most qualified workers, or why generals want their soldiers to be fit for combat. The norms of medical ethics, however, are somewhat more puzzling. I shall offer some conjectures concerning the origins of two central medical norms with important allocative consequences. Neither norm is outcome oriented, in the sense of aiming at the most efficient use of scarce medical resources. Instead, one might say that the norms are *patient oriented*, in a sense that will become clear in a moment. [Italics in the original.]

> The first is what I have called "the norm of compassion," that is, the principle of channeling medical resources toward the critically ill patients, even when they would do more good in others. In addition to spontaneous empathy, I believe some cognitive factors could be involved in this norm. . . . Instead of comparing the fates of different individuals if treated, doctors compare their fates if left untreated."

> Next, there is what I shall call "the norm of thoroughness." Rational-choice theory tells us that when allocating scarce resources, whether as input for production or as goods for consumption, one should equalize the marginal productivity or the marginal utility of all units. . . . A rational consumer would, therefore, spread his income more thinly over a large number of goods, rather than concentrate it on just a few.

> We can apply similar reasoning to the behavior of doctors. With respect to any given patient, the doctor's time has decreasing marginal productivity, at least beyond a certain point. . . . This implies that if a doctor makes a very thorough examination of his patient, his behavior is not instrumentally rational with respect to the objective of saving lives or improving overall health. Other patients might benefit much more from the time he spends on the last and most esoteric tests. Nevertheless, doctors seem to follow a norm of thoroughness, which tells them that once a patient has been admitted, he or she should get "the full treatment."

> In Norway, a recent parliamentary commission found that eye specialists tend to admit too few patients and treat each of them excessively thoroughly. When I confronted my own eye doctor with this claim, she refuted it by telling me about a case in which she had been able to diagnose a rare eye disease only after exhaustive examination, thereby saving her patient's sight. I did not remind her of

the cases that go undetected because the patient never gets to see a doctor at all. (pp. 146-48)

In the 1950s such an application of economic theory to medicine was unlikely. Even today, many clinicians would be upset at the conclusions Elster has drawn, but he is not alone. As F. H. Bradley once said, "When you are perplexed, you have made an assumption and it is up to you to find out what it is." Elster's assumption, which led to his puzzlement about the norms of medical ethics and on which his argument stands, is that medicine is devoted to saving lives and promoting overall health.

Historically, *clinical* medicine has been devoted to caring for individual patients, one at a time. Elster can be excused his error. He has probably been reading medicine's public relations slogans, in common with the rest of the population. The medical industry—clinical, teaching, and research—supports itself by spreading the belief that it is about saving lives and promoting health. The error is really an error in systems theory. The level of the medical system devoted to these goals is not medicine as a profession of individual doctors treating individual patients—what most people think of when they speak of medicine. It is medicine as a social system, concerned with keeping the population alive and healthy. The United States does not have an institution responsible for the social system of medicine—certainly is not the Surgeon General's Office or the Department of Health and Human Services. The nation depends instead on the outmoded and demonstrably false assumptions that the health of the population is the sum of the health of individuals and that lives are best saved by the actions of individual physicians.

In the last few decades, however, as the economics of medical care have come under increasing scrutiny, addressing questions of equity and efficiency in the car of patients has come to be sen as necessary and reasonable. But the goal has not necessarily been the best medicine for the overall health of the population and the lowest death rate, but the most medical care for the money. Perhaps the closest thing to an arbiter of medicine as a social system has been the Healthcare Financing Administration, in conjunction with various organizations concerned with technology assessment, epidemiology (The Centers for Disease Control), and health policy.

It is probably true that at the present time more than one set of norms are applied to clinical medicine and the care of patients—patients who persist in clinging to historical values in the belief that when they are actively the patient they are their doctor's primary concern. Their health insurance organization is probably dedicated primarily to efficiency and, hopefully, equity—whatever its public advertising may say. But the matter does not end here. A recent paper by Lynn Jansen, a nurse who has a doctorate in political theory, allows us to move a step further.[3] Drawing on Elster's work, she applies the concept of local justice to the treatment of pain. As have many other, she finds that pain is under treated. She states that "an important factor affecting the distribution of [pain management] resources was the decisions made by individual clinicians at the bedside. Since these decisions affect the distribution of important health care resources, they should be understood as raising an issue of justice." After citing as an objection to her conclusions the belief of others that individual treatment decisions should be discussed in terms of beneficence, she states, "It is the actual distribution of resources, however, that should be assessed in terms of justice. *Ultimately, what matters from the standpoint of justice is who actually gets what resources.* If, therefore, this distribution is influenced in part by the decisions of individual physicians then it is entirely appropriate that these decisions be assessed in terms of justice" (italics in the original). (In a footnote she states that not every decision by a physician raises an issue of justice.)

Why does it matter whether the local decisions are viewed in terms of justice?" As the case of pain management resources aptly demonstrate many of these resources cannot be distributed properly according to a uniform policy or guideline. Yet they are sufficiently important to require stronger distributive justification than simply relying on market forces or professional discretion." And finally, "When decisions . . . come to be viewed in terms of justice, there is greater pressure, both social and legal for those who make these decisions defend and justify them in public."

Whether one agrees with Jansen's argument is not the issue; what is important is the concept on which her discussion is based. For Jansen, and for many others in these last decades, the actions of the doctor have become *resources* for which physicians are socially and legally accountable. Take away the concept of resources and the argument that the idea of justice applies at the bedside disappears. The overriding belief that physicians' acts represent the exemplification of the *personal* duties of individual physicians toward individual patients—that this is the moral framework of clinical medicine—has lost considerable currency.

A number of things follow from the shift to a framework of justice. It presupposes people or groups pressing claims for scarce goods as their *right* and justifying those claims by rules or standards. It suggests the utility of rules and guidelines, and evidence-based medicine that can provide the basis for the social and legal evaluation of the distribution of the physicians' resources. It provides a basis for diminishing the importance of the personal judgment of physicians.

Chapter 5

Respectful Treatment Values Inherent in Medical Education

Martin R. Lipp

Life was something you dominated, if you were any good.
> - F. Scott Fitzgerald

We simply can't get around the fact that we are overpaid and overtrained for most of our practice.
> - David W. Crippen

Medical schools in my experience have had a discouragingly similar character. The students begin the first year with laudable amounts of intellectual curiosity, optimism, and empathy for patients; and, for far too many, leave at the end of the fourth year feeling cynical, regarding many patients with blatant hostility, and viewing the process of patient care as perhaps interesting but not a whole lot of fun. It's not a universal pattern, but I believe it to be distressingly common. I also believe it to be a product of our medical-education system itself.

While students may be the relatively more innocent victims, the faculty often becomes victimized too. Even the best potential clinicians among junior faculty members because of institutional pressures tend to become insensitive and impatient with both individual patients and individual students, withdrawing from continuing empathetic care of the one in favor of the processing of the many. Time for clinical work is likely to be regarded as a duty rather than as an opportunity, and heavily weighted toward episodic care with unfamiliar patients, using a disease-oriented focus. Conflicting administrative and research obligations account for too many demands on time and are too important for progress up the department ladder. Human and family-oriented care inevitably is slighted, and the young faculty member's development of potential humanistic traits tends to be neglected. How, then, can the young faculty member teach these qualities to students?

Students learn values by example, and examples tend to be consistent from one department to the next. Clinical care is relegated to the least-experienced persons around—students and house officers—with faculty members darting in and out to provide episodic supervision. The result is a subtle downgrading of the value of patient contact; anyone with seniority and clout soon flees from continuing daily contact with patients to other and presumably more attractive and important activities.

Faculty members seldom can get to know their students as human beings or watch them evolve over four years. Instead, they measure the students by the amount of data the students can master and divulge on request, and by the technical procedures they can perform. Faculty members, because of their other obligations, seldom have the time to assess more subtle skills derived from patience, empathy, understanding, and integrity. By implication, the student finds these qualities less of an asset in getting through medical school than mastery of cognitive detail; and, even if the former qualities don't wither, they are unlikely to flower in a medical school setting.

Intensive involvement with patients who are sick and in pain and need is often itself painful, even for an experienced clinician, and certainly for a novice. Where is the student to learn to experience such involvement with an acceptable degree of comfort? Who among the professors or junior faculty have both the time and skill to demonstrate the process? Students who suffer noisily, like patients who suffer noisily, are commonly either ignored, regarded as a pain in the neck, or referred to a psychiatrist. Suffering is seldom viewed as a potentially enriching experience for a clinician, which calls for patient and empathetic listening by colleagues. The unspoken message is, "If you're having troubles, keep them to yourself. Suffering shows weakness, and a real professional has to be tough." I believe that message provides a lousy standard for an evolving physician, and I think the values on which the message is based serve our profession poorly.

Medical school usually teaches you that you can never be bright enough, never knows enough, never work hard enough to be worthy to practice medicine. The explicit message is that every missed fact, any oversight on your part, can be the death of someone—literally! You are told that perfection is not merely the elusive ideal, but rather, the daily standard by which you must measure your performance. You neither expect nor receive plaudits for a job "just" well done when perfection alone is the standard. Only deviation from perfection stands out, and that constitutes disaster. You are not permitted to see yourself as what you are: bright, capable, hard-working, but nonetheless a human being and therefore fallible, vulnerable and subject to making judgments distorted by fatigue, personal values, and considerations other than merely "objective" measures of health.

In many respects, you are not only too smart for much of what you need to do in the practice of medicine, your intelligence is too restless. By virtue of getting into medical school, you are a straight A undergraduate student or nearly so, and capable of a stunning performance in your Medical College Admissions Test. By virtue of getting through medical school, you demonstrate your mastery of the Krebs cycle and an unending flow of exotica. As you go through one class, one rotation after another, your mind becomes accustomed to constant stimulation, the recurrent exposure to new and obscure conditions and diseases. Yet these qualities will not help you in the *practice* of 90% of what you will do. Whether you are a family practitioner or a thoracic surgeon, after your apprenticeship is complete, the measure of your happiness will lie in the mastery of what after a while becomes routine. The stuff you see day in and day out, the things that you do almost as a matter of habit, make it seem easy because you know it so well and can do it so well without being bored by the repetition.

But medical school's biggest failing, in my view, is its emphasis on pathology. Not only the focus on disease per se, but on patients as bearers of disease, as persons who are themselves diseased. In the process, we neglect to see our patients as colorful human beings, living lives of quiet and personal drama and comedy, each with their own very human stories to tell. Someplace in the curriculum, students should be helped to focus on the wonder of it all—not just the wonder of the electrons spinning in their orbits and electrolyte transport at the cellular membrane, but the extraordinary ability of people to cope in the face of illness and the mundane stresses of life. Most of us find it difficult to see heroism in the low-back-pain sufferer, but that doesn't mean it isn't often there. We only begin to understand the phenomenon when we ourselves develop some sciatic pains and somehow manage to discharge our responsibilities despite the aggravating burden of day-in-and-day-out discomfort. If we look for valor of spirit in our patients, expecting to find it, we will often be successful; if we look for psychopathology in our patients, expecting to find it, we will be successful in that search too. But we will seldom find the discovery ennobling to ourselves or our patients.

Models of the Doctor-Patient Relationship

It is an occupational hazard, I thought. Everyone gets contemptuous after a while of his clients. Teachers get scornful of students, doctors of patients, bartenders of drinkers, salesmen of buyers, clerks of customers.
Robert B. Parker

So what does all this have to do with the kinds of relationships we have with our patients? The one truth which surely must be apparent from what has been discussed so far is that our relationships with out patients can be extraordinarily complex and necessarily evolve not only with our own personal development, but also with the changing realities of contemporary medical care.

The central issue in these relationships is how responsibility and authority for decision making are allocated. Each physician will approach the issue in a personal fashion, but one hopes with flexibility enough to adjust personal style to the needs and wishes of individual patients and families.

The pleasure a physician gets from contact with a patient reflects not only the kind of individual each may be, but what each wants from the other. The manifest requests are important, but so are unspoken and perhaps more amorphous interests and needs. Every patient comes to us with a set of expectations, conscious or not, abut what the experience will be like. The patient may approach us expecting a tender healer, a stern authority figure, an accepting parent, or a blundering fool. We, in turn, may expect the patient to act in a dependent, stoic, sneaky, seductive, or some other manner. These expectations may have little to do with any specific patient, or they may be brought out primarily by certain categories of patients.

A classic example is a case of a physician who places great emphasis on the healer role and a patient who is on the road to becoming a career disability-compensation patient. The doctor in essence says, "I'm going to cure you if it kills you," and the patient responds, "I will do everything in my power to frustrate your desire to heal me." Another common but somewhat more subtle example involves the patient who, in addition to organic disease, would also like to feel taken care of and "special" to doctors. When a patient like this is looked after by a researcher-scientist who values objectivity, personal distance, and date, there is bound to be a clash.

Such physician and patient expectations and attitudes in themselves are neither good nor bad. We can ignore them, fight them, or find someway of using them to enhance patient care and the satisfaction we get from our clinical work. In this broadened sense, these phenomena are inappropriate only when they constitute barriers to optimal health care and a sense of satisfaction in the participants.

Various models of physicianhood and patienthood are summarized. The models clearly are not mutually exclusive. Most of us will see ourselves as fitting into more than one category, and the same is true for many patients that we see. As a consequence most of us are simultaneously seeking rewards from diverse roles that call for (often) conflicting behaviors. Often it's difficult to know what we really wish for ourselves, and we end up seeking rewards that don't give us the pleasure we anticipated.

In many respects, our training years teach us to be students rather than physicians. As a consequence, our personal reward systems, as molded early in our careers, often emphasize the role of patient as "learning material" rather than human being. Some physicians can find no pleasure in contact with patients unless they have "interesting" or unusual diseases. This circumstance is truly unfortunate, because there are many potential rewards to be gotten from patient contact in addition to those sought by the pure student.

Specific kinds of illnesses often have the capacity for brining out or frustrating different kinds of role functions in patients and physicians. Depending upon the kinds of contribution each of us enjoys most, we may prefer patients with conditions which are acute or chronic, straightforward or complicated, which either do or don't foster patient neediness, or which lend themselves to clinical study or reporting in scientific journals.

One contemporary reality deserves special attention, in part because the discrepancy between physician and patient perspectives can be so profound, and in part because my personal experience with this discrepancy was so dramatic.

Several years ago, I was a member of the audience at a conference on traumatic injuries, where the following problem was presented to experts on a panel: You are an emergency physician at a small community hospital. An eight-year-old boy is brought in after a bicycle accident, from which he sustained a 15-minute loss of consciousness. The exam is entirely normal (except for minor contusions and abrasions), as are all x-rays and lab work. According to protocol, such patients are admitted for observation to the pediatric service, which in this case means old Doc Jones, who phones in orders without ever seeing the patient. To make a long story short, over the next 6 hours the patient becomes marginally more obtunded, not alert and bright as usual, and somewhat lethargic. Because you are interested and concerned, you repeat your neurologic exam, finding no "hard" signs of neurologic damage. You call Dr. Jones, describe the situation and your concern about a slowly evolving intracranial bleed, and suggest transferring the patient to the nearest hospital with a CT scanner. Dr. Jones politely but adamantly refuses, saying he is confident the patient can be safely observed in this hospital. Now, what do you do, given your concern? The expert panelists suggested a variety of options: demand that Dr. Jones come in to examine the patient himself; call Dr. Jones' department chief; call in a surgeon for a second opinion; call the hospital chief-of-staff; or as a last resort, transfer the patient to another hospital chief-of-staff; or as a last resort, transfer the patient to another hospital on your own authority, however flimsy. Then yours-truly piped up from the audience with the following suggestion: how about talking with the parents, explaining that you and Dr. Jones have a difference of opinion (as can happen between any two competent professionals), but that since it was their son who was involved, you thought they deserved to be informed, so they could influence what happened next, if they so chose.

Well, you would think I had advocated that chiropractors be allowed to perform neurosurgery. Every one of the panelists thought that my suggestion was the worst thing that could be done in the circumstances—and, if a single physician in the audience of 300 or so thought my suggestion had any merit, no one mentioned it to me. If that's all there was to the matter, there would be no point in mentioning it. I have been wrong many times in the past, and certainly could be in the present example.

The interesting thing is that as I have re-told the story to various lay people, not a single person agreed with the panelists—and many parents were vehement in asserting their "right" to know in such circumstances.

The point here simply is that there is an enormous backlash against medical paternalism, wherein a physician makes a decision for a patient, presumably with the best of intentions and for the latter's good, without the patient and the patient's family being aware of it.

As you find models of the doctor-patient relationship, which comfortably fit your own style and values, you will want to keep these ongoing developments in mind. To ignore the patient's wishes in such circumstances is to invite his or her wrath—and to burden yourself with responsibilities which can reasonably be shared with those most intimately involved: the patient and the patient's family.

Values for an Evolving Clinician

Idealism increases in direct proportion to one's distance from the problem.
                                                                  - John Galsworthy

The most utterly lost of all days is that in which we have not once laughed.
                                                  - Sebastien Roch Nicolas Chamfort

Many of our prayers were not answered, and for this we are now grateful.
                                                              - William Feather

Writers seldom come to their subjects by accident. My own interest in writing this book arose from a very early and definitely naive biopsychosocial idealism, which I found extremely difficult to implement in practice. At one stage, my natural but occasionally superficial optimism was seriously threatened by a brooding pessimism about the doctor-patient relationship as it seemed likely to unfold in the years ahead. During that period, I wrote a book about my flirtation with disillusionment called, *The Bitter Pill: Doctors, Patients, and Failed Expectations*, which was widely perceived to be about physician burnout and even impairment. As is the norm with such things these days, I was sent on the talk-show circuit by my publisher. On one such program, I was introduced by the talk-show host, who said: "And here, to talk about the important subject, is Dr. Martin Lipp, himself a burned-out and impaired physician."

The introduction caught me by surprise, and I categorically denied if, but it forced me into a careful self-assessment. I will admit to being singed about the edges even as I have avoided burnout at the core, and I certainly acknowledge that the process of relinquishing illusions has been a painful one. My point in mentioning all this here is simply to emphasize that the values I advocate below are not simply derived from scholarly study, but rather are an outgrowth of my own painful experiences and those of colleague and friends. While others with parallel experiences inevitably would come up with a different list, the following are a representative sample of ideas worth pondering, and perhaps adopting as guidelines in our continuing pursuit of satisfaction in patient care.

Respect for the patient as an individual. If you can't respect the patient, you won't respect what you do with, or for, or to the patient. If you don't respect the process of giving care, how can you respect yourself? The irony of all this is that disrespect for the patient may ultimately be more harmful to ourselves than to the patient. I need to value what I do, even if the patients don't think they need it for themselves. I need to keep alert to the person who is my patient, that amalgam of feelings and thoughts, experiences and hopes, strengths and limitations, which makes each of us unique. I need to keep open my own soul's eye for the soul who is my patient.

Acceptance of self as person. We need to accept that the demands of being a human being supersede those of physicianhood. How we practice medicine will be heavily influenced by the events in our personal lives: birth of children, death of parents and friends, disruption of important relationships, illness, joys and sorrows. Being a physician does not insulate us from the need for sympathy, tenderness, support and occasional guidance from those around us, including co-workers and patients. Learn not only how to give, counsel, and succor, but how to receive in return.

Recognition of personal vulnerability. One of the paradoxes of the good clinician is that the professionally useful quality of sensitivity to the patient as a person in turn makes the clinician potentially vulnerable as a human being who may suffer along with the patient. While recognizing that many ventures worth pursuing nonetheless involve some potential for discomfort, the pain itself never feels good and can sometimes become a major burden. Such stresses affect each of us differently, but once a certain variable threshold is passed, the stress takes its toll of physicians no less than patients. The consequences may include impaired health, depression, excessive use of alcohol or substances, and impaired clinical performance. Be alert to such difficulties in yourself and in your physician colleagues; shared concern and support can lighten many burdens.

Self-respect independent of human limitations. At various stages of my training, I was told implicitly or explicitly: "If you don't know everything, you will kill someone. If you don't know everything, you will be a lousy doctor, and you don't belong in clinical medicine." That, of course, is the Big Lie—and probably the source of more unhappiness and guilt and personal suffering in physicians than all other misbeliefs put together. Each of us has our limitations. No one knows it all, and no one can do it all. The complete physician doesn't exist. These limitations don't make us bad clinicians; they are the basis for our empathy with patients whose illnesses give them such a keen awareness of their own limitations. The only truly terrible things that happen in association with limitations come as a consequence of refusing to recognize their existence and substituting arrogance for humility.

A safe doctor is one who knows his or her limitations, and calls for help when the demands of a situation exceed ability. None of us need feel diminished in requesting assistance from others. All care must be collaborative, and we deserve to respect ourselves even as we respect the nurses, social workers, patients, and others with whom we collaborate.

Effective limit setting. Setting reasonable limits involves two steps: first, knowing what they are; and second, acting on them in a way that demeans neither ourselves nor our patient. You can't meet all of your patient's expectations or all of your own expectations, let alone do so every day. There are differences among "there is nothing I can do," "there is nothing that can be done," and "there is nothing you can do." The irony is that patients are often better able to accept our limitations than we can ourselves, as long as we don't communicate these limits in a way that implies that the patient is somehow responsible for them. Acknowledge the patient's needs and feelings, take responsibility for what you can't or don't wish to do, and then try to find some reasonable alternative. Understand that clashes between expectations and reality are inevitable. While ambition is useful and often praiseworthy, try to avoid the trap that captures so many physicians: substituting rapacious financial ambition for success in the less tangible and sometimes more elusive interpersonal arena.

Setting priorities and cultivating resources. The limits you set will depend upon what you value and what you specifically dislike. We will sometimes choose to emphasize one function of work over another, or one model of the doctor-patient relationship over another. The kinds of choices we make will depend not only upon the rewards we perceive, but also upon the resources we have to draw upon. A recurring question will be, How much can I give at the office and still be able to give at home? We must be able to give our family, friends, and colleagues enough time so that they will be able to replenish us when we need replenishment. Clinical work is hard work, often emotionally draining. We must be able to share time of high quality with those we care about, in order to get back valuable support in return. We need to honor the need for selfishness in its purest form: attention to self. When we are confident of our own resources, we will feel more comfortable "giving at the office." Take your positive strokes where you can find them. Learn to take satisfaction from small successes, even when—and perhaps especially when—larger successes seem less frequent.

Acknowledging the natural course of events. Some fights are worth fighting even though we are bound to lose by objective standards. In a clinical setting, we must acknowledge that the inexorability of some disease processes and the inevitability of death will overcome any efforts on our part. The physician who regards such an eventuality as a failure has set standards which no human being can hope to meet. We have to believe that providing palliation and comfort constitute worthy contributions, separate from the predictable conclusion of the disease process. Each of us inevitably will have our failures as a part of our professional life. The coping styles we urge upon patients faced with burdensome stresses are no less relevant for ourselves. We need to acknowledge events as they occur, acknowledge our feelings and their appropriateness, and allow them time to evolve. Time soothes wounds for us as well as for our patients.

Limitations of physician authority. In recognizing that physicians are not omniscient, not gods or even godlike, we must also understand that our patients and our nonphysician co-workers will seldom take our requests as divine instruction. Many of us entered the medical profession thinking that, by virtue of being a physician, we would be "in charge," and relinquishing control has not always been easy. The public is increasingly skeptical or our technology and wary of iatrogenesis. Fortunately, we are much less likely to harm wary patients than those who try to abdicate all responsibility to us. However, in respecting the patient's fundamental right to make decisions concerning matters of personal health, we must still live within the legal constraints that put so much of the responsibility for patient care on the physician's lap. Malpractice law must be altered to reflect the acknowledged virtue of the patients' rights movement and its claim that each patient is ultimately responsible for his or her own body.

Personal and professional evolution. A century ago, saddle sores constituted an occupational hazard for the physician on the American frontier. Today, the physician faces a new hazard: "triplicate-form amblyopia." Different times, different frustrations, different rewards. Your life will be more interesting and complicated than you ever imagined it could be, with plenty of unanticipated and unpredictable turns.

Nonetheless, the crucial importance of sustaining high morale while practicing good clinical medicine remains the same. Clinical skill evolves, and inherent in that evolution is an understanding of the universality of human suffering and an alertness to the often subtle manifestations of human nobility in its various guises. The essence is respect for ourselves, respect for our patients, and respect for the process of treatment itself.

Sense of humor. Finally, few qualities will serve you as well in the practice of medicine—and in life—as your sense of humor. You will be confronted again and again by life's absurdities, and they must be recognized for what they are. Often, laughter, if not the only response, is clearly among the best. Believe in human folly; wisdom often creeps into our foolishness if we have the wit to see it. And sometimes the reverse also is true: we who aspire to be so wise can often seem foolish and amusing to others. The practice of medicine can be, in addition to everything else, a great deal of fun, but, like so much in life, what you get out of it is largely a reflection of what you bring to it.

Bibliography

Bittker TE: The industrialization of american psychiatry. Am J Psychiatry 142:149-154, 1985.

Bosk CL: Occupational rituals in patient management. N Engl J Med 303:71-76, 1980.

Burnham JC: American medicine's golden age—what happened to it? Science. 215:1474-1479, 1982.

Cassell EJ: The nature of suffering and the goals of medicine. N Engl J Med 306:639-645, 1982.

Charles SC, Wilbert JR, Francke KJ: Sued and non-sued physicians' self-reported reactions to malpractice litigation. Am J Psychiatry 142:437-440, 1985.

Crippen DW: Emergency medicine redux—the rise and fall of a community medicine specialty. Ann Emerg Med 13:539-542, 1984.

Ehrenreich J (ed.): The Cultural Crisis of Modern Medicine. New York, Monthly Review Press, 1978.

Ginzberg E: The monetarization of medical care. N Engl J Med 310:1162-1165, 1984.

Illich I: Medical Nemesis—The Expropriation of Health. New York. Pantheon Books, 1976.

Jonsen AR: Watching the doctor. N Engl J Med 308:1531-1535, 1983.

Knowles J (ed.): Doing Better and Feeling Worse. New York, Norton, 1977.

Kramer M: Reality Shock—Why Nurses Leave Nursing. St. Louis, CV Mosby Co., 1974.

Kubie LS: The retreat from patients—an unanticipated penalty of the full-time system. Arch Gen Psychiatry 24:98-106, 1971.

Lipp MR, Weingarten R: Hazards in the practice of medicine. Am Fam Physician. 12(4):92-96, 1975.

Lipp MR: The Bitter Pill—Doctors, Patients and Failed Expectations. New York, Harper & Row, 1980.

Machie RE: Family problems in medical and nursing families. Br J Med Psychol 40:333-340, 1967.

May HJ, Revicki DA: Professional stress among family physicians. J Fam Pract 20:165-171, 1985.

Needleman J: The Way of the Physician. San Francisco, Harper & Row, 1985.

Reidbord SP: Psychological perspectives on iatrogenic physician impairment. Pharos, Summer 1983, pp 2-8.

Relman A: The new medical-industrial complex. New Engl J Med 303:963-970, 1980.

Starr P: The Social Transformation of American Medicine. New York, Basic Books, 1982.

Stephens GG: Family practice—The renaissance is over. J R Coll Gen Pract 31:460-466, 1981.

Terkel S: Working—People Talk About What They Do All Day and How They Feel About What They Do. New York, Pantheon Books, 1972.

Thomasma DC: Beyond medical paternalism and patient autonomy. Ann Intern Med 98:243-248, 1983.

Vaillant GE: Physicians' use of mood-altering drugs—A 20-year follow-up report. N Engl J Med 282:365-370, 1970.

Chapter 6

Respect for Persons: Nursing Ethics

Rose Mary Volbrecht

Rule ethics has dominated moral philosophy since its development in the eighteenth and nineteenth centuries. The goal of this ethical model is to capture our moral duties and obligations within a manageable set of rules. Thus, applied ethics, such as nursing ethics, involves the application of abstract, universal rules to particular situations or cases. This attempt to distill ethical decision making into a list of rules reflects both the strength and weakness of this theory's roots in the Western European Enlightenment period.

Like all ethical theorists, the authors of utilitarianism and Kantian ethics were thinking, discussing, and writing within a particular historical, cultural context. These two theories of rule ethics clearly reflect their origin in the modern Enlightenment period. This does not make them irrelevant for our contexts; it does mean that we must be aware of their context in order to understand the concepts and principles that they highlight. We must then ask how these are relevant to our contexts and whether any modifications of them are needed in light of our different experiences.

Utilitarianism begins with the basic insight that acting morally should make our world a better place by increasing human happiness. The classical utilitarians, Jeremy Bentham and John Stuart Mill, believed that the one thing that has value in itself—the one thing that we desire for itself and not as a means to something else—is pleasure. Therefore, they believed that increasing happiness meant maximizing pleasure and minimizing pain. Utilitarianism begins with the *principle of utility:* Actions are right in proportion to their tendency to promote the greatest good for the greatest number of persons affected by these actions.

Thus, for the utilitarians, *consequences* alone are what is important. It is the utility of actions—their likely ability to produce good consequences (pleasure/happiness) and not bad ones (pain/unhappiness)—that is morally relevant for utilitarians. Box 2-2 illustrates this key utilitarian principle.

It is easy to see how utilitarianism supports the rules related to beneficence and nonmaleficence. Beneficence involves acting in ways that benefit others, including both acting to prevent some harm as well as producing positive benefits for others. Clearly, beneficence is a primary obligation of nursing and other health professions. Nurses are committed to acting for the benefit of patients, families, and communities by addressing health needs. Nonmaleficence is a corollary to beneficence: It directs us to refrain from actions that cause harm. This includes not merely avoiding malicious actions that intend to harm, but also exercising due care and caution to avoid causing harm while working to benefit someone. For the utilitarian, it is the consequences that count: A careless disclosure of patient information can be equally as harmful as an intentional disclosure.

Beneficence as an ideal in nursing is uncontroversial. In practice, nurses face difficult decisions when conflicts occur. A decision to choose or refuse treatments may appear to be contrary to well-being. Or actions that support patient well-being may conflict with family or community needs. These conflicts will raise important issues about patient autonomy and justice or fairness. Utilitarianism places the rules of autonomy and justice as secondary to and derived from the primary obligation to maximize pleasure and minimize pain.

Kantian Ethics

Kantian ethics, like utilitarianism, begins with a basic principle and derives rules from it that guide actions. Immanuel Kant (1724-1804) was the most influential modern deontologist. His ethics is referred to as *deontological* because it emphasizes what we are supposed to *do* (from the Greek, *deon*, meaning *duty*). While utilitarianism advances the belief that only the utility of actions has intrinsic value, Kant believed that some actions are in themselves right or wrong and not simply because of their consequences. In fact, Kant took the rather extreme view that some ethical rules should never be broken regardless of the consequences. Most contemporary deontologists argue that since ethical rules are intended to protect and benefit human beings, even the most basic ethical rules may need to be broken in unusual circumstances to avert major human catastrophes. In all but very extreme cases, however, deontologists regard respect for individual human beings as taking priority over maximizing happiness.

Kant's ethical theory reflected the optimistic confidence in the objectivity of human reason and the value of individual autonomy, which was characteristic of the Enlightenment. His basic principle, summarized in Box 2-5, is one of universal respect for all persons.

From this principle, duties not to harm and duties to help all human beings can be derived. It is difficult to overestimate the influence of Kant's ethics in Western cultures. Recognizing persons as autonomous beings, capable of deliberation and choice, rationally demands that we treat them as worthwhile in themselves. Kant described this as treating persons as "ends-in-themselves," rather than as mere means to other persons' ends as the children at Willowbrook were. This core Kantian insight has had a profound impact on Western moral, political, and legal traditions. Furthermore, it has been absolutely central in modern health care ethics.

Kant's Categorical Imperative

Unlike utilitarianism, wherein one's motives are irrelevant and only consequences matter, in Kant's ethics, motives are everything. An action is morally good and praiseworthy only if it is done from a sense of duty, or what Kant calls a "good will." It is not enough to do the right thing; it must be done because the one who acts believes that this action is morally right and that it is, therefore, his or her duty. Kant proposes a test for determining whether our will is good or whether an action is our duty. The test that he outlines, called the *Categorical Imperative*, has two requirements that he discussed in his book *Groundwork of Metaphysics of Morals* (1785/1964).

UNIVERSALIZATION

The first requirement is that when we are considering an action we must ask whether we can imagine our intentions for an action as a general rule for everyone. This is the requirement of *universalization:* Could my intention be stated as a principle—or maxim, as Kant called it—that could be generalized to apply to all cases of the same kind? Kant's examples of universalization emphasize the need for logical consistency. For instance, Kant argues that you could not will that you allowed to lie when it serves your interests while, at the same time, willing that all other people tell the truth even when it is to their disadvantage to do so.

Kant's argument here is not the utilitarian one that a lie will be effective only if people can generally assume that others are telling the truth. Utilitarians note that if we all agree to lie when it suits us and we all know that this is going to happen, then we will stop trusting each other and our attempts to get away with a lie will not work. But Kant's argument is not about the bad consequences of universalizing our intention to lie. Rather, his argument is that it is logically inconsistent to apply one rule to yourself and a different rule to other persons. Logical consistency is a requirement that rational people impose on their own actions. Kant concluded that the universalization of our moral maxims is also then a requirement that we impose on ourselves simply because we are rational beings.

How exactly we should understand and apply Kant's Categorical Imperative is controversial among Kant scholars. But it is clear that one of the basic insights behind the Categorical Imperative is the claim that we cannot make arbitrary exceptions for our own actions. This is consistent with one of our first moral lessons about fairness. Parents encourage their children to think about fairness when they ask a child to stop and consider "How would you feel if your brother or sister did that to you?" This simple lesson encourages children to universalize their actions—to imagine that their actions are open to assessment by any rational person. Would that person see the action as one that says "what's fair for me is fair for you?" Or would that person see an action that says "my interests and preferences count more than yours?" Fairness is a consistency requirement that is embodied in Kant's requirement of universalization.

Of course, some exceptions to rules are legitimate. Ambulances should be allowed to run red lights, surgeons should be allowed to cut into abdomens with a knife to remove inflamed appendices, and nurses should be allowed to spend more time with a patient in critical condition than with one whose condition is stable. However, these are all exceptions that we expect *any* rational person to recognize as legitimate. The ambulance rushing to the hospital is in a different situations deserve different considerations. We can still say that drivers generally should not run red lights, while allowing exceptions that are of the same kind as the ambulance, that is, a lifesaving kind. Our maxim would then be that "Drivers should not run red lights unless it is necessary to save a life." This maxim can be universalized and, thus, passes this first requirement of Kant's Categorical Imperative test.

RESPECT FOR PERSONS AND AUTONOMY

The second requirement of the Categorical Imperative is one of *respect for persons*. To be morally praiseworthy, the maxim of your action must not only be universalizable to all persons in the same type of situation, but it must also contain the intention to show respect for all persons as rational beings.

The Moral Value of Rationality

Without doubt, Kant was an Enlightenment man who reveled in the power and potential of human reason. But why did he think that our rationality is morally relevant? Why does the fact that beings have the capacity for reasoning make them valuable and deserving of respect? Is it simply that reasoning ability is what makes human beings unique? If so, this may seem rather self-serving. (Today, we are beginning to appreciate that dolphins and whales may have similarly complex reasoning capacities.) Does the fact that other living beings have unique characteristics make them objects of respect as well? Kant tells us to respect others and ourselves *as rational beings*. Should we then respect horses and lions as swift and graceful beings or bats as echo-locating beings? Do their unique characteristics endow these animals with a morally relevant value? What *moral* value does human rationality have? We can see how Kant answered this by looking at what he thought it meant to treat rational beings with respect.

One formulation of the Categorical Imperative, which Kant provides in *Groundwork of Metaphysics of Morals* (1964, p. 96), is the following:

Act in such a way that you always treat humanity, whether in your own person or in the person of any other, never simply as a means but always at the same time as an end.

This formulation suggests that treating rational persons with respect means that we treat them as "ends" and never as mere "means." An end is a goal or something that is value for itself rather than valued only as a means to another goal or value that motivates a person's action. Kant thought that human rationality had moral value precisely because their capacity for rationality makes human beings capable of being goal setters. Rationality enables human beings to deliberate about what actions to take and about what ends or goals are worth pursuing. Our behavior is not simply the result of instincts, biological conditioning, or learned responses to environmental stimuli. We are capable of choosing our goals and not merely following ones that are imposed on us by nature or environmental conditioning. If we are capable of deliberating, choosing our ends, and determining actions consistent with these ends, then it is also appropriate for us to be held accountable for these choices and actions.

Persons As Mere Means

This is exactly what it means to be a moral agent. Ethics is the process of reflecting and deliberating about what has value, what end is worth pursuing and how it should be pursued. A moral agent is someone who is capable of entering into this process of reflection and deliberation and, then, of being held accountable for his or her actions. This is why Kant thinks that rationality is morally relevant. It is what makes human beings capable of moral reflection and action. This is what gives us value and makes us "ends" deserving respect. When we treat people simply as "means," we deny them the respect that they deserve as deliberators, goal setters, or moral agents. In fact, it means that we act as if they have no goals or values of their own, but stead that they value is merely their usefulness in helping truly autonomous beings to achieve their own goals.

We have all likely experienced both being "used" and using others as mere means. Service roles especially lend themselves to this treatment. It is not wrong, of course, for others to expect those in service jobs to do their jobs. But bosses, customers, and patient can sometimes forget that secretaries, clerks, and nurses are more than just providers of service. When they do forget, they treat these people as mere means to their own ends. If we treat our secretaries as mere means, we treat them like Xerox machines that exist solely to serve our production needs. We fail to remember that they are also agents who are capable of deliberation and goal choosing. This is, in fact, why many employees feel alienated from their daily work when they are not invited to be part of the process of choosing goals and the effective means to achieve them. They are simply assigned tasks and expected to carry them out. Kant regards treating people this way as demeaning and immoral.

Human beings have an absolute value, according to Kant, because of their ability to reason and, on the basis of this, their ability to choose actions. This, Kant suggests, is the basis of human dignity. Each human being is unique and is, therefore, irreplaceable. One human being cannot be substituted for another or traded off for another. The unique, intrinsic value of each human being imposes limits on the means that we may choose to pursue our goals. We may never violate the autonomy of any rational human being as a means to achieving other goals, even if these goals are themselves for the benefit of other human beings. On the other hand, we must also recognize that there are limits on individual autonomy: Individuals may not exercise their autonomy in ways that cause significant harm to others.

Sadly, the history of medicine, is filled with examples of exactly this. In the Willowbrook case, the mentally retarded children were deliberately harmed in order to benefit other, "less expendable" human beings. Before the institutionalization of informed consent, the autonomy of many patients was violated in the interests of training health care personnel or advancing medical knowledge. Medical interns routinely performed multiple pelvic exams on women anesthetized for surgery, without their knowledge or consent. Indigent patients were frequently used to test new drugs or procedures that had no therapeutic value for these patients, again without their consent and sometimes, without their knowledge. The case study of the deceptive use of a placebo with Ms. Reed suggests that all such violations of patient autonomy have not disappeared today.

Obligations Related to Autonomy

For Kant, respect is a feeling, , but it is most of all a way of acting required by the Categorical Imperative. An action will be moral if it satisfies the tests of universalization and respect for persons. Most importantly, respect for persons *as rational beings* requires that we do not take away the conditions of their moral agency or autonomy. Autonomy is the ability to choose one's actions based on relevant information. It is easy to see why lying, deception, withholding relevant information, and paternalistic treatment of autonomous patients are all fundamentally wrong from this perspective. It should also be clear why informed consent and the right of patients to refuse treatment have been recognized in contemporary health care as basic patient rights. Ensuring privacy and confidentiality are two other moral obligations that respect for autonomy prescribes. Respecting patients (and colleagues) as autonomous decision maker includes respecting the decisions these persons make about what information they wish to provide about themselves, for whom, and for what purposes.

PRINCIPLES OF UNIVERSALIZED RESPECT

Kant did not attempt to summarize his ethical theory into the four principles of autonomy, nonmaleficence, beneficence, and justice, which are ubiquitous in contemporary rule-based bioethics. But, as noted earlier, the rules derived from

Kant's principle of universalized respect can be grouped into these four categories. We have already seen that respect for autonomy is inherent in Kant's basic principle of universalized respect for persons. We will briefly discuss the other three categories and note the distinction that Kant makes between "perfect" and "imperfect" duties.

Nonmaleficence

The injunction to "do no harm" has been the most basic principle in the history of health care ethics. Because human beings have intrinsic value and dignity, we demonstrate respect for this value by taking care not to harm these persons. The category of nonmaleficence will include rules that prohibit killing, physical and emotional harm, negligence, stealing, sexual exploitation, and breaking promises or contracts.

Beneficence

The provision of health care is as fundamentally tied to beneficence as it is to nonmaleficence. Health care professionals commit themselves to the care of the sick and to the promotion of health. Our duty of universalized respect for persons implies that we all have duties to promote the well-being of others as well as our own well-being. This duty follows both from our recognition that each human being has intrinsic value and from our recognition that physical and mental health is a necessary foundation to our autonomy. Healthy bodies and minds enable us to pursue our chosen goals.

Patients do not have an unlimited obligation to promote their own well-being. Neither is the obligation of health care providers to promote their patients' well-being unlimited. Kant distinguished two kinds of duties, perfect and imperfect (1964, p. 91; 1797/1964, pp. 48-53). *Perfect duties* must be observed at every opportunity. These are duties not to harm. Every time that we have the opportunity to murder, rape, steal, deceive, and so on, we have an obligation not to do so. On the other hand, *imperfect duties* are duties that we are obligated to perform, but the time and manner are more open. These are duties of benevolence and self-development. For example, as you leave a department store during the holidays, the Salvation Army bell ringer may not grab your scarf and bark "Fulfill your duty of benevolence. Put some money in the kettle." You do have an on-going duty of benevolence, but you are not obligated to be benevolent at every opportunity. Some choice about how and when is permitted. Benevolence is a duty as long as there are others who need help, but you are permitted to make choices about where you will invest your time, effort, and money. A rational, responsible person will not overlook grave and urgent needs for trivial ones. In some cases, you will be obligated to help a person, here and now. If the need is urgent, if you have the ability to help and no other help is available, and if the cost of helping would not be too great, then you are obligated in a particular situation to give help.

Respect for persons requires that we do our part to give aid to others and ourselves, but there are some limitations. The first is that we may not violate a perfect duty in order to fulfill an imperfect one. Consequently, it is impermissible to intentionally lie, deceive, exploit, or physically or emotionally harm an innocent person (one not threatening any other person) in order to give help to that person or other persons. The researchers at the Willowbrook Institution clearly violated their perfect duty not to harm its residents when they intentionally infected children with hepatitis as a means to potentially benefit others. Less dramatic but equally significant violations of perfect duties may occur as a result of misguided attempts by health care professionals and families to protect patients. Consider the following case:

> Mr. Gahn, 79, is in your care following an episode of angina. He is alert and talks of being discouraged because he feels so tired recently. He lives with his son and daughter-in-law, Jeb and Stacie. Dr. Bender has told them that Mr. Gahn's angina is well managed, but that recent tests she reviewed revealed untreatable pancreatic cancer. Jeb informs the physician that his father is planning to leave with a friend of his on a Caribbean cruise in two weeks. It is a trip that his father had dreamed of taking for many years. Mr. Gahn and his friend have been planning this trip for two years. Jeb and Stacie ask the physician if Mr. Gahn is strong enough to make the trip. Dr. Bender states that he is. The couple begs the physician not to tell Mr. Gahn about the cancer until he returns from the trip, saying that it would be a huge disappointment if he could not go, and receiving the news about his cancer will certainly ruin the trip for him. Dr. Bender thinks that Mr. Gahn should have an accurate diagnosis of his condition and be free to make his own decisions about how he will spend his remaining time. But Jeb and Stacie persist in their request that he not be told. The physician reluctantly agrees to abide by the family's wishes and instructs the nurse to do so as well. She agrees not to reveal the cancer diagnosis to Mr. Gahn.

Jeb and Stacie clearly believe that withholding the truth about Mr. Gahn's condition is in his best interests. Although the physician is not so sure that it is, she goes along with the family's request and the nurse follows suit. For Kant, this is a violation of Mr. Gahn's autonomy. Jeb and Stacie presume to substitute their judgments for Mr. Gahn's. In doing so, they deny him both the respect that he is due as a competent adult and also the opportunity to use his remaining time as he judges most appropriate. For their part, the physician and nurse respect the family's autonomous choice at the expense of their patient's autonomy. Consequently, although Jeb and Stacie are motivated by genuine concern for Mr. Gahn, the mean used is unacceptable. Furthermore, although the physician and nurse may believe that their actions are necessary in order to respect Jeb and Stacie's autonomy, this is false. Jeb and Stacie's autonomous choice in this instance violates their perfect duty not to violate Mr. Gahn's autonomy by withholding critical information about his health status. Consequently, their action is unjustified, and Mr. Gahn's health care provider should not cooperate with this deception.

Finally, although Kant argued that no violation of perfect duties is ever justified, most contemporary Kantians believe that catastrophic (not merely serious) costs to others may sometimes justify violation of a perfect duty.

Principle of Justice

Also a critical responsibility in health care, justice requires that we give each person his or her due. This includes an obligation to distribute the benefits, risks, and costs that belong to a community and to allocate health care resources fairly. Universalized respect for persons demands that we give each person his or her fair share. Since individuals have intrinsic and equal value, individuals in similar circumstances will require similar treatment. Kant did not offer any particular model for how shared resources should be fairly allocated. Contemporary deontologists, however, have offered a variety of models, which vary depending on which "similar circumstances" are considered most relevant. Is it similar needs, similar talents, similar efforts, similar promises by others, or similar achievements that should be given priority? Does it make a difference what is being allocated so that we might emphasize need in the case of health care, but emphasize talent in the case of education? These are critical questions for our communities faced with growing needs and limited resources. Ultimately, they can be answered only in the context of careful community dialogue.

Box 1 summarizes rules that are relevant to nursing practice. All of these rules can be derived from both the utilitarian principle of utility and from the Kantian principle of universalized respect for persons. The lists are illustrative and do not necessarily include all the moral rules that could be derived. It is important to note that rule utilitarians and Kantians produce similar lists of rules, but also to keep in mind that their justifications for these rules are quite different.

Box 1   Summary of Moral Rules
Relevant to Nursing Practice

Requirement of Nonmaleficence: **Do not intentionally inflict harm.**

- Do not kill or physically harm others without justified cause (e.g., self-defense or the use of physically harmful treatment as a necessary and consented means to promoting patient welfare).
- Do not impose unreasonable risks of harm. Negligence is conduct that falls below a standard of due care.
- Do not harm others by slander, insult, or ridicule.
- Do not break a freely made promise or contract to do something in itself morally permissible.
- Do not engage in sexual acts that are exploitative or life diminishing. This includes all sex with patients.

-   Do not steal the legitimately obtained property of others, including their intellectual property (e.g., published ideas, research data, and computer programs).

Respect for Autonomy: **Respect the ability of competent patients to hold views, make choices, and take actions based on personal values and beliefs.**

-   Respect the choice of competent patients to refuse medical treatment and/or nursing care.
-   It is impermissible to treat competent patients without their adequately informed consent. Such consent requires disclosure of relevant information, probing for and ensuring understanding and voluntariness, and fostering adequate decision making.
-   Establish a clear process for the identification of surrogate decision makers in the case of incompetent patients.
-   Respect and protect patient privacy and confidentiality, providing confidential information to others only as required by law or to prevent grave harm to others.

Requirement of Beneficence: **Promote the well-being of others and oneself, using morally permissible means, insofar as one can do so without disproportionate cost.**

-   Maintain one's competence in nursing; participate in efforts to maintain and improve standards of nursing; participate in efforts to maintain working conditions that support quality nursing care; support the development of nursing's body of knowledge.
-   Make reasonable efforts to protect patients and the public from harm due to incompetent or unethical practice by other health care professionals.
-   Participate in efforts to promote the health needs of one's communities.
-   Promote one's own mental, physical, emotional, and spiritual development.

Requirement of Justice: **Distribute benefits, resources, and burdens fairly.**

-   Nursing resources should be allocated fairly among patients served.
-   Communities should develop processes for the fair access and allocation of health care to all members of the community.
-   Workplaces should ensure that all health care providers receive fair compensation for their work and that appropriate appeal processes are in place to ensure fair distribution of wages, compensation, and workloads.

Chapter 7

Respect and Caring: Ethics and Essence of Nursing

Brighid Kelly

Respect for persons and caring are ideally integral to nurse practice. It remains puzzling, however, that these concepts are so noticeably absent from most theoretical descriptions of nurse. Nursing theorists have, for the most part, concentrated their attention on the roles of nurse and client, with little discussion of the ethical and moral dimensions inherent in the relationship. This has not always been the case, as many of our early nursing leaders including Florence Nightingale discussed the ethical role of nursing (Nutting 1916; Nightingale 1969). One explanation for the regrettable oversight is that, while nursing scholars reject the medical model and its influence on nurse, a review of knowledge development in nursing provides ample evidence of reductionism and empiricism. One may well conclude, as did Freire (1970), that oppressed groups, such as nurses, tend to emulate the values of the dominant group. In nursing, as in medicine, ethics and the broader concept of morals were typically classified under the category of metaphysics and consequently ignored. Thus, the scientific method and positivism became the dominant approach to inquiry in nursing.

Respect and caring are familiar concepts and thus may be taken for granted as found in nursing. Respect is an ethical concept, which is not only "the paramount moral attitude but all other moral principles are to be explained in terms of it" (Downie and Telfer 1970,2). One could easily spend a day browsing through books and articles on nursing ethics and never read ore than a sentence or two on the concept of respect. On the other hand, the concept of caring has been well explicated philosophically and anthropologically (Leininger 1977; Watson 1979, 1985; Ray 1981; Gaut 1983; Bevis 1981). Recently a few empirical studies have surfaced in the nursing literature, which provide insight into the phenomenological experience of caring (Drew 1983; Gardner and Wheeler 1981; Reimen 1986). However, the view of caring as a nursing ethic is a relatively recent occurrence (Carper 1986; Fry 1988).

The purpose of this paper is to show that respect and caring are the ethics and the essence of nursing. It is the author's position that if respect and caring are absent, nursing does not occur. The essential nature of respect and caring to the practice of nursing will be explicated by initially clarifying the concepts of respect and caring. Empirical evidence, derived from a recent research study (B. Kelly 1987), will be provided to support respect and caring as the ethics of nursing. Finally, the paper will end with a theoretical commentary on the relationship among the concepts respect, caring, and nursing.

CONCEPT CLARIFICATION

Respect for persons. Downie and Telfer (1970, 87) describe the components of respect for persons as follows:

> In so far as persons are thought of as self-determining agents who pursue objects of interest to themselves we respect them by showing active sympathy with them; in Kant's language, we make their ends out own. In so far as persons are thought of as rule-following we respect them by taking seriously the fact that the rules by which they guide their conduct constitute reasons for which may apply both to them and to ourselves. . . . These two components are independently necessary and jointly sufficient to constitute the attitude of respect which it is fitting to direct at persons.

Kant (1965), in distinguishing respect for persons from admiration or esteem, says respect for humanity is really for respect for the moral law. Williams (1962, 159) says, "Each man [sic] is owed an effort at identification and not regarded as the surface to which a label can be applied." For the attributes of respect one can say that all persons are morally obligated to take seriously the values and goals of all other persons and in addition to be conscious that respect if not a reward for a particular behavior but is in fact a right.

> First condition: S must be aware, either directly or indirectly, of the need for care in X.
> Second condition: S must know that certain things could be done to improve the situation.
> Third condition: S much intend to do something for X.
> Fourth condition: S must choose an action intended to serve as a means for bringing about a positive change in X, and then implement that action.
> Fifth condition: The positive change in X must be judged on the basis of what is good for X rather than for S or some other Y or Z.

In briefly analyzing this view of caring one can say that Gaut believes that: (1) knowledge of the cared-for is necessary; (2) hope is necessary; (3) intention to act is necessary; (4) a "proper" action has been identified and implemented by the care-er; and (5) a judgment is made by the care-er that the positive change is what is good for the cared-for. What is not clear, however, is the role of the cared-for. Does *X* have a voice in the action intended to bring about "this positive change"? This raises the question of what part the cared-for plays in "caring."

Mayeroff (1971) identifies the major ingredients of caring as: knowing, patience, honesty, trust, humility, hope, and courage. He says that care-er and cared-for exist on the same level. They exist in equality. Noddings (1984) also refers to equality in the relationship between adults but also described how the cared-for may not be able, because of developmental maturity or other reasons, to respond as an equal to the care-er.

Overview of the Study

The purpose of the study was to investigate, describe, and explain what senior baccalaureate nursing students internalize as professional values and to describe what they perceive as a commitment to professional ethics in nurse practice. The problem was explicated as a discrepancy between how nursing is expounded by the profession, particularly nursing educators, and how nursing is actually experienced by the general staff nurse. Since the aim of the study was to explore the experiences of the informants from their perspective, the qualitative method was chosen. Specifically, the design was a blend of inductive as described by Glaser and Strauss (1967) and deductive as outlined by Miles and Huberman (1983). The sample consisted of 23 senior baccalaureate nursing students of a total population of 120 who were in the final clinical rotation before graduation. Subjects were volunteers who gave informed consent, having been briefed on the purposes of the study and how their confidentiality would be protected. Data were collected in two ways: audiotaped, in-depth, open-ended interviews and written clinical logs. Content analysis was conducted on all data.

While a detailed description of data collection procedures and data analysis is beyond the both the scope and the purpose of this paper, there is one element that had an important bearing on the findings. The bulk of data in this study was in response to the following statement. "I want you to think of nursing as you have experienced it and then tell me what you believe good nursing to be. I also want to know what you believe bad nursing to be. In other words what, in your experiences, are examples of nursing as you believe nursing ought be done and likewise examples of nursing as it ought not be done."

The study began as a study of ethics. Since the aim of the study was to have the informants express their views on professional values yet avoid an *a priori* fallacy, the investigator had each subject define the concept as it had meaning for him or her. The words *ethics* was not used in the early part of the interview because the investigator believed that the informants, being students, would become preoccupied with providing the researcher with the "classroom" answer instead of their actual lived experiences. Each informant's date was classified under his or her code initials as either interview or log data and further organized by a coding system that identified the page number and the line number.

THE FINDINGS

Results of the study revealed that informants perceived two concepts to be central to their view of "good" nursing, namely respect and caring. Data to support these concepts are presented in the informants' words.

Respect. The need to respect patients and families, self, colleagues, and the profession was identified as the most basic professional value. For example, respect for patients was described in terms of what the "ideal" nurse would do:

> The first nurse was ideal. She came in and she listened to whatever the patient had to say to her. Even though she didn't understand it, she'd say "I didn't understand that please speak slower so that I can understand what you are saying to me." She was candid on the phone with the family. She gave her respect by pulling curtains when some procedure had to be done. She always explained from beginning to end. (N.O., interview, 2.20.).

Informants said respect was evidenced in the manner of interaction with the patient, i.e., listening, being honest, candid and "treating them like human beings." The importance of respect for these subjects was the message conveyed to the patient in the initial interaction, i.e., recognizing the patient as a person. However, these students were even more conscious of the need for respect when they perceived that it was absent. "The first thing that comes to mind . . . that really makes me angry is the nurses that don't listen to the patients. They go in the room and they want to hear a certain thing and no matter what the patient says that is the way they come out." (J.E., interview, 1.15.).

Another concern identified by these students was the manner in which patients were addressed: "Instead of calling the patients by their name, they—a lot of nurses—call the patients by their first name or they call them "honey." I work with a lot of older patients and I don't like that belittling. I think we should show respect. I wouldn't call my grandmother "honey"! I wouldn't call anyone older then me "honey." I hate it when people do it to me." (K.P. interview, 6.25.).

Respect for self, colleagues, and profession was described by most of the students in terms of self-respect as a professional, respect for colleagues, and "professional" behavior in general. Self-respect was described as assertiveness, continuing one's education, and promoting the rights of the nurse. Respect for colleagues was described in terms of collaborative, "professional" communications. Disrespect was evidenced by "backbiting" and lack of professional unity. Respect for colleagues was described in terms of collaborative, "professional" communications. Disrespect was evidenced by "backbiting" and lack of professional unity. Intra-professional respect was of considerable concern to these nursing students, as any perceived that nurses did not support each other. One subject said, "I don't think nurses are half as kind to each other as they are to the patient. I think there is a little lacking there that I wish were untrue . . . but I see a lot of backbiting of one another which is very distressing to me." (E.A., interview, 7.1.)

Respect for the profession was defined as striving for professionalization, subscribing to the professional values, and being involved in the professional organization. Disrespect for the profession was viewed as seeing nursing as a "job" rather than a career and not evidencing one's knowledge by assuming responsibility for decisions. Informant's were conscious of the need to be respected as professionals. Keeping standards high was viewed as a professional obligation, and students were aware of the constant need for vigilance in this area.

Caring. In analyzing informants' accounts, it was concluded that caring was closely aligned with respect in the minds of these subjects. In fact, the concepts were intertwined. The informants did not describe their experiences in terms of conceptual themes; it was the task of the investigator to separate and classify. In this case the investigator saw sufficient differences in the expression of these two concepts to separate them. The concepts of respect and caring were differentiated on the basis of conceptual quality. Caring was associated with showing "concern and love," providing psychological support, getting involved, being cheerful and friendly, and "taking the time" to do a good job. The concept of caring for these nursing students was best understood as all "the little things" as exemplified by the following: "It's the little things that are important to the patient—This man I had—he couldn't walk—he had been bedridden for a month—he couldn't even stand up and use his urinal. He needed help to walk and nurses didn't have the time to do it. Yet, there are nurses at the nurses' station just sitting and yakking. . . . Nurses need to have time to take care of patients." (K.P. interview, 15.25.) Another student said, "The exceptional nurses did those things, holding hands, talking to them, telling them what was going on. Being real open and honest with the families. Giving them psychological kind of support along with the physical." (F.V., interview, 1.11.)

The importance of the concept of caring for these nursing students was clearly evident. It would appear that they perceived caring as an essential ingredient to "good" nursing and as the "right" thing for a nurse to do. The pain of caring was another dimension expressed through the voices and experiences of these students. The dictionary defines caring as a state of mental suffering. To care is to be burdened, to be involved with someone. Noddings (1984) talks of caring as "engrossment." It would appear that caring is not easy. When one cares, one experiences pain as indicated from these findings:

I was terribly sad when I went in a room with one family whose 50-year-old daughter was the patient. She had lung cancer which had metastasized. They brought along a long page of questions which the doctor faithfully answered—the hardest one being the life expectancy which turned out to be only about six months with no treatment. I went out to try to comfort them. I felt so helpless. I ended up just simply staying with her for a while because she didn't want to talk. (L.T., log, 4.14.).

In the case of the young man dying on the unit now, the frustration and anger is very evident in their voices and the way they talk. As I said this is new to me. It is all very hard to sort through at times. The pain, the grief of the staff and the parents. The frustrations and helplessness felt when a kid is dying and you can't do anything. (H.G., log, 10.5.).

These findings reflect helplessness, underlying pain, and confusion as to the appropriateness or acceptability of these feelings: Am I supposed to feel this way? There also is an inference that nurses handle these feelings "in their own way."

In summary the results of the study revealed that the nursing students perceived respect and caring as the most basic professional values. Respect was empirically defined by these students as the message received by the other in initial interaction. It was described in terms of interactive demeanor, and the verbal and non-verbal message conveyed. Caring was perceived as multidimensional. It was described as "little things." It was empirically defined by these subjects as having the dimensions of "taking time," showing love and concern, getting involved, being open and honest, being empathic and a good listener, being cheerful and friendly, and being a safe, competent nurse. Caring was found to be painful and was described not only as subjects perceived it, but through their voices in experiencing it.

DISCUSSION

The significance of the findings may be obscured by their apparent simplicity and by the current emphasis on task completion and technical competence. Is that all there is to good nursing? The most significant finding was that "good nursing" was perceived as an ethical concept. In other words, the students had integrated ethics into their concept of nursing.

Students' perception of caring as a nursing ethic was an unexpected finding. Although informants' familiarity with the concept of caring was in no small way related to their nursing education, the fact that they associated caring with ethics was interesting because this connection is not apparent in the nursing ethics literature. The recognition of caring as a moral duty has not been identified by nursing ethicists. Gilligan (1977) found that women's moral development centers around an ethic of care and a responsibility for not hurting others. According to Gilligan, the ethic of care becomes a universal obligation for women. Noddings (1984), in her feminist approach to ethics, describes the ethic of caring as "I must." She is, in many ways, advocating an ethic of virtue.

Although a few nursing scholars are beginning to discuss caring as an ethic (Carper 1986; Fry 1988; Watson 1988), the nursing ethics literature does not include caring as an ethic. Nurse ethicists are fairly consistent in their view of the guiding moral principles, which are usually identified as respect, beneficence, and justice. The ethical principles of autonomy and veracity tend to be incorporated under respect (Benjamin and Curtis 1982). The concept of caring is to included in the ANA *Code for Nurses* (1985). The word *care* appears once as in "health care." Moreover, in the ICN *Code for Nurses* (1973), although the term *care* appears four times, the concept of caring is not included. The question, With so little connection between caring and ethics in the nursing ethics literature, why have the nursing students in this study made such a conceptual leap? Data from this study support that subjects believed a "good nurse" was a caring nurse. Therefore, it follows that in their minds caring and good nursing are one and the same. A logical conclusion would be that for these students ethical practice as caring is the essence of nursing.

Theoretical Commentary

In qualitative research, theory should emerge from empirical data Patton says: "The cardinal principle of qualitative analysis is that causal relationships and theoretical statements be clearly emergent from and grounded in the phenomena studied. The theory emerges from the data: it is not imposed on the data" (1986, 278).

With these thoughts in mind, the following propositions form the basis of the theory emerging from the findings of this study. These propositions describe the relationship among the concepts respect, caring and nursing.

The practice of nursing is essentially moral in nature.

Respect for persons and caring are the ethics of nursing.

Respect, as a nursing ethic, is evidenced by respect for clients and families, self, colleagues, and the profession.

Caring, as a nursing ethic, is evidenced by caring for clients and families, self, colleagues, and the professions.

Respect and caring are necessary but no sufficient elements of nursing.

Respect precedes caring in the nurse-client relationship.

In the absence of respect, caring cannot take place.

In the absence of caring, nursing does not take place.

PROPOSITION 1: THE PRACTICE OF NURSING IS ESSENTIALLY MORAL IN NATURE.

Silva (1983) described nursing as a duty, a moral art, and an autonomous profession. Her thesis is that nursing owes society a duty to care because society and nursing have a social contract. She describes the moral art of nursing as taking care of patients by touching, teaching, comforting, listening, diminishing, suffering, and generally doing for persons what they cannot do for themselves. Nightingale saw nursing in her own life as a "call from God" (Woodham-Smith 1983). On May 29, 1900, she wrote the following letter to her probationers at St. Thomas' Hospital:

> My dear children:
> You have called me you Mother-Chief. It is an honour to me and a great honour to call you my children. Always keep up the honour of this honourable profession. . . . We dishonour [it] when we are had or careless nurses, we dishonour [it] when we do not do our best to relieve suffering even in the meanest creature. (Schuyler 1975, 166)

That statement by Nightingale supports the notion that nursing is essentially a moral activity. Prior to the influence of Nightingale, nursing was provided by religious orders because ministering to the sick was viewed s the essence of moral obligation. The history of American nursing is replete with examples of women who risked everything to focus their lives on service to others (Kalisch and Kalisch 1986). Ministering to the needs of others is the essence of nursing.

PROPOSITION 2: RESPECT FOR PERSONS AND CARING AND THE ESSENTIAL ETHICS OF NURSING.

This statement was supported by data in this study, but there is much wider support for such a proposition.

Respect. The first ethical injunction of the *Code for Nurses* speaks to the provision of respect for all humans. The ethics of nursing refers to the conduct of nurses while they are nursing and to the motives and ends of their professional decision making. L. Kelly (1975, 208) says, "The true ethical core of all professional codes derives from the rights and dignity of the individual—treating the patient as a person." Curtin (Curtin and Flaherty 1982, 3) has consistently stated that ethics in nursing is more evidenced by the day-to-day activities among nurses and patients than "fabulous life and death issues."

Caring. The connection between caring and ethics was made by Gilligan (1977). She described a model of moral development for females based on caring. Gilligan believes that females have had to develop a sense of responsibility based on the universal principle of caring in order to survive. Noddings (1984), an educationist, also proposes a feminine view of ethics based on caring. Her argument is that the basis of all moral action is the memory of being cared for. Her belief is that all moral decisions are grounded in natural caring. This view of ethics is similar to the psychological view that one needs to be loved in order to love. Montagu (1975, 2) says, "She knows how to love, for the only way one learns to love is by being loved." This leads one to conclude that caring is taught by example. The implications are clear for nursing instructors whose clients are nursing students.

Are nurses ethically obligated to "care" for their clients? Before answering this question one must be clear on the meaning ascribed to *care* in this context. Leininger (1981) has studied and identified the essential characteristics present in care such as comfort, compassion, concern, empathy, enabling, involvement, and facilitating. Caring is philosophically defined as being concerned, involved, having an active sympathy, which manifests itself in supporting the cared-for's goals for growth, and self-actualization (Ray 1981). It may be equated with being concerned about someone or charged with the protection of a person. The idea that "caring" involves some element of personal giving of oneself or sacrifice has also been discussed by philosophers. Downie and Telfer (1970) describe this as an "active sympathy" with others and call it *agape*. May (1969) says the opposite of caring is apathy or indifference. The answer to the above question is a resounding "yes". Nurses are ethically obligated to "care" for their clients.

PROPOSITION 3: RESPECT, AS A NURSING ETHIC, IS EVIDENCED BY RESPECT FOR CLIENTS AND FAMILIES, RESPECT FOR SELF, COLLEAGUES, AND THE NURSING PROFESSION.

Since respect for clients and families has been discussed above, a brief clarification of the concept of self-respect is in order as viewed by several philosophers and analyzed in relation to the findings. Kant's views on self-respect are found in *The Doctrine of Virtue* (1964, 434): [A person] possesses, in other words, a dignity (an absolute inner worth) by which he [sic] expects respect for himself from all other rational beings in the world." In discussing one's duties to oneself, Kant lists vices one should avoid, that is, vices that degrade one's moral being. Among these are servility, avarice, and lying. Although Kant discusses self-deception at length, he says that no violation of a person's duty to self is worse than dishonesty. Downie and Telfer (1970, 87) believe that self-respect involves being one's own master and being self-determining. Hill (1982) believes that self-respect is when the person has personal standards or ideals and believes that he (or she) lives by them. Sachs (1982), in analyzing whether self-respect and respect for others are independent, concludes that persons deficient in self-respect are "sorely lacking" in formal object.

The informants in this study provided evidence of how nurses ought to respect colleagues and the profession. They identified the need to see oneself as professional, to act in a professional manner toward one's colleagues, to continue one's education, to strive for unity among nurses, and to be active in one's professional organization. Collegiality was perceived as manifested by respect for others' knowledge and the sharing of ideas through networking and professional cooperation. Respect for the profession entailed not merely viewing nursing as a profession, but acceptance of the professional values of professional growth and a commitment to the professional code.

PROPOSITION 4: CARING AS AN ETHIC IN NURSING IS EVIDENCED BY CARING FOR CLIENTS AND FAMILIES, SELF, COLLEAGUES, AND THE PROFESSION.

Caring for clients and families has been discussed above. Caring for self, colleagues, and the profession is ideally integral to a caring profession. Kelsey (1981) says that caring for self involves listening to ourselves and forgiving ourselves. Healthy persons knows themselves and exhibit trust and confidence in their own ability to deal with situations when they come along, says Tubesing (1983). He also says that self-are involves practicing self-disclosure, reflection, developing healthy relationships, and nurturing support groups.

Caring for colleagues was described by informants as involvement and support in professional relationships. Mayeroff (1971, 3) states: "caring is helping others to grow and to actualize themselves." With regard to manifesting caring toward the profession ANA *Code of Ethics* specifies that nurses have an ethical obligation to contribute to the development of the profession's body of knowledge, to participate in the profession's efforts to implement and improve standards of care, and to participate in efforts to improve standards of employment conducive to high-quality nursing care. These are the goals of the nursing profession, and nurses who participate in any or all of these efforts are demonstrating a "caring" attitude to the profession.

PROPOSITION 5: RESPECT AND CARING ARE NECESSARY BUT NOT SUFFICIENT ELEMENTS OF NURSING.

Respect and caring are essential elements of nursing, but these properties alone are not enough. Professional status is not determined by merely subscribing to the values of a profession. Nightingale said, "Nature has laws or conditions for health and for sickness as for everything else. We have to learn them." (Schuyler, 1975, 165)

The nursing students in this study identified their educational program as the most influential force in shaping their view of themselves as nurses. Many students also made reference to the baccalaureate as the minimum educational qualification for entry into the profession. In the absence of knowledge, respect and caring are insufficient for nursing to take place.

PROPOSITION 6: RESPECT FOR PERSONS PRECEDES CARING IN THE NURSE-CLIENT RELATIONSHIP.

The findings of this study confirm the primary nature of respect. Kant claimed that every human being was an end in himself [sic] and therefore worthy of respect, and he distinguished persons from things in asserting that "respect always applies to persons, never to things." According to Hill (1982, 129), a philosopher, basic respect as a human being does not have to be earned. Humans need not participate in order to be respected. One can, therefore, respect another human being without knowing him or her. On the other hand, caring cannot take place without knowledge. To illustrate this concept one might recall a moving scene in the film *The Elephant Man* (1980, directed by David Lynch). The "creature" is being chased by a mob through the London underground and when cornered, cries out in desperation, "I am not an animal, I am a man." As the story unfolds, one is truck by the way in which the "creature" is treated when it is discovered that not only is e to an imbecile, he is brilliant. He is then addressed a "Mr. John Merrick" and held in high esteem. In examining the doctor's attitude, one deduces that the doctor respected "the creature" from the beginning because of his humanity, but it was only when he began to know John that a caring relationship was evident.

PROPOSITION 7: IN THE ABSENCE OF RESPECT, CARING CANNOT TAKE PLACE.

The essence of caring is wishing a person well—wanting what is best for him or her. This attitude is logically impossible in the absence of respect. Mayeroff (1971) believes that respect is primary in a caring relationship and says a person needs to be viewed as an individual and not "used" by the care-er. He provides the example of a father caring for his child. Instead of dominating and wanting to possess the other, the father wants the child to grow in his or her own right.

PROPOSITION 8: IN THE ABSENCE OF CARING, NURSING DOES NOT TAKE PLACE.

Caring as the essence of nursing has been discussed by several nursing leaders (Leininger 1977; Watson 1979; Ray 1981; Boyle 1981). Carper says: "This basic dictum to be compassionate, humane and caring toward those for whom we provide care is most often expressed in the phrase 'treat the person not merely the patient.' To be concerned with the 'whole person' and to practice with consideration and sensitivity for the integrity of the human self is basically an ethical injunction" (1986, 1).

According to Leininger (1981), caring is the central and unifying focus for the body and practice of nursing. Ray (1981) says caring is perceived as involving a process of co-presence, giving, receiving, communication, and in essence lov-ing. Bevis (1981) says concern is the closest to being synonymous with caring and compares it to Tillich's use of the term *ultimate concern*. Although Bevis does not use the term *duty*, she says *caring* is a force, a compelling action. Watson (1979), in explicating ten curative factors integral to the nurse-client relationship, says that focusing on feelings promotes self-awareness in the nurse and thus is con-ducive to acceptance of client's feelings—both positive and negative. She says nursing is the science of caring.

The ANA social policy statement (1980) describes the nature of nursing as interactive and says that nursing has historically focused on nurturing and creat-ing a physiologic, psychologic, and sociocultural environment in which the pa-tient (and family) can gain or maintain health. The students in this study valued caring as the essence of nursing for them. In fact, when they were asked to iden-tify the one value so important to them that they could not practice nursing without it, more of them identified caring than any other value. Ozar (1987) speaks of the fundamental values and principles of the nursing profession. He says that in order to truly be a nurse, one needs to have a wholehearted com-mitment to the principles and values of the profession. He goes on to say that one who enters with reservations about these values and principles cannot be viewed as a full member of the nursing profession. A logical inference from this state-ment is that a person who does not practice according to the values and principles of nursing is not practicing nursing. In the absence of caring, nursing does not take place.

Summary

The findings of this study and the emergent theory together provide a tapestry of nursing. First, nursing is a caring ministry. Second, nursing requires a specia-lized body of knowledge. Third, nursing respects the uniqueness and wholeness of all persons. And fourth, nursing recognizes and respects the nurse's role in manipulating environmental forces. These assumptions and beliefs about nursing are stated in terms of the ideal, i.e., what nursing ought to be. One could make a case for the notion that the results of this study more accurately reflect the reality of nursing.

The thesis of this paper is that ethical decision making is central to every nursing act. Decision making grounded in ethics is not a particular mode of rea-soning to which one refers in certain situations. It is an element of nursing. The nursing students in this study perceived that ethical nursing was evidenced in ordinary, everyday nurse-patient interactions and in collegial relationships. Le-vine said: "Ethical behavior is not the display of one's moral rectitude in times of crises. It is the day-by-day expression of one's commitment to other persons and the ways in which human beings relate to another in their daily interactions" (1977, 847).

Bibliography

American Nurses' Association. 1980. *Nursing: A social policy statement.* Kansas City, MO: American Nurses' Association.

American Nurses' Association. 1985. Code for nurses with interpretative statements. Kansas City, MO: American Nurses' Association.

Benjamin, M., and J. Curtis. 1982. Ethics in nursing. New York: Oxford University Press.

Bevis, E. 1981. Caring: A life force. In Caring: An essential human need, edited by M. Leininger. Thorofare. NJ: Charles B Slack.

Boyle, J. 1981. An application of the structure-functional method of the phenomenon of caring. In Caring: An essential human need, edited by M. Leininger. Thorofare, NJ: Charles B. Slack.

Carper, L., and M. J. Flaherty. 1982. Nursing ethics: Theories and pragmatics. Bowie, MD: Robert J. Brady Co.

Drew, N. 1983. Exclusion and confirmation. A phenomenology of patients experiences with caregivers. Image 18(2): 39-43.

Downie, R. S., and E. Telfer. 1970. Respect for persons. New York: Schocken Books.

Freire, P. 1982. Pedagogy of the oppressed. New York: Continuum Publishing.

Fry, S. 1988. The ethic of caring: Can it survive in nursing? Nursing Outlook 36(1): 48.

Gardner, F., and E. Wheeler. 1981. Patients and staff perceptions of supportive nursing behaviors. In Caring: An essential human need, edited by M. Leininger. Thorofare, NJ: Charles B. Slack.

Gaut, D. 1983. Development of a theoretically adequate description of caring. Western Journal of Nursing Research 5(4): 313-324.

Gilligan, C. 1977. In a different voice: Women's conception of self and morality. Harvard Educational Review 47: 481-517.

Glaser, B., and A. Strauss. 1967. The discovery of grounded theory. Chicago: Aldine.

Hill, T. 1982. Self-respect reconsidered. In Respect for persons, edited by O. H. Green, New Orleans: Tulane University Press.

International Council of Nurses. 1973. The code for nurses. Geneva, Switzerland.

Kalisch, P., and B. Kalisch. 1986. The advance of American nursing. Boston: Little, Brown.

Kant, I. 1964. The doctrine of virtue, translated by McGregor. New York: Harper and Row.

Kant, I. 1965. The metaphysics of morals, translated by J. Ladd. Indianapolis: Bobbs-Merrill Co.

Kelly, B. 1987. Perception of professional ethics among senior baccalaureate nursing students. Ph.D. diss., Ohio State University.

Kelly, L. 1975. Dimensions of professional nursing. New York: Macmillan.

Kelsey, M. 1981. Caring. Ramsey, NJ: Paulist Press.

Leininger, M. 1977. Caring: The essence and central focus of nursing. American Nurses' Foundation Nursing Research Reports. 12(1): 2-14.

Leininger, M. 1981. Caring: An essential human need. Thorofare, NJ: Charles B. Slack. Reprint 1988 by Wayne State University Press.

Levine, M. 1977. Nursing ethics and the ethical nurse. American Journal of Nursing 77(5): 846-847.

May, R. (1969). Love and will. New York: Norton.

Mayeroff, M. 1971. On caring. New York: Harper and Row.

Miles, M., and A. Huberman. 1983. Qualitative data analysis. Beverly Hills, CA: Sage Publications.

Montagu, A. 1975. The practice of love. Englewood Cliffs, NJ; Prentice Hall.

Noddings, N. 1984. Caring: A feminine approach to ethics and moral education. Berkeley: University of California Press.

Nightingale, F. 1969. Notes on nursing: What it is and what it is not. New York: Dover Publications.

Nutting, A. 1916. Some ideals in training school work. Annual Report. New York: National League of Nursing Education.

Ozar, D. 1987. The demands of professions and their limits. In The professional commitment, edited by Quinn and Smith. Philadelphia: W.B. Saunders.

Patton, M.Q. 1986. Qualitative evaluation methods. Beverly Hills, CA: Sage Publications.

Ray, M. 1981. A philosophical analysis of caring within nursing. In *Caring: an essential human need,* edited by M. Leininger. Thorofare, NJ: Charles B. Slack.

Reimen, D. 1986. The essential structure of caring interaction: Doing phenomenology. Munhill, *Nursing research: A qualitative respective,* edited by Munhall and Oiler. Norwalk, CT.: Appleton Century Croft.

Sachs, D. 1982. Self, respect and respect for others: Are they independent. *Respect for persons,* edited by O.H. Green, New Orleans: Tulane University Press. 100-128.

Schuyler C. 1975. *Molders of modern nursing: Florence Nightingale and Louisa Schuyler,* Ann arbor, MI: University Microfilms International.

Silva, M. 1983. The American Nurses' Association's position on nursing and social policy. *Journal of Advanced Nursing* 8(2): 147-151.

Tubesing, D. 1983. *The caring question.* Minneapolis: Augsburg Publishing.

Watson, J. 1979. *Nursing: The philosophy and science of caring.* Boston: Little, Brown.

Watson, J. 1985. *Nursing: Human science and human care. A theory of nursing.* Norwalk, CT: Appleton-Century-Crofts.

Watson, J. 1988. New dimensions of health care theory. *Nursing Science Quarterly* 1(4): 175-181.

Williams, B. 1962. The idea of equality. In *Philosophy, Politics and Society,* edited by Laslett and Runceman. New York: Barnes and Noble.

Woodham-Smith, C. 1983. *Florence Nightingale 1820-1910.* New York: Atheneum.

Chapter 8

Respecting Ethnic Elders:
A Perspective for Care Providers

Jo Ann Damron-Rodriguez

INTRODUCTION

Can professionals provide care to older persons in ways that respect, not diminish, their dignity? To do this calls for an appreciation of the elder's strengths won from a life lived, as well as an assessment of late life frailties. Additionally, it requires an appreciation of the great diversity of the older population (Yee & Gelfand, 1992).

The older minority population is growing at a more rapid rate than the majority elderly population (American Association of Retired Persons, 1989). From 1970 to 1995 African American elderly increased 40%, Asian American 109% and Hispanic American elderly increased 98% (Valle, 1989; AARP, 1988). Diversity for all older persons is based not only on ethnicity but on gender, age, health status/functioning and socioeconomic status as well.

In order to develop a perspective for respectful care provision with attention to the breadth of these issues, key concepts which will help us to understand ethnic aging will be defined. These concepts will then be translated into a practice perspective and service relevant considerations for care providers.

DIGNITY AND RESPECT:
AN INTERACTIONAL PERSPECTIVE

The definitions of dignity and respect set the foundation for understanding the interactional nature of respectful care. Dignity comes from the Latin *dignities* meaning worth, merit, or *dingus*, worthy (Neufeldt & Guralnik, 1991). Thus, dignity is defined as the quality of being worthy of esteem or honor; worthiness. In its smallest sense dignity means loftiness of appearance but in the larger sense it means proper pride and self-respect. Dignity is then an inner quality which arise and is maintained by the individual in interaction with her/his world. In late life care providers can make significant contributions or diminutions to the maintenance of the dignity of the older person. However, older persons themselves are the source of dignity.

Respect comes from the Latin *respectus* to look at, to look back on (Neufeldt & Guralnik, 1991). To respect is to feel or show honor or esteem for, hold in high regard or to show consideration for. Respect also admonishes us to avoid intruding upon or interfering with the respected one. In its least shallow sense and yet its most cliched form, "respect your elders" means only deference or dutiful regard. In its deepest sense respect means to attend to another honoring their worth and their separateness.

It is not the job of service providers to dignify or "to give dignity to, to make seem worthy or noble" as in a false sense of awarding dignity to another. Rather, it is the service provider's, health care professional's and clergy's role to respect the intrinsic dignity residing in the individual. Use of the term elder denotes this respect. Elder is defined as "one having authority by virtue of age and experience" (Neufeldt & Guralnik, 1991). Ethnic elder appropriately connotes the respect given to older persons within many ethnic and cultural groups (Gelfand & Yee, 1992).

AGING, DIGNITY AND INTEGRITY:
A LIFECOURSE PERSPECTIVE

To find one's life worthy of respect is defined by Erikson (1963) as the distinctive virtue of late life, "ego integrity." His eloquent description as follows provides a theme for this discourse:

> Although aware of the relativity of all the various life styles which have given meaning to human striving, the possessor of integrity is ready to defend the *dignity* of his own life style against all physical and economic threats. For he knows that an individual life is the accidental coincidence of but one life cycle with but one segment of history; and that for him all human integrity stands or falls with the one style of integrity of which he partakes. (Erikson, 263-269)

In Erikson's view a life is the person's "one and only adventure in history." An older adult who possesses ego integrity accepts the good and the bad of their life events as contributing to the creation of who he or she has become. Erikson emphasized that this meant "the acceptance of one's one and only life cycle as something that had to be and that, by necessity, permitted of no substitutions" (1963: 263-269). In contrast, for those who enter late life in despair the focus is on the life not lived, a sense of having abandoned their own life.

In either case Erikson's perspective is one of the life course. From this perspective, the end of life must be seen as connected with the whole of life. This life course perspective broadens our view of aging by including personal biographies, cultural factors, and sociohistorical context (Stoller & Gibson, 1997). Integrity and dignity are actualized by the individual but in interaction with others. Erikson as a social psychologist views human development as an interactive process between the individual and the significant others who person his/her social world. In late life, care providers are often a significant part of this social world.

Two more recent works add to the Eriksonian perspective of late life development and relate to ethnic aging. Kaufman (1986) finds themes in older adult's live which create an "ageless self." Bateson (1990) describes women's work of "composing a life" through improvising with the materials allocated to them. She emphasizes the discontinuities or transitions as particularly significant in defining a life. Both the continuities and the transitions for ethnic elders may be ways to understand how they have built a life with what they have taken from their culture of origin and has been presented to them in their country of residence.

This cultural and ethnic identity is particularly rich background for late life self-respect and pride. It relates the individual life to the life of the group as it continues over time. In the cultural perspective the individual history interfaces with cultural events shared be a people. Developmentally cultural heritage and ethnicity can be adaptive resources for elders in reaching a sense of wholeness with the past and well-being in the present which is the essence of integrity.

If our environments for children are designed to facilitate their growth at each particular stage of development, then should not our environments for elders provide opportunities for them to accomplish late life developmental tasks such as the development of integrity over the life course (Damron-Rodriguez, 1991)? Instead it could be asserted that many care environments for elders are designed for childlike activities, e.g., coloring, simple crafts.

The professional's assessment of the patient, though decidedly not a life review, should include major life transitions and social roles. Long term care settings could incorporate recognition of the importance of historical events, and past individual accomplishment through the display of photographs, posting of bio-sketches, gathering of reminisce groups and taking oral histories. In addition to present tense activities, incorporating life review as a real developmental task respects the elder's process rather than discarding the developmental work as "dwelling in the past."

AGING AND ETHNICITY

An important aspect of what Erikson describes as "the dignity of his/her own life style" is cultural and ethnic identity. Ethnic identification based on race, religion, or national origin distinguishes individuals with a group membership classified by their degree of affiliation (Cox, 1993). Hollsberg (1982) distinguishes a criteria of ethnicity as its sense of peoplehood with a shared history. Cultural elements related to ethnic identification are distinct values, beliefs, language, and religion (Gelfand, 1994). These cultural elements may be woven into the fabric of individual integrity. The transitions of the life course for ethnic elders may have been modified significantly by need to take on responsibilities of adulthood early and aborting their childhood (Barresi, 1987). These can influence the aging experience and definitions of health and dependence in late life (Gelfand, 1994).

The importance of religion in the lives of older persons relates to their ethnic identity (Chatters & Taylor, 1994; Levin, Markides & Ray, 1996). Judaism is an example of how religion may be a primary ethnic identification which is the core of the sense of peoplehood (Gelfand, 1994). Religion is historically an integral component of the social support system of ethnic elders as documented for African Americans (Chatters & Taylor, 1994).

The Cross-Cultural Exchange of Provider and Elder

Health professionals and other care providers also bring cultural and ethnic identity to the process of care provision (Grant & Finocchio, 1995). Thus, it is a cross-cultural exchange to give and receive assistance. Generational, as well as ethnic, differences add to the complexity of accomplishing elder care based in respect (Gelfand, 1994).

For both clients and professionals, cultural is part of determining what they see as a health problem. What a symptom is and what it means and what to do about it is a judgement call and each analysis will be based on past experience as well as current options. For ethnic elders this analysis is often done with the assistance of family or other members of their support system who hold similar views. For elders, most beliefs about health and illness come from everyday experiences and most health care occurs at home. In a diverse population health and service decisions are made using widely varying criteria.

Biomedical health care providers have a specialist cultural viewpoint driven from orientations, expectations and organization of Western (America) society (Barker, 1994). This contrasts with the generalist viewpoint held by many patients, especially the elderly and non-Western groups. She points to incongruities that may arise in relation to the basic life trajectory, the meaning of health, family roles, dependence and notions of time.

Examples are the general beliefs of forces that contribute to ill health by creating imbalance such as the Chinese expansion and contraction or some groups in Mexico that speak of hot and cold. Chinese elders may use foods to control equilibrium (Chau et al., 1990). To address these causal factors for health problems traditional folk remedies such as herbal teas may be used.

A recent study (Frank et al., 1995) examined the meaning of late life health for Eastern-Euro-American, African-American, Chinese-American and Hispanic-American community-dwelling older persons. Although many had been living in the U.S. for years, most were immigrants. The definition of the meaning of health in late life that emerged from the focus groups for all ethnic groups encompassed physical, psychological, spiritual, and social aspects. There were marked similarities, related to defining health in late life, as well as ethnic group differences. The following quotes by ethnic elders illustrate the differences.

> Chinese-American Elder: I'm up there in age and my heart is content at this age. I realize that at this age, if I didn't have my mind and my health I would not be happy. The most important thing is being content. The mind and the body work together and must be in balance. If your heart is to good then it will affect your physical health. Don't be too serious about your life.

> European-American Elder: Being healthy means that you can go on, get up in the morning, do what you need to do to take care of yourself then go out and meet people, be among organizations and activities.

The emphasis on activity, to some degree present in all groups, was emphasized most in the Eastern-Euro-American group. The definitions of health embraced by the European-Americans in this research may more closely reflect the values of the planners of senior activities at senior centers than values of non-western older adults.

Professionals based in a Western perspective are more likely to talk about the specific virus and how to kill it. Aspects relevant to this health professionals' culture are: cure rather than palliation, returning the patient to productivity as soon as possible, constant monitoring and alteration of treatment, technology, and strict controls on who will provide treatment (Barker, 1994). These relate in many ways to the difference in the nature of informal or personal care giving and formal or professional roles as described by Litwak (1985).

Facilitating cross-cultural communication is based in understanding both worldviews and negotiating any miscommunications. Culturally congruent care involves interventions that are acceptable to the consumer and appropriate for the provider (Kavanagh & Kennedy, 1992). To reach cultural congruence the older adult's original perspective must be accommodated, negotiated with the provider, or the provider or client must restructure their beliefs. Berlin and Fowkes (1983) present the LEARN model to accomplish the necessary negotiations between provider and ethnic class. The LEARN model consists of the following steps: (1) Listen with sympathy to patients explanations; (2) Explain your perceptions;

(3) Acknowledge and discuss differences; (4) Recommend treatment or service and (5) Negotiate agreement.

DIVERSITY AND ETHNICITY

Erikson calls us to recognize diversity by appreciating that each person must understand the "relativity of all the various life styles" while being prepared to "defend the *dignity* of his own life style." Diversity is related not only to differences between ethnic groups but within ethnic groups. Ethnicity has relative value based on a variety of factors. Each individual ethnic elder brings a unique combination of a myriad of factors to create their life.

Clearly one important factor in diversity of ethnic elders is country of origin. Hispanic American elders may identify as Mexican American, Puerto Rican American, Cuban American, Spanish American or from one of any of the Central and South American countries. Asian and Pacific Islander Americans are composed of 22 distinct ethnic groupings. Urban versus rural differences for African American older persons may have significant cultural implications. European American elders will vary greatly based on generation in this country ad other distinguishing factors in the degree of assimilation or ethnic identification. Ethnic elders also vary based on generation in this country, cohort, religion, language, and socioeconomic status. Ethnic differences also relate to immigration status and pattern, including age of immigration. The family pattern of migration is important, whether the elder came first alone, later after others were economically established or if he/she was brought to this country for elder care.

Gender is another major aspect of difference in aging process and also relates to ethnicity (Dressel, 1988). Men and women both biologically and socially experience age in significantly different ways. Further gender roles may be more firmly delineated among ethnic elders than among the broader culture and than among subsequent generations of their own culture. Barker (1992) urges us to consider the complexity of the concept of ethnicity as it relates to age and gender as well as the acculturation process. Developing a perspective that considers both sameness and difference, both within and between ethnic groups, is important because a focus on either without attention to the other will lead to distortion.

Diversity for Care Providers

Historically, responsibility for the ethnic client tended to be apportioned to the professional who shared the identifying characteristic, i.e., race. Congruity of provider/care recipient continues to be a strength in any delivery system. However, this match may be difficult, even when it appears congruent. African American health care providers know the variability of African American older persons. Language differences may make racial similarities an important but not sufficient basis for communication, as an example. Yet it is crucially important that the health care work force represent the ethnic diversity of the older population it serves. More than half the U.S. work force now consists of minorities, immigrants and women (Thomas, 1990). It is important that diversity is represented within professions at all levels of status and authority (Antonucci & Cantor, 1994).

In Los Angeles 40% of the total population are non-Hispanic whites; this does not even account for the number of European immigrants. In this metropolis, the interface of ethnicity in service provision in long term care is often striking. At Keiro, a Japanese Nursing Home located in East Los Angeles, a Latino neighborhood, most of the residents are first generation Japanese and are monolingual Japanese, professionals are bilingual English and Japanese, and most of the aides are predominantly Spanish speaking Mexican American and El Salvadorian immigrants. A related issue is the beliefs of elders that limit their access to multicultural assistance. Prejudice based on a life lived disproportionately in the acceptance of segregation may limit some persons' acceptance of diversity in late life leading them to not accept a provider of another racial or ethnic group.

Kavanaugh and Kennedy (1992) challenge professionals to affirm diversity not be proud to ignore it and state that "everyone is alike." Through reflective practice care providers must assess their shortcomings and stereotypes that limit their ability to appreciate difference. This can lead to a fuller appreciation of the variety of individual elders we have the opportunity to care for. Though diversity can beget conflict its acknowledgment can also promote and confirm difference in ways that may avert noncompliance to our care plans and interventions.

BI-CULTURAL AGING

The "one and only adventure in history" (Erikson, 1963) may have taken the older person across continents to build their life. Many ethnic elders have a life style created both from their country of origin or their families' country of origin and their country of residence. Confounding the elder's experience of ethnic identification in the U.S. is this biculturization or the different degrees to which the person is socialized in two cultures, contemporary American culture and the elder's culture of origin (Parillo, 1996). The acculturation process produces the dual identity symbolized by the nomenclature of Chinese American or Hispanic American. Certainly a major dynamic in the understanding ethnic differences is the variation among elders in the degree of acculturation and ethnic identification (Kitano, 1985). Ethnic identification of older adults must be viewed within this changing and sometimes conflicting context (Gelfand, 1994).

Even if the elder remained in the country of origin, industrialization, urbanization and modernization would take place and alter traditional cultural beliefs and create differences between generations and an emerging ethnic shift (Gelfand, 1994). Frequently cultural descriptions are taken unchanged from the country of origin and applied to the ethnic experience of an elder in this country.

Many have been influenced profoundly by sociopolitical and historical events in this country and abroad. Isei and Nisei or first and second generation Japanese American elders' dignity as well as economic status were shattered with the bombing of Pearl Harbor and the subsequent move to internment camps (Kitano, 1985). Immigrants of choice must be distinguished from those fleeing their country in need of political asylum. Cambodian elders immigrated to the U.S. fleeing war and torture (Lew, 1991). Refugees may have little social support, have left with out cherished belongings, and be psychologically bereft.

The strength of ethnic identification varies over the life course for any individual, by social context and within the historical context. For persons born at the turn of the century, assimilation based on a "melting pot" ideology was a cherished virtue (Healey, 1995). Not until the 1960s did ethnic pride emerge as an attribute of social value. Older persons as a cohort may have a much different view of the place of ethnicity in American culture than the baby boom generation. As older persons live outside of their traditional environments the saliency of ethnicity to their lives may weaken (Gelfand and Barresi, 1987). As an example, in a study of Japanese older adults they were found to use a combination of traditional and professional treatments reserving the later for more severe symptoms (Sakauye, 1990). The following examples of rituals and family care present additional ways in which bicultural influences apply to the care of ethnic elders.

Emerging Rituals in Providing Care

Rituals provide resources for ethnic identification and social exchange. Rituals are not immutable but can present the same fundamental symbolic meanings in a variety of forms tailored to suit various social circumstances. People old and young reshape aspects of their culture based in new environments (Gelfand, 1994). The rituals described here are in transition much as the individual's ethnic identification is modified not only by interaction with the majority culture but also by even broader contemporary dynamics.

Chin (1991) reveals changes in the hwangap or 70th birthday ritual for Korean elders that relate to industrialization and urbanization in Korea as well as to migration to the US and community formation in this country. Doi (1991) describes Japanese American kanreki or 60th birthday rituals which have changed between generations. In both these cases the birthday party which is distinctly western is substituted for aspects of the traditional celebration. The use of ritual to create community and late life integrity should be examined by service providers.

The blanket use of contemporary American traditions for all elders, many of which are organized as child's play, may lead to alienation rather than community. Social activities in senior centers and residential facilities which center around Halloween or St. Patrick's Day may totally lack meaning for the ethnic elder. A life without meaningful cultural ritual and ceremony, substituted with Valentine parties or Bingo, may add a sense of despair rather than integrity (Damron-Rodriguez, 1991). Doi's (1991) description of the making of a thousand cranes in celebration of old age for Japanese elders is an example of a culturally meaningful activity. In multiethnic facilities cultural exchanges between elders might facilitate communication between individuals and groups.

Emerging Family Care Issues

The family is a primary context for older persons care and is frequently viewed as particularly important for ethnic elders (Kahn & Antonnuci, 1980; Lubben & Becerra, 1987). Ethnic elders may be less likely to perceive themselves as frail within the context of culturally supported family care. Cambodians have expectations about independence that are markedly different from mainstream American views which form the basis for policy and program development in the U.S. (Lew, 1991). Southeast Asian elders value interdependence above independence. To be valued and respected is to be cared for by family. Thus, for these elders, promoting program participation on the basis of "maximizing independence" and avoiding being cared for by others would *not* increase participation.

A significant difference between minority and majority elder care is the number of older persons cared for in the home of children or younger family members (Hooyman & Kiyak, 1996). Unmarried older African-Americans are twice as likely to live with family as whites. Asians and Latinos are three times more likely than Anglos, even after controlling for income, health status, and other characteristics (Worobey & Angel, 1990).

There is reason to believe that this intergenerational living is a benefit and a challenge to family members (Brubaker, 1990; Cantor, 1994). In some cases for low income families the older person in the home may be an economic benefit as well as providing instrumental assistance (Worobey & Angel, 1990). The multiple responsibilities of minority families may also create significant costs in health and opportunity for the caregiver (Antonucci & Cantor, 1994). A distinction must be made between values and beliefs related to filial piety and what is actually realistic for families with multiple economic and role responsibilities in post-industrial society. (Strawbridge & Wallhagen, 1992). Community based services will need to integrate with the informal network including not only family but friends, neighbors, churches and temples and other community services (Antonucci & Cantor, 1994). The family may need to be the "unit of care" not assuming that no community support is needed for immigrant families because "they take care of their own."

MINORITY ELDERLY

The "good and the bad" of ethnic elders' lives may be associated with, among other aspects of living, the positives and negatives of status in their adopted country. Minority status differs markedly from ethnicity. Ethnicity is predominantly self identification in contrast to minority status which is a comparison of differential power relationships between groups (Healey, 1995). Minority status limits access to a society's resources. Some ethnic groups, though few in relative number, do not experience minority status. Many ethnic elders experience poorer income and health in late life based on a lifetime of marginalized economic and social opportunities (Markides, Liang, & Jackson, 1990). Multicultural perspectives may appear to view ethnicity as an area of difference among equals (Parillo, 1996). However, minority status is not to be overlooked because of its hard outcomes in differential morbidity and mortality throughout the life cycle (Wykle & Kaskel, 1994). Yet ethnicity in and of itself should not be conceived as a liability (Gelfand, 1994).

Thus, it is imperative to consider both the beliefs and values of ethnic elders which may furnish adaptive resources for challenges presented by minority status and aging itself (Stoller & Gibson, 1997). It is also important to view the integrity of a minority elders' lives within the context of a social structure of disadvantage and privilege. For African American elders their childhood was lived within a racially segregated world which presented a struggle to maintain self respect. Some adaptive resources to combat disadvantage are strong filial and religious ties. Yet many survivors of this hostile world over the life course often show in late life a remarkable resilience and strength (Antonucci & Cantor, 1994). This extraordinary survivorship has been related to the morbidity crossover for older African Americans who are often healthier in late life than would be projected (Markides, Liang, & Jackson, 1990).

Hooyman and Kiyak (1988) integrate these two contrasting dimensions of ethic aging:

> Based on its unique history, each ethnic minority population developed its own methods of coping with the inevitable conflicts between traditional and adopted ways of life, leading to both vulnerabilities and strengths in the ways they adjust to aging. (p. 475)

Poverty

Minority elders in late life must attend to age discrimination and frailty along with minority status and thus, face what has been termed double jeopardy (Tally & Kaplan, 1956; Bengston, 1979). Even further triple jeopardy has been associated with older minority women who are confronted with a life course of gender as well as race description (Dressel, 1988). Though double and triple jeopardy have been questioned as an over arching framework to view ethic aging (Kiyak & Hooyman, 1996), minority older persons have significantly higher rates of poverty. In 1987, 10% of elderly whites, 34% of elderly African Americans, and 27 percent of elderly Hispanics were poor (AARP, 1989). Poverty is highest for older women in all groups (Quinn & Smeeding, 1994). Older African American men and women are the most likely to live in poverty. Of older African American women who live alone half live in poverty (Quinn & Smeeding, 1994).

Service Accessibility and Acceptability

Although minority older adults have higher service needs based on medical problems and functional limitations, they have lower utilization of key geriatric services (Damron-Rodriguez, Wallace, & Kington, 1994). Professionals must deliberately address two elements of the delivery system in order to provide equitable services for minority populations. The metaphor of the service door will be used to illustrate these elements. Accessibility requires opening the door to services for older adults while acceptability means that ethnic elders want to walk through the door (Damron-Rodriguez, Wallace, & Kington, 1994). Many service doors have signs that say welcome but to a pace that is culturally closed. Opening the door requires that services are located in the community where the elders live, that admission procedures do not exclude elders based on immigration status and that language barriers do not bar admission.

Accessibility is created by addressing structural barriers including income, health care coverage, location of service, and transportation including accessibility for functional limitations including cognitive limitations. Kramer (1991) describes American Indian elders' abhorrence of the "white" tape that surrounds services and elders' unwillingness to accept services delivered as charity.

To create acceptable services, cultural barriers must be addressed. These include ethnic factors such as language, religion, family and acculturation. Some provider interventions include: outreach, translation, interpretation, transportation, cultural training for health professionals, and the use of bilingual/bicultural para-professionals. To maximize the quality and the equity of services to ethnic minority elderly, providers must accommodate racial and ethnic diversity while standardizing the provision of health services to assure equity in the types of services and interventions available to all older persons (Damron-Rodriguez, Wallace, & Kington, 1992).

CONCLUSION

Modernization theory (Cowgill & Holmes, 1972) reminds us that urbanization, medicalization, a and secularization are major social forces which reduce the worth of older persons. This challenge to the value of the aged is particularly salient to ethnic elders as they age in contemporary society. How then can care providers respect the dignity of ethnic elders who bring hard won strengths and frailties to late life and are tremendously diverse?

Barker (1994) provides a metaphor to help understand the cultural differences between care providers and ethnic elders. The "shooting star" describing the life trajectory of the professions will be compared with the "roller coaster" orientation of many ethnic elders.

The shooting star has a straight path trajectory to the top always aiming to reach the best in life or the highest achievement. The steeper, straighter the trajectory the better. Life's path might be hard work and not much fun but the endpoint of unlimited resources and freedom are what counts. Time is of the essence and becomes a commodity that must be spent. Rationality, efficiency, and economy are prized. Keep your eye on the goal.

Contrast that to the roller coaster model which sees life events as a series of ups and downs. These are endured and experienced and lived through. Where one is heading is constantly changing. There is no glorious destination. There are good times and bad times and nothing is forever. One person is not in control One needs to be mobile and adjustable to contingencies. A person's life is best when part of a group. When none's own luck is out, someone else will be there. Pooling resources makes the ride smoother for all. Go with the flow enjoy the ride. (Paraphrased, Barker, 1994, 15-17)

These different life views have consequences in their approach to providing care in late life. The medical model is based in doing "to" or "for" patients rather than "with" and as such may mitigate against respect. The approach of individual treatment planning and goal setting in order to maximize independence is a model for success to most care providers. The wait and see, more accepting approach of many elders may be viewed as resistance or noncompliance by the professional who proposes his goals to the elder and meets with less than enthusiasm. Leaving the family ut of the plan as a short cut to intervention may lead to ultimate failure in the long run. These differences must be negotiated; both views may be valuable and contribute to the positive care (Berlin & Fowkes, 1983).

The American health care system has traditionally acknowledged and emphasized individuals as the locus of problems and interventions (Kavanaugh and Kennedy, 1992). Organizational and disciplinary culture focus on individuals as the "units of service." In the changing health care environment health care providers are asked to change perspective, if not paradigm, to view the individual within the context of their community (Grant & Finnocchio, 1995).

The dynamics of dignity and respect appreciate that care provision is an interpersonal/interactive process. It requires the care provider to be reflective and appreciate the way in which their own beliefs and values influence the care. Increasingly, in late life a person's worth is mirrored by professionals who know little about the individual the richness of a long life must be brought to the foreshortened life perspective of the very old. Communication and meaning in the delivery of care is an important interactional process in religion the tremendous ethnic and cultural diversity of those served. It requires the skill of inquiry, asking others for their view of the care they receive and its meaning. This can be done in groups when we seek direction for our programs and individually in our practice. We must be watchful for constrictions in our services which require elders to adapt and conform to a limited set of norms in order to access resources.

Wu (1975) described the process of adjustment to life in Los Angeles for Chinese elders as the "adaptable rt of living" that was required to grow old gracefully in a foreign country. This is exemplified in the Chinese proverb "Youth is a gift of nature; Age is a work of art." A similar artful adaptation is required of service providers in order to adapt care that is both accessible and acceptable for ethnic elders. Care providers may give valuable materials or resources for this "work of art." However, they do not supply the canvas or the background for the elder's life. The canvas is the life course or history of each ethnic elder. The form and texture of the work is envisioned through the cultural lens of the elder. The artist is the elder who alone, but with support, can create the life of integrity and dignity. It is the care provider's work to appreciate the contribution and preserve the creation. That is respectful care. In the end, any contribution to the dignity of our elders will be an intergenerational one. For as Erikson (1963) proposes, "children will not fear life if their elders have the integrity not to fear death."

Epilogue or Something

But in the main, I feel like a brown bag of miscellany propped against a wall. Against a wall in company with other bags, white, red and yellow. Pour out the contents, and there is discovered a jumble of small things priceless and worthless, a first water diamond, an empty spool, bits of broken glass, lengths of string, a key to a door long since crumbled away, a rusty knife-blade, old shoes saved for a road that never was and never will be, a nail bent under the weight of things too heavy for any nail, a dried flower two still a little fragrant. In your hand is the brown bag. On the ground before you is the jumble it held so much like the jumble in the other bags, it could be emptied and all might be dumped into a single heap. Perhaps that is the way the Great Stuffer of Bags filled them in the first place—who knows?

- Zora Neale Hurston, How it Feels to be Colored Me (c. 1922)

Nowhere to put this but couldn't quite get rid of it yet. Says something to our uniformity as well as our diversity—wanted to share it!

References

AARP Minority Affairs Initiative (1988). A portrait of older minorities. Washington, DC: American Association of Retired Persons.

Antonucci, T.C., & Cantor, M.H. ((1994)). Strengthening the family support system for older minority persons. In Minority elders: Longevity, economics, and health (2nd Ed.). Gerontological Society of America, p. 40.

Barker, J.C. (1994). Recognizing cultural differences: Health-care providers and elderly patients. Cultural Diversity and Geriatric Care: Challenges to the Health Professions. New York: The Haworth Press, Inc.

Barresi, C.M. (1987). Ethnic Aging and the Life Course. pp. 18-34.

Bateson, M.C. (1990). Composing a Life. New York: Plume.

Bengston, V.L. (1979). Ethnicity and aging: Problems and issues in current social science inquiry. In D.E. Gelfand and A.J. Kutzik (Eds.), Ethnicity and aging: Theory, research and policy. New York: Springer, 9-31.

Berlin, E.A., & Fowkes, W.C. (1983). A teaching framework for cross-cultural health care. The Western Journal of Medicine, 139, 934-938.

Brubaker, T.N. (1990). Families in later life: A burgeoning research area. Journal of Marriage and the Family, 52, 959-981.

Cantor, M. ((1994)). Family caregiving: Social care. In M. Cantor (Ed.), Family caregiving: Agenda for the future. San Francisco, CA: American Society on Aging, 1-9.

Chatters, L.M., & Taylor, R.J. (1994). Religious involvement among older African-Americans. In J.S. Levin (Ed.) Religion in aging and health: Theoretical foundations and methodological frontiers. Thousand Oaks, CA: Sage, pp. 196-230.

Chau, P., Lee, H., Tseng, R., & Downers, N.J. (1990). Dietary habits, health beliefs, and food practices of elderly Chinese women. Journal of the American Dietetic Association, 90(4), 579-580.

Chin, S.Y. (1991). Korean birthday rituals. Journal of Cross-Cultural Gerontology, 6(2), 145.

Cowgill, D., & Holmes, L. (1972). Aging and Modernization. New York: Appleton-Century-Crofts.

Cox, C. (1993). The Frail elderly: Problems, Needs, and Community Responses. Ethnicity and Frailty. Westport, CN: Auburn House, pp. 125-145.

Damron-Rodriguez, J.A. (1991). Multicultural aspects of aging in the U.S.: Implications for health and human services. Journal of Cross-Cultural Gerontology, 6(2), 135-145.

Damron-Rodriguez, J.A., Wallace, S., & Kington, R. (1994). Service utilization and minority elderly: Appropriateness, accessibility, and acceptability. Cultural diversity and geriatric care. Challenges to the Health Professions. New York: The Haworth Press, Inc.

Dressel, P. (1988). Gender, race and class: Beyond the feminization of poverty in later life. The Gerontologist, 28(2), 177-180.

Erikson, E. (1963). Childhood and society. New York: Norton.

Frank, J., Damron-Rodriguez, J.A., Hirsch, S., & Reuben, D. (1995). A paper presentation at the 50th Annual Scientific Meeting of the Gerontology Society of America in Los Angeles, CA.

Frank, J., Damron-Rodriguez, J.A., Levin, J., Hirsch, S., & Reuben, D.B. (1995). Multicultural perceptions of the meaning of health. A presentation at the 48th Annual Scientific Meeting of the Scientific Meeting of the Gerontology Society of America, Los Angeles, CA.

Gelfand, D.E. (1994). Aging and ethnicity: Knowledge and services. New York: Springer Publishing Company.

Gelfand, D.E., & Yee, B. (1992). Trends and forces: Influence of immigration, migration, and acculturation on the fabric of aging in America. Generations, 15(4), 7-10.

Grant, R.W., & Finocchio, L.J. (1995). The California Primary Care Consortium on Interdisciplinary Collaboration: A Model Curriculum and Resource Guide. San Francisco, CA: Pew Health Professions Commission.

Holzberg, C. (1982). Ethnicity and aging: Anthropological perspectives on more than just the minority elderly. The Gerontologist, 22, 249-257.

Hooyman, N., & Kiyak, H.A. (1988). Social gerontology. Boston: Allyn & Bacon.

Kahn, R.L., & Antonucci, T.C. (1980). Convoys over the life course: Attachment, roles, and social support. In P.B. Baltes & O.G. Brim (Eds.), Life span development and behavior (Vol. 3, pp. 253-286). New York: Academic Press.

Kaufman, S.R. (1986). The Ageless Self: Sources of Meaning in Late Life. Wisconsin: University of Wisconsin Press.

Kavanagh, K.H., & Kennedy, P.H. (1992). Promoting Cultural Diversity: Strategies for Health Care Professionals. Newbury Park, CA: Sage Publications.

Kramer, B.J. (1991). Urban American Indian aging. Journal of Cross-Cultural Gerontology, 6(2), 205.

Levin, J.S., Markides, K.S., & Ray, L. (1996). Religious attendance and psychological well-being in Mexican Americans: A panel study analysis of three-generations data. The Gerontologist, 36(4), 455-463.

Levin, J.S., & Tobin, S.S. (1995). Religion and psychological well-being. In M.S. Kimble, S.H. McFadden, J.W. Ellor & J.J. Seeber (Eds.), Aging, spirituality, and religion: A handbook. Minneapolis: Fortress Press, pp. 30-46.

Lew, L.S. (1991). Elderly Cambodians in Long Beach: Creating cultural access to health care. Journal of Cross-Cultural Gerontology, 6(2), 199.

Litwak, E. (1985). Helping the elderly. New York: The Guilford Press.

Lustbader, W. (1991). Counting on kindness. New York: Free Press.

Markides, K., Liang, J., & Jackson, J. (1990). Race, ethnicity and aging. In R. Binstock, R. & George, L. (Eds.), Handbook of aging and the social sciences: Third edition. San Diego, CA: Academic Press.

Neufeldt, V., & Guralnik, D.B. (1991). Webster's New World Dictionary. New York: Simon & Schuster.

Osako, M.M. (1979). Aging and family among Japanese Americans: The role of ethnic tradition in the adjustment to old age. The Gerontologist, 19(5), 448-455.

Quinn, J.F., & Smeeding, T.M. (1994). Defying the averages: Poverty and well-being among older Americans. Aging Today, September/October, XV(5), 9.

Sakauye, K. (1990). Differential diagnosis, medication, treatment, and outcomes: Asian American elderly. In Minority aging. Rockville, MD: U.S. Department of Health and Human Services.

Stoller, E.P., & Gibson, R.C. (1997). Worlds of Difference: Inequality in the Aging Experience. Thousand Oaks, CA: Pine Forge Press.

Tally, T., & Kaplan, J. (1956). The Negro aged. Gerontological Society Newsletter, 3.

Thomas, R.R. (1990). From Affirmative Action to affirming diversity. Harvard Business Review, March-April, pp. 107-117.

Valle, R. (1989). U.S. ethnic minority group access to long-term care. In Caring for an aging world: International models for long-term care, financing and delivery. New York: McGraw-Hill Information Services Company.

Worobey, J.L., & Angel, R.I. (1990). Poverty and health: Older minority women and the rise of the female-headed household. Journal of Health and Social Behavior, 31(4), 370-383.

Wykle, M., & Kaskel, B. (1994). Increasing the longevity of minority older adults through improved health status. In Minority elders: Longevity, economics, and health (2nd Ed.). Gerontological Society of America, p. 32.

Chapter 9

Social Workers Demonstrate Respect for Elderly Clients

Kyu-taik Sung

Introduction

For the elderly in all cultures, the quality of treatment they receive in their later years is critically important. For service providers also, providing respectful services for clients is an important issue. In the social work profession, this issue is continuously under review and scrutiny. In this chapter, the way social service providers express respect for their elderly clients is discussed based on data from a survey of purposefully selected social workers in the United States.

Although respect is a crucial aspect of social work practice, few studies have examined how social workers convey their respect for elderly clients. This study explored the various forms of respect demonstrated by social workers when they were with older clients. Fifty social workers serving elderly clients were surveyed by a questionnaire with closed- and open-ended questions. Based on data on the way the social workers respected their elderly clients, the study identified seven forms most frequently practiced and considered most important. They are linguistic respect, care respect, acquiescent respect, salutatory respect, presentational respect, spatial respect, and consultative respect. The key expressions of these forms are introduced in quantitative data and a narrative form. This finding provides insights as to how social workers exhibit respect for elderly clients in their practice. The results of this exploration may be useful in developing a more comprehensive typology of the forms signifying respect for elderly clients.

Many seniors have a variety of social and psychological problems. To resolve these problems, they most often depend on social service providers. Hence, social workers become a significant part of the social world of the elderly in their later years. While elderly persons need food, shelter, health care, and social services, they also need to be treated with respect. The extent to which the service providers treat elderly persons with respect, therefore, becomes a significant psychosocial factor that affects the quality of their later life (Cassel 1990; Noelker and Harel 2000).

In social work, respect for the client has, in fact, been considered to be the very beginning of the service process (NASW 1996; Mayeroff 1971). That is, respect is to precede all forms of care and service (Gambrill 1983; Reichel 1995; Rogers 1961). With respect, service providers can demonstrate a positive attitude toward their clients, treat them with propriety, and serve them as dignified persons. Clients treated with respect by a provider will increase their own sense of self-esteem and life satisfaction, and also their sense of usefulness and involvement in community and significant others (Applegate and Morse 1994; Ghusn, Hyde, Stevens, Hyde and Teasdale 1996; Damon-Rodriguez 1998).

Thus, respect becomes an important message to the clients that brings about a sound and productive provider-client relationship. In a helping situation, whenever the provider demonstrates to her clients by her actions that she respects them, a relationship grows. The clients treated with respect will be more likely to freely discuss difficult topics, explore their own contributions, and involve themselves in a cooperative effort to achieve desired service outcomes (Gambrill 1983).

A study found that the way in which a client was shown respect was often more important to the client than what the therapist did to help her solve her problems (Gibbard 1990). As an evidence of this, clients' perception of the therapist's level of regard for them was significantly related to their ratings of their change at completion of treatment (Rogers 1961: 36).

Respect, although important throughout all phases of service, it is particularly appropriate to interactions among newcomers or strangers (Dillon 1992: 107). Carkhuff and Pierce (1976) suggested that respect, along with empathy and warmth, is essential in the first interview. And, the initial contact is important as providers often use it to establish an ongoing relationship with the client.

In practice, however, social workers have difficulty in specifying expressions of this essential message; they often struggle to operationalize respect for clients (Campton and Gallaway 1984). One of the least discussed issues in social work has been respect paid to persons receiving the services. Consequently, little has been known how social workers show respect for their clients.

Respect is a benevolent, altruistic, or sympathetic expression of regard for other persons (Downie and Telfer 1969). To respect a person, we treat that person in a certain manner or act in a particular way. Dillon (1969) describes that a person who respects another person pays careful attention to that person and takes the person seriously. Respect, however, calls for more than our attention. As Gibbard (1990) states, respect requires certain actions or forms of conduct. Respect, then, needs to be manifested in concrete behavioral expressions oriented toward caring for and serving others (Silverman and Maxwell 1978). Such expressions would include vocal sounds (ex. greeting, calling), physical movements (ex. serving, guiding), bodily movements (acknowledging, polite posture), appearance (ex. proper dressing, grooming), and so forth (Sung 2001). A respectful person exhibits such explicit gestures or expressions that connote respect. Both the respecter and the respected would perceive these gestures as significant symbols (Hewit 1988), allowing the meaning of respect to be shared with others who make the same gestures or expressions.

Accordingly, social workers should be able to say by what concrete gestures and expressions they can demonstrate respect for their clients (Hugman and Smith 1995). Only when the general concept of respect is specifically defined and related actions implemented on a daily basis, would respect become meaningful to the service provider as well as the client (Gambrill 1983). .

The present study will explore expressions of respect for elderly clients that pervade social workers' attitudes and behaviors toward elderly clients. (In this paper, we refer to those expressions 'elder respect'.) The paper addresses the following questions: (1) What are the kinds of expressions that social workers show in their interaction with elderly clients in order to connote respect for them?; (2) What forms of elder respect are most often practiced and considered important to social workers? The focus of the present study is on the identification of the expressions of elder respect and forms thereof demonstrated by social workers. It is not the purpose of this study to discuss the philosophy of respect or to conduct a causal analysis of respect-related variables.

This exploration, therefore, will provide information on specific forms of expressions connoting social workers' respect for elderly clients and the extent to which the social workers give importance to the forms. This information could be useful to the future development of a more comprehensive typology of forms of respect that social workers practice in their services for elderly clients.

DIFFERENT FORMS OF ELDER RESPECT

To date, little research has been done on the forms of elder respect. The review of the literature uncovered four empirical studies which reported forms and expressions by which people respect older persons. Silverman and Maxwell (1978) identified seven forms of elder respect based on qualitative data from a sample 34 societies selected from Murdock and White's (1969) cross-cultural sample of 186 world areas.

The seven forms are service respect (housekeeping), victual respect (serving drinks and foods), gift respect (presenting gifts), linguistic respect (using respectful language), presentational respect (showing courteous manners), spatial respect (furnishing honorable seats or places), and celebrative respect (celebrating birthdays).

Other studies led by social work researchers—two in Asia and one in the United States—also reported expressions of elder respect (Ingersoll-Dayton and Saengtienchai 1999; Mehta 1997; Sung 2002). Ingersoll-Dayton and Saengtienchai (1999), using a focus group approach and individual interviews, distinguished various expressions of elder respect based on their study in four Asian countries. Mehta based on her sample of Singaporeans only, reported expressions of elder respect similar to what Ingersoll-Dayton and Saengtienchai discovered. Sung (2002), based on data from a survey of American college students, identified 12 forms of elder respect.

Although the four studies were conducted in different cultural contexts and in non-social work settings, they taken together yielded parallel results, identifying similar expressions of elder respect forms thereof as shown below:

* Care respect (providing care and services for elders),
* Acquiescent respect (assenting, listening to elders),
* Consulting respect (seeking elders for advice),
* Precedent respect (providing services to elders first),
* Salutatory respect (greeting, saluting elders),
* Linguistic respect (using proper language in addressing to elders),
* Victual respect (serving drinks and foods of elders' choice),
* Gift respect (presenting gifts to elders),
* Presentational respect (holding proper manners before elders),
* Celebrative respect (celebrating elders' birthdays),
* Spatial respect (furnish elders with comfortable seats),
* Public respect (serving neighborhood elders and elders at large)

These 12 forms, all important corollaries of elder respect, replicated and added to the seven forms which were cross-culturally distinguished by Silverman and Maxwell (1978).

Building upon the above findings, the present study explored specific forms of respect most often practiced and considered most important by social workers.

Study Method

We used a convenience sampling strategy to identify social workers providing services to elderly clients. Data were collected from a sample of 50 social workers in two different locations: 25 in a town in the Midwest and 25 from a city on the West Coast. The participating social workers met the following criteria: (1) licensed professional social workers, (2) currently providing direct services to elderly clients, and (3) had practiced for 3 years or longer.

In each of the two areas, 20 social workers were selected from two community health clinics, two state and county agencies, a mental health clinic, and a senior day care center, and a family service agency. In addition, five solo-practitioners serving elderly persons were selected. From each one of the agencies or clinics (sizes ranging from 1 to 30 social workers), one to five social workers were selected at random from those willing to respond to the questionnaire with a pre-addressed envelope with a stamp on it. They were asked to mail it after answering all the questions.

Both areas combined, 50 percent of all social workers were practicing in public agencies and the rest in private agencies (30%) and in solo practice (20%). The average years practiced was 9 years; 72 percent of the respondents had an MSW degree and the rest had a BSW degree; and 84 percent were female. In terms of ethnicity, 68 percent were White, 12 percent African American, 12 percent Latino, and 8% Asian American.

A 12-item questionnaire consisting of closed-ended and open-ended questions was administered to the social workers. The close-ended questions related to the 11 forms of elder respect—care, acquiescent, consultative, precedent, salutatory, linguistic, victual, gift, presentational, celebrative, and spatial—were included. Each form was accounted for by two questions. (Of the 12 forms previously described, public respect for neighborhood elders and elders at large was excluded as the elderly under study were all served within the setting of agency or clinic).

The following are examples of questions:

Sample Questions:

1. Please, list two or more behaviors or gestures by which you most often express your respect for older clients. (A list of the 11 forms of respect was provided.)

2. Please, indicate the degree of importance you give to this form of respect. (Choose one.)

   __very important __important __fairly important __not so important

3. Please, comment on your practice of this form of respect.

Thus, two measures of elder respect were used on each form: (1) frequency with which a form was cited and (2) the degree of importance given to the form. As shown above, the levels of importance were rated on a 4-point scale (4=very important . . . 1=not so important). In addition, on each form of respect, the respondent gave free, unstructured comments on the practice of the form.

Analysis and Findings

RESPONSES TO THE CLOSED-ENDED QUESTIONS

In response to the closed-end questions, the social workers cited a variety of forms by which they demonstrated elder respect. Table 1 highlights an overview of these forms: descriptive statistics based on frequency with which the forms were cited and the rating of importance given to the form, and the ranking of the forms by frequency size and importance rating.

The forms are ranked from the 1st to 11th according to frequency (percent size) and importance (mean rating by the 4-point scale) (Table 9-1).

First, in terms of frequency, social workers indicated that they most often demonstrated respect linguistically. Specifically, 82% of them reported that they used this form. The second most often cited form was salutatory respect, the third, care respect, the fourth, acquiescent respect, the fifth, presentational respect, the sixth, spatial respect, the seventh, consultative respect, the eighth precedential respect, the ninth, celebrative respect, the tenth, victual respect, and the last, gift respect.

Thus, seven forms of respect—linguistic, salutatory, care, acquiescent, presentational, spatial, and consultative—whose frequencies ranging from 82% to 62%, were clearly more frequently demonstrated than the rest of the forms ranging from 42% to 12%).

Next, in terms of importance, linguistic respect is the highest or the most important form (m=3.78), and salutatory respect is the second most important one. The third-ranking form was presentational respect, and the fourth is care respect. These four forms were given ratings ranging from m=3.78 to m=3.57, which are nearly "very important" according to the four-point scale. These are followed by acquiescent respect (the fifth), consultative respect (the sixth), and spatial respect (the seventh). These three forms, ranging from m=3.37 to m=2.97, are "important to fairly important. The rest—precedential, celebrative, victual, and gift ranging from m = 2.73~m = 1.84—are rated "fairly important" to "not so important."

In Table 9-1, the two rankings are compared—one based on frequencies with which the forms were cited and the other based on the ratings of importance of the forms. Spearman rank-order correlation between the two rankings [.67, RHO (.05)] for the 11 categories suggests similarity or comparability between the two rankings.

Results of these analyses clearly suggest that the following seven forms of respect were more frequently practiced and considered more important than other forms: 'linguistic', 'salutatory', 'care', 'acquiescent', 'presentational', 'spatial', and 'consultative'.

RESPONSES TO THE OPEN-ENDED QUESTIONS

The social workers' answers to the open-ended question provided the following qualitative information on the practice of the forms (in order of the number of the respondents answered.

With respect to linguistic respect, 14 social workers made comments. Four social workers shared their comments:

"When we are in doubt about how to address elderly clients, we usually consider using their surname along with their title, e.g., Mr., Mrs., Dr., or Miss. After elderly clients become familiar with us, some of them insist on being called by their first name."

"It is important to consider differences in age and status when addressing Latino and Asian clients. For example, the head of the family (e.g., the father or the mother) should always be addressed using his or her last name and any title."

"In Asian American families, it is often more respectful to refer to their members by their roles, such as father, mother, old sister, or brother than by their first name."

"I am bilingual. When I talk to an elderly Japanese client, I usually use honorifics in Japanese. This is a cultural norm that must be observed when I interact with Japanese seniors. The same applies to the cases of elderly Chinese and Koreans."

   "Naturally, we need to have caring minds and attitudes toward elderly clients."

Table 9-1.
Frequency and Importance of Forms of Elder Respect: American Social Workers*

Forms of Elder Respect	Frequency[1]		Importance[2]		
	Rank	%	Rank	Mean	S.D.
Linguistic	1	0.82	1	3.78	0.46
Salutatory	2	0.78	2	3.73	0.45
Care	3	0.74	4	3.57	0.53
Acquiescent	4	0.72	5	3.37	0.93
Presentational	5	0.68	3	3.61	0.63
Spatial	6	0.64	7	2.97	0.72
Consulting	7	0.62	6	3.35	0.82
Precedential	8	0.42	8	2.73	0.8
Celebrative	9	0.28	9	2.33	0.86
Victual	10	0.16	10	2.18	0.79
Gift	11	0.12	11	1.84	0.73

*N = 50

[1] Frequency with which each form is cited by the subjects; only forms cited by 5% or more are included.

[2] Importance given to each form based on the 4-point scale (4 = very important . . . 1 = not so important)

With regard to care respect (being kind and considerate to the client; having attention to and concern for the client), 10 social workers made comments. Four social workers shared their comments:

"I make phone calls to them occasionally and try to check on if they are all right."

"The elderly deserve our attention and support."

"I do my job in a multi-cultural setting. Elderly clients, many being immigrants, tend to carry on values and family orientation they brought from their motherland. I have to provide services that fit into their cultural backgrounds."

On acquiescent respect (listening to the client's opinion and suggestions; following rules and proceedings mutually agreed upon; honoring the client's ideas, beliefs, and values), nine social workers made comments; the following shared their comments:

"I let my elderly clients do story telling. I listen and follow their wishes."

"I let my clients participate in setting the goals of services to be attained. Once the goals are set, I pursue those goals in cooperation with them."

"I listen to them. But, I do not blindly agree. Sometimes, I disagree in a nice manner and by speaking moderately."

With regard to salutatory respect (greeting the client, exhibiting proper body language of respect), the focus of eight social workers' comments was on the importance of appropriately greeting their clients. Three respondents shared their comments.

"Saluting and greeting my clients is the first action I take to develop a positive relationship with my client."

"I usually say to my elderly client 'How are you?' looking at her with an expression of intimacy."

"I shake hands with my client and hug her when she comes to my office."

On presentational respect (exhibiting polite and courteous manners to the client; wearing appropriate dress when meeting with the client), six social workers commented. The following comments were shared:

"I think it is important for us to show proper postures and manners as these reflect our interest and concern for clients.

"We need to dress in the way the client's culture says is appropriate to a helping professional."

On spatial respect (furnishing the client with a comfortable seat; securing a comfortable atmosphere for the client), five social workers gave comments. The following shared their comments:

> "I usually furnish my client with a comfortable chair and provide services in a quiet room for privacy and confidentiality."

> "I try to secure a distract-free environment for my clients."

> "I pay attention to the arrangement of seats in a family or group treatment situation, particularly in dealing with Asian American elderly clients. I let the father, who has authority, occupy a center seat and the mother next to him."

On consulting respect (seeking out the client's opinion or suggestion; consulting over procedures for services), five social workers gave comments and the following shared their comments:

> "Clients should always be consulted."

> "I try to give the client the feeling that she or he is important part of my decision."

> "I try to find out my client's frame of reference and values."

> "In services for Latinos and Asian Americans, who generally place great emphasis on the individual family relationship, I often consult the members of their family on my treatment plan."

On victual respect (serving coffee or tea), they gave the following four comments:

> "My agency funded by the state and the county does not have administrative approval for doing this."

> "I don't think doing this form is appropriate."

> "We should practice this form all the time."

> "I am in favor of practicing this form. In doing this sort of extra service, we must take into consideration of the client's cultural and ethnic background."

On celebrative respect (celebrating clients' birthdays or special events), three social workers gave comments:

> "In an event that makes a significant change in the client's life, I sometimes express my goodwill to celebrate or to attend such an event for some of my clients."

"Sometimes I send small flowers or cards to my clients to express my goodwill."

"In our agency, we do not celebrate clients' birthdays or special events."

On gift respect (sending cards or flowers to recognize certain achievements or merits, or to express sympathy), there were two comments:

"I send Christmas cards and sympathy cards with some regularity. I think doing this increases a client's self-esteem and helps promote a strong relationship with the client."

"Sometimes, I get respect from my clients. Some Asian American clients offer me presents as their expression of gratitude for my services. I accept it when it is culturally appropriate. Rejection of such gifts may hurt their feelings."

There was no comment on precedential respect (serving first).

The above comments reflect the social workers' personal feelings and views with regard to the practice of the forms. They nevertheless provide important clues as to the ways in which certain forms of respect need to be conveyed or expressed in practice situations.

Significantly, ethnic and cultural differences are repeatedly cited as factors that influence the practice of several forms. The practice of the forms varied by ethnic and cultural backgrounds of practitioners as well as elderly clients, and the agency setting in which they practice.

Discussion

The present study was undertaken to determine what forms of elder respect social workers most often use in their interaction with elderly clients and which forms of respect they consider to be more important. Based on quantitative and qualitative data from a questionnaire survey, this study provided a set of specific forms of respect that social workers demonstrated and their views and opinions on the practice of these forms.

Of the 11 forms explored, seven forms—linguistic, salutatory, care, acquiescent, presentational, spatial, and consultative—were most often demonstrated and considered more important than other forms.

The distinctions between the various forms highlight specific ways in which older clients were respected by social workers. In the description of the holistic meaning of respect for the client, all these forms would have to be considered as they portray elder respect in combination. The forms may be interrelated in their meanings and practices. However, each of them seems to reflect an action or a behavior of the service provider that demonstrates a particular way in which older clients are respected.

The specific forms identified in this exploratory study provide us with insights into the respect for elderly clients that has, heretofore, been discussed in invariably abstract or unspecific terms. These behavioral forms could be useful in developing a comprehensive typology of elder respect that can assess the propriety of the provider and the quality of the relationship between the client and the provider. By practicing these forms, a provider could treat his or her elderly clients with benevolence and altruism imbued with a sense of humanity and professional ethic.

In addition, the qualitative data provided useful information on the practice of certain forms of respect. Some of the social workers commented that such forms as victual respect, gift respect, and celebrative respect were not appropriate to practice or not practiced, while others gave importance to practicing these and other forms. At least two factors seemed to explain such a variation in the social workers' views.

The first reason was cultural. Some social workers took into consideration the ethnic background of the client in the practice of those forms of respect. At the same time, the practitioners' own background seemed to affect the use of those forms as well. Thus, some Latino and Asian American respondents cited the importance of practicing certain forms not cited by White respondents. There was a noticeable variation in the social workers' responses by their ethnic background; Latino and Asian Americans tended to give greater importance to using respectful language, properly greeting clients, arranging a seat, and serving tea and coffee. Thus, this finding reflects the diversity not only of the elderly clients but also social workers in terms of cultural differences (Gomez, Zurcher, Farris and Becker 1985). To many Asian clients, the respect they receive from a therapist is often more important than what the therapist does to help them solve their problems (Berg and Jaya 1993; Leininger 1990). Similarly, for Hispanic Americans, respeto (respect) dictates the appropriate behavior toward persons, particularly parents and those who are older (Paniagua 1998).

The second factor was organizational constraint. As some respondents commented, certain forms, such as victual respect (serving coffee and tea), gift respect (gift giving), and celebrative respect (celebrating birthdays or events), are difficult to practice due to the absence of agency approval or resources. Thus, in this case, some providers' respecting expression is defined and limited by the employing agency. In other agencies, however, the use of such forms seemed tacitly or informally approved, to the extent that the resources needed to practice the forms were available.

As the practitioners' comments suggest, the practice of elder respect needs to be consistent with the lifestyles and values of the client being served. Social work has historically been based on values that appreciate differences among clients including cultural backgrounds, race, and ethnicity (NASW 1996). The social worker who deals with specific ethnicity will need to understand the relevant subtleties inherent in the practice of respect for the elderly. In this context, considering social work solely in terms of technical competencies would fail to do justice to the value complexity of social work practice.

The finding of this exploratory study provides preliminary information as to the way in which social workers respect their elderly clients. The general concept of respect is defined in the forms of specific behavioral expressions, which can be implemented on a daily basis. Thus, the forms of elder respect provide us with insights into how social workers practice elder respect that has been discussed in an invariably abstract form.

The findings of the present study are based on the result of an exploration of a delimited set of eleven forms of elder respect. Data were drawn from a convenience or purposive sample of social service agencies. Therefore, the findings need to be carefully used in a discussion of elder respect among social workers. Further research, based on a larger sample representative of social workers in a variety of practice settings, is needed to develop a more comprehensive typology of forms of elder respect. As the findings suggest, it is important to investigate the extent to social workers' practice of the forms vary by their ethnic background and agency setting. Furthermore, it is necessary to explore appropriate forms of respect for elderly clients.

References

Applegate, M., & Morse, J. M. (1994). Personal privacy and interactional patterns in a nursing home. *Journal of Aging Studies*, 8, 413-434.

Berg, I. K., & Jaya, A. (1993). Different and same: Family therapy with Asian American families. *Journal of Marital and Family Therapy*, 19, 31-38.

Campton, B., & Gallaway, B. (1984). *Social work process.* (3rd Ed.). Chicago, IL: Dorsey Press.

Carkhuff, R. R., & Pierce, R. H. (1976). *Teacher as person.* Washington:: National Education Association.

Cassel, C. K. (1990). Ethical issues in the medicine of later life. In Evans, J. G., & Williams, T. F. (Eds.), *Oxford Textbook of Geriatric Medicine*. New York: Oxford University Press. Pp. 717-719.

Damron-Rodriguez, J. A. (1989). Respecting Ethnic Elders. *Journal of Gerontological Social Work*, 29, 53-72.

Damron-Rodriguez, J. A. (1998). Respecting ethnic elders: A perspective for care providers. In Disch, R., Doborof, R., & Moody, H. R., *Dignity and Old Age*. New York: Haworth.

Dawnie, R. S., & Telfer, E. (1969). *Respect for persons*. London: Allen and Unwin.

Dillon, R. S. (1992). Respect and care: Toward moral integration, *Canadian Journal of Philosophy*, 22, 105-132.

Dunkle, R., Roberts, B., & Haug, M. (2001). *The oldest old in everyday life: Self perception, coping with change, and stress.* New York: Springer.

Gambrill, E. (1983). *Casework: A competency-based approach.* Englewood Cliffs, NJ: Prentice-Hall.

Ghusn, H. M., Hyde, D., Stevens, E. S., & Teasdale, T. A. (1996). Enhancing life satisfaction in later life: What makes a difference for nursing home residents? *Journal of Gerontological Social Work*, 26, 27-47.

Gibbard, A. (1990). *Wise choices, apt feelings.* Cambridge, MA: Harvard University Press.

Gomez, E., Zurcher, L. A., Farris, B. E., & Becker, R. E. (1985). A study of psychosocial casework with Chicanos, *Social Work*, 30, 477-483.

Hewit, J. P. (1988). *Self and society: A symbolic interactionist social psychology.* (4th Ed.). Boston: Allen and Bacon.

Hoffman, L., & Long, L. (1969). A systems dilemma. *Family Process*, 9, 211-234.

Hugman, R., & Smith, D. (1995). Ethical issues in social work: an overview. In Hugman, R. and Smith, D. (Eds.), *Ethical Issues in Social Work.* London & New York: Routledge.

Ingersoll-Daton, B., & Santienchai, C. (1999). Respect for the elderly in Asia: Stability and change. *International Journal of Aging and Human Development*, 48, 113-130.

Josssey-Bass Publishers.

Kelly, B (1990). Respect and caring: Ethics and essence of nursing. In Leininger, M., *Ethical and moral dimension of care.* Detroit: Wayne State University. Chapter 6

Leininger, M. (1990). *Ethical and moral dimension of care.* Detroit: Wayne State University.

Marshall, E. K., & Kurtz, P. D. (1982). *Interpersonal helping skills.* San Francisco:

Mayeroff, M. (1971). *On caring.* New York: Harper & Row.

Mehta, K. (1997). Respect redefined: Focus group insights from Singapore. *International Journal of Aging & Human Development*, 44, 205-219

Mendelsohn, A. R. (1980). *The work of social work.* New York: New Viewpoints.

Murdoch, G. P., & White, D. R. (1969). Standard cross-cultural sample. *Ethnology*, 8, 329-369.

NASW (1996). *The NASW Code of Ethics.* Noelker, L. S., & Harel, Z. (2000). *Linking quality of long-term care and quality of life.* NewYork: Springer, Chapter 1.

NASW Code of ethics of the National Association of Social Workers (1996). Value: Dignity and worth of the person, Ethical Principles.

Older Americans Month (1982). *A Proclamation by the President of the United States.*

Paniagua, F. A. (1998). *Assessing and treating culturally diverse clients.* (2nd Ed.) Thousand Oaks, CA: SAGE.

Pray, J. E. (1991). Respecting the uniqueness of the individual: Social work practice within a reflective model. *Social Work*, 36, 80-85.

Reichel, W. (1995). Essential principles in the care of the elderly. In Reichel, W., Gallo, J. J., Busby-Whitehead, J., Delfs, J. R., & Murphy, J. B. (Eds.), *Care of the elderly: Clinical aspects of aging.* (4th Ed.)

Rogers, C. (1961). *On becoming a person: A therapeutic view of psychotherapy.* Boston: Houghton Mifflin Co.

Silverman, P., & Maxwell, R. (1978). How do I respect thee? Let me count the ways: Deference towards elderly men and women. *Behavior Science Research*, 13, 91-108.

Sung, K. T. (2001). Elder respect: Exploration of ideals and forms in East Asia. *Journal of Aging Studies*, 15, 13-27.

Sung, K. T. (2002). Elder respect among American college students: Exploration of behavioral forms. *International Journal of Aging & Human Development*, 55, 367-383.

PART III

Expressions and Practices

In this part we will examine specific ways in which respect for the elderly is expressed in different nations and cultures. Chapter 10 introduces how American young adults in the West express their respect for elderly persons; Chapter 11 presents how Chinese young adults pay their respect for the elderly; Chapter 12 describes how Japanese people express elder respect; Chapter 13 is about the way in which Korean young adults respect their elderly people; and Chapter 14 is on the practice of respect for the elderly in Singapore. Chapter 15 presents findings from a cross-cultural study on the ways of respect for the elderly.

These chapters describe specific ways in which young people convey respect for elderly persons in respective countries and cultural contexts. All these studies identified a comprehensive set of forms of respect, as well as a number of categories indicating these forms. Moreover, they specified the extent to which individual forms were practiced and the level of importance given to the forms based on empirical studies conducted in the respective nations and cultures. Clearly, there is commonality among nations of East Asian culture in terms of similarity in the kinds of forms and expressions of respect for the aged. Although Asian young adults practiced respect for the elderly in a more salient and diversified way, the American young adults did practice most of those forms and gave importance to the forms as well. But the Americans evidently practiced several forms minimally, if at all, reflecting their cultural orientation toward egalitarian and nonhierarchical interpersonal relationships. Thus, the studies provide insights into the ways in which the elderly are respected by young adults in the United States and Asian countries.

Chapter 10

Elder Respect Among American College Students: Exploration of Behavioral Forms

Kyu-taik Sung

Introduction

This chapter presents the full report on the study of the American young adults with whom the Korean young adults were compared in Chapter 10.

In recent years, the issue of respect for the elderly has been gaining increased attention from gerontologists (Belmont Report 1974; McKee 1982; Silverman and Maxwell 1978; Strahmer 1985; Palmore and Maeda 1985; Wilson and Netting 1986; Streib 1987; Post 1989; Chipperfield and Haven 1992; Freedman 1996; Mehta 1997; Sung 1998; Palmore 1999; Ingersoll-Dayton and Saengtienchai 1999; Ikels 2004; Sung 2004).

Most of the elderly people have contributed to their families, communities, and nations. They suffered to raise, educate, and care for the younger generations. Without respect, society cannot have positive attitudes toward these people or treat them as dignified members of society. In our aging society, respect for the elderly remains as a key element in uplifting their statuses and integrating them more fully into society (Nydegger 1983; Palmore and Maeda 1985; Leininger 1990; Ghusn, Hyde, Stevens, Hyde and Teasdale 1996).

However, the theme of respect for elders has been noticeably absent from most discussions on aging. There has been little systematic research focused on respect by the young for the old. Consequently, little has been known about how young Americans respect the old.

How young people treat the elderly is very important because the younger generations will soon be responsible for caring for and supporting their elders. They will be an essential part of the support system (Bell and Garner 1996;

Montgomery and Kamo 1989). Their willingness to respect the aged is a critical factor. It is, therefore, important to begin to understand the behaviors demonstrating elder respect by young people which has been, for the most part, overlooked.

As discussed in previous chapters, elder respect has been a concept too general and abstract to inform people of its specific implications and to provide clear guidance for practice and research. That being the case, we need to distinguish between varying forms of respect the young accord the aged, and develop a set of behaviors reflecting these forms.

This paper reports on the results of an exploratory study of how American young adults (university students) demonstrate respect for the elderly. Since the present study was to exclusively explore the respectful treatment of the aged, an understanding of elder respect among the young adults and the means by which they convey respect to the elderly were of central importance. First, by a questionnaire, the study explored the behaviors that young people exhibit to convey their respect. Following the survey, additional data were collected by interviewers to test the reliability of the findings from the survey and to explore which factors influenced them to respect the elderly. This combined approach allowed the present study to explore specific ways in which the young adults respect the elderly, to gain insights into elder respect among them, and to identify issues to be examined in future studies.

PREVIOUS STUDIES

Respect comes from Latin 'repicere', which means to look back at or to look again. The idea of looking to, or giving attention to, can be used synonymously with words such as regard and consideration (Webster's 1996: 1640). So attention is a central aspect of respect; we respect a person by paying careful attention to the person and taking the person seriously (Dillon 1992; Downie and Telfer 1969: 23). Respect, however, calls for more than our attention; it requires certain actions or forms of conduct to be practiced which are deserved by the person (Gibbard 1990: 265; Dillon 1992).

Respectfulness is referred to as moral behavior in so far as it is not based on external rewards but on the person's internalized values of what a younger adult should do for the elderly (Kunda and Schwartz 1983; Raphael 1955). The behavior is intended to convey an altruistic and benevolent sense of regard and reverence to an elderly person.

Elder Respect encompasses esteem of the aged in general and esteem for one's own kin. It may be expressed in a variety of forms, e.g., by showing consideration for them, by caring for them, by complying with their wishes, by showing them courteous manners, or by giving them seats of honor. It is an open, visible, and matter-of-fact behavioral expression (Silverman and Maxwell 1978: 96; Ingersoll-Dayton and Saengtienchai 1999). The expression can be observed and recorded. Elder respect, on the other hand, can be subtle, private, carry an affective charge, and be culture-based (Leininger 1990; Silverman and Maxwell 1978; Downie and Telfer 1969). To assess the level of respect one connotes to an elder, it would take an in-depth inquiry.

A few studies have analyzed specific forms of elder respect. Over two decades ago, Silverman and Maxwell (1978) identified seven forms of expressing reverence towards elderly persons based on data from a cross-cultural study of 34 societies in various regions of the world. The forms were derived inductively from having observed the way the aged were treated. Specifically, they developed a typology consisting of seven behavioral forms: service respect (housekeeping), victual respect (serving drinks and foods of elders' choice), gift respect (bestowing gifts), linguistic respect (using respectful language), presentational respect (holding courteous appearances), spatial respect (furnishing honorable seats), and celebrative respect (celebrating birthdays).

After several years, Palmore and Maeda (1985) described a dozen of ways in which the Japanese expressed their respect for parents and elders. Over a decade later, Mehta's (1997) study reported on several forms of elder respect in Singapore. Ingersoll-Dayton and Saengtienchai (1999) reported on multiple forms of elder respect based on their extensive study of Taiwanese, Singaporeans, Thais, and Filipinos. This study grouped the forms of elder respect into several types including gestures and manners, customs and rituals rooted in the Asian culture. Lately, Sung and Kim (2003) identified 14 forms of elder respect ranging from care respect to ancestor respect, based on data from a survey of South Korean young adults.

The above four studies conducted in East Asia have clarified the multiple forms in which adults respected their elders. They furthermore demonstrated the usefulness of qualitative approaches, including the focus group method, in the analysis of behavioral expressions of elder respect interlaced with personal and affective qualities of intergenerational exchanges. The various forms distinguished by them include the seven forms previously identified by Silverman and Maxwell (1978) and at least the following six new forms: care respect (caring and serving), acquiescent respect (obeying), consulting respect (seeking advise), salutatory respect (greeting), public respect (respecting elders at large), and ancestor respect (respecting ancestors).

Care respect includes service respect. Thus, all the forms presented by Silverman and Maxwell have been replicated by the forms distinguished by the four studies suggesting cross-cultural similarity among the forms.

According to the reports of Ingersoll-Dayton and Saengtienchai (1999), and Mehta (1997), although the elderly are still respected by the young in East Asia, the meaning of respect is changing. For instance, obedience and subservience are being modified to mean courtesy and kindness. Palmore and Maeda (1985: 97) described, "Most Japanese have modified the more extreme expressions of subservience toward elders." Therefore, those forms of respect taken to be important today may not be considered so tomorrow.

The above pioneering studies have clarified that elder respect is expressed in multiple behavioral forms and that the meanings and expressions of the forms do change. While the studies made significant contributions, they commonly suffer from not explicating forms of respect based on quantitative data derived from a random sample and not examining it in the United States.

Study Method

A survey was given to a sample comprised of 621 university students (361 juniors and seniors, and 160 graduate students). The students were attending 28 randomly chosen classes in social sciences at two universities selected purposively for this study—one in the Midwest and the other on the West Coast. Older students were selected because they are more mature and better able to comprehend and judge moral values and behaviors of respect than younger ones (Hunt, 1993: 377-384).

A questionnaire consisting of the following structured questions was administered:

(1) Please list two important behaviors or gestures by which you most often express your respect for your parents and elders.

(2) How important, would you say, is each of the behaviors or gestures you cited? Please give a rating on their importance.

The first question identified the forms of elder respect the students most often practiced. The second question assessed the importance given by the students to the forms. Their levels of importance were rated on a 4-point scale (1=very important . . . 4=not so important). Added to these items were age, gender, and race. A concise questionnaire was constructed to enable the students to respond quickly and easily in a classroom situation. The questionnaires were group administered in the classroom. At the beginning of a class, the instructor explained the voluntary nature of participation and asked the students to complete the anonymous, self-administered questionnaire. In all, 90 percent or more students in each class returned completed questionnaires.

In the second phase, interviews were conducted by the author with 62 students (30 and 32 at the two respective universities) selected at random from those who responded to the questionnaire (2-3 students from each classroom). Their telephone numbers were secured, and they were subsequently called and interviewed by appointment. There were two purposes for undertaking this second phase of the study: (1) to test the reliability of the findings from the survey and (2) to gather information about an unanticipated finding. In each interview, the author outlined two questions. The first was, "What are the most important forms or ways in which you express your respect for elders? Please, give two examples of the forms or ways." A list of the 11 forms identified in the survey was provided in a randomized order. The second was to ask them to reminisce upon a personal experience: "From your recollection, who has taught or influenced you to respect parents and elders? Please state the relationship of one or more such persons." At the beginning of the survey, it was presumed that some of the students would not respond to the questions either because they do not respect the aged or for other personal reasons. However, as the survey proceeded, it was noticed that, contrary to the presumption, nearly all of the students cited some forms of elder respect, which they practiced and considered important. To interpret this unanticipated finding, face-to-face interviews (Merton, Fiske and Kendall. 1990) were carried out to clarify a major question, "Who or what has influenced the students to respect the elderly?" Their opinions and experiences relevant to elder respect were also obtained through interviews. The interviews lasted on the average of 20 minutes at locations selected by the subject and the researcher. The interviews were taped, transcribed, and then compared with field notes for accuracy.

Findings

Data from the Survey

The sample (graduate students: 32%; seniors and juniors: 68%) ranged in age from 20 to 44; their median age was 23. Male students numbered more than female students (56 to 44). In terms of race, about 72 percent were Caucasian, 12 percent African Americans, 12 percent Latinos, 4 percent Asian Americans, and less than one percent was others. Based on their responses, the following 11 forms of elder respect were identified and named referring to the titles and meanings of elder respect described by the previous studies (Refer to Table 10-1):

* Giving care and services for elders (Care respect)
* Complying with and listening to what elders say (Acquiescent respect)
* Seeking advice (Consulting respect)
* Greeting elders (Salutatory respect)
* Using respectful language in speaking to elders (Linguistic respect)
* Holding courteous appearances (Presentational respect)
* Giving precedential treatment to elders (Precedential respect)
* Bestowing gifts on elders (Gift respect)
* Furnishing elders with honorable seats or places (Spatial respect)
* Serving foods and drinks of elders' choice (Victual respect)
* Celebrating elders' birthdays (Celebrative respect)

Table 10-1.

Forms and Expressions of Elder Respect: American Respondents

Forms of Elder Respect	Descriptive	Expressions of Elder Respect
Acquiescent respect	(complying, listening)	Complying with directives of elders Listening when they talk
Care Respect	(care and service)	Being kind and considerate to elders; paying attention to them; having concern for them Taking care of elders when ill Assisting elders when they need help; doing housekeeping for them Maintaining contact with elders; spending time with them; living closer to them
Linguistic Respect	(using respectful/ honorific language)	Cordially addressing mother and father Using the title (Mrs., Mr., Dr., or professor, chairperson, etc.) or proper name of elders Avoiding inappropriate language and negative feedback to elders; not swearing at them Saying thank you for even small things
Salutatory Respect	(greeting)	Greeting elders by hugging and kissing; shaking hands with them Making eye-contact; looking at them with an expression of intimacy; acknowledging them on sight Saying "How are you?"
Consulting Respect	(consulting, asking advice)	Consulting elders over personal matters Asking them for advice
Presentational Respect	(showing courteous manners)	Wearing plain, neat, and proper attire Doing ordinary or moderate grooming Exhibiting polite and deferent postures
Precedential Respect	(serving elders first)	Allowing an elder to go through doorways first; to get in and out of cars first Cutting off friend's call when a call from an elder comes in
Public Respect	(serving elders at large)	Providing voluntary services for elders in community Providing personal assistance to elders at large (e.g., giving up seats for elders on buses, helping them to carry heavy things, providing them with transportation)
Celebratory Respect	(celebrating birthdays)	Celebrating elders' birthdays Visiting elders on their birthdays
Gift Respect	(presenting gifts)	Providing cash allowances and/or living expenses Providing clothes and daily necessities Sending cards and/or presents on their birthdays
Spatial Respect	(offering a seat, a place or a role of honor)	Furnishing elders with head seats Furnishing them with a central role to play Including them in activities, e.g., conversation, eating meals together, family gatherings, outings, etc.
Victual Respect	(serving choice foods and drinks)	Serving drinks and foods of elders' choice. Treating them at their favorite restaurants

Table 12-2.

Frequency of Citing and Rating of Importance per Forms of Elder Respect Practiced by American Respondents*

Forms of Elder Respect	Frequency[1]		Importance[2]		
	%[a]	Rank[b]	Mean[c]	Mode[d]	Rank[b]
Acquiescent	53	1	1.35	1	3
Care	32	2	1.19	1	1
Linguistic	27	3	1.44	1	5
Salutatory	17	4	1.41	1	4
Consulting	13	5	1.25	1	2
Presentational	11	6	1.47	1	6
Precedential	4	7	1.55	2	8
Public	3	8	1.64	2	9
Celebrative	3	9	1.67	2	10
Gift	3	10	1.71	2	12
Spatial	2	11	1.69	2	11
Victual	1	12	1.53	2	7

*N=521
[1] Frequency with which each form was cited by the subjects; only forms cited by 5% or more are included.

[2] Importance given to each form based on the 4-point scale (1=extraordinarily important ... 4=fairly important)

[a] The percentage of the subjects who cited the form. Most subjects cited more than one.
[b] The rank based on the size of the percentage
[c] The average rating of importance
[d] The statistical mode of the rating

First, the frequency with which each form was cited was assessed in terms of percentage. Based on the percentage, the forms were rank-ordered. Second, based on importance or weight given to the form, the forms were ranked.

In the ranking based upon frequency, acquiescent respect was the most frequently cited form (53% of all the respondents). The second most often cited form was care respect (32%), the third, linguistic respect (27%), the fourth, salutatory respect (17%), the fifth, consulting respect (13%), and the sixth, presentational respect (11%) (Table 12-2). The rest of the forms were cited by less than five percent of the respondents: precedential (4%), public (3%), celebrative (3%), gift (3%), spatial (2%), victual (1%). Thus, six forms, acquiescent, care, linguistic, salutatory, consulting, and presentational, were cited by more than 10 percent of the respondents, which makes these forms of elder respect more common and practiced more often by those surveyed.

In the rating based upon importance, care respect was the highest ranking form (rated 1.19), followed by consulting (1.25), acquiescent (1.35), salutatory (1.41), linguistic (1.44), and presentational (1.47) (Table 12-2). All these forms are roughly rated as between "very important" and "important" from the 4-point scale used. The 7th~11th ranking forms were given ratings ranging from 1.55 to 1.71, which were roughly rated "important" or "fairly important." Thus, all the forms were considered by the students as "very important" to "fairly important." (The original question was to elicit only important forms.) Although differences between the ratings are small, the statistical mode (Table 12-2) clearly differentiates the relative levels of importance given by the respondents.

Next, the ranking of frequencies and that of ratings on importance were compared. Spearman rank-order correlation between the two rankings [.82, RHO (.001)] suggests a fairly high level of similarity or consistency of the rankings.

Of the 11 forms of elder respect, six stand out: care, acquiescent, consulting, linguistic, salutatory, and presentational. Therefore, these six forms were selected for further analyses.

To examine the comparability of the findings at the two universities, a statistical analysis was undertaken by dividing the sample into two groups: one comprised of the students in the Midwest and the other of those on the West Coast. In order to examine differences in the mean rating of importance on each of the six forms, the Midwestern group was compared to the West Coast group. Results of a t-test showed that only the ratings of acquiescent respect—the former with a mean score of 1.51 (SD=.80) compared to the latter with a mean of 1.31 (SD=.53)—were different at the statistically significant level (t=2.24, df=226, p<.05, 2-tailed). These findings suggest that overall the two groups were similar in terms of citing various forms of elder respect, except for acquiescent respect. Those on the West Coast gave a greater weight to acquiescent respect than those in the Midwest. In the West Coast group, Latino and Asian American students accounted for 23.6% as compared to 10.6% in the Midwestern group. These groups gave higher ratings on importance of acquiescent respect. Probably because of the inclusion of these ethnic groups, the West Coast group as a whole had a higher importance rating of acquiescent respect: Latinos 1.30 and Asian Americans 1.35. (Cf., Caucasian and African Americans 1.43 and 1.41).

Results of an ANOVA test comparing importance scores on the six forms by gender, only acquiescent respect had a statistically significant variation between males and females (F=9.44, p<.01). Male students tended to give greater importance to acquiescence than did female students (mean rating: male 1.29 vs. female 1.56). By age groups, there were significant differences between the groups in rating consulting respect (F=3.02, p<.05). In terms of race, the rating of care respect had also statistically significant differences (F=3.59, p<.01). Latino and

Asian American students respectively (1.09, 1.12) gave higher ratings on importance of care respect than did Caucasian and African-American students (1.21, 1.19).

Information from Interviews

Results of interviews conducted by the author were summarized by three major points: (1) a review of the most important forms of elder respect, (2) factors which influenced the students to respect elders, and (3) anecdotes and quotations from their upbringing and experiences about elder respect.

Overall, the interviewer elicited detailed information to determine which forms of respect were most often cited by the interviewees and whether the influencing factors had a central or peripheral significance to their respecting behavior toward elders. Data for this phase was drawn from a sample of 62 students comprised of males (53%) and females (47%), and four age groups (20-24, 68%; 25-29, 27%; 30-34, 3%; 35+, 2%). Ratios of sex and age groups resembled those found in the survey.

In terms of racial composition, however, there were more Latino and Asian American students in the West Coast group than in the Midwestern group (Latino: 8 vs. 17; Asian American: 3 vs. 6).

An array of altruistic behaviors of care respect was cited by the students. They may be broadly classified into two types: (1) caring for elders with affective touches involving attention, concern, and resolving anxiety, and (2) providing service in terms of doing work or taking action for elders, such as housekeeping, spending time with them, and assisting them to cross the road. Both types are needed to practice care respect. For a graduate student of psychology who visited her parents once a month, care respect meant telling her parents that she cares about them and doing something beneficial for them. She described:

> "I spend time with my parents by talking with them over the phone. I visit them and lend a hand with cleaning, washing, or organizing something in their house that needs order. If they want something, I get it for them. I try to provide them with help before it is needed."

Another considerate student stated:

> "My parents' biggest worry seems to be my safety and health. I don't want them to worry about me all the time. So, I often talk to them about what I do and how I feel. I also discuss with them things that concern me. By doing so, I feel I can reduce their anxiety about me."

A graduate student who lived far from his parents voiced a similar sentiment when he said:

> "I call my parents frequently. I keep in touch with them. I tell them that I want to be home to help them . . . When they become older, I am going to live closer to them so that I can take care of them."

Although not all the interviewees visited aged parents frequently, nearly all of them recognized the importance of keeping in touch with their parents to alleviate their isolation and to keep them as part of their lives.

Of the students who cited acquiescent respect, 58 percent indicated `compliance' and 42 percent cited `listening.' Thus, one way of expressing acquiescent respect was complying with rules set by parents. Asked how she practiced acquiescent respect, a junior majoring in sociology said:

"I follow family rules and what my parents tell me to do, including keeping curfew."

A graduate student studying social work described:

"My parents usually discuss with me before setting up rules to be observed by family members. So I obligingly comply with most of those rules."

The data and these instances suggest that many of the young people tend to follow the wishes and directives of their parents. Another way acquiescent respect was shown was by listening to parents and elders when they talked. Although listening would not always mean complying with what the elderly directed, the young people obviously understood that listening is a way of respecting elders. For a large proportion of the students, listening appeared to be a very important form. They seemed to prefer this less subservient and more interactive form. The following remarks reflect this point:

"When my parents talk, I listen to them even when I am bored. I do not interrupt them"

"I listen to my parents' advice and opinions even when they might not seem very helpful. I occasionally nod or smile while listening to them."

A graduate student of urban planning described his feelings about consulting respect:

"I ask my parents and grandparents for their opinions and advice on decisions I have to make on my personal matters because I value their experience, wisdom, and willingness to help me."

Meanwhile, the elderly who are consulted often feel respected for their age and experience. Hence, the practice of consulting respect would bring forth beneficial results for both the young and the old.

Greetings reflect the social worth of the elderly toward whom they are directed. The respondents cited several ways of greeting elders which connoted respect ranging from hugging and kissing to saying "How are you?" A junior from Arizona stated,

"The first thing I learned from my parents was saying `Hi' to visitors. I think this is a basic way of interacting with others."

For a student who emigrated from Asia, greetings were more formal. He said, "When I meet my older relatives, I bow and bend my body forward."

To convey respect, they used proper verbal and body language when they addressed or spoke to the elderly. They mentioned several behaviors of this frequently cited and highly important form of respect. A senior studying political science described,

"I try to be sensitive to the kinds of words I use in talking to elders including my parents and teachers. Once I was paddled by a teacher for swearing at others. I don't raise my voice when I speak to them."

Proper and modest apparel and good grooming were cited as ways of connoting elder respect. A graduate student said,

"I think proper attire and manners are basics of our social life. These are what I learned from my parents."

Meanwhile, an Asian American student said,

"I usually give something to my grandparents and parents with two hands. I stand erect when they enter the room."

Precedential respect, gift respect, spatial respect, victual respect, and celebrative respect—mostly symbolic displays of elder respect—are forms of elder respect widely practiced among older adults. However, in the present study, these forms were cited by a small number of the young adults. For financial and physical reasons, many of them would not be able to practice these forms.

The rankings of the two sets of the forms—one based on data from the first phase study (the survey) and the other based on data from the second phase study (interviews)—were compared by a cross-check. Spearman rank-order correlation between the two rankings [.93, RHO (.001)] for the 11 forms suggests high similarity or consistency of the rankings.

The interviewees cited factors that influenced them to respect elders. The three most frequently cited factors were teachings by parents (91%), grandparents (33%), and other relatives (13%). Less frequently cited factors were friend's advice (9%), self-awareness (6%), influence from mass media (6%), and learning at the school (5%). Five percent (3 persons) stated that nobody taught them how to respect the elderly. A further analysis was conducted by dividing the subjects into the Midwestern group (30) and the West Coast group (32). The two groups were compared using the frequencies with which influence factors were "cited" or "not cited." The key factors—teaching by parents (Chi-square=.916, df=1, sig.=.338, 2-tailed), teaching by grandparents (chi-square=.089, df=1, sig.=.765, 2-tailed), and teaching by other relatives (Chi-square=.265, df=1, sig.=.338,

2-tailed)—were found not differentiated by the two groups. Similarly, all other influence factors were not statistically differentiated by the two groups.

The following are anecdotes and quotations regarding the general meaning of elder respect obtained from interviews. These were selected on the basis of their relevance, or how representative or insightful the statement:

"People should treat each other on an equal footing. But my parents are a different case. I respect them more than anybody else. They work hard and care for me. I started to respect them as I became older and more conscious of their love and aid for me. It was a natural awakening on my part."

"My parents were particular about my manners toward elders and my language in speaking to them. I think my elder respecting values and behaviors have been built up under the influence from my parents."

"My grandparents always told me to respect the elderly. Once when their friend visited our home, I refused to kiss the visitor's cheek. For this misbehavior, I was deprived of Coke for two days."

"Elderly persons deserve kind and friendly treatment for their age and wisdom. They deserve social respect. But I have higher regard for those elderly who care for me and pay attention to my concerns."

"I lived separately from my parents who were divorced when I was young. I learned how to treat others courteously through television and movies."

"I would like to know more about older generations—their wisdom and experience as well as their issues and concerns. Some form of school teaching on how the young and the old can understand and relate to each other would be desirable."

"We Americans need to teach the next generation respectful behaviors, so that when they grow up, they would pass the value to their children. Much depends on how we bring up our children."

Although the findings cannot be generalized, they do reflect the students' perceptions and feelings on elder respect.

Discussion

The present study was undertaken to explore the forms of elder respect frequently used and considered important by the American young adults. A set of 11 forms of elder respecting behavior was measured and the six of them were strikingly important. Thus, almost all the forms (except public respect and ancestor respect) described by the previous studies reemerged and have been included in the set. This suggests the cross-cultural resemblance of the 11 forms. In the description of the holistic meaning of elder respect, all these forms would have to be considered as each of them indicates a different way in which the American young people convey their elder respect. Some of the young adults might also display a lack of respect. But, the present study did not take into account the other side of elder respect.

The findings suggest that there are two types of elder respect: (1) one involving some activity or work, such as caring, serving, and consulting, and (2) symbolic displays of respect—those falling into acquiescent, linguistic, salutatory, and presentational types. The typology of the forms is a mix of these two types reflecting the necessity for fulfilling both types.

It is noteworthy that, of all the forms, care respect was given the highest degree of importance also by the American young people, and it was their second most frequently cited form. Respect, closely interrelated with care, reflects the value of caring for others with benevolence and sympathetic concern. Caregivers of elderly who are ill need to make a renewed moral commitment to the practice of this particular form.

Certain cultural differences in the expression of elder respect were noticed: Latino and Asian American students consistently expressed their tendency to respect elders in the forms of acquiescent respect and care respect. Also Caucasian American students emigrated from such countries as Lithuania, Hungary, and Armenia expressed a similar tendency. Peoples of various cultural backgrounds apparently share common values of elder respect. However, as the finding suggests, there are differences in meanings and expressions of elder respect between cultures or subcultures. The differences would probably be a matter of degree than of direction.

The meanings of certain forms may undergo modification over time. Those taken to be important today may not be considered so tomorrow in the changing society of the United States. Listening has emerged as a modification of the traditional form of obedience. And, consulting respect has emerged as the second most important form, which involves open communication and mutually beneficial exchange between generations. Thus, expressions of elder respect appear to be shifting from subservient forms to reciprocal or egalitarian ones. They also appear to be shifting from complex forms to simpler ones. For instance, complicated lingual expressions of greeting and paying courtesy are not as frequently heard and seen as they were decades ago. Also, the young people studied were selective in practicing elder respect. They would not express respect to every elderly person automatically. Most of them seemed to define the extent to which they respect someone based on the proximity of familial and social relations, i.e., parents and grandparents first, other older relatives next, and thereafter, teachers and seniors, community elders, and elders in the larger society. Their feelings and expressions of respect toward their parents reflected the natural and instinctual relationship between the child and the parent. Some asserted that elder respect would depend on the behavior of the elderly in terms of proper attitude and manner they hold toward the young. Hence, conducts of the elderly would seem to condition the amount of respect the elderly receive.

Identification of the various forms of elder respect leads us to understand that, in practicing elder respect, an adult might give more emphasis to certain forms while giving less to other forms for tactical and situational reasons. It may be a great challenge for many to practice all the forms because of constraints associated with family relations, their work situations, and social and environmental factors including financial capability and long-distance living.

Nearly all the students expressed their eagerness to convey their care respect more to their mothers suggesting greater care respect often accorded to mothers. More men than women and more Latino and Asian Americans than Caucasian and African Americans tended to follow directives of their elders and listen to what the elders said to them. Future studies should include an examination of the gender and ethnic-cultural backgrounds of the subjects in order to produce valid assessment of elder respect.

In the process of dynamic social changes, the young seemed to be modifying their expressions of elder respect to reflect the culture and subculture in which they reside. In what manner and to what degree the effect of such shifts engenders positive or negative effects on the well-being of the elderly is an empirical question to which gerontologists need to be sensitive.

The overwhelming majority of the subjects cited family influence—teachings by parents, grandparents, and other relatives—as the key factor which influenced them to respect elders. Clearly, socialization and role modeling by family members emerged as the most important factor. This underscores the crucial role of the family in instilling the value of elder respect at an early age (Harre and Lamb 1983). As the finding of the present study indicates, children who were taught to respect their elders did respect the elders. An interesting corollary is that there is little evidence of influences from school.

Conclusion

Elder respect will remain a vital issue in our aging society. The elderly in civilized societies must be ensconced in the moral domain (Post 1989). There have been statements of concern by gerontologists over declining elder respect. As Palmore (1999: 20-30) described, people often ignore, isolate, and discriminate the elderly. Range and Vinovkis (1981) criticized that frequently the image of the older person is portrayed negatively in the media. And, Nydegger (1983) pointed out, "Only those elderly who possess resources and social status are respected." These tendencies are believed to render the elderly valueless to society.

But the issue of "declining elder respect" is an age-old concern of human society. More than two thousand years ago, Plato showed his insight by fixing on youth as the impressionable period when reverence should be stamped on the mind of a learner. He trusted reverence to check the rise of insolence in the young (Hastings 1908: 752). In the East, before Plato, Confucius stressed the need for elder respect in young adults. He said, "Filial piety today is taken to mean providing nourishment for parents. . . If it is not done with reverence for parents, what is the difference between men and animals?" (Analects, Bk. 2. Ch. 7; de Bary 1995). The concern expressed by these great scholars seems to be still with us as has been for many generations and eras.

However, one should not be overly critical, for there is a convincing indication that the young adults respect their parents and elders. In America, numerous adults care for and support their ill old relatives, and young adults are watching this and learning from it. Impressively, Chipperfield and Havens (1992) found in Canada that the level of older people's perceived respect increased. These facts would seem to support the finding of this exploratory study. Hence, there is room for optimism as long as there are such positive signs. We must struggle to preserve these signs, for without them the mistreatment of the elderly may increase.

This exploratory study does have limitations: the sample was drawn at only two universities selected purposively, and situational factors surrounding the subjects were not fully accounted for. Besides, the basic principles applied to the study design were to focus the respondents' attention to a few most important forms they most often practiced and to allot limited time and cost to the survey and interviews. These constraints could have delimited the scope and depth of exploration.

Given the limitations, the results were found to be similar whether they were compared by the students' age, gender or geographic area, suggesting the consistency of the findings. An effort was made to explicate the forms based on quantitative data in combination with information from a qualitative exploration. The gamut of the forms ranging from care respect to consulting respect may be useful in developing a more systematic typology of forms of respect. The findings reflect a fairly large number of young adults' feelings, values and practices of elder respect. By understanding these referents of elder respect, the old may be able to develop a more progressive and harmonious relationships with young people.

The present study is an initial step toward a more systematic study of elder respect by the young, about which little has been known in the United States. Future research should use a wider range of representative samples that include older adults who assume greater caring obligations and young adults not attending college, and carry out longitudinal studies to account for the changing process of elder respecting expressions and behaviors. The following issues might be addressed in the future research:

* Forms of elder respect presently changing in their meanings and expressions
* The extent to which the elderly are respected in comparison with the degree to which they are devalued
* The extent to which the young devote their time and energy to elder respect
* Impact of elder respect on well-being and life satisfaction of the elderly

* Distance between elders and children, and the practice of elder respect
* The extent to which socialization and education influence the young to respect the elderly
* Society-wide willingness to develop policies and strategies to stress elder respect
* Cross-cultural differences and similarities in ideals and practices of elder respect
* Forms of elder respect with universal applicability

References

Applegate, M., & Morse, J. M. (1994). Personal privacy and interactional patterns in a nursing home. *Journal of Aging Studies, 8,* 413–434.

Becerra, R. M. (1988). The Mexican American family. In C. H. Mindel, R. W. Habenstein, & R. Wright, Jr. (Eds.), *Ethnic Families in America: Patterns and Variations* (3rd ed.). New York: Academic Press.

Bell, W., & Garner, J. (1996). Kincare. *Journal of Gerontological Social Work, 25,* 11–20.
Butler, R. (1995). Ageism. In G. Maddox (Ed.), *Encyclopedia of aging.* New York: Springer.

Chipperfield, J. G., & Havens, B. (1992). A longitudinal analysis of perceived respect among elders: Changing perceptions for some ethnic groups. *Canadian Journal on Aging, 11,* 15–30.

Cortese, A. J. (1999). Ethical issues in subculturally diverse society. In T. F. Johnson (Ed.), *Handbook on ethical issues in aging.* Westport, CO: Greenwood Press.

Dillon, R. S. (992). Respect and care: Toward moral integration. *Canadian Journal of Philosophy, 22,* 105-132.

Downie, R. S., & Telfer, E. (1969). *Respect for persons.* London: Allen and Unwin.

Finkel, A. (1982). Aging in Jewish perspective. In F. V. Tiso (Ed.), *Aging: Spiritual perspectives.* Lake Worth, FL: Opera Pia International/Sunday Publications.

Gekoski, W., & Knox, V. (1990). Ageism or healthism, *Journal of Aging and Health, 2,* 15–27.

Ghusn, H. M., Hyde, D., Stevens, E. S., Hyde, M., & Teasdale, T. A. (1996). Enhancing life satisfaction in later life: What makes a difference for nursing home residents? *Journal of Gerontological Social Work, 26,* 27–47.

Gibbard, A. (1990). *Wise choices, apt feelings.* Cambridge, MA: Harvard University Press.

Hummert, M. (1994). Stereotypes of the elderly and patronizing speech. In M. Hummert, J. Wieman, & J. Nussbaum (Eds.), *Interpersonal communication in older adulthood.* Thousand Oaks, CA: Sage.

Ingersoll-Dayton, B., & Saengtienchai, C. (1999). Respect for the elderly in Asia: Stability and change. *International Journal of Aging and Human Development, 48,* 113–130.

Jecker, N. S. (1991). *Aging and ethics.* Clifton, NJ: Humana Press. Kauh, T. O. (1997). Intergenerational relations: Older Korean-Americans' experiences, *Journal of Cross-Cultural Gerontology, 12,* 245–271.

Kelly, B. (1990). Respect and caring. In M. Leininger (Ed.), *Ethical and moral dimension of care.* Detroit: Wayne State University Press.

Kim, K., & Hurh, W. (1991). The extended conjugal family: Family-kinship system of Korean immigrants in the United States. In T. Keak & S. Lee (Eds.), *The Korean-American community: Present and future.* Pusan, Korea: Kyungnam University Press.

Lawrence, R. H., Bennet, J. N., & Markides, K. S. (1992). Perceived intergenerational solidarity and psychological distress among older Mexican-Americans, *Journal of Gerontology, 47,* 555–565.

Leininger, M. (1990). Culture: The conspicuous missing link to understand ethical and moral dimensions of human care. In M. Leininger (Ed.), *Ethical and moral dimension of care.* Detroit: Wayne State University Press.

MacNeil, R., Ramos, C., & Magagas, A. (1996). Age stereotyping among college students: A replication and expansion, *Educational Gerontology, 22,* 229–243.

Mehta, K. (1997). Respect redefined: Focus group insights from Singapore. *International Journal of Aging and Human Development, 44,* 205–219.

Montgomery, R. J., & Kamo, Y. (1989). Parent care by sons and daughters. In J. A. Manchini (Ed.), *Aging parents and adult children.* Lexington, MA: Lexington Books.

Murdock, G. P., & White, D. R. (1969). Standard cross-cultural sample. *Ethnology, 8,* 329–369.

Nydegger, C. N. (1983). Family ties of the aged in the cross-cultural perspective. *The Gerontologist, 23,* 26–32.

Palmore, E. B. (1999). *Ageism: Positive and negative.* New York: Springer.

Palmore, E. B., & Maeda, D. (1985). *The honorable elders revisited.* Durham, NC: Duke University Press.

Post, S. G. (1989). Filial morality. *Journal of Religion and Aging, 5,* 15–29.

Raphael, D. D. (1955). *Moral judgement.* London: George Allen & Unwin.

Riley, M., & Riley, J. (1994). Age integration and the lives of older people. *The Gerontologist, 34,* 110–115.

Rowe, J., & Kahn, R. (1998). *Successful aging*. New York: Pantheon Books. Schonefield, D. (1982). Who is stereotyping whom and why? *The Gerontologist, 22*, 267–272.

Silverman, P., & Maxwell, R. (1978). How do I respect thee? Let me count the ways: Deference towards elderly men and women. *Behavior Science Research, 13*, 91–108.

Silverstein, M., Burholt, V., Wenger, G. C., & Bengtson, V. L. (1998). Parent-child relations among very old parents in Wales and the United States: a test of modernization theory. *Journal of Aging Studies, 12*, 387-409.

Simic, A. (1990). Aging, world view, and international relations in America and Yugoslavia. In J. Sokorovsky (Ed.), *The cultural context of aging: Worldwide perspectives*. New York: Bergin and Garvey.

Strahmer, H. M. (1985). Values, ethics and aging. In Losnoff-Caravaglia (Ed.), *Values, ethics and aging*. New York: Human Sciences Press.

Streib, G. F. (1987). Old age in socio-cultural context: China and the United States. *Journal of Aging Studies, 7*, 95–112.

Sung, K. T. (1995). Measures and dimensions of filial piety. *The Gerontologist, 35*, 240–247.

Sung, K. T. (1998). An exploration of actions of filial piety. *Journal of Aging Studies, 7*, 95–112.

Sung, K. T. (2001). Elder respect: Exploration of ideals and forms in East Asia, *Journal of Aging Studies, 15*, 13–27.

Vasil, L., & Wass, H. (1993). Portrayal of the elderly in the media: A literature review and implications for educational gerontologists. *Educational Gerontology, 19*, 71–85.

Webster's new universal unabridged dictionary. (1996). New York: Barnes & Noble Books.

Chapter 11

How Do I Respect Thee? Let Me Count The Ways: Deference Towards Elderly Men and Women

Philip Silverman[1] and Robert J. Maxwell[2]

Introduction

Over the past two years we have been engaged in a study to determine the position of the aged in the variety of cultural contexts. In attempting to explain the treatment of the elderly, we were well aware of the considerable range of treatment modes the aged can expect as one moves from the enviable state of veneration so often associated with traditional (and perhaps even contemporary) Chinese culture, to the depths of contempt we too frequently tolerate in our own society.

After struggling with this treatment variable in a previous paper (Maxwell and Silverman 1970), we realized that the nature of the question we were posing had enormous significance, even beyond the peculiar position of the aged. For we were clearly raising issues which were fundamental in social life: How does one confer, or deny, social honor in any society? Does the distribution of such honor differ by sex? And since our approach is both anthropological and cross-cultural, there was a necessary corollary question: Are there categories of social honor with universal applicability?

Social honor, prestige, status are all more or less interchangeable concepts enjoying an "honorable status" in sociological theory. In a much respected synthesis of social stratification theory, Gerhard Lenski begins with the assumption that men seek three great rewards—power, privilege, and prestige or honor. It was not reassuring, however, to find in this book devoted to understanding the nature of these three rewards, in a volume that runs to almost 500 pages that no more than two pages are allocated to studies of "prestige stratification" (Lenski 1966: 430-31).

Earlier, Max Weber had defined the three major stratification concepts of class, power, and status, each having a separate, if mutually influencing, set of determinants in the social structure. Status is determined by the social order which he defined as: "The way in which social honor is distributed in a community." (Weber 1972: 45). Accordingly, the specification of status must be sought in the "style of life" (Weber 1972: 53) pursued by a group of individuals. Despite the amorphous nature of lifestyle as a concept, we felt compelled to develop a set of categories that would allow us to tap the varying kinds of social honor accorded the aged as a status group in the Weberian sense of a plurality of persons, who, within a larger group, claim a special social esteem (Weber 1968: 307).

Our previous study and the work of others concerned with the variable cross-culturally (see, for example, Stephens 1963: 291ff.), had treated the conferral of social honor (which we shall refer to henceforth as deference) as an indefinite set of behavioral acts which could be interpreted as reflecting the social worth of those toward whom these acts were directed. These procedures yielded a potpourri of items, any one of which could be found in only a rather limited number of cultures. Clearly, the power of broad-scale comparisons is vitiated by keeping one's nose too close to the empirical richness of the ethnographic corpus. Thus, our initial task was to develop a set of finite categories that would not exclude relevant data, yet wold allow us to compare data from a large number of societies realistically and systematically.

The Information-Esteem Hypothesis

A brief description of the broader investigation which provides the framework for this study of deference may be in order. In a series of earlier papers we had viewed culture as a system that depends for its functioning on the processing of information (Maxwell and Silverman 1970; Silverman and Maxwell 1971, 1972). This perspective derives for the most part from general systems theory, an interdisciplinary attempt to develop an interrelated set of hypotheses relevant to living systems at various levels of complexity. James G. Miller described the relevance of information for social systems rather well in the following statement: "In systems that survive, the component with the most relevant information available to its decider is the one most likely to exercise power over or elicit compliance from other components in the system" (Miller 1972: 4).

Our major concern was to subject to empirical test the proposition: that when old people know something which younger people consider relevant, the position of old people in the community is enhanced and that this will be reflected in the treatment they receive at the hands of their neighbors and kinsmen. Secondarily, we were interested in the influence of a number of other variables upon this relationship, including the social isolation of the community (i.e., the extent of its involvement with adjacent communities or with the state) and the rigidity of its social structure (i.e., the strength of barriers to communication between community sub-groups [Young and Bacdayan 1965]).

Earlier criticisms of our hypothesis focused rather consistently around the idea that "power" was a prepotent factor in determining the status of old people. Some of these objections were the result of confusion concerning our unit of analysis, which was the community rather than the nation-state. Thus, it is hardly relevant to our hypothesis to point to the "nine old men" of the Supreme Court or to the elderly rulers of many contemporary counties, and claim that the proposition is refuted. Our current investigation has attempted to take "power" into account as a test variable. We found the concept rather difficult to operationalize adequately. A study group based at the University of Southern California has also paid attention to the idea (Abarbanel 1974; Dowd 1974; Sheehah 1975).

It is unnecessary to treat the rationale of this larger study in any greater detail here. Suffice it to say that an understanding of deference and the means by which it is signalled is of central importance, as it is the dependent variable.

Since our investigation dealt exclusively with the treatment of the aged, it is unfortunately not possible for us to compare their status with the status of younger persons. However, since we differentiated deference displays towards old people by the sex of the person addressed, our data do discriminate between old men and old women. Considerable importance has been attached to sexual differences in the activities and status of the aged in Leo Simmons' cross-cultural study, *The Role of the Aged in Primitive Society.* Simmons reports that:

> The mother-family system which has safeguarded higher rank and more rights for women, has generally tended to be associated with simpler types of maintenance such as collection, hunting, and possibly fishing. The father-family system, which has usually enhanced rank and rights of men—not infrequently at the expense of women—has shown a strong tendency to prevail among herders and probably farmers (Simmons 1945: 210).

He cautions, however, that his findings should be considered tentative, since their statistical support is neither strong nor consistent.

We hope to examine the determinants of differential status by sex more closely in later publications. For the moment, we are chiefly concerned with demonstrating that such differences do in fact exist.

Some remarks may be in order concerning differences as reported. Although some of our sources were written by women, and some tend to focus on the behavior of women, it is true that most were written by men and are primarily about men. It is possible that this tendency to focus on the behavior of males might introduce a bias into our findings, skewing them in the direction of greater deference accorded men, since such behavior is more likely to be reported than deference accorded women. To the extent that this is the case, there is no justification for treating "missing data" as indicative of the absence of the item. However, whether or not such a bias is present in any cross-cultural study dealing with sex differences depends a great deal on the nature of the variables. This bias is likely to have more of an impact on the study of, say, attitudes towards sexual behavior, than on the study of household management or socialization practices. To the extent that the behavior under scrutiny is subtle, private, and carries an affective charge, then what is reported in ethnographies will tend to be descriptive of men, rather than of women. The present study, however, deals with behavior that is relatively open, public, and matter-of-fact. We suspect, therefore, that the findings reflect real differences in behavior, rather than differences in reporting.

Methods

Turning to our procedures, we drew a 55% random sample (N = 103) from Murdock and White's Standard Cross-Cultural Sample of 186 "distinctive world areas" (Murdock and White 1969). A rather lengthy codebook, the Bakersfield Aging Study Schedule, using a pre-coded format, is being completed for each of our sample societies, and an additional 25 will be duplicated in an attempt to establish reliability. A further check on reliability has been provided by a short reliability estimate, which is essentially a list of 80 statements relevant to the aged, drawn at random from our ethnographic sources. All of our staff are in the process of coding this set of statements independently. We also attempted to overcome order effects by drawing at random one society from each of the 6 major ethnographic areas and combining them into sets. Coders were instructed to complete all of the societies within a given set before proceeding to the next. This procedure also reduces the possibility of bias in the subsample to be examined here.

Definitions

We defined deference as a type of behavior that is intended to convey respect and appreciation on the part of one person or persons for another. This is a broad category of acts in the course of which younger people (in the context of this study) indicate they hold old people in esteem by communicating to them a sense of integrity and worth. Terms like "respect" and "esteem," are expressions meant to suggest the hypothetical construct indexed by varied forms of deference behavior. It follows logically that younger people may also display negative deference by communicating a sense of the elderly's devalued position in society. Although we have also collected data on negative deference, we do not take account of it within the scope of this paper.

The set of generalized categories we developed have been derived inductively from having looked at the treatment of the aged in many cultural contexts. We have now coded data from over ninety societies using this typology; although some tinkering could improve the logic of the set, we feel it is useful heuristically as an initial attempt to describe the behavioral acts in the literature which seem to reflect the notion of deference as defined here. The typology includes the following categories:

1. *Spatial Deference:* behavior directed towards the prerogatives held by the aged with respect to territory, domestic area, individual distance, or relative position in a group. Several examples of spatial deference can be found in Ireland. Writing of the western countries in the 1930s, Arensburg states:

> Ireland is in many ways an older person's country. . . . We remember that the household and the family centres itself in them. Their room is semi-sacred in the fairylore; it is the best in the house. The chair by the fire, the seat of honour and most comfort is theirs (Arensburg 1968: 110)

2. *Victual Deference:* behavior directed towards the prerogatives held by the aged with respect to the consumption of food and drink. We may draw an example of victual deference from the Samoans, among whom chiefs of varying ranks are the most important figures of political and social authority. Chiefs are appointed by the members of their families, and since the appointment is ordinarily a lifetime one, chiefs tend to be older men, sometimes older women. Most of the significant events in Samoan public life are accompanied by the serving of kava to the assembled guests. This is a very formal procedure, each guest having his name called out by the steward and served in turn, in order of his rank. Since chiefs are served first, it happens that, de facto, older men are given precedence in the serving order (Grattan 1948: 48-49).

3. *Linguistic or Communicational Deference:* behavior directed towards the aged which conveys a sense of esteem through speech or other communicational behavior, such as writing or drawing. The most common form that this deference takes is in the terms of reference or address used for the elderly which communicates their social worth: e.g., "the honored ones." Another form this takes is the restraint expressed by younger people when the elderly are present, such that certain words, or certain types of conversation, are taboo. Communicational deference is encountered fairly commonly. Meyer Fortes reports that the Tallensi of Ghana:

> Always show off an old parent, own or classificatory, with great pride to a visitor. I have often ben led out of my way to shake the hand of a blind and senile old man or woman who was too bemused with age to understand the speech with which we were presented to each other (Fortes 1949: 48).

4. *Presentational Deference:* behavior directed towards the aged with reference to clothing, grooming, posture, and other modifications of appearance and motor behavior which communicates information about the self, usually in face-to-face situations. This includes any sort of behavior that must be performed or avoided in the presence of the elderly, excluding of course the linguistic forms specified above. Presentational deference of a particularly interesting sort is found among the rural Japanese, where old people are rather well off. At the end of the working day, the half dozen people of the family line up for their evening

baths. There is ordinarily only a single large Japanese tub and enough warm water to fill it only once. The old men bathe first, and the others follow in order of seniority and sex, all of them using the same water (Beardsley *et al.* 1959: 88-89).

5. *Service Deference:* any kind of work performed for the benefit of old people. It includes such chores as housekeeping, property maintenance, grooming, special medical treatment, and others. Empirically, we found that most service medical treatment, and others. Empirically, we found that most service deference boiled down to drudgery: cooking, mending clothes, and so on, as among the Pawnee (e.g., Weltfish 1965: 319). Though instances of service deference do appear, it evidently is rarely extended to *all* old people in a society, but usually only to the infirm or the fatigued. Most old people continue to help with household chores as long as they are able. On the other hand, where there are periodic cooperative tasks involving heavy labor or endurance, such as battles or big game hunts, old people tend to be routinely excused.

6. *Prestative Deference:* the bestowing of gifts or other favors on old people, excluding instances of the exchange of goods or favors of equal value. These gifts may be of real or symbolic value, including money. Because they fall under victual deference, we must exclude food and drink from this category. We distinguish two kinds of prestative deference: material and non-material. The first refers to artifacts, precious metals or other material goods. The second refers to the bestowal of favors and privileges, such as the right to sing certain songs, or utter certain prayers, or otherwise appeal to supernatural forces.

Material prestation occurs among the Huron, who live on the Canadian side of the Great Lakes; old men are given gifts during the celebrations that follow a battle, and old women receive gifts during the performance of a curing ritual for the sick (Tooker 1964: 107). Although non-material prestation does occur, we have few instances of it among the societies in our sample that we have examined so far.

7. *Celebrative Deference:* displays through ritual or ceremonies, one of the purposes of which is to dramatize the esteem accorded to old people. Some examples are ceremonies marking the entrance into old age, marking some crucial event within the elderly life-cycle, or providing more elaborate funerals or those who die at an advanced age.

Some of the categories were devised on an a priori basis, such as spatial and victual deference, but most were derived from a preliminary reading of some of the ethnographic material. We also included an item in our code book indicating that "the ethnographer reports that there is a display of deference towards old people but does not elaborate his statement." This item was designed to cover such statements as: "young people show a great deal of respect towards old people." It has proved to be a most useful category.

Once we had managed to construct a typology of deference behavior that seemed workable, our pre-test results uncovered a dimension which it appeared crucial to account for, but at fist glance technically impossible to operationalize. Regardless of the domain covered in the typology, it is obvious that any given deference act varies according to the amount of energy invested by those conferring the social honor. Weber referred to the development of status as essentially resting on some form of usurpation (Weber 1972: 51). Deference can only occur if time, resources, or motor energy is usurped or diverted for its expression.

Unfortunately, it was far from obvious how we could derive this dimension from ethnographic data, which are so often reluctant to yield the precise expenditure of *anything* let alone such a comprehensive factor as energy. After deliberating over the problem for a considerable time, we finally decided on a trinary set of energy expenditure categories which allows for modest but, we believe, useful discriminations within each deference act. Thus, every item is coded according to one of the following procedures:

A. *Active Deference:* refers to going out of one's way to express respect for one another. During a display of active deference, one is socially engaged and/or working. What we are trying to code here is something similar to what Goffman (1956: 473) called "presentational rituals."

B. *Passive Deference:* refers to refraining from any exercise of censure of otherwise avoiding what one ordinarily would do if the situation involved younger people. In a sense, this involves excusing old people from obligations and responsibilities that other adults must observe, and although it means ignoring old people and their behavior, it is done to benefit them rather than to degrade them. Passive deference generally takes the form either of not correcting or commenting upon errors old people make, or of excusing old people from participation in onerous or strenuous tasks. People do not go out of their way for the benefit of the aged, they simply ignore their behavior or treat them as if they were not in fact there. For example, when a young person kills a big game animal and brings the choicest part to the old people, it is active deference. But when all the adult men go on a communal hunt except for the aged—who are excused from participation, even though they will get a share of the meat when it is distributed following the hunt—the deference is passive.

Certainly, what we refer to here as "passive deference" is universal, or nearly so, for decrepit elderly. However, our codes refer to prestative deference passive deference as it is extended to the aged who are still active, so far as can be determined. The investigation does, in fact, take account of the treatment of the decrepit aged; these data have not yet been analyzed, but will be reported upon subsequently.

C. *Moderate Deference:* this category falls in between active and passive and has been most difficult for us to define in a conceptually respectable way. It is actually a form of active deference in that it involves some noticeable deprivation or discomfort on the part of those showing deference, but it does not necessarily involve the repetitive doing of something, nor necessarily, work or social engagement.

It might be possible to make this category clear by an example. We find empirically that moderate deference tends often to be expressed in "taking turns" or "getting the lion's share" of something, in which cases old people have the advantage. It occurs chiefly in situations in which a number of people participate in the same event but the old people are shown favoritism, resulting in some degree of inconvenience for the non-aged participants. The Samoan example, in which old people tend to be served kava first, and the Japanese example in which old men are the first to bathe, will serve as typical instances.

The above set of operational definitions provide the framework for the coding of the deference variable. However, as we continue to examine the ethnographic literature, new data suggest additional ways to combine these finite categories of deference in order that they might be more applicable to modern societies. There seems to be two basic types of deference within our existing categories, and these allow for an alternative pi of energy expenditure. First, there is deference involving some actual work, such as cooking a meal or building a house; and second, there are numerous types of symbolic displays—particularly falling in the linguistic, presentational, and celebrative categories. We give deference of both types to demonstrate our recognition of older people, but usually only the work type of deference is given to those needing custodial care.

Analysis

We can present here only a preliminary analysis of our data. Since we are still in the process of coding data, we had available for this analysis 34 societies, or approximately 1/3 of our total sample.[4] The most consistent finding so far is the presence of a substantial difference in deference behavior directed towards the elderly according to their sex. Sex was not coded for celebrative deference. However, elderly men receive deference in over 50% of our cases for five of the types of deference for which sex was coded, including spatial, victual, linguistic, presentational, and service. By contrast, elderly women receive deference in an equally high proportion of our cases for only one type, service deference. The percentage of cases in each type run from 44% to 76% for males, and only 18% to 59% for females. In one sub-type, non-material prestation, we have yet to find an item relating to females. It should be pointed out that our units of analysis are not societies but subsystems of elderly males and elderly females. Since there are 34 societies in the subsample, and each society has two such subsystems, our N is 68, rather than 34.

The most frequent type of deference found for males is victual, which is the one present in 76% of the cases, and not too far behind is linguistic or communicational deference. The victual type is also relatively high for elderly women, falling in second place with 38%. However, females do manage to outstrip the males, although by only one case, in the category of service deference where we find items in 59% of the cases.

Now service deference is a category essentially concerned with providing various kinds of custodial care for the aged, and together with certain sub-categories of victual deference, it comprises one of the two basic types of deference discussed earlier and is associated with some form of work. Possibly, this relatively high percentage of work deference available to older women can be explained by the fact that, generally, they represent a higher proportion of all elderly, and the very least that is provided for those with longevity is some form of custodial care. The interesting corollary to this is that we find very little evidence of deference directed towards old women in the various categories that comprise the second basic type, which we referred to earlier as symbolic deference. This latter is the ode of respect wherein the old men command most of the prerogatives a society has the potential to provide.

When we have completed the coding of data for the remainder of our sample, we hope to isolate those societies which allow for the more generous displays of symbolic deference directed towards old women, so that eventually it might be possible to uncover the factors associated with this relatively rare state of affairs.

Let us end by stating that we have made some other attempts at preliminary analysis of data growing out of this project. These include a previous paper on deference behavior, upon which this article is based (Silverman and Maxwell 1975), and one on the intensity of funeral behavior (Maxwell and Maxwell 1976). Although space does not allow us to consider the full range of our research concerns here, we expect, needless to say, to provide a more detailed discussion of these matters in the near future.

Notes

1. Philip Silverman (Ph.D., Cornell University) is Professor of Anthropology at California State University, Bakersfield. His research interests include political anthropology, particularly tribal-national relations, gerontology, and cross-cultural methods. He has done field work in rural Canada and among the Lozi in Zambia, and will shortly begin a study of the aged among ethnic groups in Bakersfield.

2. Robert J. Maxwell (Ph.D., Cornell University) is Research Anthropologist at California State University, Bakersfield. Is research interests include the perception of time and the management of spatial relations. He has done field work among Samoans and Tlingit and is presently enrolled in a graduate program in clinical psychology.

References

Abarbanel, Jay S. 1974. Prestige of the Aged and Their Control Over Resources. Paper presented at the annual meetings of the Gerontological Society, Portland, Oregon, October.

Arensburg, Conrad. 1968. The Irish Countryman. Garden City, New York: Natural History Press.

Beardsley, Richard K., John W. Hall and Robert E. Ward. 1959. Village Japan. Chicago: University of Chicago Press.

Dowd, John J. 1974. Aging as Exchange: A Preface to Theory. Paper presented at the annual meetings of the Gerontological Society, Portland, Oregon, October.

Fortes, Meyer. 1949. The Web of Kinship Among the Tallensi. London: Oxford University Press.

Goffman, Erving. 1956. The Nature of Deference and Demeanor. American Anthropologist 56: 473-502.

Grattan, Francis J.H. 1948. An Introduction to Samoan Custom. Apia, W. Samoa: Samoa Printing and Publishing Co.

Lenski, Gerhard. 1966. Power and Privilege: A Theory of Social Stratification. New York: McGraw-Hill.

Maxwell, Robert J., and Eleanor K. Maxwell. 1976. Constituents of Funeral Rites. Paper presented at the annual meetings of the Southwestern Anthropological Association, San Francisco, California, April.

Maxwell, Robert J., and Philip Silverman. 1970. Information and Esteem: Cultural Considerations in the Treatment of the Aged, Aging and Human Development 1 (No. 4) 361-92.
1971. An Informational Approach to the Treatment of the Aged, Paper presented at the annual meetings of the Gerontological Society, Houston, October.

Miller, James G. 1972. Living Systems: The Organization. Behavioral Science 17 (1): 1-182.

Murdock, George Peter, and Douglas R. White. 1969. Standard Cross-Cultural Sample. Ethnology 8 (4): 329-69.

Sheehan, Thomas. 1975. Senior Esteem as a Factor of Societal Economic Complexity. Paper presented at the annual meetings of the Gerontological Society, Louisville, Kentucky, October.

Silverman, Philip, and Robert J. Maxwell. 1971. Models of Aging. Paper presented at the annual meetings of the American Anthropological Association, New York City, November.1972. An Anthropological Approach to the Study of the Aged. Paper presented at the annual meetings of the Gerontological Society, San Juan, Puerto Rico, October. 1975. A comparative Study of Categories of Deference Displays Towards Old People. Paper presented at the annual meetings of the Gerontological Society, Louisville, Kentucky, October.

Simmons, Leo W. 1945. The Role of the Aged in Primitive Societies. New Haven: Yale University Press.

Stephens, William N. 1963. The Family in Cross-Cultural Perspective. New York: Holt, Rinehart and Winston.

Tooker, Elisabeth. 1964. An Ethnography of the Huron Indians. Bulletins of the Bureau of American Ethnology 190: 1-183.

Weber, Max. 1968. Economy and Society. Edited by Guenther Roth and Claus Wittich. Vol. I. New York: Bedminster Press. 1972. Class, Status, Party. In Status Communities in Modern Society. Holger R. Stubb, ed. Pp. 44-57. Hinsdale, IL: Dryden Press.

Weltfish, Gene. 1965. The Lost Universe. New York: Basic Books.

Young, Frank W., and Albert A. Bacdayan. 1965. Menstrual Taboos and Social Rigidity. Ethnology 4: 225-40.

Chapter 12

Chinese Young Adults and Elder Respect Expressions in Modern Times

Kyu-taik Sung

Introduction

China has been known to the world for its tradition of filial piety (孝)—the ideal and practice of the family-centered care and respect for the elderly. While the influence of this tradition has been weakened somewhat in the course of social and economic changes, it remains as the most important value that regulates young people's attitudes and behaviors toward the elderly in China (張文范, 1988; Chow, 1991; de Bary, 1995; Kong, 1995; Wang, 2001).

Teachings in filial piety originated in China. Confucius and his followers wrote the classics which prescribed moral cultivation, propriety, education, and filial piety, e.g., the Teachings of Filial Piety (孝經), the Book of Rites (禮記), Analects of Confucius (論語), Mencius (孟子), Doctrine of the Mean (中庸), and Great Learning (大學). For many generations, the teachings prescribed in these widely-quoted classics have greatly influenced family life and the moral aspect of the parent-child relationship of Chinese people, along with peoples of neighboring nations, e.g., Korea. Japan, and others in East Asia. [Chinese people include those in Hong Kong, Taiwan, and Singapore, and other Chinese communities in Asia.] Thus, Chinese people have a distinct cultural legacy.

Filial piety is essentially to direct young adults to have gratitude for the care and aids they received from their parents and, in return, to respect and care for the parents in old age (Li, 1985; Kong, 1995; Sung, 2001). The values of filial piety

have been shared by the Chinese and other East Asian people for many generations. The care and support for parents is a universal value in human society.
However, in China and East Asia the value has expanded its influence to every
sphere of people's life. It is reflected in their rituals, propriety, and even minute
details governing their manners of daily living (Streib, 1987; de Bary, 1995;
Kong, 1995; Chang, 1998).

In the teachings of filial piety, elder respect is the most stressed point.

Confucius prescribed the widely known five cardinal relationships, *wu lun* (
五倫). These are relationships between kings and subjects, fathers and sons,
husbands and wives, between brothers, and among friends. In these relationships,
three apply to family members, with the most fundamental relationship being that
between parents and children, wherein children are expected not only to care for
their parents but also to respect them.

The author does not intend to burden this chapter with a lengthy introduction
to issues associated with aging in the PRC. However, it is felt that readers in the
West might need additional information about the broad social and cultural context, in which the Chinese young adults practice elder respect.

China has gone through turbulent political changes. Following a series of the
changes in the early part of the past century, the nation has been under the rule of
the socialistic state, The People's Republic of China (PRC). At the wake of the
rule, Chinese people were discouraged to hold the traditional Confucian values
and the family-centered living style which the values upheld. Filial piety practiced in the family setting was seen to be incongruent with the ideology of the
state.

Traditionally, the family has been the arena wherein filial piety is practiced.
In recent decades, the family and its social environment have been changing along
with industrialization and urbanization in many regions of the PRC (Goldstein &
Ku, 1993; Leung, 1997; Pei & Pillai, 1999). In particular, socio-demographic
changes are noteworthy. As a result of family planning, fewer children are born.
The size of the family has declined dramatically while that of older population is
increasing fast (Cheng, 1995; Yi & Wenmei, 1994). Another major cause of the
reduction of family size is housing shortage, particularly in large cities, such as
Shanghai and Beijing (Wang, 2001). Consequently the burden of eldercare is
being placed on the shoulders of fewer adults. More married children are living
apart from their aging parents. The number of elderly people residing in old-age
homes is increasing (Eckholm, 1998). Younger generations are less dependent on
older generations for economic and social support. Now, they have more say over
their own lives and family matters. More women are working outside their home.
Younger generations appear less welded to the tradition than were their parents
and grandparents (Ma & Rosenberg, 1998). As the urban population grows and
the economy shifts away from farming; the source of wealth is moving from land
to money. This weakened elders' hold on their children, and led to the general
decline of the authority and status of the elderly within the family (Cai, Song,
Luo, & Jiang, 1994; Jia, 1988; Fei, 1985). Along with the changes, the ability of
the family to care for elderly members is weakening (Wang, 2001). In most

families, filial piety has been unquestioned. But, now, concerned Chinese feel that the cultural heritage is endangered.

However, the change has not induced a revolutionary shift in the way of caring for parents, as the following facts indicate.

Parents, whether they live together with their adult children or not, they still maintain frequent interactions with their adult children. In villages as well as in cities, parents still receive support from their children, despite that they have their own income (Goldstein & Ku, 1993; Leung, 1997; Pei & Pillai, 1999). Every age cohort has the value that it is their important role to support aged parents—a nationwide and common phenomenon in China.

Scholars insist that the traditional value continues to exert its influence as a regulator of behaviors of the young and the relations of family members (Liu, 1985; Kong, 1995; Chow, 1991; Olson, 1993; Parish & Whyte, 1978; Streib, 1987). Chow (1991) states that, except for the 10 years of the Cultural Revolution when the family system was in disarray and children were told not to respect heir parents, filial piety has generally been observed in China.

Most central to Chinese culture is the family, the fundamental unit of society. The family is chiefly responsible for socializing its members and for providing care and support for them. In most Chinese families, filial piety is still emphasized and family obligations remain strong (Whyte, 1995; Olson, 1993; Xie et al., 1996; Leung, 1997).

Riding on this cultural background, the principle policy orientation of the government of the PRC has been attaching great importance to the role of the family in caring for the elderly. In order to resolve the issue of population aging and the weakening self-supporting capability of families, various forms of social security measures are being instituted and a high priority is given to such public programs.

The fundamental principle of the PRC government is to facilitate the viable working relations between family support and social support. With this principle, the government is putting in order a new environment in which the at-home eldercare can be better provided. That is, the limitation of the family's caregiving capacity is augmented by the social support system which provides public services from the outside of the family, e.g., social and health care service agencies. (Wang , 2001)

Emphasis on family support for the aged is directly connected to the need to re-illustrate the Chinese family ethics rooted in filial piety.

The fundamental ideal underlying the support for the aged reflects the traditional Chinese values of "benevolent government" (仁政). The cardinal component consisting of the values is respect for the elderly. As discussed elsewhere in this book, 'care'—a synonym of providing care, services, and support—is a indispensable part of respect (Downie & Telfer, 1969; Li Chi 禮記).

In China, the first source of care for the aged is, thus, the family. In the family, care giving is taken for granted, as motivated by a sense of filial obligation and duty (Leung, 1997). The vast majority of elderly persons are legally to be supported by their own children. Elderly persons who do not have families are provided with food, clothing, medical care, housing, and burial expenses (The Five Guarantees, 五 保 戶). They are also provided with a retirement home—Homes for the Respect for the Elderly.

In villages, family ties are still strong, so that help is readily available to the rural elderly. Parish and Whyte (1978: 777) wrote, "Peasants in need continue to rely on their own families, and secondly the nearby families. Furthermore, they noted, "Parents expect to live with and be supported by their sons in their old age." Families still provide such support for older members. Not just people in rural areas do so. Even educated urbanites see strong family bonds as both natural and important (Streib, 1987). In Chinese culture, such a support relationship between parents and adult children is very much reciprocal. That is, what adult children do for their aged parents is believed to be a natural way of making repayment for the aids and support they received from their parents.

The bondage parents and children is thus underscored by reciprocity and interdependence between generations, a distinct cultural trait that persists among Chinese people (Pedersen, 1983). The Chinese accept dependency as a norm of reciprocity (Streib, 1987). The elderly do not view their dependency as a fatal attack on their self-esteem, and the young and middle-aged do not entertain illusions of perpetual self-sufficiency or disengagement from the old. Because of the norm of reciprocity and orientation to the family group, there is an acceptance of dependency as an inevitable part of growing old. This is in contrast to Western countries where the ideology of self-reliance and economic independence are fostered. Chinese society carries advantages for the frail or dependent elderly.

In this cultural context, adult children play a major role; they assist elderly parents and provide a safety net for them as their physical capacity wanes (Goldstein & Ku, 1992). Chinese sociologists, Pan and Pan (1984, p. 65) believed that the emphasis on mutual responsibilities between the generations will allow China to avoid the current serious social problems of Europe and America where many elderly people have no one to look after them and must spend their later years in solitude.

Meanwhile, the government of the PRC has made improvements in enlarging the sources of support available to the elderly and has been pragmatic in accepting the role of the family and making the children perform their filial duties. Though the state has found filial piety ideologically repulsive, it has tolerated it. What is more significant is that filial piety is used as the basis for the welfare network to support the elderly (Chow, 1991; Leung, 1997).

The policy for the pursuance of this national goal was clarified by the vice-premier Mr. G. Q. Wan (萬國權) of the government of the PRO, as follows (人民日報, 1999):

"As the structure of the traditional family changes, the population aging in our nation has already reached a very critical state. We Chinese people have a long tradition of respect and care for the elderly. We need to uphold this virtue and endeavor to enable our elderly people to be cared for, enjoy their life, and have meaningful later years."

The Constitution of the PRC states that the old have the right to material assistance from their adult children and be supported by them in old age. Article 49 of the constitution states that parents have the duty to rear and educate their minor children, and children who have come of age have the duty to support and assist their parents. Identically, Article 15 of the Marriage Law of the PRC promulgated in 1981 states that parents have the duty to rear and educate their children and children have the duty to support and assist their parents.

While the imposition of filial responsibility does not necessarily imply an acceptance of the value of filial piety, the two Articles show that the state has not found it necessary to suppress or counteract the influences of filial piety directed to respect and care for elderly parents and the aged at large (Chow, 1991).

The goals of the state coincided with the informal support for the elderly, in addition to the family support. Various informal support groups are involved in nationwide support programs for elderly persons, and this resulted in keeping the elderly integrated into the society (Olson, 1987; Leung, 1997).

In China, of all the elderly who are 60 years and older, only 1/3 receive pension, and the rest of them depend on family support. Even those who are pensioners receive care and support from their family. There are disparities among localities in terms of support for the aged. For instance, in Sandong Province, the aged received public support, e.g., pension, support from village, and five types of guarantees from the community (The Five Guarantees). Still those elderly persons who could not lead financially independent living reached 70%. However, the majority of the aged in the province depended on family support. (薛興利, 新相木, 劉桂鉋, 1998).

Leung (1997) states, "Policymakers of the PRC wish to endure that the traditional Chinese virtue of caring for the old remains intact." They have not turned children against their parents inasmuchas the socialist policies regarding distribution maintain the importance of old people's roles in the families and also help to maintain intergenerational bonds.

In parallel with such these familial and communal endeavors to care for the elderly, the government is developing the social security system, improving services for the elderly, providing allowances and tax benefits to caregivers.

Mr. W. F. Chang (張文范, 1998), Chairperson of Chinese Association of Aging, reiterated the societal purpose to pursue such a pluralistic goal.

> "The format of the Chinese eldercare is a combination of family care and social care. The care largely depend on the family. In the family, consisting of blood relations and marital relations, young members should fulfill the responsibility of providing elderly members with economic support, support for daily living, and emotional support. Such filial conducts form the foundation of the traditional Chinese way of eldercare, i.e. filial piety. We need to inherit this way of caring for elderly persons and promoted this way in this time when we construct the socialistic spiritual culture. In order for us to ensure happy old age for the elderly, we need to adopt the way, that is, a combination of two essential measures—family eldercare and social eldercare."

In Teachings of Filial Piety, a Confucian classic which laid down a number of roles and duties to be performed by filial children, is the following passage:

> "A filial son serves his parents by paying utmost respect for them, by happily serving them with foods and drinks, with concern and anxiety when they are ill, and in sorrow and mournfulness when they pass away."

In Book of Rite, another major Confucian classic, which also prescribed how parents are to be served, is the following passage:

> "There are three forms of filial piety. The first great form is respecting parents, the second form is to not put parents to shame and disgrace, and the third form is to serve them with sufficient nutrition."

Thus, the first and foremost duty of a son is to revere parents. In the long history of China, Chinese people have practiced filial piety in an expansive and inclusive way. A son must fulfill not only the duty of supporting parents with materials but also the duties of holding emotional feelings of respect toward them, behaving properly in the interaction with them, and not making them anxious and uncomfortable. These duties are broadly categorized into material support and spiritual support.

Material Support(膽養):

The fulfillment of these categories of filial piety is described in The 24 Stories of Filial Piety, widely read and endeared by Chinese people over several hundred years. The majority of Chinese young adults (20 years and older) responded to a questionnaire that children should care for and support parents in old age (亞細亞女性交流研究王刊, 1994).

Emotional support (安老): This means that the aged need to be provided not only with material support but also with emotional stability. That is, the young should secure the non-material aspect of the living of the aged. Traditionally, this type of support is provided in three ways: 1) Complying with the directives of parents, 2) Not making parents anxious and worry, and 3) Treating parents with propriety, i.e., respect and proper conducts.

A survey conducted in Jiangsi Province (江西省) found that adult children had expressed their concern over the emotional support to be provided to their parents. Of the 667 subjects, 86% responded that elderly support consists of not only material support but also spending time with parents, helping them to have comfortable life, having concern and worries over their well-being, and providing them with emotional support (人民日報, 1999). Under the law of the PRC

(高齡者權益保障法), the aged should be provided with emotional comfort along with financial support, care for daily living.

China's collective responsibility will continue to prevail and an individualist approach to provision for one's old age will not be as salient as in Western countries (Streib, 1987). It may be a little early to determine the full impact of this general trend upon the continuity of filial piety and elder respect.

As we look ahead into the twenty-first century, what changes can we forecast for the elderly in China? As the policy of modernization continues and the level of productivity rises, the implementation of social welfare programs is likely to continue. In this process, there will be the debate on how to share responsibilities for caring for elderly persons between the state and the family. Coale (1984) estimates that about 20% of China's population will be over 65 by 2035, partly as a consequence of the one-child family policy. This will profoundly affect the traditional norms, roles, and relationships.

However, traditional cultural patterns consisting of norms, roles, and relationships—those ways of organizing social life—tend to persist from generation to generation in China (Streib, 1987). Some of these patterns are deeply embedded in centuries of Chinese tradition. Filial piety has been a paramount value in China for centuries and welded the generations together (Hsu, 1948). However, the value is so deeply embedded in Confucian norms that it remains a strong theme that results in an almost automatic sense of obligation to care for one's frail parents, and also in the automatic expression of elder respect (Streib, 1987).

In Western countries, the ideology of self-reliance and economic independence are fostered. In contrast, Streib (1987) raised two determinants that greatly affect the living of the elderly in rural China—(1) traditional cultural patterns which are rooted in the values of filial piety and (2) economic conditions under which the aged live in agricultural economy. As consequences of these living patterns, Chinese families, particularly those in rural areas, are maintaining traditional lifestyles in terms of 'respect and care' for elderly parents.

Several studies of contemporary China (Kirkby, 1985; Liang et al., 1985; Parish & Whyte, 1978; Streib, 1987) pointed out that urban China is probably changing at a faster pace than other parts of China, yet this has not resulted in major destabilization of the relations between the generations. Similarly, Whyte and Parish (1984) noted, "The power of the aged has clearly softened somewhat, but strong feelings of respect and mutual obligation remain to bind the generations together." A similar view was expressed by Chow (1991), Xie et al. (1996), and Ng et al. (2002).

The views presented above attests the persistence of the Chinese tradition.

It is intriguing to see to what extent the tradition of filial piety is being preserved by contemporary Chinese people who have gone through the turbulent political changes. Are they still practicing the traditional virtue of elder respect? Empirical data on elder respect among the Chinese introduced in western journals and books is very scarce.

To examine changes occurring in any given society, one would have to look into younger people to find the potential source of the changes. They are likely to contract new values that are different from their parents' and be less supportive of the traditional norms governing the ways of treating older adults. However, they will be an essential part of the support system for the old. For the present study, Chinese young adults—college students—were chosen as study subjects for the present study. These young people are soon to assume great responsibilities for running various sectors of the national life of their country, wherein the ideology of filial piety originated and which has influenced other nations to practice the ideal of parent care. How properly these young people treat and care for the elderly is a critically important issue not only for elderly people but also for the nation as a whole.

The issues raised for the present study are threefold:

(1) Do young Chinese respect the elderly?

(2) If they do, in what way do they express their respect for the elderly? That is, what are the forms of elder respect by which they connote elder respect?

(3) How do certain personal characteristics of the study subjects differentiate the way they respect elders?

To answer these questions, the present study explored behavioral expressions that Chinese young adults exhibited to convey elder respect.

Identification of Traditional Forms

The following are the classics which laid down a number of rules and pre-scripts that adults were to follow in order to fulfill their filial duties, which included respect for parents, ancestors, elderly relatives, and teachers: The Book of Rites (Li Chi 禮記, Confucian teachings on rites or propriety), Teachings of Filial Piety (Hsiao Ching 孝經, guidelines for the practice of filial piety), Analects of Confucius (Lun Yu 論語, sayings and deeds of Confucius and his disciples on a scope of subjects including education and moral cultivation), Works of Mencius (Meng Tzu 孟子), a collection of opinions and conversations of Mencius, a principal disciple of Confucius), Doctrine of The Mean (Chung Yung 中庸), Confucius' dis-courses on the universal moral order—the cultivating the person, regulating of the family, ordering the state, and pacifying the world), and Great Learning (Ta Hsueh 大學), prescribing the aims of human existence and steps and methods that should be adopted to achieve them, the gate through which first learners enter into Confucian virtue.). The two of the above classics—The Book of Rites and Teachings of Filial Piety—elaborately prescribe the ideals of filial piety and the ways in which the ideals should be put into actions in the family setting. And, Analects of Confucius, Works of Mencius, Doctrine of The Mean, and Great

Learning are the well-known 'Four Books' most cherished by Confucian scholars. These classics are widely quoted in discussions of the meanings and practices of filial piety, and they contain discourses on the way of elder respect.

Passages in the above classics were explored to identify the forms and expressions of elder respect. Initially, the seven cross-cultural forms distinguished by Silverman and Maxwell (1978) were chosen as reference forms, which are service respect (providing housekeeping service), victual respect (serving drinks and foods), gift respect (bestowing gifts), linguistic respect (using respectful language), presentational respect (showing courteous appearances), spatial respect (furnishing honorable seats or places), and celebratory respect (celebrating birthdays). These forms were identified based on data from 186 distinctive world areas which included China, Korea, and Japan.

The author collaborated with two Neo-Confucian scholars to explore forms of elder respect. Relevant passages in the classics describing forms and expressions of elder respect that fit into the seven reference forms were located and compared to delineate specific forms of elder respect. While the reference forms guided the analysis, other forms were allowed to emerge in the process of the exploration. For instance, the form of care respect was distinguished by one or more expressions directed to provide care and services for parents. In the case of Teachings of Filial Piety, all but one of its chapters were dedicated to the prescriptions of various types of care and services for parents. All these chapters combined were categorized as the form of care respect, which includes service respect that Silverman and Maxwell distinguished. Excerpts of some of these chapters are presented in the following section. In other instances, an entire paragraph or a whole chapter described how to connote a single form of respect. For instance, in The Book of Rites, Chapters 20, 21, and 22 dealt with respect for parents after their death. These chapters were transformed into ancestor respect. In contrast, the following single passage was considered to reflect two different ways of elder respect—salutatory respect and presentational respect: "When a son is called by parents, he should answer 'Yes' politely and greet them in a courteous manner. In entering and exiting their room, the child should keep sincere and respectful posture" (Book of Rites, Bk. 2, Ch. 12). An inference was made based on the meanings of two or more sentences or passages. For instance, the statements "A child should use proper language" (Teachings of Filial Piety, Ch. 4) and "A gentleman should speak the proper words in the proper tone of voice" (Analect, Bk. 8, Ch. 4) were interpreted as expressions of linguistic respect. Similarly, precedential respect was inferred from "Allowing visitors to enter a room first" (Book of Rites, Bk. 1, Ch. 1) and "Not leaving a drinking table before the elderly had done so" (Analect, Bk. 10, Ch. 13). Passages prescribing the same form and expression of elder respect were found in two or more of the four classics. In this case, only one of those passages was quoted.

The interpretation and categorization of the forms and expressions of elder respect were cross-checked by independent testimonies of the author and the two analysts who conducted the exploration separately. Any form cited by two or more of the analysts was counted for. Forms and expressions of elder respect were subsequently defined.

The following are various expressions of respect discovered in passages in Chinese and English versions of the classics (Legge, 1960; Sung, 2000, 2001). In the exploration of the classics, the following 15 forms and expressions of thereof were identified.

Traditional Forms of Elder Respect

FORMS AND EXPRESSIONS OF ELDER RESPECT

Form 1   Care respect (Providing care and services)
    1. Providing affective care
       * Making elders comfortable
       * Being considerate to elders
    2. Providing instrumental services
       * Housekeeping for elders
       * Spending time with elders

Form 2   Consulting respect (Asking for consent and advice)
    1. Consulting with elders
    2. Asking elders for advice

Form 3   Victual respect (Serving foods and drinks)
    1. Serving foods and drinks of elders' choice

Form 4   Acquiescent respect (Complying with elders' wishes)
    1. Being obedient to elders
    2. Listening to elders' words

Form 5   Gift respect (Bestowing gifts on elders)
    1. Providing parents with material things

Form 6   Celebrative respect (Celebrating birthdays in honor of elders)
    1. Celebrating elders' birthday

Form 7   Linguistic respect (Using proper language to convey a sense of respect)
    1. Using respectful language
    2. Calling elders by their titles

Form 8   Precedential respect (Giving precedential treatment)
    1. Bestowing services or convenience first

Form 9 Presentational respect (Holding proper manners to convey respect)
  1. Holding respectful manners
  2. Showing proper physical appearance

Form 10 Salutatory respect (Greeting elders with respect)
  1. Greeting
    * Placing hands together
    * Bowing or bending body forward

Form 11 Spatial respect (Furnishing elders with honorable seats)
  1. Furnishing with a seat of honor

Form 12 Ancestor respect (Worshipping ancestors)
  1. Paying respect to ancestors
    * Commemorating ancestors' death anniversaries
    * Attaining wishes of ancestors

Form 13 Public respect (Respecting elders of larger society)
  1. Respecting elders of other families
  2. Caring for neighborhood elders

Form 14 Identifying respect (Identifying with elders)
  1. Identifying with elder's values
  2. Identifying with elder's lifestyles

Form 15 Privacy respect (Respecting privacy of elders)
  1. Respecting elders' personal privacy

Conception of Elder Respect

As discussed elsewhere, elder respect is intended to convey an altruistic and benevolent sense of regard to older persons (Downie & Telfer, 1978; Dillon, 1992). It involves practical concerns as well as emotion or feeling; the practical concerns and emotion tend toward outward expressions of and actions for respect (Dillon, 1992; Gibbard, 1990: 264-69). Hence, respect is an open, visible, and matter-of-fact behavioral expression toward elder persons (Silverman & Maxwell, 1978: 96).

Cultural influence has a significant effect on such expressions of elder respect (Streib, 1987; Sokolovsky, 1990; Homes & Holmes, 1995; Palmore & Maeda, 1985). In a culture, values, norms, roles, and patterns of social interactions associated with elder respect persist from generation to generation. Chinese people have a distinct tradition of elder respect. The Chinese shared this tradition with other East Asian nations (Silberman, 1962; Lang, 1946; Park, 1983). The traditional basis of elder respect is Confucian teachings of filial piety discussed above.

Until now, elder respect has been described in abstract terms; it has been a concept too general to provide clear guidance for practice and research.

Respect comes from the Latin 'respectus', which means "to look back at or to look again" (Webster's). The idea of looking to or giving attention to is synonymous with words such as regard and consideration (Webster's). As Downie & Telfer (1969) and Dillon (1992) state, attention is a central aspect of respect; we respect a person by paying careful attention to the person and taking the person seriously. Furthermore, these scholars defined that care is one kind of respect.

Respect, however, calls for more than our attention; it requires certain actions or forms of conduct, e.g., personal service or some actual work (Gibbard, 1990: 265; Kelly, 1990; Finkel, 1982; Sung, 1998; Ingersoll-Dayton & Saengtienchai, 1999). As Silverman and Maxwell (1978) define, elder respect is an open, visible, and matter-of-fact behavioral expression or action. In respecting a person, we consider and take certain forms of conduct deserved by or appropriate to the person (Gibbard, 1990). That is, we treat a person in a certain manner or act in particular ways to respect the person. Respect, then, needs to be manifested in concrete behavioral expressions oriented toward caring for others (Downie & Telfer, 1969; Dillon, 1992). Such expressions would include vocal sounds (ex. greeting, calling), physical movements (ex. serving, guiding), bodily movements (acknowledging, polite posture), appearance (ex. proper dressing, grooming), and so forth (Sung, 2001; 2004). A respectful person exhibits these explicit gestures or expressions that connote respect. Both the respecter and the respected would perceive these gestures as significant symbols (Hewit, 1988), allowing the meaning of respect to be shared with others who make the same gestures or expressions. Accordingly, a respecter should be able to say by concrete gestures and expressions they can demonstrate elder respect. Only when the concept of respect is specifically defined and related actions are implemented by such behavioral expressions, would respect become meaningful to the respecter as well as the respected.

For older persons, food, clothing, shelter, health care, and security are all necessities. But they have another cardinal need. That is, the need to be treated with respect (Reichel, 1995; Leininger, 1990; Sung, 2001; 2004). Significantly, the elderly respected tend to have greater life satisfaction, which in turn enhances their sense of usefulness and involvement in community, family, or significant others (Applegate & Morse, 1994; Ghusn et al., 1996). Elder respect is, therefore, an important factor in uplifting their status, improving their sense of well-being, and integrating them fully into family and society (Nydegger, 1983; Leininger, 1990; Riley & Riley, 1994).

A reason for elder respect may arise from a young person's inner feeling of respect for elders, willingness to repay the debt to them, or personal desire to please them. In contrast to this voluntary and truthful expression, a young person, who has to express respect without such feelings or under pressure, his other expression may turn to be an outward gesture only without the true feeling.

The expressions of elder respect are considered to be person related. That is, the expressions are connected to a social order in which there are distinct types of interpersonal relations governing at least the four groups aforementioned: i.e., the primary group (parents, elderly relatives), a secondary group (teachers, closely related seniors), a tertiary group (seniors at work places, formal organizations), and a fourth group (seniors at large). In most instances, the extent of respect might be considered to vary in this order. One would then analyze the extent to which the respecter is related to the respected, elder(s), who belongs to the primary group or other groups in the social order taking into account caring attitudes and behaviors, intimacy, indebtedness, and affection of the former toward the latter.

The present study explored the form of elder respect most frequently used by the respecter in conveying respect to elderly persons belonging to the groups. In addition, the study assessed the degree of importance (or the weight) given to the forms by the respecting person. The objective of the assessment of importance was to see to what extent the respecter considered the form of respect to be important to himself or herself according to his or her own judgment. In this way, this study explored explicit forms of elder respect practiced by Chinese young adults.

Methods

In this study, identifying the most widely practiced forms of elder respect was of central importance. For this purpose, the study surveyed college students in three different locations in the PRC: Shanghai, Nanjing, and Qindao in Shandong Province.

Before undertaking the construction of a questionnaire, 28 students from the PRC, who were studying at two different universities in the United States, were asked to provide a list of expressions of elder respect they most often used when they were in their mother country. The researcher provided them with a list of various expressions of elder respect reported by the above mentioned studies. The students, selected at random from the Chinese students at the universities, were asked to give expressions of elder respect which they practiced often and felt important. They were also asked to give one of more forms of elder respect other than those shown in the list. In this preliminary exploration, two new items which have not been reported by the previous studies emerged: 1) identifying with elders' ideals and lifestyles (identifying respect) and 2) respecting elders' privacy and personal life (privacy respect).

In translating the questions, the translation-back-translation procedure was employed; the bilingual investigator prepared the questions in Chinese and then had another bilingual to translate them into English. A third bilingual translated the translated questions back into Chinese. The three translators compared the questions in both language versions and judged that both were culturally appropriate and linguistically equivalent.

Two sets of questionnaires were administered to the study subjects. Each questionnaire contained 29 items asking 'frequency' with which the respondents practiced each of the expressions of elder respect. These questions were followed by the identical 29 items, which asked to rate the degree of 'importance' they assigned to each of the items. The first four expressions (spending time, housekeeping, being considerate, and making comfortable) indicated the form of care respect, the next two expressions (obeying and listening) indicated acquiescent respect. These were followed by two items (using respectful language and using titles) indicating linguistic respect. Similarly, the rest of the forms, (except victual respect, privacy respect, and identifying respect), were indicated by two indicators.

These items were followed by six items regarding socio-demographic items, e.g., gender, age, marital status, education, living arrangement (whether or not living with parents), and residential area (urban or rural). Last three items were regarding the quality of supporting relationship between the respondents and their parents.

Frequency with which they practiced each item was rated on a 5-point scale *(5=practiced always, 4=practiced often, 3=practiced sometimes, 2=practiced rarely, 1=never practiced),* and the level of importance assigned to the item was rated on a five-point scale *(5=very important, 4=rather important, 3=neither important nor unimportant, 2=no so important, 1=not important at all).* The extent to which each of these forms was associated with the socio-demographic characteristics was checked. The instructor explained the voluntary nature of participation and asked the subjects to complete the anonymous, self-administered questionnaire. Over 90 percent of the subjects in each class returned completed questionnaires.

The questionnaires were administered at universities in three different cities in the PRC to find out the forms of elder respect commonly used by the young adults: Shanghai, Nanjing, and Qingdao. The cities are situated in the Central-Eastern China, where the most dynamic social and economic changes are taking place. By and large, Shanghai, the Metropolis of the PRC, is the most industrialized and urbanized; Nanjing, a medium-size city, holds cultural, intellectual, and trade centers; and Qingdao, a smaller industrialized city is surrounded by largely rural communities. Thus, the study subjects were young adults studying at universities in the highly urbanized social environment. In each of the cities, two universities were selected at random. Data were collected from a sample of altogether 1,202 students from the three locations: 402 in Nanjing, 405 in Shanghai, and 404 in Qingdao. At each university, the subjects were selected at random from 4~6 classes in social sciences and business administration. All these universities are state-supported coeducational institutions with socially and economically diverse student bodies.

Analyses and Findings

RESPONDENTS' BACKGROUND

The study subjects cited a variety of behavioral forms by which they expressed elder respect and on which they gave importance. In the following, results of analyses of their responses to the questionnaires, subsequent identification of the forms of elder respect, and exploration of association between the ratings of the forms and sociodemographic characteristics of the respondents are described.

The majority of the respondents were young adults attending colleges; 89% of them were between 20 and 29 years of age (20-24: 70%; 25-29: 19%); 59% were undergraduate students, 25% graduate students, 5% doctoral degree holders, and 11% with other degrees; 57% were male and 43% female; 68% were single and 32% married; 63% were living separately from their parents and 37% living with their parents; 83% were living in urban area and 17% in rural area.

To examine the comparability of sociodemographic characteristics of the respondents in the three geographic locations, analyses were undertaken by dividing the sample into three groups. Chi-square tests were performed to compare the groups by socio-demographic variables. The respondents in the three locations varied by marital status, living arrangement, and area of residence. In other characteristics, there was no difference among the groups at the statistically significant level.

By marital status, the group in Shanghai had more unmarried respondents than the groups in Nanjing and Qingdao respectively (Unmarried: Shanghai 83%; Nanjing 64%, Qingdao 49%; Married: Shanghai, 17%; Nanjing 36%, Qingdao 51%), [Results of Chi-square test: $X^2=228.06$, df=2, sig.= .001]. Thus, those in Shanghai had substantially more unmarried respondents than two other areas. The three groups varied by living arrangement as well. The group in Shanghai had much fewer respondents living with their parents than did the groups in Nanjing and Qingdao respectively (Living together: Qingdao 51%, Nanjing 39%, Shanghai 12%; Living separately: Shanghai, 88%, Nanjing 61%, Qingdao 49%) [$X^2=80.02$, df=2, sig.=.001]. These data indicate that the group in Shanghai, the most urbanized metropolis of the PRC, had considerably fewer respondents living with their parents than those of Nanjing and Qingdao respectively. By residential area, Nanjing had more rural-area dwellers than did the two other areas; conversely Shanghai and Qingdao respectively had more urban-area dwellers (Rural residents: Qingdao 46%, Nanjing 25%, Shanghai 13%,; Urban residents: Shanghai 87%, Nanjing 75%, Qingdao 54%) ($X^2=27.43$, df=2, sig.= .001). Thus, there were more urban residents in Shanghai and Nanjing than in Qingdao. As the prominent names of the three cities in PRC signify, the majority of the respondents schooling in these cities are unmarried young adults who dwell in the urban areas afar from their home.

Table 12-1. Ratings of Frequency and Importance per Forms of Elder Respect
Chinese Respondents (N=1,202)

Forms of Elder Respect	Frequency			Importance			Overall* Ranking
	Rank	Mean	S.D. (%)	Rank	Mean	S.D. (%)	
Presentational	1	4.25	.85	5	4.06	.85	2
Linguistic	2	4.09	.89	3	4.10	.81	1
Precedential	3	3.95	.90	7	3.89	1.01	5
Spatial	4	3.90	.89	4	4.08	.91	4
Salutatory	5	3.87	.88	6	3.91	.92	7
Care	6	3.74	.99	1	4.21	.77	3
Acquiescent	7	3.72	.96	14	3.39	1.16	10
Privacy	8	3.65	1.04	9	3.82	1.36	5
Victual	9	3.64	1.67	2	4.12	.89	7
Celebrative	10	3.63	1.09	12	3.57	.99	11
Identifying	11	3.60	1.05	11	3.76	.98	11
Ancestor	12	3.58	1.15	8	3.88	1.02	9
Public	13	3.46	1.09	10	3.77	1.19	13
Consulting	14	3.37	.98	15	3.29	.99	15
Gift	15	2.79	1.23	13	3.40	1.04	14

* Overall rank: (rank on frequency + rank on importance) / 2

RATINGS OF THE FORMS

Table 12-1 highlights an overview of the 15 forms that emerged in the exploration, and descriptive statistics about the forms, which are based on frequencies (means) of practice and ratings (means) of importance given to the forms.

In order to have an overview of the similarities between the young people of China and those in Japan in the way they expressed elder respect, the forms of elder respect that the two groups practiced were compared (Sung et al., 2006). The levels of the ratings based on the frequency with which both groups practiced the forms are by and large similar, although there is minor noticeable differences. The Japanese group practiced five forms (precedential, victual, celebrative, consulting, and gift) fewer times than the Chinese group. Overall, however, the differences between the two groups appear to be a matter of degree.

Ratings on Forms: Frequency and Importance

In the following, data on the 15 forms are analyzed in terms of two measures: the frequency with which the respondents cited the forms and the importance they gave to the forms. First, based on data on frequency (on the 5-point-scale), percentage was calculated; then, based on the size of percentage, each form was ranked. Secondly, based on importance ratings (based on another 5-point scale), percentage was obtained, and the form was ranked according to the size of the percentage (Table 12-1).

In terms of '*frequency*,' *presentational* respect (showing polite manners) was the most frequently cited form (the mean rating based on the 5-point scale = 4.25) and the second most often cited form was *linguistic* respect (using respectful language) (4.09). These two forms were practiced slightly more frequently than 'often.' They are followed by *precedential* respect (giving precedence) (3.95, the 3rd), *spatial* respect (furnishing seats & places tied to honor) (3.90, the 4th), *salutatory* respect (greeting) (3.87, the 5th), *care* respect (giving care & services) (3.74, the 6th), *acquiescent* respect (obeying orders & listening) (3.72, the 7th), privacy respect (respecting privacy) (3.65, the 8th), *victual* respect (serving choice foods and drinks) (3.64, the 9th), *celebrative* respect (celebrating birthdays) (3.63, the 10th), *identifying* respect (identifying with elders' values and lifestyles) (3.60, the 11th), and *ancestor* respect (worshipping ancestors) (3.58) the 12th. These 10 forms were practiced fairly 'often.' The rest of the forms—*public* respect (respecting elders at large) (3.46, the 13th), *consulting* respect (seeking advise and consultation of elders) (3.37. the 14th), and *gift* respect (bestowing gifts) (2.79, the 16th)—were practiced close to 'sometimes.'

Next, in term of "*importance*," *care* respect was the highest rated form (4.21), followed by *victual* respect (4.12), *linguistic* respect (4.10), *spatial* respective (4.08), and *presentational* respect (4.06). These five forms were rated roughly 'rather important'—care respect being the most important of all. The 6th~13th ranking forms are *salutatory* respect (3.91), *precedential* respect (3.89), *ancestor* respect (3.88), privacy respect (3.82), *public* respect (3.77), *identifying* respect (3.76), and *celebrative* respect (3.57). These forms were rated nearly 'important' to fairly 'important.' The rest—*gift* respect (3.40), *acquiescent* respect (3.39), and *consulting* respect (3.29)—were rated close to "neither important nor unimportant."

The 12 of the 15 forms were accounted for by two or more indicators in order to replenish information on the expressions of elder respect. (Forms conveying victual, identifying, and privacy respect were accounted for by a single indicator. Regarding indicators of the forms, refer to the questionnaires in Appendix.). Overall, the majority of the 15 forms were practiced often and rated important.

Mean ratings of all the forms (based on importance) were positively correlated with each other at the statistically significant levels (<.05~<.001), correlation coefficients ranged from .63 to .41 (N=1191~1203). Similarly positive correlations were found among the ratings of all the 15 forms (on frequency) (r=.55~.37, p<.001, N=1191~1203). These data suggest that, although each of the forms reflects an action or a behavior that demonstrates a particular way in which older adults are respected, the forms are interrelated in their meanings and practices. In the description of the holistic meaning of elder respect, all these forms would have to be considered since they in combination portray elder respect expressed by the young adults in China.

Meanwhile, the mean ratings of frequency and those of importance are positively correlated at the statistically significant level (r=,77, p<.01). The results of the following basic analyses also suggest that the two separate ratings are positively associated. The association is suggested by the similarity between the ranking of the 15 forms based on frequency and the ranking of those forms based on importance. Spearman rank-order correlation between the two rankings—Rho=.67—suggests the association between the two ratings. These findings furthermore suggest that the extent to which the respondents practiced the 15 forms roughly explains the degree to which they gave importance to the forms.

Forms and Indicators: Meanings and Practices

In the following, data on indicators of the 15 forms and the meanings and practices of these forms are summarily discussed.

Care respect was accounted for by four indicators: 1) making elders comfortable, 2) being considerate to elders, 3) doing housekeeping for elders, and 4) spending time with elders (Table 12-2). Scores on these indicators were collapsed or averaged to obtain a mean score, i.e., the overall rating of care respect. As the table in Appendix shows, making elders happy and comfortable and being considerate to elders (the affective side of care respect) were practiced more often than spending time with elders and housekeeping for elders (the instrumental side of care respect). Despite that the ratings on the frequency with which the forms were practiced are relatively low, the ratings on importance given to these indicators are high; importance given to 'being kind and considerate to elders' is the highest of all the indicators. These high ratings led the form of care respect to be the highest ranking of all the 15 forms in terms of importance.

Care respect has significant implications for family members as well as for caregivers whose duties are to provide care and services for elderly persons. Respecting the elderly, particularly those who are in declining physical capacity, would allow the caregiver to make significant differences. Many elderly persons have a variety of problems. To resolve the problems, they most often depend on care providers. When they are dependent on the providers, respectful care has even more significant implications as one of psychosocial sources of the quality of their later life.

Acquiescent respect was accounted for by two indicators: 'being obedient to elders' and 'listening to what elders say.' Both were practiced similarly fairly 'often,' but the ratings on importance given to these indicators were respectively low, close to 'neither important nor unimportant.' To obtain an average score on this form, the two indicators were collapsed (as in the cases of other forms with two or more indicators). In the family- and group-oriented, and hierarchical society of the PRC, acquiescent respect has been a social norm. The young listen to the parents' advice and usually follow them. They tend to accept even scolding from elderly relatives and seniors, and do not talk back. In workplaces, informal advice from seniors is often obediently followed. And, at school, students obey their teachers almost unreservedly. Such behaviors' reflect young persons' deference and acquiescence toward parents and seniors. This behavioral pattern has been part of the traditional Chinese culture rooted in Confucian teaching. In this study, however, the young respondents gave a low rating on the importance of acquiescent respect, which is expressed by such deferent and assenting behaviors. Is this response reflecting a new trend of the young Chinese adults' attitude toward the elderly? We need to conduct a more careful exploration of the meaning of this response.

Victual respect—'serving drinks and foods of elders' choice'—was practiced fairly 'often' to 'sometimes,' and rated 'important.' In old age, receiving the foods and drinks of one's choice is a blessing. This form has been a highly admired and praised way of caring for elderly persons. Stories of filial children in China invariably describe how devoutly they served their aged parents with foods and drinks of the parents' choice.

Linguistic respect was accounted for by 'using respectful languages' and 'calling proper titles of elders.' Both were practiced 'often' and rated more than 'important.' The young commonly use honorifics when they salute, have conversation with, and write letters to elders so as to convey a sense of respect. The level of respect is reflected not only in different nouns but also verbs, prefixes, and suffixes, and even phrases and sentences when these are used in interaction with parents, teachers, seniors, elders or superiors. Elder respect is built into Chinese language. The traditional way of conveying this form of respect is much more complex, although the use of honorifics has been considerably simplified.

Table 12-2 Ratings (Means) of Indicators of Elder Respect
(N=1,202)

Indices of Forms of Elder Respect	Means (SD) (Frequency)	Means (SD) (Importance)
Care Respect		
* Spending time with elders	3.47 (.84)	4.24 (.80)
* Doing housekeeping for elders	3.57 (.89)	4.10 (.88)
* Being kind and considerate to elders	3.93 (.99)	4.41 (.79)
* Making elders happy and comfortable	4.00 (.86)	4.09 (.97)
Acquiescent Respect		
* Obeying what elders say	3.68 (1.09)	3.36 (.89)
* Listening to what elders say	3.76 (.87)	3.42 (.91)
Linguistic respect		
* using proper language	4.10 (.90)	4.13 (.80)
* calling elders by title	4.08 (1.10)	4.06 (1.03)
Salutatory Respect		
* acknowledging elders	3.84 (.89)	3.97 (.82)
* greeting elders	3.90 (.88)	3.85 (.96)
Consulting Respect		
* consulting with elders	3.21 (1.09)	3.32 (1.06)
* asking elders for advice	3.53 (.98)	3.26 (1.05)
Presentational Respect		
* holding polite manners	4.24 (.85)	4.28 (.89)
* wearing proper dress	4.26 (.1.14)	3.83 (1.03)
Precedential Respect		
* serving elders first	3.96 (1.00)	4.02 (.85)
* allowing elders to go first	3,94 (.90)	3.76 (1.06)
Public Respect		
* serving neighborhood elders	3.25 (1.09)	3.65 (.91)
* giving up seats for elders	3.68 (.89)	3.88 (.94)
Celebrative Respect		
* visiting elders on birthdays	3.62 (1.03)	3.57 (.90)
* making calls on elders' birthdays	3.65 (1.06)	3.58 (.92)
Gift Respect		
* presenting gift to elders	2.68 (1/13)	3.22 (.92)
* attaining elders' wishes	2.90 (1.00)	3.58 (.97)
Spatial Respect		
* Letting elders chair meetings	3.82 (1.10)	3.80 (1.02)
* Offering honorable seat	3.98 (1.04)	3.99 (.95)
Victual Respect		
* serving drinks and foods	3.64 (.95)	4.12 (.82)
Identifying Respect		
* identifying with elders	3.60 (.96)	3.76 (.98)
Privacy Respect		
* respecting elders' privacy	3.65 (1.06)	3.82 (.89)
Ancestor Respect		
* paying calls to ancestors' graves	3.45 (1.15)	3.79 (1.06)
* Commemorating death anniversaries	3.72 (1.06)	3.97 (.98)

Salutatory respect was indicated by 'acknowledging elders when one sees them' and 'calling them properly by title (Mr., Mrs., Dr. Prof., Chairperson, etc.).' Both indicators were practiced 'often' and rated 'important.' The use of honorifics and showing courteous manners and appearances are not enough. One must also exhibit the proper body language; the level of deference is usually determined by the degree to which one bows or raises the placed hands. Often such a salutatory movement is repeated or continued to convey deep respect or deference. This form has been the first social behavior that Chinese children learn at early ages from their parents and teachers. In recent years, some expressions of this form have been simplified. For instance, young people, as a gesture of acknowledging elders, shake hands with them instead of bowing. However, the traditional values still influence young people to perform in the old way. The young need to be aware of the importance of expressing these expressions timely and properly.

Consulting respect was indicated by 'consulting with elders' and 'seeking their advice.' Both were practiced close to 'sometimes' and given a rating close to 'neither important nor unimportant.' The young seek out elders' opinions on personal and family matters. By consulting, they implicitly show their respect to the elderly. Both the young and the old benefit from consultation: the former receive knowledge and assistance, and the latter feel appreciation, personal fulfillment, and respect. However, in this study, both indicators were rated not very positively.

Presentational respect, indicated by 'holding polite manners' and 'wearing proper dresses,' was practiced more than 'often.' But they decided that holding polite manners were more important than wearing proper dress. Young persons coming into contact with elders are expected to have dressed properly and to maintain a posture that is polite and deferent. Thus, arrogant and indifferent manners, and any type of appearance that would cause displeasure or disapproval of elders is considered not respectful. This form of respect is important to Chinese culture where deference and ritualistic mores are valued.

Precedential respect was indicated by 'serving elders first' and 'allowing elders enter a room or an elevator first.' Both indicators were practiced 'often' and rated 'important.' The gist of this form is 'to serve elders first.' Exemplars are providing foods, drinks, and assistance to elders first, giving precedence to their tastes and convenience; for instances, by allowing them to go through doorways first, to get in and out of cars first, and to use a shower or Bath first. Such precedential treatment is arranged often in order of seniority or age, or the amount of respect bestowed upon the elderly. In China, where elderly persons tend to be conscious of age-related prestige, such a treatment is taken to be important.

Public respect was indicated by 'serving neighborhood elders' and 'giving up seats for elders on buses or street cars.' These were practiced close to 'sometimes' and given ratings close to 'neither important nor unimportant.' In modern China, this form reflects societal efforts—the public as well as the private—to promote the status of the elderly at large and to provide the elderly with services outside the family. Public and private groups provide a range of community-based services for needy elderly persons, educate the young to treat elders properly, and issue a warning on abuse and neglect of the elderly. The values of public respect are rooted in traditional Confucian tenets. The Master envisioned respectful relations between all members of the family and society. He said, "Treat with reverence the elders in your own family, so that elders in other families shall be similarly treated" (Teachings of Filial Piety, Ch. 2). Thus, propriety extends beyond the boundary of the family.

Celebrative respect was indicated by 'visiting elders' and 'making telephone calls' on elders' birthdays. Both indicators were practiced a little more often than 'sometimes' and given a fairly 'important' rating. The birthday event signals the entrance into old ages marking a crucial event within a parent's life-cycle, and it becomes a special occasion for family celebration to honor the aged parent. Throughout the year adult children make telephone calls and visit their parents to celebrate their birthdays and other family events. An important purpose of such events is to dramatize the esteem accorded to elderly parents.

Gift respect was indicated by 'presenting gift' and 'attaining elders' wishes.' Gift giving was practiced 'sometimes' and rated 'neither important nor unimportant.' Attaining elders' wishes was rated a little more 'important' than giving gifts. The usual types of gifts are artifacts, e.g., clothes, money, and other things of symbolic values. Other types can be achieving their wishes or desires. Giving pocket money and monetary gifts have become a popular way of practicing this form of respect. Presenting gifts for seniors has been endemic to Chinese people.

Spatial respect, indicated by 'offering the role of chairing meetings' and 'offering honorable seats,' was practiced close to 'often' and rated fairly 'important.' In the Chinese culture, where much energy is expended to select auspicious sites for houses and graves, this form has been an important way of conveying respect. In gatherings, elders are furnished with center or head seats, chairs by the fireplace, or quiet rooms. Ancestors' graves are built on well-drained and sunny hillsides. The provision of such seats and sites reflect adult offspring's respect, obligation, and sacrifice for elderly relatives and forebears.

Identifying respect—'identifying with elders' values and lifestyles'—was practiced fairly 'often' and given a fairly 'important' rating. A young person expresses respect by following the path of or by identifying with values, beliefs, thoughts, behaviors, and lifestyles of closely related elderly persons, e.g., parents, teachers, seniors, or respected leaders. One can find many cases of this way of elder respect in Chinese historical writings, literary works, and folk stories. Thus, this form has been an age-old way of manifesting one's respect for elders with a distinguished status or a remarkable achievement.

Privacy respect—'respecting elders' privacy and personal life'—was practiced fairly 'often' to 'sometimes' and rated fairly 'important.' The respondents would respect the privacy of elders by providing them with a quiet room or a comfortable place for rest, by keeping confidential about personal matters of elders, or by making a certain arrangement for them to maintain their personal privacy and confidentiality. Traditionally, the matter of privacy has been considered alien to Chinese culture, wherein people kept closely knit, interdependent intergenerational relations. But, the Chinese young adults in this study placed a high rating on this form of respect. This way seems to be a newly emerged form of respect.

Ancestor respect was indicated by 'visiting ancestors' graves' and 'commemorating their death anniversaries.' Calling to the graves was done 'sometimes' and death anniversaries were observed fairly 'often.' They gave a rating of fairly 'important' to both indicators. Respecting ancestors is a core form of filial piety in Chinese culture. Ancestors are worshipped in order to repay the debt that descendents incurred from them and other forebears. On the anniversary rite for a deceased ancestor within a certain generation, family members gather in a clean room or a Buddhist temple, where their ancestor's tablet and the picture are kept, arrange prepared foods and drinks on a table for sacrifice, and make bows to the tablet or the picture. After the rite, parents introduce to their children memorable stories about the ancestor, so that the younger generation does not forget their origin and the favor they received. Rebuilding or decorating ancestors' graves is also an important way of paying respect. The keeping genealogy and the maintenance of the clan society, still extensively practiced in the PRC as well as in Hong Kong, Taiwan, and Singapore reinforce ancestor worship. An attribute of this form of respect is carrying out the wishes of ancestors mindful of family continuity.

It is noteworthy that care respect emerged as the highest ranking form in terms of importance. The second most important form was victual respect. Thus, providing care and services, and serving foods and drinks were taken to be more important than all other forms of respect. These are, indeed, the types of respect that elderly persons would most likely be in need of and appreciative of.

These two forms are followed by five forms, whose ratings of importance are also 'important,' e.g., forms of linguistic, spatial, presentational, salutatory, and precedential respect. Thus, they gave importance to the ways of conveying respect by using proper language, offering seats tied to respect, showing proper manners, greeting elders, and serving elders first. These forms reflect symbolic displays of respect.

The rest of the forms were considered to be fairly important as well. Specifically, worshipping ancestors, respecting elders at large, identifying with elders' values and lifestyles, and celebrating elders' birthdays were rated nearly important. Only forms of consulting, acquiescent, gift, and celebrating were given a rating of close to not so 'important.' One might conjecture that some respondents might have ambivalence in practicing those forms. On would also surmise that, as they were away from their parents and financially unable to purchase gifts or make a trip to their home, they had few chances for practicing these forms, whereby they could not give a high rating to the forms. Nevertheless, importance given to these forms is slightly higher than 'neither importance nor unimportant.'

In terms of frequency, the most-often practiced forms were presentational respect and linguistic respect. Both forms are symbolic expressions of elder respect. So are precedential respect, spatial respect, and salutatory respect, which follow the above two forms. It is noteworthy that the young Chinese adults practiced these symbolic expressions of elder respect most often. These are outwardly and professed expressions that are easily perceived and observed by the elderly who are respected. Such symbolic expressions often turn to be ostensible and ritualistic behaviors demonstrated toward elders and seniors.

Ancestor worshipping would be done at their homes with their parents. The relatively infrequent practice of ancestor respect might be due to the fact that they could not hold ancestor worshipping rites as they were away from their parents under whose direction they practice this form of respect. However, they assigned a rating of 'important' to this form.

Personal Characteristics and Ratings of Selected Forms

In the following, the relations between the respondents' sociodemographic characteristics and four selected forms of elder respect are explored. These forms are care respect, acquiescent respect, ancestor, and public respect.

As has been described, care respect has special implications for care providers whether they are family members or professional care providers. The extent to which the care provider treats an elderly person with respect becomes a significant factor that affects the quality of the elderly person's later life.

Acquiescent respect has been a key expression of elder respect in Chinese culture. Traditionally, the nexus of propriety is deference, as prescribed in the following excerpt from a Confucian classic: "If a man is governed by showing deference, what difficulty would there be in performing propriety?" (Analect, Bk. 4, Ch. 13). As China modernizes rapidly, to what extent would young people retain this age-old virtue? This has become an issue of major concern for gerontologists as well as for concerned people in East Asia.

Ancestor worship is a prominent cultural heritage and a cardinal family ritual that Chinese people continue to treasure and uphold. It is a foundation of the family-centered practice of filial piety. The practice of it binds family members together to form an interdependent family system. It furthermore leads to the stability and continuity of the family. It is likely that Chinese people continue to practice this particular way of elder respect for a long time to come.

In contemporary China, public respect has emerged as an important way of lifting the status of the elderly and providing them with informal as well as formal care and services. China has been promoting community-based services for elderly persons at large beyond the boundary of the family. Public respect has special implications for the PRC under the socialistic political system, whose aged population is growing fast while the numbers of children and family caregivers are remarkably decreasing.

In the following how certain sociodemographic characteristics of the respondents are associated with these four forms will be explored.

Care Respect

A multiple regression analysis was conducted to predict the rating of care respect from the respondents' sociodemographic characteristics (age, marital status, gender, living arrangement, area of residence, and education). In the process of the analysis, these personal characteristics were entered along with area of residence–gender interaction factor. The results of the analysis suggest that, marital status and gender respectively accounted for significant variability of the ratings of care respect (explaining 33% of the variance). It is conceivable that the personal characteristics of the respondents other than gender and marital status are associated in some way with care respect. However, in the presence of all the characteristics, only the two characteristics emerged as the predictors of the rating of care respect at the statistically significant level.

Separate analyses showed that female respondents tended to give higher ratings on care respect than did male respondents. The mean rating on care respect based on importance ratings was 4.16 for the female and 3.88 for the male: mean difference= + - .28. Similarly, married respondents rated care respect higher than did unmarried ones. The mean on importance was 4.12 for the married and 3.93 for the unmarried: mean difference= + - .19.

With respect to the four indicators of care respect, 56% of female respondents gave a high rating on 'spending time with elders of care respect,' compared with 44% of male respondents who gave the same rating on the indicator [X^2=3.32, df=1, sig.<.50]; 58% of the females gave high rating on 'housekeeping for elders,' compared with 42% of the males [X^2=8.25, df=1, sig.<.08]; 57% of the females gave high rating on 'being considerate to elders,' compared with 43% of the males [X^2=20.50, df=1, sig.<.001]; and about 60% of the females gave high ratings on 'making elders comfortable,' compared with 40% of the males [X^2=89.10, df=4, sig.<.001]. Married respondents gave higher ratings on all the four indicators of care respect.

Acquiescent respect

This form was rated close to 'somewhat unimportant.' Despite such a low rating on importance, the respondents practiced this form fairly 'often.' Results of regression analyses suggest that gender (t=3.16, B=.097, p<.002) and marital status (t=2.44, B=.074, p<.015) respectively predict the rating of acquiescent respect at the statistically significant level (R^2=.523, F=8.18, p<.001). The sociodemographic characteristics excluded from these analyses are age, education, area of residence, and living arrangement. In these analyses also, the females and the married are found to have rated acquiescent respect higher in terms of both frequency and importance (the females: 3.94, the males 3.63, based on importance; the females 3.93, the males 3.74 based on frequency; the married: 4.10, the unmarried 3.84, based on importance; the married 4.11, the unmarried 3.93, based on frequency).

Ancestor respect

Ancestor respect was practiced a little more often than 'sometimes,' but it was rated close to 'important.' The results of a regression analysis show that gender (t=44.95, .099, p<.001)) and marital status (t=25.14, B=.157, p<.001) respectively predict the rating of this form at the statistically significant level (R^2=3.63, df=1, F=8.57, p<.003). The males and the married rated the form higher than did the females (3.98 vs. 377) and the unmarried (3.95 vs. 3.81), in terms of importance.

Public respect

Predictors of the ratings of public respect were also gender (t-26.22, B=.164, p<.001) and marital status (t=.28.4, B=.17.2, p<.001); (R^2=16.39, F=26.44, p<.001). The males and the married respectively rated importance of this form higher than did the females (3.89 vs. 3.65) and the unmarried (3.84 vs. 3.70).

Thus, gender and marital status were two factors which predicted the ratings of the four forms. However, the effects of gender were mixed. That is, the females tended to rate care respect and acquiescent respect higher than did the males, where as the males tended to rate public respect and ancestor respect higher than the females.

With regard to other personal characteristics (age, education, residential area, and living arrangement), differences between the mean ratings of the 15 forms and the subcategories of the characteristics were found to be statistically not significant, in the presence of all the characteristics. Ratings of the subcategories of age (20-24, 25-29, 30-34, 35-39, 40+) were not statistically associated with the mean ratings (X=22.84, df=16, sig.=.12). Similarly, the subcategories of education (undergraduate, graduate, post-graduate) were not associated with the mean ratings (X^2=9.52, df=8, sig.=.25). So are the cases of the subcategories of residential area (rural and urban) (t=-.480, df=1097, sig.=.631) and living arrangement (living with parent and living separately from parent) (t=-1.75, df=1094, sig.=.083).

To explore the underlying dimensions of the 29 indicators or expressions of elder respect, an orthogonal Varimax rotated factor analysis (with the principal component solution) was conducted based on the data on importance. Five factors with eigenvalue over 1 emerged. Of the 29 indices, 26 had loadings .50 or larger, which were chosen to indicate factors. The first factor, with eight loadings, labeled "symbolic respect," represents a set of eight expressions. These expressions reflect the observance of forms of elder respect ranging from greeting to proper manners. It has symbolic and ritualistic implications. The second factor, with six loadings, named "presenting respect," denotes offering material and non-material things that are tied to elder respect. The third factor, with five loadings, titled "obeying respect," embodies acquiescent and deferential behaviors. The fourth factor, with four loadings, labeled "caring respect," represents affective and instrumental caring behaviors. And, the fifth, with three loadings, labeled "ancestor respect," symbolizes ancestor worship. The five factors together accounted for 55% of the total variance. Thus, five factors or dimensions of elder respect emerged. The various expressions of elder respect may be reduced to these five dimensions—(1) symbolic respect, (2) presenting respect, (3) obeying respect, (4) caring respect, and (5) ancestor respect.

Intergenerational Support Relations

In order to obtain information on the support relationship between the respondents and elderly people, three questions were administered along with the 29 items on elder respect: (1) the respondent's satisfaction with attention and consideration given by elderly people (affective care); (2) the respondent's satisfaction with material support given to them by the elderly (material support); (3) the respondent's willingness to care for and support the elderly in old age (willingness to repay).

The first two variables—(1) and (2)—indicating support given by elderly relatives are positively correlated with the respondents' willingness to support for the elderly at the statistically significant level ($r=.317$, $.366$, $p<.01$, 2-tailed, $n=1,202$). This result suggests that the respondents who are cared for and supported by elderly relatives are likely to have willingness to provide support for the parents in old age. This, in turn, suggests that the young Chinese adults judged that the kindness received from their parents should be repaid. This response further indicates that the reciprocal nature of the intergenerational support relationship.

It might be added that parent's concern for respondents and their provision of material support for the respondents are positively correlated with the two indicators of acquiescent respect: obeying elders' orders ($r=.224$, $.202$; $p<.001$, 2-tailed, $n=1201$) and listening to what elders say ($r=.194$, $.221$) respectively.

Discussion

The forms of elder respect identified in the present study are not any different from, if not similar to, the traditional forms distinguished by the author in the study of South Korean young adults (Sung & Kim, 2002) and those forms reported by other researchers who studied how people express elder respect in Japan, Taiwan, Singapore, and Japan (Ingersoll-Dayton & Saengtienchai, 1999; Mehta, 1997; Palmore & Maeda, 1985). Almost all the forms previously distinguished are replicated in the present study. In addition to the forms, two new forms were included in the present study, i.e., privacy respect and identifying respect.

The findings on the Chinese young adults are, thus, consistent with findings on people of other East Asian nations. Thus, the present study and the previous studies yielded parallel results for the identification of a set of similar, if not identical, forms of elder respect, enlarging the power of the interpretation and confirmation of forms of elder respect widely practiced throughout East Asia.

A typology of 15 various forms of elder respect emerged. The typology sheds light on the long standing question on how the people in China wherein the traditional Confucian culture originated treat the elderly. The finding provides an empirical evidence to support the distinction of various ways of connoting elder respect by the young adults in China. It also reveals data on certain behavioral patterns that have not yet been reported by other studies of elder respect.

Multiple Ways of Elder Respect:

Overall, the majority of the forms identified in this study were frequently practiced and considered important by the Chinese young adults surveyed for this study.

The outstanding forms of elder respect emerged in this study are *presentational* respect (maintaining polite and deferent posture and dressing neatly and simply) and *linguistic* respect (using honorifics to convey the proper degree of respect when addressing to elders). The highest frequency and a very high rating of importance were assigned to these forms. Both behavioral expressions reflect symbolic displays of elder respect. These forms are followed by precedential respect (providing assistance to elders first, giving precedence to their preferences), spatial respect (furnishing elders with seats of honor or giving the central role to play in gatherings), and salutatory respect (exhibiting proper body language to convey respect in greeting elders), which are also symbolic expressions. In the case of linguistic respect, for instance, the expression is not simple in China. There is an abundance of honorific words and phrases in Chinese language that one is expected to properly use in the interaction with elders. Elder respect is built into Chinese language. By the degree of proficiency with which one uses honorifics in addressing elders and seniors, the propriety exercised by that person is usually judged. Although some expressions of linguistic respect are modified or simplified in recent years, by and large this form of respect remains part of Chinese culture.

Thus, the five outstanding forms—presentational, linguistic, precedential, spatial, and salutatory—turned out to be all symbolic displays of elder respect. Such displays of elder respect would seem to reflect the social structure of China, in which interpersonal relations between the old and the young tend to be conducted most often in a vertical social relation that demands the latter's deference, courtesy, and loyalty to the former. In these relations, symbolic expressions often transform into ritualistic manners and behavioral formalities. In the Chinese cultural context, one has to exhibit these types of elder-respecting forms properly and in a timely manner when he or she encounters elderly relatives, teachers, and related seniors. If the young person does not do so, he or she is violating the code of proper conduct.

The forms have deep roots in the traditional Chinese culture influenced by the Confucian teachings. Although young Chinese would seem to adhere to the practice of the forms less rigidly these days than their parents and grandparents did, the tradition of elder respect appears to persist, as the findings from the present study evidently suggest.

Care respect is the sixth most frequently practiced form. But, impressively, the young people assigned to this form the highest rating on importance. These respondents were young adults in colleges, who were living at distance from their elderly relatives. For them, it is not easy to provide care and services directly to the relatives living far away. Probably because of this reason, the frequency on care respect was relatively low. Nevertheless, the majority of them assigned the highest importance rating to this form. Care respect has significant implications for family members as well as for caregivers not only in Chinese culture but also in all other cultures. Specific indicators of care respect—spending times with elders, doing housekeeping for elders, being kind and considerate to elders, and making elders happy and comfortable—are all actions for caring and supporting elders. They reflect the values of caring for the elderly with benevolent actions and sympathetic concern deeply imbued with the sense of filial obligation to elderly relatives, repayment of debt to them, and affection toward them. These actions indicate two types of care: 'caring for elders with affective touches involving attention and concern' and 'providing them with instrumental services, e.g., housekeeping, spending time with them, assisting them to cross the road, etc.' Both types would have to be practiced in order to holistically convey care respect.

Acquiescent respect (obeying orders, listening to what elders say) is the 7th ranking in terms of frequency and the 14th in terms of importance. Traditionally, being acquiescent to elders was a major form of respect one should express toward parents and elders. The finding suggests that, although they practiced acquiescent respect relatively often in their college life, they did not feel this form was very important to them. The rating assigned to this form is close to 'neither important nor unimportant.' Should this rating be seen as an indication that the Chinese young adults were no longer taking obedience or deference to elders seriously, or as a sign of their ambivalence to the form of acquiescent respect?

Privacy respect has not been cited by any of the previous studies. In this study, this form was fairly often practiced and given a rating of 'important.' Traditionally, privacy of individuals was believed to be not akin to Chinese culture. Butterfield (1982, p. 42) notes, "The Chinese simply do not recognize privacy; indeed, there is no word for privacy in the 50,000 characters of the Chinese language." This statement may imply that Chinese people are highly interdependent with each other and that they maintain closely-knit support networks, whereby privacy is not a major concern. However, one notices that Chinese people traditionally respected the privacy of elders in the forms of providing elders with a quiet place for rest or keeping confidential about their personal matters (Book of Rites, Bk. 2, Ch. 12). It is impressive that the young people took this form as a very important way of respecting elders. This is a sign that the young of modern China conceive and practice the way of elder respect differently from the way their parents and grandparents did.

Victual respect (serving drinks and meals) and celebrative respect (celebrating birthdays) are practiced fairly often and given ratings which are close to important. Both forms have cultural implications. Serving foods and drinks of elders' choice is taken to be an important service for parents in old age. In Confucian classics, such as Teachings of Filial Piety, Book of Rites, and Twenty-Four Stories of Filial Piety (a widely-read folk stories about highly filial sons), the importance of serving foods and drinks of elders' choices is stressed and recurrently described.

Identifying respect is another newly found form which has not been reported by previous studies. By identifying oneself with values, lifestyles, and conducts of an elderly person, a young respecter conveys respect for the elderly. Because one reveres and has high regard for an elder—who can be parent, teacher, senior, elder brother, elderly teacher or master—he or she adopts the way the elder thinks, values, sees the world, or performs certain activities. The elder is taken as a model for the young respecter to emulate and identify with.

Ancestor respect followed these forms. This deeply culture-rooted form of respect was practiced fairly often and rated close to important. The Chinese young adults would seem traditional, if not conservative, in that they gave a high importance rating to this form. Ancestor worship is a cardinal ritual and a core expression of elder respect. In recent years, rituals and procedures held for worshipping ancestors have been simplified and economized. However, it still is widely practiced in Chinese communities within and outside the PRC.

Acquiescent respect was practiced more often and rated higher by the female and the married respectively. This finding seems to suggest that the female and the married were more likely to assent to elders' wishes or orders, and listen to what the elders say to them. However, in the cases of public respect and ancestor respect, the male and the married respectively practiced these forms more frequently and rated higher than did the female and the unmarried. The male, who are more active outside the family and the married who are more mature to understand the needs of elderly people at large, would have practiced these forms more often and rated higher. The higher rating of ancestor respect by the male and the married might be seen as reflecting the male-centered family system wherein married sons are responsible for carrying out rituals and events for worshipping ancestors, including commemorating ancestors' death anniversaries, maintaining ancestors' graves and family shrines, participating in the clan association, and keeping family genealogy, which are still widely practiced in Chinese communities. Variant effects of sociodemographic characteristics of young people upon practices of the various forms of elder respect need to be more analytically explored in future studies.

Consulting respect was practiced sometimes. Such a relatively low frequency with which they practiced this form might also be due to their living far away from their parents and related elders, to whom they could turn for advice and consultation.

Finally, gift respect was practiced sometimes and rated close to neither important nor unimportant. Such a low frequency and a low importance rating may also be due to the fact that they are leading college life away from their elders back home.

The distinction of these various forms of elder respect leads us to understand that, in practicing elder respect, an adult might give more emphasis to certain forms while giving less to other forms for situational and tactical reasons.

It must be noted that there was a difference in the ranking of frequency scores and the ranking of importance scores on several forms of elder respect. For instance, linguistic respect was ranked the first on frequency whereas its rank on importance was the fifth, and acquiescent respect was ranked the seventh on frequency but its importance rating ranked the 14th. In the case of care respect, the rank on importance was the first whereas its rank on frequency was the sixth. There were similar differences in the cases of public respect and privacy respect. It is probable that, as the respondents were physically separated from their elderly relatives, they were not able to practice these forms frequently in direct contact with their elderly relatives, although they recognized that the practice of these forms was important.

Ratings of the forms varied by sociodemographic characteristics of the respondents. The ratings were closely associated with gender and marital status. In particular, female respondents and married ones respectively rated care respect higher than male respondents and unmarried ones. The differences by gender and marital status might be attributed to the common role women play in the Chinese family system. Women are still the major source of filial care in China. Sons provide emotional and financial support and resources outside the family, but they are less likely to help with instrumental, hand-on care and services. Women, particularly married ones who are daughters-in-law, are likely to continue fulfilling the age-old family obligation of caring for aged parents-in-law. The finding may reflect this family role that the respondents' mothers are still playing and which the female respondents themselves will carry on. Meanwhile, married respondents are likely to be more mature and have better understanding of the needs of elderly family members for care and services. In newly urbanized areas in China, the declining availability of women to serve as primary caregivers for aged parents has emerged as a major social concern.

Unexpectedly, age, education, area of residence (rural or urban) and living arrangement (living with parent or living separately from parent) statistically did not predict the ratings of the forms.

The overwhelming majority of the respondents were unmarried young college students between 20 to 24 years of age attending colleges located in urban areas at distance from their elderly relatives.

Therefore, the findings might be seen as the common behavioral expressions of elder respect demonstrated by this particular group of young adults with such background characteristics. Future studies need to conduct an in-depth analysis of the effects of the personal background factors of the respondents upon elder respecting behaviors by using more qualitative methods, such as face-to-face interviews and the focus group approach.

Meanwhile, in the interaction with elders, the young persons' expressions of elder respect would more likely be person related. That is, the expressions of respect are connected to a social order in which there are distinct types of inter-personal relations governing at least the following groups, as described earlier: the primary group (parent & elderly relatives), a secondary group (teachers, closely related seniors), a third group (seniors at work places), and a fourth group (seniors at large). In most instances, the extent of elder respect might be consi-dered to vary in this order. One would then analyze the degree to which the respecter is related to the respected who belongs to any one of these groups in the social order.

Continuity and Change

The cultural and social environment, in which the young adults live and work appears to be in general conducive to the practice of elder respect. Political leaders, educators, and gerontologists in the PRC positively advocate the re-illustration of the traditional values of respect and care for the elderly, as part of their effort to increase the ability of the family to provide family support for the elderly. This approach is taken in parallel with the development and provision of public support which augment the weakness of the families in providing fami-ly-centered eldercare.

For long the Chinese have had a cultural ideal that support of parents comes before other obligations. This ideal has been emphasized in literature, theater, paintings, and poetry. Parents and family members involve socializing a child to fit into the family culture wherein elderly relatives are respected. Children are taught to conform to prescribed expressions of elder respect at an early age; a typical way is greeting elderly relatives, teachers, and neighborhood elders, and using respectful words, phrases, and sentences toward them. Slowly, the tradi-tional culture structures their behaviors, thoughts, and values.

The traditional family values encourage the desirability of having the elderly live with married sons. Pei and Pillai (1999) found that living with married sons makes positive contributions to the sense of well-being among the elderly in China. By living together with adult children, an aged frail elderly can receive a hand-on care and direct services (care respect), and have protection and security. The majority of elderly in China are still living with their children, although the number of distant-living adult children has been increasing (Yuan, 1994).

Goldstein and Ku (1993) found in rural China that while the elderly derived most of their income from their own farming and sideline work, children also assisted elderly parents and provided a safety-net for them as their physical ca-pacity waned. Davis-Friedman (1983. p. 103) presented a similar view: "The general patterns of interaction between elderly parents and their adult children continue to show high levels of solidarity between generations and pronounced preference for parent and son interdependence."

Thus, the support of the elderly—a key dimension of elder respect—in rural China has undergone little change, and the introduction of the filial responsibility system in 1979 was reported to have made the elderly more secure within their own families (Nee, 1984).

During the 10 years of the Cultural Revolution notwithstanding, the family system appears to have survived unscathed (Chow, 1991). The Chinese family continues to be the key source of social support for the elderly (Pei & Pillai, 1999 IJAHD). Overall, the PRC government policies supported stable households and parent-child obligations (Davis-Friedman, 1983).

Thus, the government of the PRC is clear in its wish to maintain the tradition of respecting the old, though it has been reluctant to employ the ideal of filial piety (Chow, 1991). However, in the past several years, influential officials of the government have been openly advocating the restoration of the traditional values in order to increase the capability of the Chinese families to provide family support for the elderly.

They promote mutual assistance among relatives, friends, and neighbors, and place them side by side with the help provided by the state. Thus, the public and private efforts are concerted to provide care and support for the elderly within and outside the family system. Tang's (1959) comments underscores this trend: "While the functioning of filial piety was limited to relationship between parents and children, their veneration of age was traditionally a means of inspiring respect and obedience by the young toward all other senior members of the family and society as a whole" (Yang, 1959b). In this way, the application of filial piety in the PRC is not confined within the periphery of the family system.

In such a sociocultural environment, the practice of elder respect persists.

However, the elderly are living a changing society. Although the influences of the traditional family values persist, the family's support function is weakening due to problems caused by socioeconomic and situational factor of the industrializing and urbanized society of modern China. One of the most disturbing changes is the increasing number of distant-living adult children who cannot provide direct care and services for their aged parents. The state would have to continue to emphasize the integration of family support with social support for the elderly, and decisively assume greater responsibility for supplementing family support for aged parents of distant-living children.

Elder respect is likely to be practiced in modified forms in adaptation to changing economic conditions, living arrangements, mobility, lifestyles, technology, and other extra-familial conditions. Hence, one cannot assume that the way of elder respect found among the young adults would continue unaltered. The process of alteration, if not modification, will go on as China continues its modernization.

Relatively high weight was given to the form of privacy respect, a newly emerged form of elder respect which reflects an individualistic concern over a family member's personal convenience or indulgence – a deviation from the

traditional Chinese family values of interdependence and sympathetic concession. Similarly, low weight was placed on acquiescent respect, which has been
the core tenet of filial piety and a basic obligation of the young, stressed in the
traditional teaching of propriety. And, emphasis was given to the symbolic displays of respect in terms of high frequency and importance ratings assigned to
forms of respect, such as presentational, linguistic, precedential, spatial, and
salutatory. Often, expressions of these forms tend to be minute attention to observances and ritualistic formalities. But importance of the practice of these
forms has grown in the contemporary commercialized social world. These examples among others, which indicate a shifting concern, a deviation from the
tradition, and a newer emphasis on certain forms, might be seen as some of the
signs of changes taking place among the young adults in the way of conceiving
and practicing elder respect.

Chow (1997) expressed his concern over the likelihood of Chinese families
to not show older people the same respect as before. Three generation households
are more likely due to economic necessity and/or shortage of housing than a
desire on the part of adult children to live together with parents (Davis, 1993;
Selden, 1993). The values of the elderly themselves appear to be shifting, too.
Many elderly, particularly those in urban areas, now prefer the 'intimacy at a
distance.'

While the values and lifestyles might change, feelings of respect for elders
would continue to bind generations together. Chow (1995) aptly summed up the
communalities in this respect between East Asian peoples: "Taiwan, Hong Kong
and Singapore, all with a predominant Chinese population, have emphasized the
importance of respecting one's elderly parents. As for other Asian countries,
similarly influenced by the Chinese culture, like Japan and the Republic of Korea,
the notion of filial piety has also been regarded as an important value influencing
the way in which the elderly are being treated."

Indicative of this commonness of the cultural tradition among East Asian
nations, the forms of elder respect found among the Chinese young adults show
similarities with the forms of elder respect practiced by South Korean young
adults (Sung & Kim, 2002) and Japanese young adults (Sung & Hagiwara, 2006).
Scholars, in fact, indicate a number of similar values the majority of Asians still
hold, including filial piety, high regard for elderly persons, teachers, and seniors,
the centrality of family relationships and responsibilities, and interdependence
among members of the family and social groups (Dhooper & Tran, 1986; Ho,
1976; Tsui & Schultz, 1985). The finding of the present study, hence, presents
another indication that East Asian people share similar cultural values. The intent
of the authors is not to deny the existence of differences among the Asian nations,
but rather to describe the commonly held values regarding elder respect.

De Vos' (1988, p. 346) view of cultural influence seems to be pertinent here.
He stated that modernization will have a greater effect upon the social structure of
the more public (occupational) than upon private (familial) nature. According to
him, the culturally pattern behavior of family members is more likely to persist.
This view is in accord with the perspective of Kirby (1985), who said, "Urban

China is changing at a faster pace than other parts of China. Yet this has not resulted in major destabilization of the relations between generations."

In fact, the findings of the present study suggest that the deep values of elder respect rooted in the private social structure of China are being preserved even while its manifestation is being modified. The slowness of these values to change may guarantee that modern China will remain different from nations in the West as far as the way it treats elderly people.

Bendix (1987) aptly pointed out that even though industrial countries may all face similar problems, the persistence of social, cultural, and ideological differences are likely to result in different responses to the problems. Findings of the present study suggest that the young Chinese are likely to respond to the issue of 'how to treat elderly persons properly' differently from their counterpart in the Western world.

However, it appears young people in modern China are adapting to changes occurring in the process of industrialization and urbanization. In this process, they are likely to modify their expressions of elder respect. Certain expressions taken to be important today may not be so tomorrow (Mehta, 1997).

An important agendum for gerontologists in the coming decades will be to research the extent to which young people uphold the traditional value of elder respect. Will the value continue to be transmitted to future generations? Many gerontologists and concerned people in Asia as well as other parts of the world are watching China—the origin of the culture of filial piety—to see how she deals with this critical issue.

This exploratory study was based on a sample of college students—a delimited subset of the young adult population—drawn at only three locations in PRC, the most populous nation in the world. The study is an initial step toward a more systematic exploration of elder respect in China. Although the subjects for the present study were randomly selected at the college level, the majority of them represent young adults only of those attending the universities in the three purposefully selected geographical areas. Future studies need to substantially increase the size of the sample of young adults that include those who are not in school, living in rural areas, and older adults. Besides, how the forms and the extent of elder respect vary by characteristics of elders as well as adult children and by residential areas (urban and rural), resources of parents and children, social support networks, family solidarity. Furthermore, we need to conduct cross-cultural comparison to ascertain which forms of elder respect might be universal and which reflect ethnographic qualities specific to Chinese people. China, with its unique cultural background rooted in the Confucian ideal, would be a significant case for such a cross-cultural comparison involving Western nations with a different cultural tradition.

References

Analects of Confucius (Lun Yu) [English translation] (1996). Beijing: Sinolingua, 2nd ed.

Asian Women Exchange Research (1944). *A study of consciousness and life of modern Chinese urban families* (現代中國에서의 都市家族의 意識과 生活에 관한 研究). 亞細亞女性交流研究호럼發行 1994.

de Bary, W. T. (1995). Personal reflections on Confucian filial piety. In: *Filial piety and future society* (pp. 19-36). Kyunggido, Korea: The Academy of Korean Studies.

Book of Rites (Li Chi) [Collection of Confucian Teachings of Rites] (1993). O. S. Kwon (trans.) Seoul: Hongshin Moonwha-Sa.

Caudill, W. (1973). The influence of social structure and culture on human behavior in modern Japan. *Ethos*, 1, 343-382.

Chang, W. F. (1998). For services of Chinese elderly people—We welcome the event of the International Year of Aging to China. President of Gerontological Society of China. *Renminribao* (People's Daily). (張文范 做好中國老齡工作, 喜迎國際老年人年— 訪中國老齡協會會長. 人民日報 1998年10月28日).

Choi, S. J. (2001). *Changing attitudes to filial piety in Asian countries*. Paper presented at 17th, World Congress of International Association of Gerontology. Vancouver, Canada, July 1-6.

Chow, N. (1995). *Filial piety in Asian Chinese communities*. Paper presented at Symposium on Filial Piety, 5th Asia/Oceania Regional Congress of Gerontology, Honk Kong, 20 November.

Doctrine of the Mean (1960). The doctrine of the mean [Trans. By J. Legge]. In J. Legge (Ed.), The Chinese classics (3rd Ed.). Hong Kong: Hong Kong University Press.

Downie, R. S., & Telfer, E. (1969). *Respect for persons*. London: Allen and Unwin.

Elliott, K. S., & Campbell, R. (1993). Changing ideas about family care for the elderly in Japan. *Journal of Cross-Cultural Gerontology*, 8, 119-135.

Goldstein, M. C., & Ku, Y. (1993). Income and family support among rural elderly in Jheziang Province, China. *Journal of Cross-Cultural Gerontology,* 8, 197-223.

Great Learning (1960). Great learning [Trans. By J. Legge]. In J. Legge (Ed.), *The Chinese classics* (3rd Ed.). Hong Kong: Hong Kong University Press.

Holmes, E. R., & Holmes, L. D. (1995). *Other cultures, elder years*. Thousand Oaks: Sage.

Ingersoll-Dayton, B., & Saengtienchai, C. (1999). Respect for the elderly in Asia: Stability and change. *International Journal of Aging and Human Development*, 48, 113-130.

Kong, D. C. (1995). The essence of filial piety. In: *Filial piety and future society* (pp. 127-137). Kyunggido, Korea: The Academy of Korean Studies.

Lang, O. (1946). *Chinese family and society*. New Haven, CT: Yale University Press.

Larson, R. (1978). Thirty years of research on the subjective well-being of older Americans. *Journal of Gerontology*, 33, 109-125.

Legge, J. (1960). *The Chinese Classics*, 3rd ed. Hong Kong: Hong Kong University Press. Bk. 1.

Leininger, M. (1990). Culture: The conspicuous missing link to understand ethical and moral dimensions of human care. In: M. Leininger (Ed.), *Ethical and moral dimension of care*. Detroit: Wayne State University.

Lew, S. K. (1995). Filial piety and human society. In: *Filial piety and future society* (pp. 19-36). Kyunggido, Korea: The Academy of Korean Studies.

Liang, J., & Jay, G. M. (1990). *Cross-cultural comparative research on aging and health*. Institute of Gerontology and School of Public Health, The University of Michigan.

Liang, J., Tu, E. J., & Chen, X. (1986). Population aging in the People's Republic of China. *Social Science Medicine*, 23, 1353-1362.

Liu, W. T., & Kendig, H. (2000). *Who should care for the elderly? An East-West value divide*. Singapore: Singapore University.

Maeda, D. (1997). *Filial piety and care of aged parents in Japan*. Paper presented at Symposium on myths, stereotypes, and realities of filial piety. The 16th World Congress of Gerontology, Singapore, August 17.

Mehta, K. (1997). Respect redefined: Focus group insights from Singapore. *International Journal of Aging and Human Development*, 44, 205-219.

Noelker, L. S., & Harel, Z. (2000). Humanizing long-term care: Forging a link between quality of care and quality of life. In: L. S. Noelker & Z. Harel (Eds.), *Linking Quality of Long-Term Care and Quality of Life*. New York: Springer.

Palmore, E. B., & Maeda, D. (1985). *The Honorable elders revisited*. Durham, NC: Duke University Press.

Parish, W. L., & Whyte, M. K. (1978). *Village and family in contemporary China*. Chicago: The University of Chicago Press.

Renminribao (People's Daily 人民日報). 1999. "Elderly people's desire, Emotional care" (老年人渴望精神呵護). 海外版 11月8日

Renminribao (People's Daily 人民日報). 1999. "Re-illustration of traditional virtue, For services for the elderly" (發揚傳統美德, 做好老齡工作).. 2月14日

Silverman, P., & Maxwell, R. (1978). How do I respect thee? Let me count the ways: Deference toward men and women. *Behavior Science Research,* 13, 91-108.

Silverstein, M., Burholt, V., Wenger, G. C., & Bengtson, V. L. (1998). Parent-child relations among very old parents in Wales and the United States: A test of modernization theory, *Journal of Aging Studies,* 12, 387-409.

Sokolovsky, J. (Ed.) (1990). *The cultural context of aging.* New York: Bergin and Garvey.

Streib, G. F. (1987). Old age in sociocultural context: China and the United States. *Journal of Aging Studies,* 7, 95-112.

Sung, K. T. (2004). Elder respect among young adults: A cross-cultural study of Americans and Koreans. *Journal of Aging Studies,* 18, 215-230.

Sung, K. T., & Kim, H. S. (2003). Elder respect among young adults: Exploration of behavioral forms in Korea. *Ageing International,* 28, 279-294.

Teachings of filial piety [Hsiao Ching]. [Translated by J. Legge.]. (1989). *Sacred books of the east,* Vol. III. London: Oxford. Originally published 1879-1885.

Twenty-four stories of filial piety. (1956). Taipei: Chen Ta Press (Bilingual edition).

Wang, W. Y. (王文茨). (2001). *China and social security for the aged: Culture and direction of the institution* (中國의 高齡者社會保障: 制度와 文化의 行方). Tokyo: Hakuteisha (東京: 白帝社). 2001.

Works of Mencius. (1932). [Translated by L. Lyall.] London: Murray.

Xie, X., Defrain, J., Meredith, W., & Comb, R. (1996). Family strengths in the People's Republic of China: As perceiv3d by the university students and government. *International Journal of Sociology of the Family,* 26, 17-2.

Xue, H. L., X. M. Xin, and G. S. Liu. (薛興利, 新相木, 劉桂鉋). (1998). *Empirical analysis and basis of elder care problems in farming villages: Investigation of documents on Shandong farming villages* (農村老年人口養老問題的實證分析與基本對策—山東農村的文卷調查). 科學.經濟.社會 1998年 第1期.

Chapter 13

Respect for the Elders in Japan

Erdman B. Palmore and Daisaku Maeda

The traditional respect for elders in Japan is famous. In this chapter we will examine the extent to which this traditional respect is still reflected in actual practice and the extent to which practice and attitudes are changing.

Respect and affection are difficult concepts to measure, even within one culture. Comparable cross-cultural statistics on respect for elders are nonexistent. However, we can describe typical practices and attitudes and give our impressions about how widespread they are and how they are changing.

Family Respect

We have already described how most older Japanese continue to live with their children, how most of these arrangements appear to be motivated more by desire for companionship, for mutual aid, and attitudes that it is "natural" than by the housing shortage or financial necessity, and how the aged perform many valued services in the household (chapter 4). We believe this is indirect evidence of a continuing high level of respect and affection for the elders by their families.

Perhaps the most pervasive form of respect for elders in the family (as well as outside the family) is the honorific language used in speaking to or about elders. English and other languages have polite and impolite forms for some words, but Japanese is unusual in its extreme elaboration of different forms to show the proper degree of respect or deference. Differential respect is reflected not only in the different nouns, verbs, prefixes, suffixes, and other parts of speech, but also in the basic grammar and syntax of the language. There are three basic forms of speech in Japanese: the honorific form, which is used in speaking to or referring to someone who is older or otherwise socially superior to the speaker; the middle form, which is used in speaking to someone on approximately the same social level; and the plain or blunt form, which is usually used in speaking to younger persons and others socially inferior to the speaker. There are many other complications, depending on whether the speaker and listener and person referred to are in the same or different "in-group" or whether the setting is formal or informal, etc. Nevertheless, respect for elders is one of the basic dimensions built into the Japanese language. This is one of the main reasons why it is so difficult for foreigners to learn to speak proper Japanese: not only must they learn the many different forms, but they also must understand the culture enough to know which relationships call for which form.

Another traditional form of respect for elders family members is seating arrangement. The main room of a Japanese house, which usually doubles as a dining-living room during the day and a bedroom at night, contains a *tokonoma*, an alcove in which various scrolls, art objects, or flower arrangements are displayed, depending on the season or occasion. The seat nearest the *tokonoma* is the seat with the highest honor is occupied by the oldest male in the family. His wife would usually occupy the second highest seat, and all the other household members would be arranged in descending order according to age and sex. In many modern households, if the oldest male has retired from being head of the household, the highest seat will be given to the present head of the household, and the oldest male (retired) will be moved down to the second or third highest seat.

The same order of prestige is followed in serving. The oldest male is usually served first; the youngest female is served last. An exception is made for an infant who is usually not made to wait as long as others who are actually higher in status. Not only are the elders served first, they also get the choicest portions of whatever is served.

A similar order of precedence is usually followed in all health matters. The elders and head of household go through doors before younger persons and walk down the street in front of younger persons. The elders and head of household also get to use the family bath (*ofuro*) first. The advantage of this requires some explanation: The *ofuro* is a deep tub of very hot water in which Japanese soak after washing and rinsing off outside the tub. This same water is used for soaking by every one bathing during one evening. Therefore, each person soaking in the *ofuro* leaves a residue of body oils, perspiration, etc., which gradually reduces the purity of the water. Thus, the first user gets the cleanest water.

In cooking, also, the tastes of the elders are often given precedence. If the elders like the rice cooked soft for easier chewing, it will usually be salty or sour regardless of the others' tastes. The elders and head of household usually get the rooms with the best exposure (usually the sunny one or the one with the best view). They also usually get the best silks, decorations, and bedding (*futon*). When guests bring gifts, the gifts will often be chosen primarily to please the elders.

Adult children who have left the family home show respect and affection for their parents by returning to the family home to celebrate their parents' birthdays and special holidays, such as Respect for the Aged Day, *O-bon* festivals, New Year's Day, and Christmas. Throughout the year dutiful sons and daughters keep in close contact with their parents through frequent visits, letters, and phone calls. Many adult children call their parents every day even when they must use long distance.

There are four special birthday celebrations in old age. Age seventy is called *koki*, which means "rare old age," because in the past it was rare for anyone to live to that age. The seventy-seventh year is called the "pleasure age" (*kiju*) because the character for seventy-seven is similar to that for rice. Since rice is the basic food in Japan (indeed, the word for cooked rice, *gohan*, can also mean food in general), the "rice year" is considered to be a fortunate and important year. The ninety-ninth year is the "purity year" (*haku ju*) because the character for white or purity has one less stroke than the character for one hundred and therefore can represent ninety-nine. The birthdays marking the beginning of these special years become special occasions for family celebrations to honor the elder parent.

In the United States there is usually little ceremony at family occasions. In Japan it is precisely in the family where respect for elders is learned and meticulously observed. Benedict (1946) observed:

> While the mother still carries the baby strapped to her back she will push his head down with her hand (to bow), and his first lessons as a toddler are to observe respect behavior to his father or older brother (or grandparents). . . . It is no empty gesture. It means that the one who bows acknowledges the right of the other to have his way in things he might well prefer to manage himself, and the one who receives the bow acknowledges in his turn certain responsibilities incumbent upon his station. Hierarchy based on sex and generation and primogeniture are part and parcel of family life. (pp. 48f)

This is still generally true today. When a younger person bows to his elder, the younger person bows lower and stays down longer than the elder. The elder may acknowledge the bow with a simple nod of his head.

There are popular sayings that illustrate family respect for the elders. One riddle says, "Why is a son who wants to offer advice to his parents like a Buddhist priest who wants to have hair on the top his head?" (Buddhist priests, of course, shave their heads.) The answer is, "However much he wants to do it, he can't" (Benedict, 1946). The following dilemma is often posed: If a man's mother and his wife were both drowning at the same time, whom should the man rescue first? In earlier times the answer usually given was his mother because she is elder to his wife. These days the proper answer is not so clear, and there is considerable debate about whether a man's mother or his wife should take precedence. This may be contrasted with the United States where the usual answer would clearly be his wife because a man's primary loyalty is expected to be to his wife.

You may notice that we have often used the terms *respect* and *affection* together, and you may question whether these two different attitudes can go together or whether they are mutually incompatible. To contemporary Americans with their strong egalitarian values, it may seem unlikely that you could be truly affectionate toward one before whom you must bow and continually demonstrate subservience. The Japanese do not usually view this as a problem. In fact, they tend to regard a vertical relationship, with authority and responsibility on one side and respect and subservience on the other, to be conducive to affection between the persons involved. They simply do not value independence and equality in personal relations as much as Americans do, but rather they value dependence and deference in most relationships (Nakane, 1972).

It should be understood that the prerogatives of age are usually balanced by responsibilities and concepts of fairness.

> The prerogatives of generation, sex, and age in Japan are great. But those who exercise these privileges act as trustees rather than as arbitrary autocrats. The father or the elder brother is responsible for the household, whether its members are living, dead, or yet unborn. He must make weighty decisions and see that they are carried out. He does not, however, have unconditional authority. He is expected to act responsibly for the honor of the house. . . . The master of the house saddles himself with great difficulties if he acts without regard for group opinion. (Benedict, 1946, p. 54)

Thus, the elder normally "earns" affection and respect from younger family members through his fairness, wisdom, and aid. Hearn describes the ideal traditional Japanese family in utopian terms that show how respect, mutual aid, and affection ideally reinforce one another:

> Of course, the old family organization had certain advantages which largely compensated the individual for his state of subjection. It was a society of mutual help; and it was not less powerful to give aid, than to enforce obedience. Every member could do something to assist another member in case of need: each had a right to the protection of all. This remains true of the family today. In a well-conducted household, where every act is performed according to the old forms of courtesy and kindness—where no harsh word is ever spoken—where the young look up to the aged with affectionate respect—where those whom years have incapacitated for more active duty, take upon themselves the care of the children, and render priceless service in teaching and training—an ideal condition has been realized. The daily life of such a home—in which the endeavour of each is to make existence as pleasant as possible for all—in which the bond of union is really love and gratitude—represents religion in the best and purest sense; and the place is holy. (Hearn, 1955, p. 76)

It seems unlikely that such a utopian household was ever widespread, but the mere existence of such an ideal illustrates the power of respect and affection for elders as motivating forces in Japanese family life.

The question remains: How widespread is such family respect for elders in contemporary Japan? Our interviews with Japanese of all ages in rural and urban areas found estimates ranging from 90 percent in rural areas to a minority among young urban people. It is safe to say there is more respect for elders in rural areas, in traditional occupations and households, and among middle-aged or older persons than in urban areas, "modern" households, and younger persons. This can also be inferred from the statistics showing differences by place of residence and age as to living arrangements and support patterns.

Public Respect

The amount of public respect in Japan for elders may be best documented by quoting from the 1963 National Law for the Welfare of the Elders (Number 133): "The elders shall be loved and respected as those who have for many years contributed toward the development of society, and a wholesome and peaceful life shall be guaranteed to them. In accordance with their desire and ability, the elders shall be given opportunities to engage in suitable work or to participate in social activities."

This law also declares that "any person who is engaged in a service which directly affects the life of the elders shall endeavor to promote the welfare of the elders in the management of that enterprise." Also, "the Central Government and local public bodies have responsibility to promote the welfare of the elders" (Article 4).

In contrast, the comparable law in the United States, the Older Americans' Act of 1965 (U.S. Public Law 89-73), does not make any mention of love and respect for the aged. Nor does it even attempt to *guarantee* a "wholesome and peaceful life." Rather it states only that the duty of the government is to *assist* older people to secure equal opportunity to adequate income, health, housing, employment, etc. (Title 1). This does seem to reflect a basically different attitude toward older people in Japan and the United States.

In order to fulfill its "guarantee" of a wholesome and peaceful life, the Japanese government has undertaken a series of programs for elders:

1. *Health Examination.* Cities and towns hold annual health examinations for those who are forty years of age or older. Individual guidance is then given to those who need further diagnosis or treatment.

2. *Home for the Aged.* For those sixty-five or older who need to find a protective environment other than their home, the following three kinds of institutions are provided by the law: Nursing Home (*Yogo Rojin*); Special Nursing Home (*Tokubetsu Yogo Rojin*) for those who are in need of constant medical supervision; and Home with Moderate Fee (*Keihi Rojin*) for those who choose to live in the institution and are able to afford a moderate charge.

3. *Family Foster Care.* For those who have no family to live with.

4. *Grant of Medical Cost.* Free medical care for most persons over age seventy.

5. *Home Helper.* Housekeeping help for old people living alone.

6. *Welfare Centers for the Aged.* Over 1,600 such centers have been established throughout Japan to provide various educational, recreational, and consulting services.

7. *Rest Houses and Homes.* Over 3,500 rest houses (small neighborhood centers for the elders) and sixty-nine rest homes (vacation houses for elders in areas of scenic beauty or hot springs) existed as of 1983.

8. *Old People's Clubs.* There are over 125,000 such clubs to promote community activities, social services, education, recreation, and sports for elders.

9. *Employment Opportunities.* See chapter 5.

10. *Other Programs.* There are numerous other programs for elders, including free "gadget beds" and special equipment for the bedfast; short-stay services and day care service at special nursing homes; telephone centers to provide counseling service to lonely elders; temporary home care service for elders living alone; adult education programs; subsidies for sports meetings for elders; and designation of September 15 as Respect for Elders Day.

Respect for Elders Day (Keiro No Hi) is one of the most dramatic expressions of respect and affection for the elders. Ceremonies in honor of the elders have been widespread for more than three hundred years, but in 1963 Respect for Elders Day became a national holiday. The law specifies that "the governments of various levels should hold suitable activities to evoke the people's interest in and understanding of the welfare needs of the aged as well as to encourage old people to improve and enrich their own lives." On each September 15 the Ministry of Health and Welfare presents a silver cup and a letter from the premier congratulating each person who reached the age of one hundred during the past year. In Tokyo the Metropolitan Government presents a silver fan to those who became one hundred during the year; a "respect for elders" medal to those who became seventy-five; and gifts of 5,000 yen (about $20) to each of the more than 200,000 persons over the age of seventy-five in the city. Newspapers run feature articles on the aged and on the celebrations and rallies that are held in most cities. Even small hamlets usually have some kind of ceremony and celebration with gifts of honor for the elders in the community. In large cities there are usually several different celebrations, which include music and entertainment, speeches by important officials, and gifts to honor the very old and those who have worked to help elders during the year.

A more traditional form of respect for elders was the practice of younger persons giving their seats to elders on public vehicles such as buses, subways, and trains. Traditionally, all younger persons were supposed to give their seats to any older person when there were no other seats, simply to show their respect, regardless of whether they appeared infirm or not. In recent years there have been many complaints, especially from older persons, that younger people were no longer giving their seats to elders.

As a result, starting on Respect for the Elders Day in 1973, the Tokyo railways and subways reserved six seats on every fourth care for use by the aged and the physically handicapped. The seats are silver-gray in color (instead of the usual blue) and are called "silver seats." Prominent signs on the outside and inside of the cars explain that the aged and physically handicapped have priority in the use of these seats.

The program has been quite successful, so successful that there is now talk of eliminating them because most people now give their seats to elders and handicapped regardless of whether the seats are designated as "silver seats" or not.

One indirect indicator of rising concern for the elders is the recent growth in gerontology. In the past twenty to thirty years Japan, like the United States and several other industrial countries, has had a rapid increase in the number of scientists and other professionals doing research and education in gerontology. There are two aspects of this growth, however, that show unusual strength in Japan. One is the fact that the Japanese government now does an annual survey of some aspect of the aged and their problems. Another is the impressive size and resources of the Tokyo Metropolitan Institute on Gerontology. Begun in 1971, this institute now has a staff of 156 professionals plus another 35 research associates. It is devoted entirely to research, although some of the staff also engage in treatment and teaching. It is housed in a large modern building adjoining several other facilities for the aged, including a geriatric hospital, a special nursing home, and a home for the aged. The institute contains departments of biology, pathology, biochemistry, pharmacology, physiology, nutrition, psychology, psychiatry, sociology, epidemiology, rehabilitation, and nursing. It also has special laboratories for electronic microscopy, radioisotopes, computer science, and animals. This institute is much larger and more comprehensive in its research than any institute of gerontology in the United States (except for the National Institute on Aging in Washington, D.C.).

Another indicator of public respect for elders is the previously mentioned fact that the legislature, corporations, universities, religious organizations, and other such institutions are largely controlled by elders (Christopher, 1983). This is a result of the seniority system in which prestige and power tend to increase with age. Japan does not have a true gerontocracy in which elders have all the power, but it is clear that they have a greater share o the power and prestige than other age groups. Most Japanese believe this is as it should be, since they assume that maturity and wisdom tend to increase with age and that power should be given to those with the most maturity and wisdom—the elders. It is true that some younger people criticize this system; but the system endures basically unchanged. Younger people in most societies tend to criticize the establishment when they are outside it, and then tend to join the establishment and defend it as they grow older.

Summary

Traditional practices in the family that show respect for elders include honorific language, giving the best seats to elders, serving elders first, allowing elders to bathe and go through doors first, catering to the tastes of elders in cooking, children returning to parents' homes for holidays and birthdays, the special celebration of the sixty-first and other birthdays, and bowing to elders. Family respect for elders is also reflected in several popular sayings. Respect for elders is usually accompanied by affection based on the elders' fairness, wisdom, and aid. Respect for elders is more widespread in rural areas than urban, more in traditional households than modern, and more among the middle-aged than among the younger children. Patterns of respect appear to be changing, especially since World War II, so that the more extreme forms of subservience are declining, and some elders are no longer respected if they are viewed as unjust, immoral, or unpleasant.

Public respect for elders is demonstrated by the National Law for Welfare of the Aged, Respect for Elders Day, the practice of younger persons giving their seats to elders on public vehicles, and the many special programs and services for elders by the government and other agencies. The growth of gerontology reflects the growing concern in Japan for the problems of the aged.

In contrast to the traditional respect for elders, there is also a theme of resentment and desire to abandon senile and incapacitated aged that can be found in many stories and novels. Furthermore, there have been substantial declines in the amount of respect for elders.

Nevertheless, there are still basic differences between Japan and the United States in attitudes and treatment of the aged.

There is evidence in both countries that the status of elders is beginning to return toward relatively higher levels.

References

Benedict, J. (1946). The Chrysanthemum and the Sword. Boston: Houghton Mifflin.

Christopher, R. (1983). The Japanese Mind. New York: Simon and Schuster.

Hearn (1955). Japan: An Interpretation. Rutland, Vt.: Charles E. Tuttle.

Nakane, C. (1972). Japanese Society. Berkeley: University of California Press.

Chapter 14

Elder Respect Among Young Adults: Exploration of Behavioral Forms in Korea

Kyu-taik Sung and Han Sung Kim

Cultural change has a significant effect on how people respect the elderly (Streib, 1987; Palmor & Maeda, 1985; Sung, 2001). Elder respect is interpreted and practiced in diverse cultural contexts and varies by culture (Sokolovsky, 1990; Holmes & Holmes, 1995).

Koreans in East Asia have a notable tradition of elder respect rooted in the Confucian teachings of filial piety (Lew, 1996; Choi, 2001; Sung, 2001). The values of Asian filial piety have greatly influenced the way in which Koreans, along with the Chinese and Japanese, treat their parents and elders. Filial piety essentially directs young persons to be grateful for the care and aid received from their parents, and in return to care for and support their parents in old age. In the Confucian teachings, the most stressed point is respect for parents and the elderly (Teachings of Filial Piety, Ch. 7, Ch. 9). (Hereafter respect for the elderly is called elder respect. "Elders" here denotes parents, elderly relatives, elders in the neighborhood and workplace, and the elderly at large.)

Elder respect has been accepted as a customary and normative duty of the young in Korean culture. In recent years, however, treatment of the elderly has been gaining increased attention from policy-makers and gerontologists, as the nation has undergone dynamic social changes in the process of industrialization and urbanization. Concerned Koreans feel that the age-old tradition of elder is endangered.

In Korea, more elderly people are living longer and fewer children are being born (Kim, Liang, Rhee, & Kim, 1996). Consequently, elder care responsibilities are placed on the shoulders of fewer younger people. Along with these demographic shifts, Koreans are undergoing social changes, including movement toward smaller families, growth in the number of children living a distance from their aging parents, and the emerging tendency among the young to have individualistic lifestyles. Heavy burdens of providing elder care combined with these social changes might tempt some of the young to unravel the traditional values affirming elder respect.

Recent studies have reported on the tendencies of some Korean young people to disrespect older persons by disregarding their problems, neglecting and abusing them, and showing prejudice against them by negative attitudes and discriminatory practices (Kim & Han, 1997; Kim, 1998; Han & Kim, 2000). Negative concepts of ageism held by younger people, particularly college students, are critically discussed within and outside the country (Han, 2000; Hummert, 1994; Koyano, Inoue, & Shibata, 1987; Lee, 2000; Palmore, 1999).

Without respect, positive attitudes toward the elderly cannot exist, nor can elders be treated with propriety. Studies have found that respect was a key factor in determining an elderly person's life satisfaction (Ghusn, Hyde, Steven, Hyde, & Teasdale, 1996). The elderly who are respected are likely to increase self-esteem and involve themselves in a cooperative effort with caregivers to achieve a desired outcome whereby treatment benefits can be increased (Cohen-Mansfield, Ejas, & Werner, 2000; Gambrill, 1983; Reichel, 1995). How the young treat elders is, therefore, important not only to the elderly but also to caregivers and to society.

Growing concern over elder respect has prompted a critical review of how young Koreans respect the elderly, a basic moral issue which until recently has not been questioned.

Until now, writings about elder respect have dealt with the ideals and precepts of the traditional value in an invariably abstract form. Hence, elder respect has been a concept too general to enlighten people regarding its specific implications. However, there has been no empirical analysis of how Koreans in modern times practice the traditional value of elder respect.

Do young Koreans of today respect the elderly? If they do, in what way do they respect the elderly? Specifically, what are the behaviors or actions by which they convey elder respect? Can we develop a typology of the forms of elder respect most often practiced by the young?

To obtain answers to these questions, this study explored specific behavioral forms by which young adults, college students, convey elder respect. In this study, identifying the most widely practiced forms of elder respect was of central importance. Based on the results of a questionnaire survey given at Korean universities, the common forms of elder respect were distinguished and the meanings of the forms and changing trends of elder respect are discussed. It is to the purpose of this paper to conduct a causal analysis of respect-related variables, but rather to obtain a preliminary inventory of the explicit forms of elder respect practiced by young adults in their daily lives in the Korean cultural context.

Expressions of Elder Respect

Elder respect is intended to convey an altruistic and benevolent sense of regard to older persons (Dillon, 1992; Downie & Telfer, 1978). It involves practical concerns, distinguished from emotion or simple feeling, which tend toward outward expressions of and actions for respect (Dillon, 1992; Gibbard, 1990: 264-69). Hence, as Silverman and Maxwell (1978: 96) stated, respect is an open, visible, and matter-of-fact behavioral expression toward elder persons. However, few studies have empirically explored such expressions.

In recent years, the ways in which the young respect the elderly have been explored by a group of scholars in East Asian countries. Palmore and Maeda (1985) described Japanese forms of elder respect. Mehta (1997) discussed on such forms based on her study in Singapore. And, Ingersoll-Dayton and Saegntienchai (1999) reported on the forms based on their study of Taiwanese, Singaporeans, Thais, and Filipinos. These three rare studies have introduced a variety of forms by which Asians conveyed elder respect. They employed qualitative approaches in their studies of the forms that were interlaced with affective qualities of intergenerational exchanges. The forms they described included (1) caring and serving, (2) obeying, (3) consulting, (4) greeting, (5) using respectful language, (6) displaying courteous manners, (7) celebrating birthdays, (8) furnishing honorable seats or roles, (9) giving preferential treatment, (10) serving foods and drinks of the elders' choice, (11) bestowing gifts, (12) respecting elders in general, and (13) honoring deceased ancestors.

While these studies have made significant contributions, they have not presented quantitative data on the extent to which individual forms of elder respect are practiced and the degree to which importance is given to these forms. They also did not research younger or older adults in Korea.

Building upon the findings of these studies, the present study explored the forms of elder respect among the young Korean adults.

Methods

Data were collected from a sample of 401 students who were attending 12 randomly chosen classes (sizes: 9-58) in social sciences in the undergraduate and graduate programs of two universities—one located in downtown Seoul and the other in a local city south of Seoul. Both universities, selected purposively from area universities, are accredited coeducational institutions with socially, economically, and religiously diverse student bodies. Fifty-five percent of the subjects were male and 45% were female; 44% were seniors and 56% were graduate students. Their average age was 23.5 years. The majority (65%) were living with their parents.

The following questionnaire was administered to the subjects.

Questions:

1. Please list two or more behaviors or gestures by which you most often express your respect for older adults.

2. How important, would you say is each of the behaviors or gestures you cited? Please give a rating on their importance.

Answers:

Respecting Behaviors	Rating (Check one.)			
List two or more	extraordinarily important	highly important	averagely important	fairly important

---

The first question identified the forms of elder respect that the subjects most often practiced. The second question assessed the levels of importance the subjects assigned to these forms. Their levels were rated on a 4-point scale (4 = extraordinarily important, 3 = highly important, 2 = of average importance, 1 = fairly important). Added to the questionnaire was constructed to enable the students to respond quickly and easily in a classroom. The instructor explained the voluntary nature of participation and asked the subjects to complete the anonymous, self-administered questionnaire. On the average, 95 percent of the subjects in each class returned completed questionnaires.

Analysis and Findings

In response to the questions, the subjects provided a variety of behavioral forms by which they conveyed elder respect. These forms were categorized into specific forms by carefully scrutinizing the meanings and intentions of the forms and kinds of behaviors cited to convey elder respect. For categorization, a set of forms identified by Silverman and Maxwell (1978) was used as a reference. They identified seven forms, based on their study of how old persons were respected in different cultural contexts: *service respect* (providing services), *gift respect* (bestowing gifts), *linguistic respect* (using honorifics), *spatial respect* (offering seats and places of honor), *victual respect* (serving choice foods), *presentational respect* (showing courteous manners), and *celebrative respect* (celebrating birthdays). These forms guided the categorization of various forms. Other forms emerged throughout the process of categorization. Ten randomly selected subjects were employed to help the authors maintain accuracy and consistency in the interpretation of questionnaire responses and subsequent categorization. An effort was made to distinguish mutually exclusive behaviors of respect that fit into the forms.

Analyses of the subjects' responses and subsequent identification of the forms of elder respect are described in the following.

First, based on frequency with which each of the forms was cited, a percentage was calculated; then, based on the percentage size, each form was ranked. Next, the importance of the form was rated based on the 4-point scale, and then the form was ranked according to the rating.

In terms of the frequency, caregiver (giving care and service) was the most frequently cited (62% of all the subjects). The second most often cited form was acquiescent respect (obeying orders, 51%). Third was consulting respect (seeking advice, 41%); fourth, precedential respect (giving precedence, 36%); fifth, salutatory respect (greeting and bowing, 33%); sixth, linguistic respect (using honorific language, 31%); seventh, victual respect (serving choice foods, 23%); eighth, gift respect (giving gifts, 21%); ninth, presentational respect (showing polite manners, 20%); 10th, public respect (respecting elders at large, 17%); 11th, celebrative respect (celebrating birthdays, 15%); 12th, spatial respect (providing honorable seats and places, 13%); 13th ancestor respect (worshipping ancestors, 9%); and finally at 14th, funeral respect (holding solemn funeral rites, 7%). All of these forms except funeral respect replicate the expressions of elder respect that the three previous studies reported concerning other East Asian peoples.

In terms of importance, care respect was again the highest ranking form (3.60, nearly "extraordinarily important"). This was followed by consulting (3.41), acquiescent (3.32), linguistic (3.23), salutatory (3.15), precedential (3.10), victual (3.02), gift (2.92), presentational (2.82), public (2.72), celebrative (2.63), spatial (2.63), ancestor (2.53), and funeral (2.50). These forms were rated as roughly "very importance to of average importance." (The original question was to cite only important forms.)

Thus, in both analyses, care respect is the highest-ranking form, followed by five other outstanding forms: consulting, acquiescent, linguistic, salutatory, and precedential. These forms were practiced more often and rated more important than other forms.

To compare the findings at the two universities, analyses were made by dividing the sample into two groups. Results of Chi-square analyses suggest no difference at a statistically significant level between the two groups in terms of frequency with which the forms were cited (x^2=5.23~85, d.f.=2; p=.07~.65). In terms of the rating of importance, results of a t-test suggest that there was also no difference between the two groups (t=.42~.79, p=.67~.43, 2-tailed). These findings suggest that overall, the subjects of the two universities were similar in terms of frequency of citing and importance rating.

An ANOVA test was carried out to compare the importance scores on the 14 forms by demographic variables. By gender, there was not statistically significant variation in the ratings. By age groups (20-24, 25-29, 30-34, 35+), however, there was variation with respect to acquiescent respect (F=1.36, p=.025, d.f.=2, p<.001, d.f.=1, 301). These findings suggest that older subjects are likely to give greater importance to acquiescing, and married subjects tend to give greater weight to consulting. In the two-way analysis of variance, however, residential areas (ritual or urban) and types of living arrangements (living with elderly relatives or living separately from them) were found to have an interactional effect on mean importance ratings of care respect and acquiescent respect. This suggests that those who lives in the local city and those who are living with older relatives tended to show higher importance ratings on the two forms. Age and gender were also found to have an interactional effect on the rating of the consultative respect, suggesting that the subjects, who were older and female, tended to give weight to consulting with elders. However, these interaction effects were statistically not significant.

To explore the underlying dimensions of the 14 forms, an orthogonal vari-max rotated factor analysis (with the principal component solution) was conducted based on the data on importance. (This analysis reduces the number of variables that have high loadings on a given factor.) Three factors with eigenvalue over 1 emerged. The first factor, with four loadings, was titled "symbolic elder respect." The second factor, with three loadings, was named "engaging elder respect." The third factor, with two loadings, was titled "culture-rooted respect." The three factors together accounted for 37.2% of the variance. Thus, three factors or dimensions emerged. This result suggests that the various forms might be reduced to three dimensions.

Forms and Expressions of Elder Respect

The meanings and practices of the 14 forms will now be summarily discussed in the Korean cultural context (Jannelli, 1986; KIG, 2000; Sung, 2001).

1. Care Respect. This form involves innermost feelings of care and concern, making elderly individuals feel happy and comfortable, relieving them of anxiety, not doing something which would hurt them, maintaining contact with them, spending time with them, providing personal care for them, and providing them with nourishment, housekeeping, and health services. Thus, it involves affectionate care and instrumental services.

2. Acquiescent Respect. Commonly the young tend to listen to and obey their elderly relatives. Some identify with their elders' values and lifestyles. In workplaces, informal advice from seniors is often followed obediently. At school, students obey their teachers almost unreservedly. In the family- and group-oriented Korean culture, acquiescent respect has been a social norm.

3. Consulting Respect. The young seek out elders' opinions on personal and family matters. By consulting, the young implicitly show their respect to the elderly.

4. Precedential Respect. This form involves providing foods, drinks, assis-tance, and services to elders fist; giving precedence to their tastes; allowing them to go through doorways first, to get in and out of cars first; and to use a shower or bath first.

5. Salutatory Respect. One must exhibit proper body language, as the level of respect is usually determined by the degree to which one bows or bends the body. Often such a salutatory movement is repeated to convey deep respect or deference. This form has been the first social behavior that most Korean children learn at early ages.

6. Linguistic Respect. As in the cases of the Japanese and the Chinese, Koreans use a variety of honorific expressions elaborately differentiated to convey the proper degree of respect. Commonly, the young use honorifics to convey a sense of respect when they salute, have conversation with, and write letters to elders. The level of respect is reflected not only in different nouns but also verbs, prefixes, suffixes, and even phrases and sentences when used in interaction with parents, teachers, seniors, or superiors. Elder respect is built into the Korean language.

7. Victual Respect. Providing foods and drinks of an elder respect's choice is an age-old form of elder respect. Stories of filial children in Korea invariably describe how devoutly they served foods and drinks of their elders' choice.

8. Gift Respect. Presenting gifts, particularly to elders, has been endemic to Koreans. There are two components of this form. The first refers to artifacts, usually gifts including clothes, money, and other things of symbolic value. The second refers to the bestowal of favors, such as the right to give speeches or prayers.

9. Presentational Respect. Young persons coming into contact with elders are expected to dress simply and neatly, and to maintain a polite, deferent posture. Presentational respect has been important in Korea, where deference and ritualistic mores are still valued.

10. Public Respect. This form is reflected in societal efforts to promote the status of the elderly under the joint auspices of public and voluntary agencies in Korea, e.g., the establishment of a Respect for Elders Day or Week; the enactment of the Senior Citizens' Welfare Law and the Filial Responsibility Law; the development of the community care approach; and public campaigns to promote elder respect. Filial piety prizes awarded to exemplary filial children, programs designed to educate the young to treat elders with respect, and television dramas showing cases of elder respect are all for the purpose of promoting public respect. In addition, treating elders respectfully on a bus by giving up seats for them, helping them to cross the street, carrying heavy things for them, and providing them with transportation are personal actions for public respect.

11. Celebrative Respect. A parent's 60th birthday is the most celebrated of all family events. The birthday ceremony, signaling the entrance into old age, marks a crucial event in a parent's life cycle and is a special occasion for the family to honor the aged parent. Children frequently visit their parents throughout the year to celebrate birthdays and attend other family events. An important purpose of such events is to dramatize the esteem accorded to parents and elders.

12. Spatial Respect. Elders are furnished with seats of honor (center or head seats) in gatherings, chairs by the fireplace, or quiet rooms. They are often given the role of master of marriage ceremonies or the chair of meetings. Such physical placement and roles are tied to respect.

13. Funeral Respect. A parent's death and subsequent burial are the most emotional and of solemn times. Children do their utmost to hold a most respectful funeral ceremony and to follow the elaborate formalities in mourning for departed parents. In discharging funeral duties, the children wear special attire and express grief by wailing and weeping. Selections of funeral home, coffin, grave site, and gravestone selections are done with respect, obligation, and sacrifice for the deceased. After the funeral, many families continue mourning.

14. Ancestral Respect. Individual ancestors within certain generations are commemorated on their death anniversaries and on major holidays in order to repay the debt incurred to them. For an anniversary rite, family members typically gather in a hall, room, or a Buddhist temple where their ancestor's table and picture are kept, arrange carefully prepared foods and drinks on a table for sacrifice, and make bows to the tablet or the picture. Afterward, parents tell their children stories about the ancestor, so that the younger generation does not forget their origins and the favors they received. Rebuilding or decorating the family temple and ancestor's graves is also an important way of paying respect.

New Trends: Changing Expressions

In the process of social change, some forms of elder respect seem to be undergoing modification. For instance, listening to elders when they talk, a category of acquiescent respect, though not always obeying or following their advice, is taken as a form of elder respect. This form seems to be a modification of the traditional forms of obedience. However, a traditional form of respect—complying with elders' directives (a category of acquiescent respect)—was still frequently practiced. Consulting elders, which involves open communication and mutually beneficial exchange between generations, is another prevalent form. As more young Koreans value reciprocity between generations, consulting respect is bound to be widely practiced. Also noticeable is the visible trend of shaking hands instead of bending body forward to greet seniors. Public respect and community care are taken more seriously by voluntary and public organizations. Increasingly, the old and young alike prefer separate residencies in order to respect each other's privacy and freedom, as they do in Western countries. As more elderly live longer, many families tend to postpone the traditional celebration of parents' 60th birthdays. Even ancestor worship and funeral rites are being modified: the number of days for worship tend to be reduced and mourning rituals are simplified. The young tend to avoid time-consuming and complex ways of greeting; they prefer simpler and shorter honorific expressions. A growing number of distant living adults use telephone and other means of communication to express their respect and affection toward their relatives. They often choose paid-for services to care for their distant-living elderly relatives. As more young people value time and convenience, these modified expressions are bound to be widely practiced.

Discussion

In our exploratory study, a set of 14 forms of elder respect was distinguished. In the holistic meaning of elder respect, all these must be considered. The forms may be interrelated in their practices. However, each seems to be a distinct set of actions that demonstrates a particular behavior indicating elder respect.

Of these forms, six stand out in terms of high frequency of citing and high rating of importance assigned to them: care respect, acquiescent respect, consulting respect, linguistic respect, salutatory respect, and precedential respect. The distinction of these forms highlights specific ways in which young Korean adults respect the elderly. The behavioral forms will be useful in developing a more comprehensive typology of elder respect that can be used to assess the quality of ethic and the moral aspects of intergenerational relationships in the Korean cultural context.

The findings suggest that elder respect is multi-dimensional. The 14 forms can be categorized into three groups: First, there is respect involving some action or work, e.g., caring, consulting, and serving choice meals. Second are symbolic displays of respect—such as acquiescence, linguistic, presentational, and salutatory gestures. Third are culture-related forms, e.g., ancestral and funeral respect.

In Korean culture, if one does not exhibit these types of elder respecting forms properly and in a timely manner when they encounter elderly relatives, teachers, and related seniors, one is violating the code of proper conduct. The forms have deep roots in a culture influenced by the Confucian teachings. The cultural influence persists, although Koreans today adhere to it less rigidly (Choi, 2001; Yoon & Cha, 1999).

The present study provided quantitative data on elder respect that previous studies did not measure. Based on this data, the study specified the extent to which the forms were practiced by the subjects and the degree to which the practice of the forms was important to them. Thus it provided empirical data on the essential aspects of elder respect among the young Korean adults. In addition, the present study on Koreans and previous studies (Palmore & Maeda, 1985; Mehta, 1997; Igersoll-Dayton & Saegntienchai, 1999 on other East Asians yielded parallel results for identification of a set of similar forms of elder respect. That is, the findings about the Koreans are consistent with those on other East Asians, thus enlarging the power of the interpretation of elder respect in East Asia. Due to lack of quantitative data from previous studies, differences and similarities between the Koreans and peoples in other Asian countries could not be compared in terms of the extent to which the forms are practiced and the degree of importance given to the forms.

It is noteworthy that, of all the corollaries of elder respect, care respect was the most frequently cited and given the highest degree of importance. Care respect was expressed in a variety of ways, including caring for older adults with affective touches and providing instrumental services for them. Western writers have reported that respect is closely interrelated with care and that care reflects one kind of respect (Dillon, 1992; Kelly, 1990; Downie & Telfer, 1978). Thus, this finding regarding the Koreans coincides with the Western writers' descriptions of the connectedness of respect and care suggesting cross-cultural similarities in terms of the conception of care respect.

In the practice of care respect, however, attaining innermost feelings of caring and concern is important as well. Confucian teachings stress not only formal behavioral prescriptions for elder respect but also an inner disposition of the mind and heart for elder respect (Analects, Bk. 2, Ch. 7; de Bary, 1995). In combination, these two components seem to manifest an ideal way in which Koreans endeavor to care for their elderly.

Care respect has significant implications for family members as well as for professional caregivers whose duties are to provide care and services with respect and propriety, not only in Korean culture but also in other cultures. It reflects the values of caring for elderly clients with benevolence and sympathetic concern. However, elder respect is often difficult to practice, as in the case of caring for bed-ridden elders with chronic diseases (Chee & Levkoff, 2001). Respecting elderly persons, particularly those who are in a declining physical capacity, with a combination of engaging forms (care, consulting, and victual) and symbolic forms (acquiescent, precedential, salutatory, linguistic, etc.), would allow the caregiver to make significant differences.

Caregiving is meaningful to elderly persons only when elder respect is operationally defined and related actions are implemented. In this regard, the expressions of the 14 forms of elder respect presented in the preceding section provide us with useful references as to what sort of behavioral expressions a caregiver might consider in treating elderly persons or clients with respect. The forms also provide a set of criteria against which the caregiver's practice of elder respect might be contrasted.

A wide range of changes is taking place in the expressions of the traditional forms. If such changes continue along with changes in lifestyles and means of communication, those forms that are important today may not be considered so tomorrow. As yet, few studies have systematically assessed how much, how fast, and in what way the forms are changing.

The shifts seem to indicate a new trend: a move from authoritarian and patriarchal relationships to egalitarian and reciprocal patterns of mutual respect between generations. Overall, expressions seem to be shifting from subservient forms to egalitarian forms, and from complex to simple. In response to the challenges from social changes, young Koreans appear to be modifying their traditional forms of elder respect.

While expressions of respect are changing among the young, elder respect is a central value that continues to bind generations together in Korea. The majority of young Koreans feel strongly that parents in old age must be respected and supported by their adult children (Sung, 1995). Thus, social changes have not meant the exclusion of feelings of respect for aged kin and elders. Young Koreans appear to be adapting to changing times while searching for alternative ways to uphold their traditional values.

The values of filial piety still influence Koreans. The tradition is deeply rooted in the Korean family system and social structure, where respect as benevolent and altruistic expression is heavily imbued with the sense of filial obligation, repayment of debt to parents, and affection toward parents. In the social structure, consequential interpersonal relations tend to have a vertical structure that demands deference and loyalty to elders. In these relations, symbolic expressions of elder respect—linguistic, salutatory, presentational, precedential, celebratory, gift, and acquiescent—are shown more often and more widely in Korea than in the West. A large number of Korean adults still live with their parents and practice care respect—caring by staying close to them, spending time with them, providing hands-on care, serving them meals, etc.—more easily than do people in the West, where the majority of adults live separately from their aged parents. Korea has even institutionalized its reverence for elders by celebrating Respect for Elders Day or Week, enacting a law case of caring for bed-ridden elders with chronic diseases (Chee & Levkoff, 2001). Respecting elderly persons, particularly those who are in a declining in a declining physical capacity, with a combination of engaging forms (care, caring, and victual) and symbolic forms (acquiescent, precedential, salutatory, linguistic, etc.), would allow the caregiver to make significant differences.

Caregiving is meaningful to elderly persons only when elder respect is operationally defined and related actions are implemented. In this regard, the expressions of the 14 forms of elder respect presented in the preceding section provide us with useful references as to what sort of behavioral expressions a caregiver might consider in treating elderly persons or clients with respect. The forms also provide a set of criteria against which the caregiver's practice of elder respect might be contrasted.

A wide range of changes is taking place in the expressions of the traditional forms. If such changes continue along with changes in lifestyles and means of communication, those forms that are important today may not be considered so tomorrow. As yet, few studies have systematically assessed how much, how fast, and in what way the forms are changing.

The shifts seem to indicate a new trend: a move from authoritarian and patriarchal relationships to egalitarian and reciprocal patterns of mutual respect between generations. Overall, expressions seem to be shifting from subservient forms to egalitarian forms, and from complex to simple. In response to the challenges from social changes, young Koreans appear to be modifying their traditional forms of elder respect.

While expressions of respect are changing among the young, elder respect is a central value that continues to bind generations together in Korea. The majority of young Koreans feel strongly that parents in old age must be respected and supported by their adult children (Sung, 1995). Thus, social changes have not meant the exclusion of feelings of respect for aged kin and elders. Young Koreans appear to be adapting to changing times while searching for alternative ways to uphold their traditional values.

The values of filial piety still influence Koreans. The tradition is deeply rooted in the Korean family system and social structure, where respect as benevolent and altruistic expression is heavily imbued with the sense of filial obligation, repayment of debt to parents, and affection toward parents. In the social structure, consequential interpersonal relations tend to have a vertical structure that demands deference and loyalty to elders. In these relations, symbolic expressions of elder respect—linguistic, salutatory, presentational, precedential, celebratory, gift, and acquiescent—are shown most often and more widely in Korea than in the West. A large number of Korean adults still live with their parents and practice care respect—caring by staying close to them, spending time with them, providing hands-on care, serving them meals, etc.—more easily than do people in the West, where the majority of adults live separately from their aged parents. Korea has even institutionalized its reverence for elders by celebrating Respect for Elders Day or Week, enacting a law that mandates that elders be respected and awarding government-sponsored filial piety prizes to persons who demonstrate exemplary filial conducts (Sung, 1990, 1998).

However, it appears that the difference between Koreans and people in the West in terms of elder respect seems to be a matter of degree rather than an either or proposition. For instance, young American adults do practice most of the forms of elder respect although they practice several of the forms only minimally if at all, reflecting their cultural orientation toward egalitarian and non-hierarchical relationships (Sung, 2002). One might say that the basic human behavior displayed in treating the elderly is comparable if not similar.

But how long can the Korean family, which is becoming ever smaller and more egalitarian, continue to take respectful care of an increasingly larger number of elderly persons? Families in Korea are facing a time when those with limited resources must turn to the state for assistance in caring for elderly citizens. However, as long as Koreans practice elder respect, they are likely to have advantages over peoples not practicing elder respect in caring for elderly. For Koreans; the values of elder respect act as a driving force that minimizes the devastating effects of rapid social changes on the practice of family care for the aged, and also as an influence that facilitates the fulfillment of filial duties by stressing the importance of respectful care for the elderly. The persistence of their cultural tradition is likely to lead Koreans to respond to the issue of ethic in a way that is somewhat different from other cultures.

The present study is an initial step toward a more systematic exploration of elder respect. It has limitations; the sample was relatively small and included only students—a subset of the young adult population. Future studies should use a more representative sample that includes younger adults not attending college. Practice of the various forms of elder respect may arise from pressures from a young person's social relations, feelings of obligation and repayment, or his or her personal desires. This assumption might be tested in future studies, which should also investigate intra-family or intra-group variation in the practice of elder respect by using more open-ended, qualitative methods.

Looking ahead, young generations are likely to change or modify their emotions of elder respect. An important agendum for Korean gerontologists in the coming decades will be to research how well or to what extent young Koreans uphold the traditional value of elder respect. Will the value continue to be transmitted to future generations? This will probably depend on whether present adult generation takes the time and effort to instill the value in the next generation.

Furthermore, we need to conduct cross-cultural research to ascertain which forms of elder respect might be universal and which reflect ethnographic qualities specific to Koreans. It will be useful, for instance, to see in what patterns Koreans who immigrated to the United States and Canada uphold or shift the traditional Korean way of elder respect through the first, second, and third generations. Future studies might address the following issues as well:

· What forms of elder respect are changing? In what way? What is the impact of the change on elder care—our ultimate concern?

· Is the elder respect (in terms of the 14 forms) practiced in the extended family different from elder respect practiced in the nuclear family?

· To what extent does elder respect vary by personal backgrounds of adult children (gender, age, marital status, education, income) and by contextual variables (rural and urban residence, intergenerational relations in terms of solidarity and conflict, resources of parents and adult children, social support network, etc.)?

· To what extent, do families and schools socialize and educate the young to respect elders? How effective are such socializing and educational efforts in sustaining the tradition of parent care?

References

Analects of Confucius (Lun Yu) [English Trans.] (1996). Beijing: Sinolingua, 2nd Ed.

Applegate, M., & J. M. Morse, J. M. (1994). Personal privacy and interactional patterns in a nursing home. Journal of Aging Studies, 8, 413-434.

De Bary, W. T. (1995). Personal reflections on Confucian filial piety. In Filial piety and future society (pp. 19-36). Kyunggido, Korea: The Academy of Korean Studies.

Chee, Y. K., & Levkoff, S. E. (2001). Culture and dementia: Accounts by family caregivers and health professionals for dementia-affected elders in South Korea. Journal of Cross-Cultural Gerontology, 16, 111-125.

Choi, S. J. (2001). Changing attitudes to filial piety in Asian countries. Paper presented at 17th World Congress of International Association of Gerontology. Vancouver, Canada, July 1-6.

Cohen-Manfield, J., Ejas, F. K., & Werner, P. (2000). Satisfaction surveys in long-term care. New York: Springer.

Dillon, R. S. (1992). Respect and care: Toward moral integration. Canadian Journal of Philosophy, 22, 105-132.

Downie, R. S., & Telfer, E. (1969). *Respect for persons.* London: Allen and Unwin.

Gambrill, E. (1983). *Casework: A competency-based approach.* Englewood Cliffs, NJ: Prentice-Hall.

Ghusn, H. M., Hyde, D., Stevens, E. S., Hyde, M., & Teasdale, T. A. (1996). Enhancing life satisfaction in later life: What makes a difference for nursing home residents? *Journal of Gerontological Social Work,* 26, 27-47.

Gibbard, A. (1990). *Wise choices, apt feelings.* Cambridge, MA: Harvard University Press.

Han, E. J., & Kim, T. H. (2000). An ecological study on causes of elder abuse, *Journal of the Korea Gerontological Society,* 20(3), 71-89.

Han, J. (2000). Undergraduate students' attitudes toward the elderly, *Journal of the Korea Gerontological Society,* 20(3), 115-127.

Holmes, E. R., & Holmes, L. D. (1995). *Other cultures, elder years.* Thousand Oaks: Sage.

Hummert, M. (1994). Stereotypes of the elderly and patronizing speech. In M. Hummert, J. Wieman, & J. Nussbaum (Eds.), *Interpersonal communication in older adulthood.* Thousand Oaks, CA: Sage.

Ingersoll-Dayton, B., & Saegntienchai, C. (1999). Respect for the elderly in Asia: Stability and change. *International Journal of Aging and Human Development,* 48, 113-130.

Jannelli, D. Y. (1986). Ancestors, women, and the Korean family. In Slote, W. H. (Eds.), *The psycho-cultural dynamics of the Confucian family: Past and present.* Seoul: International Cultural Society of Korea.

Kelly, B. (1990). Respect and caring. In M. Leininger (Ed.), *Ethical and moral dimension of care.* Detroit: Wayne State University Press.

KIG (200). The rules of etiquette. *Studies of Welfare Policies for The Aged* (Noin-Bokji-Jungch'aek Yunku), 2000-04, No. 19. Seoul: Korean Institute of Gerontology.

Kim, H. G. (1998). Public perceptions of elder mistreatment and its reality in Taegu [Taegu-aesu-ui Noin-haktae-wa noinhaktae-ui Silt'ae-ui kwanhan Yunku]. *Journal of the Korean Gerontological Society,* 18(1), 184-197.

Kim, I. K., Liang, J., Rhee, K. O., & Kim, C. H. (1996). Population aging in Korea: Changes since the 1960s. *Journal of Cross-Cultural Gerontology,* 2, 131-137.

Kim, T. H. (1992). Gerontological study [Nonyun-hak]. Seoul: Kyomoon-sa.

Kim, T. H., & Han, J. E. (1997). A literature review about measurement and intervention in elder abuse, *Journal of the Korean Gerontological Society,* 17(1), 51-71.

Koyano, W., Inoue, K., & Shibata, H. (1987). Negative misconceptions about aging in Japanese adults. *Journal of Cross-Cultural Gerontology,* 2, 131-137.

Lee, I. S. (2000). Perception of rural area college students on the aged, *Journal of the Korean Gerontological Society,* 20(2), 129-135.

Lew, S. K. (1995). Filial piety and human society. In *Filial piety and future society* [Hyo-wa Mirae-Sahoe] (pp. 19-36). Kyunggido, Korea: The Academy of Korean Studies.

Mehta, K. (1997). Respect redefined: Focus group insights from Singapore. *International Journal of Aging and Human Development,* 44, 205-219.

Palmore, E. B. (1999). *Ageism: Positive and negative.* New York: Springer.

Palmore, E. B., & Maeda, D. (1985). *The honorable elders revisited.* Durham, NC: Duke University Press.

Reichel, W. (1995). *Care for the elderly: Clinical aspects of aging.* (4th Ed.) Baltimore, MD: Wilkins & Wilkins.

Silverman, P., & Maxwell, R. (1978). How do I respect thee? Let me count the ways: Deference towards elderly men and women. *Behavior Science Research,* 13, 91-108.

Sokolvsky, J. (Ed.) (1990). *The cultural context of aging.* New York: Bergen & Garvey.

Streib, G. F. (1987). Old age in sociocultural context: China and the United States. *Journal of Aging Studies,* 7, 95-112.

Sung, K. T. (1990). A new look at filial piety: Ideals and practices of family-centered parent care in Korea. *The Gerontologist,* 30, 610-617.

Sung, K. T. (1995). Measures and dimensions of filial piety in Korea. *The Gerontologist,* 35, 240-247.

Sung, K. T. (1998). An exploration of actions of filial piety. *Journal of Aging Studies,* 12, 369-386.

Sung, K. T. (2001). Elder respect: Exploration of ideals and forms in East Asia, *Journal of Aging Studies,* 15, 13-27.

Sung, K. T. (2002). Elder respect among American college students: Exploration of behavioral forms. *International Journal of Aging and Human Development, 55*, 71-86.

Teachings of filial piety [Hsiao Ching]. [Translated by J. Legge.] (1989). *Sacred books of the east,* Vol. III. London: Oxford. (Originally published 1879-1885).

Yoon, H. S., & Cha, H. B. (1999). Future issues for family care of the elderly in Korea. *Hallym International Journal of Aging,* 1, 78-86.

Chapter 15

Respect Redefined:
Focus Group Insights From Singapore[1]

Kalyani Mehta

Today when people call a man filial, they mean that he is supporting his parents. But he does as much for his dogs and horses! If he does not show respect for his parents, how is he differentiating them from the animals?

- Confucius

Respect for elders has long been recognized as a highly valued principle in Asian cultures. Within the socialization process, respectful behavioral patterns are taught to young children with the view of perpetuating these values. Much variation exists over the extent of respect accorded to elders within Asian families and Asian communities today, as compared to the past [1-3]. The available literature points to a variety of phenomena occurring in different cultural contexts in terms of the prestige accorded to the aged. In some societies, economic growth has not affected the degree of respect that the elders receive from younger generations, for example, in Samoa owing to the mitigating effects of the *matai* family system, the elders have maintained prestige [4]. Simic draws an insightful comparison of the patterns of intergenerational relations in America and Yugoslavia [5]. He encapsulates the dynamics of deference shown to elders within the cultural values of the society in question, which deepens our understanding of this topic. In America, "Most, if not all formal signs of deference toward older persons has disappeared" [5, pg 94] which the author feels is linked to the great emphasis placed on individualism and democratic ideals in the society. On the other hand, the esteem of the elder in the Yugoslavian family continues due in part to the great value placed on "family solidarity" _and "intense affect relations" between parents and children. The example of Japan is perhaps more relevant to this study, since it is also in Asia. Several authors have researched on the topic [6-9]. Recent literature seems to point to a weakening of the state of high regard which elders in the past used to command in Japan. However, relatively speaking it may still be higher than some nations where it has eroded faster.

Respect and status are sometimes used interchangeably by authors with the assumption that a positive relationship exists between the two concepts. From the perspective of the Exchange Theory, the status of an elderly individual is determined by the relative power resources he possesses e.g., socioeconomic resources, charisma [10]. It is often assumed that with rapid technological advances and higher educational levels of younger generations the elderly would become "obsolete" having reduced level of younger generations the elderly would become "obsolete" having reduced level of control over resources and decision making leading to lowered social status. However, does lowering of power and control always lead to lowered respect? It need not be the case because status refers to a person's social position or rank in relation to others whereas respect refers to regard or admiration felt or shown for a person who has good qualities or achievements. Have researchers unknowingly blurred the differences between these two distinct concepts, so much so that it is perhaps time to reexamine each of them separately?

This article reexamines the meaning of respect, based upon the findings of twenty-three focus groups conducted in Singapore in 1990-1992, as part of the qualitative dimension of an international project "Comparative Study of the Elderly in Four Asian Countries," funded by the U.S. National Institute on Aging. The goal of the overall project is to measure the social, economic, and health characteristics of the older population (aged 60 and above), to predict what changes may occur over the next decades, and to suggest implications for public policy. The four countries are Taiwan, Thailand, Philippines, and Singapore. The findings reported here refer only to the Singapore data.

In Southeast Asia, Singapore leads as the country with the fastest increasing aging population. Presently, the elderly comprise 9 percent of the total population of Singapore [11], a figure which is expected to rise dramatically to 25 percent by the year 2030. This shift in the population's age profile will have major implications for the country's economy, health services, and social welfare programs. A prominent feature of Singaporean society is its multicultural composition. The Chinese (C) consist of 78 percent of the total population, the Malays (M) 14 percent, and the Indians (I) 7 percent. The remaining 1 percent comprise smaller groups such as Eurasians, Japanese, and Europeans. Singapore is, therefore predominantly an Asian society with a fast growing economy and a greying population.

The concept of respect is an oft-discussed topic in younger as well as older circles. Therefore, it was included in the focus group guideline. Interestingly, during the discussions it emerged that perceptions of the notion of respect seemed to be changing. In response to social changes there seemed to be subtle shift taking place in the "stock-of-knowledge" of the elder and adult generations. This can be seen to have significant bearing on the dynamics of intergenerational relations. Keeping abreast with these subtle shifts is important to counselors, family therapists, and social workers who practice in this area. Although the project was focused on the issue of living arrangements, which has been published in another report [12] in this article the domain of respect will receive attention. In addition to redefining respect based on the focus group data, the hanging expressions of respect, the conditions which promote these expressions and perceptions of the prevalence of respect toward elders in terms of past, present, and future, is discussed.

Methodology

The focus group method was adopted because it is able to generate data regarding the processes involved in determining the living arrangements of elderly in Singapore. The loose structure of the guided discussion allowed participants to express freely their observations and opinions regarding matters that are familiar and intimate, offering a richness that structured surveys often cannot capture. "The focus group technique has substantial potential for providing information that is simultaneously relevant to sociological investigations and is difficult to obtain using other techniques (i.e., surveys, experiments, etc.). It offers the promise of providing definitions of the situation that would not otherwise be available to the researcher" [13].

A total of twenty-three focus group discussions (FGDs), of which two were pilot groups, were conducted from August 1990 to February 1992 by the Department of Social Work and Psychology, National University of Singapore. The exact breakdown are as follows: four groups of Chinese elderly, with two groups each of high socioeconomic status (SES) and low SES; four groups of Chinese adult children, with two groups each of high SES and low SES; four groups of Indian elderly, with two groups each of high SES and low SES; two groups of Indian adult children with one each of high and low SES; five groups of Malay elderly with three of high SES and two of low SES; and two groups of Malay adult children with one each of high and low SES.

Two more Chinese adult children groups, compared to the other ethnic groups, were conducted to obtain a wider sample of the Chinese who constitute the majority population in Singapore. One small additional Malay elderly groups which consisted of three female participants from two previously held high SES mixed gender groups was conducted because it was found that gender differences inhibited participation of the female elderly in the earlier groups. This inhibition was, however, not prominent in other groups where members had freely contributed to the discussions. The size of each group ranged_ from five to ten participants.

The major variables utilized in this research design to distinguish groups were ethnicity, economic status, and generation. The elderly participants were aged between sixty to eighty-five years and adult children, aged twenty-five to forty-nine years, who had at least one surviving parent. The age range for elderly groups was twenty-five years with the mean age being sixty-five. The age range for adult children groups was twenty-four years with the mean range being thirty-six. High and low socioeconomic status (SES) was judged according to the type of dwelling in elderly groups and, in adult children groups, according to type of occupation. The team of investigators felt that since the majority of aged in Singapore were retired their household type rather than income was a better indicator of their socioeconomic status. Those living in private bungalows, five-room or four-room flats were classified as High SES whereas those living in three-room, two-room, or one-room flats were classified as Low SES. In the case of adult children, it was felt that in the Singaporean context income is considered as "personal" information, therefore occupation was considered a good substitute. For example, a manager or professional was considered High SES while a clerk or factory worker was considered Low SES. The number of groups conducted roughly matched the ethnic complexity of our research population. The majority of elderly groups were conducted in the languages of the participants, e.g., Malay, Chinese, and Indian dialects.

The sample population was obtained largely through purposive sampling. Participants were drawn from various existing natural groups such as old folks' clubs, religious groups, neighborhood groups, and welfare recipients living in proximity. Informal contacts referred by participants were also used. Screening of participants was conducted mainly by telephone. For those who did not possess telephones, home visits were carried out.

Each moderator was trained in group dynamics and was mindful of not posing leading questions. It surfaced that during focus group discussions, some factors influenced the flow and content of discussions. These were "posturing" on the part of participants; the skills and personality of the moderator, and interruptions e.g., telephone calls. There was a marked tendency by participants to personalize their answers to general questions. The last tendency occurred more in lower educated groups, who felt inhibited by their restricted knowledge. The quest of obtaining generalized views was sometimes thwarted due to this tendency.

The impressions gathered by the research team was that focus group discussions were efficient and effective in gathering qualitative material. The discussive nature of the sessions allowed participants to interact and stimulate each other, maintaining a high level of interest throughout the session. In many groups, participants expressed good feelings and satisfaction after the session. The data on living arrangements supported, in many aspects, earlier findings of other researchers, and further shed light to the processes leading to the current living arrangements. Furthermore, focus groups provided insight to the current dynamics that are forging new forces in defining the notion of respect as perceived by young and old Singaporeans.

In the focus group guideline, there were three questions directly focused on the topic of Respect. These were:

1. How much respect do you think elderly persons receive in the community?
2. How is this shown? Please elaborate.
3. In the past, did they receive more or less respect? Please elaborate. Discuss changes in the family and community.

Although there was no direct question such as "What does respect mean to you?," in all groups, participants elaborated on the changes in the meaning and expression of respect over time. This spontaneous focus was noted by moderators and was picked up in the analysis of transcripts. Since each group produced approximately forty-five printed pages of data, a computer program Ethnograph Version 3.0 was used to enable easy retrieval of coded data. In the final analysis and report writing a summary overview grid [14] was found to be extremely useful.

Findings

The underlying theme in both the elderly groups as well as adult children groups was that while in the past "respect" for elders in the family was synonymous with obedience, today this is not so.

> Mr. U: I would say it was more blind respect in the past. Today you respect the person but if there is a bone of contention, you argue about it definitely.
> (I. Adult Children High SES)

Respect today is synonymous with courtesy, voiced the adult children participants. The younger generation would accord politeness toward elders because

> Ms. M: Respect for age is always there, it has been ingrained.
> (I. Adult Children High SES)

> Ms. A: What the old folks expect is respect. Previously they expected obedience. But now they want to be informed of everything you do.
> (C. Adult Children High SES)

Thus it emerged in the focus group discussions that in the Singapore context the old definition of showing respect through "obedience" had shifted to keeping elders informed, which symbolized consideration and courteous behavior. This impression obtained from the focus groups is in keeping with the reality of present-day Singapore, as observed in my field of social work practice.

Kindness surfaced as another important dimension of respect. Kindness, whether demonstrated at home or in a public place was acknowledged as a mark of respect.

> Mdm. S: For me, when I collect paper boxes which are rather heavy, people will offer to help me carry.

(C. Elderly Low SES)

Mrs. W: To respect them in the family is to be kind to them. Not just give them food and leave them alone.
(C. Elderly High SES)

Mr. D: If I board the bus, the driver does not ask for fare. If I ask for a lift, he just picks me up, he even asks me to sit down and when I alight he keeps quiet, very respectful.
(C. Elderly Low SES)

The shift in the perceived meaning of respect from unquestioned obedience to courtesy and kindness, which cut across generations, gender, and ethnic lines in this research can be seen to reflect the changing social reality in Singapore.

A second finding which is concomitant with the changing nature of inter-generational relations in other parts of the world is the perceived lower level esteem or respect enjoyed by the older generation as compared to the past. This will be discussed in greater detail later in this article.

Expressions of Respect

The transcripts contained an interesting variety of expressions ranging from not raising your voice when speaking to elders, to polite manner of addressing them in the appropriate terms, to not doing something which would hurt them. In the area of consultation of elderly, there were divided opinions. In one group, the idea was discussed that since elderly were not updated on contemporary issues, it was futile to consult them over certain matters. In another group, the adult children ventilated their frustration over the dogmatic attitude of parents who preferred to stick to their principles rather than be accommodating to the concern's desires. In a couple of other groups, the elderly were consulted over certain family issues. These particular issues tended to be areas in which elderly had special expertise e.g., rituals and traditions. Thus, although it was recognized that seeking advice was a definite expression of respect, various dynamics explained the reasons for adult children not practicing it. It should be noted that carrying out the advice given was not necessarily part of the notion of respect.

Sharing with elderly if one brought home some special delicacy, and giving a regular cash allowance to one's parents were other expressions cited.

Mod: What kinds of acts would you consider to be examples of respect?
Mrs. Y: When my son takes home his pay, he would give some money to me, the more the better!

Mrs. S: When you are sick, the son should come to visit you. This will be enough.

Mr. T: It has to be self-initiated. But you yourself have to behave in such a way to deserve respect from others. If you want others to respect you, you must also respect others. Don't think that because you are older you can demand respect.
(C. Elderly Low SES)

The idea of "mutual respect" was mentioned in three out of the eight adult children groups. It was also stated in two elderly groups.

Mr. RR: Elderly will get respect only if they respect other people.
(I. Elderly Low SES)

Another important dimension is illustrated in the next quotation.

Mr. C: Now you have to earn respect but you cannot buy respect. Earn it in the things you do.
(C. Adult Children High SES)

The earlier quote is insightful because it reveals that one's actions draw respect from the next generation. Money by itself is not a guarantor of respect. This link between conduct and respect is seen again in the next quotation.

Mr. S: I wouldn't respect an elderly person just for the sake of respecting the elder person. I would respect someone who understands me and does not brush me aside saying "Oh, you are young, you don't know anything." I don't think that is right.

Mod: So an elderly person who knows how to communicate with the younger person.

Mr. S: Who knows how to conduct himself. I think that is important.
(I. Adult Children High SES)

The younger generation sometimes felt that respect would depend on the behavior of the elder. A well-mannered elderly person, who "conducts himself" with propriety would be likely to draw respect from youngsters. Clearly the extension of high regard for an elder person was tied to more than his social status. In the realm of the family and kin the past nature of the relationship had bearing upon the respect accrued to the elder.

Mod: Do you respect someone for the qualities he possesses or do you respect the person who is better off financially?

Mr. H: I think you respect a person for what they have done for you.
(I. Adult Children High SES)

Conditions Which Facilitate Respectful Behavior

Closely linked to the issue of respect in the family and community, and a topic which arose spontaneously was "Do rich elderly get more respect?" While some elderly and adult children felt that possession of economic power wielded respect, others felt that it was not necessarily so.

Ms. A: I believe a lot depends on the economic power they hold. Because the respect they hold will depend on the money they have.

Mr. S: Richer older folks have more authority, but not necessarily respect.

Ms. K: It is not all money. I mean, it depends on the relationship.
(C. Adult Children High SES)

It would seem that control of economic resources did not ensure or guarantee respect from one's family members. Other considerations such as the relational factor, reciprocity, and conduct of the elderly also played a major part.

Ms. G: When parents reciprocate, children respect them.
(M. Adult Children High SES)

As compared to the higher income groups, the elderly and adult children in the lower income groups asserted the significant role economic power seemed to play in drawing respect.

Mr. N: You would only respect me if I have money.

Mdm. N: If I give my grandchildren money they would call me "granny," if not no.
(I. Elderly Low SES)

The economic exigencies of the lower income strata impinged upon the dynamics of respectful behavior toward elderly. Thus, the data suggests that the role economic resources play in determining the respect an elderly receives is contextual, as well as influenced by the presence of other factors.

A second factor which was raised in at least half of the total number of focus groups was that early socialization of younger generation influences greatly the respect they accord to elders in family and community.

Mdm. K: What we hope is that our children can follow what we teach. Like people says that Malays are rich with courtesy—it's the Malay's treasure. So we must not lose them but to improve them and pass it on to the children.

Mod: So the way we train children is important to ensure respect.
(M. Adult Children Low SES)

> Mdm. S: I was saying that it also depends on the individual. The upbringing counts a lot. If they are not properly brought up, people tend to be disrespectful, no matter if you are old or young.
> (C. Elderly High SES)

Hence, it was clear that both elderly and adult children recognized the crucial role played by instilling the value of respecting elders in the early childhood years. For the adult children, early socialization was perceived as an effective way of trying to ensure that in future their children would practice the maxim.

Closely associated with the earlier point was the notion of "role modeling" which was raised by participants. In order to inculcate values and behaviors in youngsters, e.g., to teach respect toward elders to children, one had to practice it oneself. Thus, through observation and imitation the younger generation would emulate their parents.

> Mdm. J: Yes, we have to teach our children. Like if we treat our mother like that, our children will see and say, "My mother is respecting her mother"; this way, never scold elderly; or if they see their mother scolding her mother, so they may also raise their voices at us. . . . So we must be careful as children can easily follow.
> (M. Adult Children Low SES)

> Mdm. S: I believe if you show respect to your parents, your children will imitate you. If you really don't care for them, then later they will not reciprocate.
> (C. Adult Children High SES)

Finally, the basic ingredients of a positive relationship between generations, namely love and concern, was underscored as a source of drawing respect.

> Mr. A: Love and concern wins respect from the younger generation.
> (C. Adult Children High SES)

The Impact of Social Change

As compared to the past, in the majority of focus groups, the perception was that respect for elders was decreasing. This sentiment prevailed across both generations of participants i.e., elderly and adult children, and across ethnic and economic lines. Admittedly, to some degree "romanticizing" about the high regard enjoyed by elders of yesteryears was taking place. Nevertheless, their opinion was worth noting.

There were, however, three focus groups—all Chinese—in which members expressed that elderly were still respected in society, as they were in the past. In one Low SES group, the perception was that the degree of respect accorded was even higher than the past. This group felt that the improvement was largely due to the government's efforts.

> Mr. T: The government does a very good job in educating the young people. No matter what, there is an emphasis on helping the needy people in society.

> Mr. L: For example, taking the public bus transport, the young people will offer their seats for us. Whether these same people are filial at home, I'm not sure. But they certainly demonstrate for us in the bus.
> (C. Elderly Low SES)

In the other two groups, the level of respect in general was viewed as the same as before. The three groups who differed from the rest were all Chinese and the question therefore arises whether it is an ethnic variation. The author feels that it cannot be assumed to be so because the other three Chinese groups were in tune with the majority. Their perspective reflects the diverse nature of social reality and their experiences record kindness and courtesy demonstrated to elderly in the community.

Discussion in the focus groups on the possible reasons for erosion of respect disclosed three main causes. There were first, the rising materialism in Singapore society; second, the higher levels of education of the younger generations; third, the modern lifestyle partially influenced by Western ideas. The following quotations illustrate.

> Mr. K: It (society) has become materialistic. They (children) want to achieve and produce.

> Mdm. N: The mindset of the people of the new generation are different from those of the past. They are educated, have seen enough of the world and are capable. Because they are capable, they look down on the elderly.
> (C. Elderly Low SES)

Interestingly, in one focus group the elderly reminisced upon the pre-war memories of Singapore when people had limited wealth but valued human bonds greatly. After the second world war, they began to see the society slowly change to a materialistic society. With the increasing importance of money, human relationships within family and community were transformed. These sentiments were echoed in two adult children groups too.

> Mr. F: It was not like this in the olden days. People were different then. Regardless of whether they were rich or poor—people had love.

> Mod: Which period would you classify as the olden days?

> Mr. F: Before 1945. The attitudes of the people in the olden times were different. They worked and gave some amount to their elder brother, younger brother, and relatives. But youngsters of present times only care for money—they don't bother about you.
> (I. Elderly Low SES)

With increasing opportunities for higher education, the desire of independence by younger people also increased. Hence, the earlier definition of respect as equivalent to obedience was untenable. In Singapore, the increased exposure to television has brought into the living room news of the world. Elderly felt this increased knowledge also eroded respect for elders, who were unable to keep up with the technological advances and therefore perceived as 'obsolete.'

> Mr. L: We must understand, nowadays, parents are not at home, that is one bad thing. . . . So the children go on their way. That's modern life. So they are influenced by friends, T.V. and what they see. So there's no one to teach them and they are not living with their grandmother. . . . But with modern people, they already think old people are a nuisance so they let them go to a Home.
> (C. Elderly High SES)

Closely associated to the earlier point was the perception that the television was a vehicle for propagation of Western norms and mores, which impacted upon the values of Asian viewers especially the young and impressionable. Elderly in five groups discussed the modern life styles of the adult children who had busy work schedules and little time to spend on socializing their young in the proper traditional ways.

> C: It's because of Western culture and influence, that's why we have to teach children. Even though they want to go forward, be aggressive, and be forever going forwards, we cannot forget our cultural roots and that we are Chinese.
> (C. Elderly High SES)

When asked about the future, there were no consensus. Some participants felt that it would be very difficult for the older generation to earn the respect of the young. Others felt that the current situation would continue without much changes. Some qualified their answers by saying that as long as parents taught their children the proper values, future generations would continue to respect their elders.

> Mod: Do you think the respect will change in the future?

> Mrs. P: It depends on how you bring up your children. If parents are always working, they leave the children for some other person take care. Now most parents are always working. If they have children then somebody outside looks after them. I think the time they spend with the child is not sufficient. They can only spend time during the weekends to get close to children. So when children grow old, I don't think they will have that kind of closeness with the parents to want to take care of them. Because the parents left them alone, gave them money, to do what they want. So it may be that in ten years time in future, there will be more old age people, who have nobody to take care of them.
> (C. Adult Children High SES)

Discussion

Focus group discussions are effective and economical instruments of data collection in social science research especially for the purpose of clarifications of meanings, processes, and perceptions. In the present article, the subject of respect was explored for its meaning, its manifestations, and prevalence within the family and community.

The transformation of Singapore into a highly industrialized and modernized society has probably contributed toward the perceptual shifts in the meaning of "respect" from "obedience" to "courtesy." This can be seen as both a reduction in the power of the elderly as well as a process of accommodation of elder and younger generations to the changing times. Within the Asian context of Singapore and across the three ethnic groups, this shift in meaning seemed pervasive. It may be argued that even in the past obedience toward elders must have been accompanied by "courtesy." The counter-argument would be that a term often has several meanings, and precisely which meaning is generally accepted within a societal context at any particular time is a crucial piece of information. Based on the social researcher's assumption of meanings, questions are designed in surveys using relevant indicators. For example, noting the shift in meaning, it may be more useful to ask an elder, "Do your children/grandchildren inform you of their plans?" rather than "Do your children/grandchildren accept your advice?" On the other hand, survey questions such as "Do your family members respect you?" are ambiguous and the findings reported do not throw much light on the subject because the definition of "respect" by the interviewer and interviewee may be different. In a recent survey such a question was posed to Singaporean elderly as one of the two items to measure their status in their families [15]. The other item was "participation in family matters." It is the author's contention that specific behavioral indicators in questions related to the concept of respect would be more useful than simplistic questions which are loaded in assumptions.

The research also documents the perceived lower degree of respect accorded to elderly in Singapore as compared to a recollected past existing within the subjective realms of the participants. This finding is supported in another study by Lim [16]. Although these findings cannot be generalized because of the limited sample used, it does reflect the perceptions and feelings of the majority of twenty-three focus groups. The advantage of using a qualitative instrument such as focus groups is the greater depth to which an issue/topic may be probed as well as the likelihood of capturing shifts in meaning and processes.

The findings of this study offer insights into the perceptions of intergenerational relations based on the focus group discussions. While elders continue to expect respect from their children in the form of kindness, love and concern, and some monetary gifts, there was a growing realization that respect had to be mutual. Reciprocity between generations engendered growth of respect. In addition, the discussions underscored that actions and conduct of the elderly conditioned the amount of respect he could draw. Respect rested more on relational factors for the higher income groups, while economic resources affected the level of respect received by elders in lower income groups.

Socialization and "role modeling" were cited as effective avenues for the transmission of the value of respect for elders but with the growth of dual career marriages and employed babysitters, elderly showed pessimism over the value systems instilled in their grandchildren. While the latest statistics indicate that the 84.2 percent of children below age twelve are looked after within the home [11] we have no way of gauging how many of these parents work and how much time they devote to their children. Interestingly of the 84.2 percent 10 percent are cared for by their grandparents. The concern of the elderly participants is justified if we observe the trend for greater use of childcare centers by working women in Singapore. It seems plausible that parents would in future depend upon child-care teachers to instill Asian values such as respect for elders.

Both generations upheld the conventional wisdom that younger generations learn values by imitating their own parents. Thus, "role modeling" operates when grandchildren observe their parents' behavior toward their grandparents.

In conclusion, the case of Singapore presents an example of the fast-changing social scene in developing nations. The research has highlighted the fact that a concept may undergo shifts in meaning over time, and social researchers as well as helping professionals have to monitor such shifts. In the light of this study, it wold seem that status and respect cannot be presumed to be synonymous although there is some degree of overlap. Status as a concept appears to be closely linked with roles and functions whereas respect has a personalized dimension which explains why people in authority often do not draw respect. On a societal level, whether the Asian value of respect for elders continues to be transmitted will depend on whether the present adult generation takes the effort and time to instill this in the next generation. Even then, it seems that elders in future will need to give respect to younger generations in order to receive it.

Notes

1   This research forms part of a larger project sponsored by the U.S. National Institute on Aging, the Comparative Study of the Elderly in Four Asian Countries (Grant No. AGO07637).

References

Census of Population. Statistical Release 1 6. National Printers, Singapore, 1990.

P. L. Cheung, T. L. Ngiam, S. Vasoo, and Y. Y. Chan, Social Support Networks for the Elderly in a High-Rise Public Housing Estate in Singapore, in *Social Services and Aging*

Policies in the U.S. and Asia, H. L. Sheppard (ed.), International Exchange Center on Gerontology, Florida, pp. 305-341, 1991.

J. J. Dowd, Aging as Exchange: A Preface to Theory, Journal of Gerontology, 30:5, pp. 584-594, 1975.

L. D. Holmes, Other Cultures, Elder Years: An Introduction to Cultural Gerontology, Burgess, Minnesota, 1983.

L. Holmes and E. Rhoads, Aging and Change in Samoa, in Growing Old in Different Societies: Cross-Cultural Perspectives, J. Sokolovsky (ed.), Copley Publishers, Littleton, Massachusetts, pp. 119-130, 1987.

C. W. Keifer (op. cit.)

C. W. Keifer, The Elderly in Modern Japan: Elite, Victims or Plural Players? in *The Cultural Context of Aging: Worldwide Perspectives,* J. Sokolovsky (ed.), Bergin and Garvey, New York, pp. 181-196, 1990.

J. Knodel, Conducting Comparative Group Research: Cautionary Comments from a Coordinator, *Health Transition Review, 4*:1, pp. 99-104, 1994.

B. H. Lim, *An Exploratory Study on the Quality of Life Issues of Chinese Elderly with Family: Implications for Planning Social Service Programmes,* Academic Exercise, Department of Social Work and Psychology, National University of Singapore, 1993/94.

K. Mehta, A. E. Y. Lee, and M. M. Osman, Living Arrangements of the Elderly in Singapore: Cultural Norms in Transition, Journal of Cross-Cultural Gerontology, 10:1&2, pp. 113-143, 1995.

E. B. Palmore and D. Maeda, The Honorable Elders Revisited, Duke University Press, Durham, 1985.

D. Plath, "Ecstacy Years"—Old Age in Japan, in Growing Old in Different Societies: Cross-Cultural Perspectives, J. Sokolovsky (ed.), Copley Publishers, Littleton, Massachusetts, pp. 147-153, 1987.

A. Simic, Aging, World View and Intergenerational Relations in America and Yugoslavia, in The Cultural Context of Aging: Worldwide Perspectives, Sokolovsky (ed.), Bergin and Garvey, New York, pp. 89-107, 1990.

S. Vatuk, The Family Life of Older People in a Changing Society: India, in Aging and the Aged in the Third World "Regional and Ethnographic Perspectives", J. Sokolovsky (ed.), Studies in Third World Societies Publication Number 23. Department of Anthropology, College of William and Mary, Williamsburg, Virginia, 1982.

S. Wada, The Status and Image of the Elderly in Japan: Understanding the Paternalistic Ideology, in Images of Aging: Cultural Representations of Later Life, M. Featherstane and A. Wernick (eds.), Routledge, London, 1995.

R. A. Zeller, Focus Group Research on Sensitive Topics: Setting the Agenda without Setting the Agenda, in *Successful Focus Groups: Advancing the State of the Art,* D. L. Morgan (ed.), Sage, Newbury Park, pp. 167-183, 1993.

PART IV

Comparative Study

In Part IV, we will review cross-cultural explorations of the practice of respect for the elderly. We will describe specific similarities as well as differences between peoples of varied cultures and ethnic groups.

Chapter 16 reports on a nursing researcher's study of cultural differences she found in the way families interacted with her patients. She stresses the importance of understanding ethical and moral care values specific to cultures, and the need to be culture competent in caring for patients with non-Western cultural backgrounds, including Chinese, Japanese, Koreans and other Asians.

Chapter 17 introduces a report on a cross-cultural study of the ways in which Korean young adults and American young adults respect the elderly. Both groups cited care respect, acquiescent respect, linguistic respect, consultative respect, salutatory respect and precedential respect as the most often practiced and highly important forms. However, the two groups were dissimilar in other forms. Thus, similarities as well as differences are found between the two cultural groups, although the differences were a matter of degree.

Chapter 18 reports on a finding of a study of respect for the elderly in Canada. This study assessed changes in older people's levels of perceived respect between the 1970s and the 1980s. Significant increases were found in the level of respect for some ethnic groups, namely the British, French and Germans. The results suggest that the social climate of the elderly population in Manitoba, Canada has improved at least for some ethnic groups.

Chapter 19 introduces a study of respect for the elderly in Philippines, Singapore, Taiwan and Thailand. This study examined ways in which respect for the elderly is experienced in these countries, the extent to which respect has changed over time, and the reasons for changes in respect for the elderly. The changes were attributed to variations in family structure and function, education, income and modernization. These findings are discussed in relation to changing definitions of respect and variation in the ways in which respect for the elderly is expressed in different countries and ethnic groups.

Finally, Chapter 20 brings up a paper on filial piety practiced in Chinese communities, which include China, Hong Kong, Taiwan and Singapore. This chapter stresses that filial piety along with respect for elders is still upheld as sacrosanct in all of the Chinese communities, where the values of family-centered support for parents and elders are still being preserved and fostered. These values are influencing the making of policies on the aged in all of the communities. Thus cultural dictates persist. The policies are now oriented to caring and supporting of elders in larger communities beyond the boundary of the family.

Chapter 16

Culture: The Conspicuous Missing Link to Understand Ethical and Moral Dimensions of Human Care

Madeleine Leininger

Since the late 1970s, there has been an increased focus in nursing and medicine on moral and ethical issues, dilemmas, and problems that nurses and physicians face in providing human care services to clients. The increased number of new technologies, drugs and treatments, diverse client values, and the rise in consumer human rights are a few of the major factors leading to many ethical and moral issues in nursing and the health field. Nurses have faced these ethical issues in the most intense and continuous way because of their intimate contact with clients in providing direct care.

A systematic and comparative investigation of ethical and moral dimensions of human care of diverse cultures worldwide is one of the most challenging areas in nursing. Transcultural ethical and moral knowledge of Western and non-Western cultures is greatly needed to help nurses function effectively with people of different cultural backgrounds (Leininger 1978, 1983, 1988b). A knowledge of comparative ethical and moral values of multicultures is essential today to help nurses make meaningful care judgments, decisions, and actions. Indeed, to provide culturally congruent care and increase the client's health or well-being, culture knowledge based on ethical and moral dimensions of care is imperative. Knowing what "ought or should be" appropriate ethical care, or what is a "right or wrong" moral decision, requires that nurses know and understand different culture care values of individuals, families, groups, and institutions. Thus the challenge for nurses to be knowledgeable about and skilled in giving culturally based care to clients in the home, clinic, hospital, or in other settings is a major one, and it will increase in the future.

Some Culture Specific Ethical and Moral Care Values

It is always fascinating for nurses to realize that most cultures in the world explicitly or implicitly teach sets of cultural values to guide people in their moral commitments and to uphold desired ethical behavior. Diverse enculturation processes and sanctions exist to ensure proper moral and ethical culture behavior. Some cultures are quite conscientious in teaching and monitoring ethical behavior throughout the life cycle; other cultures, such as the United States, tend to be less conscientious in their enculturation practices. In Japan, the subject of ethics and morality has been taught for a longer period of time than in the United States. In a course called *Dotoku* (referring to ethics), students receive ethical and moral instruction related to group perseverance, diligence, quietness, patience, respect for elders, and teamwork (Lanham 1986). These values are mainly derived from their social structure and worldview, but especially from their religious and kinship systems. Japanese ethical values have guided the people in decision making and actions for many years, with only slight changes. The Japanese culture shows tenacity in the teaching of ethical values and principles, which has promoted cultural identity and other benefits to their sociocultural institutions.

In the United States, I have studied Japanese-American individual and family behavior in different nursing contexts, and have identified some behaviors similar to those mentioned above, such as the ethical care value of deference to and respect for the elderly, reciprocal kindness to one another, benevolence, and a tendency to forgive easily (Leininger 1983-1989). The dominant ethical care value of Japanese families to show *respect for the elderly* was clearly apparent in the home and in hospitals. In fact, deference and respectful care were viewed as a moral responsibility for nurses as caregivers with first, second, and third generation Japanese elderly and middlescent informants. While some slight variations prevailed with these ethical care values, they remained dominant themes of Japanese-American belief and action.

In an individual context, the ethical values of *respect* and *deference* were identified as important in a large Japanese manufacturing plant in the Midwest, where many employees had recently come directly from Hiroshima, Japan. They spoke English and Japanese, and were extremely deferent and benevolent to all Japanese employees, especially older employees in authority positions. They showed strong reciprocal loyalty and respect for one another and a "family-like corporate loyalty." These values were predominant ethical care values in the management of the Japanese plant. The Japanese company president was much respected for his role with employees who were deferent to him in many ways. The president's ethical caring behaviors of mutual respect for all employees was readily identified. This care value greatly attributed to group employee solidarity and a desire among employees to achieve the state institutional goals rather than individual employee achievements or awards. The few Anglo-American employees in the plant had difficulty at first adjusting to the Japanese ethical care values because their values of *high individualism, competition, self-reliance,* and *less respect for those in authority* were in conflict with the Japanese care values had been a covert source of tension and conflict as the Anglo-American employees were the minority employees. With consultation through group discussion, the employees became aware of these transcultural value difference and began to deal successfully with ethical care differences. The dominant action plan of *care accommodation,* as reflected in my theory goals, proved to be helpful in decreasing intercultural tensions between the two groups (Leininger 1988a).

Another illustration of the meanings and expressions of ethical care was discovered in Luna's recent study (1989) of Arab-Lebanese Muslims in three urban culture contexts. This was a major longitudinal study covering a three-year period, which I monitored as a research consultant and mentor. The purpose of the study was to identify the meanings and expressions of culture care, including moral and ethical care behaviors. It soon became apparent that all ethical and moral decisions were clearly derived from the Qur'an. The Qur'an is the holy scripture that contains the tenets of the Islamic religious beliefs and practices, and it guides Arab-Muslim beliefs care and practices. Luna found that care was viewed as *responsibility* and a *universal moral obligation* with all informants. There were, however, some gender role differences. The ethical care expectations for the male Arab-Lebanese Muslims were *honor, protection,* and to be an *economic provider* and *protector* of the Lebanese family. In contrast, the female Lebanese-Arab Muslims emphasized and practiced care as *family honor, unity,* and a *social and domestic family responsibility*. These ethical care responsibilities were clearly embedded in the religious and kinship systems. They were taught at an early age to children and served as a moral care guide to their daily living. These ethical care values became of central importance in helping nurses give culturally congruent care to Arab-Lebanese Muslims.

Prior to the research, hospital and clinic nurses and physicians were unaware of these *culture-based ethical care values* and had been frustrated in trying to get clients to cooperate, comply, or to understand what the staff wanted them to do. Cultural imposition and ethnocentric practices were identified, as were client dissatisfactions. Avoiding professional-staff appointments had been a common practice of Arab clients because it was perceived that the staff offered inappropriate and questionable care practices. There were other specific ethical care expectations of the Arab clients that made them uncomfortable with physicians and nurses. These were closely related to their religious beliefs and cultural values, such as the nurse giving medications to them with her left hand and a lack of attention to the modesty of the females. The nursing and medical staff in the hospital and clinic context needed culture-specific care knowledge in order to provide meaningful care to Arab-Lebanese Muslims, and thus protect their cultural values and rights. Luna's transcultural research findings are now being used by nurses in the care of Arab-Lebanese clients and families, and clients are responding positively.

Both Luna's (1989) and Wenger's (1988) research studies are examples of in-depth ethnonursing research in discovering similarities and differences in ethical care values and of the need for culture specific care practices. These transcultural findings are helping to build knowledge to support *ethical specific care decisions and actions.* The research methods of ethnonursing and ethnography and the Cultural Care theory were extremely important and valuable to discover and confirm ethical care meanings and patterns of behavior of different cultures (Leininger 1985a, 1988a).

In the search to identify universals or commonly shared care knowledge, a few examples will be offered from my research (1983-1989) with Mexican-Americans, North American Indians, Chinese-Americans, Arab immigrants, and Vietnamese refugees. These cultures all shared the common ethical care values of *filial respect and obedience* especially to the elderly. There were some slight differences in patterns of their care expression and in the meanings from their experiences that guided their ethical cultural care behaviors. For example, the Chinese-American informants had been in America for five years, and they retained a strong ethical obligation to be *obedient* and *compliant* to government officials and to the elderly. This finding, however, was not as strongly evident in the other four cultures. But ethical care variability was clearly evident with the values of *filial respect for* and *obedience to the elderly* with all five cultures and between first and second generations. In each of the five cultures, there were explicit prescriptions for what "ought to be" or "should be" desired ethical caring behavior and moral commitments of what made their actions "right" or "wrong" (Leininger 1983-1989). The informants were able to identify and explain the meanings of ethical care expectations, but it required that the researcher sensitively tease out the embedded care values from their religious, kinship, and lived-through cultural values. Currently, these ethical care values are being used to provide culture specific nursing care to individuals and families of these five cultures.

In the hospital context, it was interesting to discover that Anglo-American nurses showed less evidence of overt respect for clients of the five cultures cited above and for Anglo-American elderly. For many Anglo-American hospital nurses, care of the elderly was viewed as a "duty" or "task," and they expressed a preference to care for young or middle-aged clients. Several nurse informants were encouraging the elderly to be *elf-reliant* and to be *self-care givers* as they had been taught Orem's self-care theory. Interestingly, the nursing ethic of self-care was very difficult for these elderly clients to accept, as it as incongruent with their cultural values and ethical expectations (Leininger 1983-1989). The Anglo-American nurses were curious about the Vietnamese and Chinese clients and tended to avoid them because they could not speak their language and did not know their culture. Because of the nurses' lack of cultural knowledge and language uses, they were greatly handicapped in giving appropriate culture care to clients of the five cultures.

In general, discovering and using appropriate ethical and moral culture care knowledge can make a major difference in ways nurses can help clients to restore their health and well-being. Knowledge of culture specifics and universals about ethical and moral care behaviors remains largely undiscovered. Research findings from diverse cultures world wide should help open the door to new modes of nursing care decisions and actions. This discovery is just beginning and will take time and diligent efforts with over two thousand cultures in the world.

Interestingly, the ethical concepts of autonomy, self-respect, and human dignity are frequently cited as universals in the nursing literature and in the Code of Ethics for Nursing (Viens 1989), however, the existence, meanings, and expressions have not been *established* by research as cultural universals. While the nursing profession undoubtedly would like to have ethical values serve as "universal" guides to nurses' behavior and actions, the epistemic cultural knowledge base with its cultural variabilities has not been verified. It is, therefore, important that nurses begin to study Western and non-Western cultures to establish the substantive foundation for ethical care constructs, meanings, and expressions. This is one of several transcultural nursing goals which the author and her graduate students have been working toward using the Theory of Culture Care with its many practical and abstract features to provide culturally congruent care.

Most importantly, ethical care concepts, principles, and practices need to be taught in schools of nursing so that nurses can learn and skillfully use ethical care concepts with clients, families, and groups of different cultural backgrounds. To achieve this goal, some major changes in nursing curricula are needed to replace vague, ethnocentric, or inaccurate ethical concepts that do not reflect diverse or similar culture values. Teaching *emically-derived* culture care knowledge is essential for beneficial client outcomes and to deal with the nurse's *etic* views derived from the profession, which may not always fit with the client's care values. Transcultural nurse specialists and generalists can be of a great help in establishing relevant teaching content and curricular changes (Leininger 1989). The use of the growing body of transcultural nursing care findings could help to advance the science of ethical care. In addition, Culture Care Theory and ethnonursing research methods are invaluable to advance the explication of specific ethical moral dimensions of care that are rooted in culture values and life ways. As clients continue to seek culture-congruent care to support their ethical and moral care beliefs, one can anticipate that all professional nurses will need transcultural care knowledge in their teaching, curricular work, and clinical practices. In general, a major gap exists in regard to ethical and moral care largely because there are still too few faculty and nurse researchers prepared in transcultural nursing, and who value ethical cultural variabilities in nursing.

Contextual Spheres of Ethical Culture Care

In this final section, four contextual spheres of ethical and moral culture care will be briefly discussed from different perspectives: (a) *personal or individual,* (b) *professional of group,* (c) *institutional or community,* and (d) *cultural or societal.* These four spheres can be viewed as differential contexts, which give meaning to and greatly influence ethical and moral decisions and actions of care. They are the reality context or perspectives in which nurses and clients function, and which need to be recognized in order to understand and accurately assess ethical care. These four contextual spheres of knowing and understanding can guide the nurses' competencies and effectiveness as they realize that differential contexts can mean shifts in the way nurses function in caring for clients, families, or groups of people.

In considering these contextual spheres of ethical and moral behavior, nurses need to recognize the principle that different contexts can lead to different meanings and behaviors (Leininger 1970, 1978, 1984, 1988b). Each sphere reflects different cultural frames of reference for ethical care decisions and actions. For example, in the United States, Americans maintain a dominant focus on the *individual* or *one's personal views, rights, beliefs, and actions,* and ethical decisions tend to be referenced to *individuals* as the sphere of knowing or understanding. In contrast, in the People's Republic of China, the Chinese maintain a dominant reference to *collective* and *societal norms* in any decision or action, and personal or individual rights receive limited attention and are not of prime consideration. Indeed, individual rights in China are deferred to what is "best for society," or the *collective societal good.* Any decisions regarding individual rights become part of a communal obligation and a right of the central government, based on well-known and explicit cultural rules and regulations (Leininger 1983-1989). Thus any individual ethical rights and freedoms in China are of limited importance and deferred to the collective needs in the Chinese society with reinforced rules, sanctions, and obligations.

These care expectations were identified in the author's research with the dominant Chinese culture values of *obedience* and *compliance* within the country and for recent Chinese living in the United States. Interestingly, these cultural values were evident during the recent (June 1989) pro-democratic students' movement in China in which the central political committee of the communist government (Politburo) denied any individual or personal wishes of students as they rallied for a more democratic government. Such strong collective central government rules were alarming to many Americans and especially to American students who greatly value freedom and the rights of individuals to be heard, to make choices, and to receive due consideration of their needs. For American students, the Chinese cultural norms or rules of *obedience, compliance,* and *deference to authority* were extremely difficult to accept; however, the Chinese students in the People's Republic of China should have been keenly aware of them. It was interesting to find in my study that Chinese-American students, who had come from China since 1980 and who were studying at a Midwestern university, had retained these values of obedience to the government as an obligation, but they were also looking for future changes toward more democratic principles when they returned to China (Leininger 1983-1989).

Turning to the Western world of nursing, especially in the United States, the nurse's individual and professional values and perceived personal rights are dominant spheres that tend to govern what nurses should or ought to be. In the culture of Western nursing, most nurses become upset and protest today if their perceived individual or professional rights are violated (Leininger 1970, 1984). Collectivities, institutions, or group values are often viewed with suspicion, especially if individual rights are perceived to be threatened. Many ethical issues, conflicts, and dilemmas become major problems to the nurse when his or her individual rights and autonomy are not fully considered. The nurse usually has to deal with at least three major sets of ethical rights. First, there are the *personal* home cultural values that the nurse learned when growing up in the family culture. Second, there is the *professional set of cultural values* that the nurse learns in schools of nursing. Third, the nurse is expected to live by and value the *American or societal cultural values* as a U.S. citizen. The latter contextual sphere is important for the nursing profession to become culturally and socially relevant to humanity. In addition, the nurse is also challenged by the *public or private institutional value system* of hospitals, agencies, or wherever the nurse is employed. These different sets of cultural and ethical values often differ greatly, and nurses can experience cultural value conflicts or stresses. Cultural conflict in ethical values is often a major reason for nurse turnover on resignation, but it is not always recognized. Hence the nurse can get caught in different contextual ethical spheres of knowing and experiencing what is "good" or "bad," or "right" or "wrong," or what threatens the nurses autonomy or rights. These different cultural contexts of ethical knowing need to be recognized by nurses to prevent cultural burnouts, cultural imposition practices, cultural conflicts, and even serious legal problems.

In these different contextual spheres of ethical thinking and decision making, the nurse may need to *compromise* personal ethical values for another perceived good or benefit. Sometimes the nurse works out what Ray (1988) calls a "bonding" relationship with the client. Sometimes, the nurse avoids ethical dilemmas by not dealing with them or figuratively "running away from" the ethical conflicts. And sometimes nurses live almost perpetually with unresolved ethical care conflicts that reduce their energies, freedoms, professional skills, and work satisfaction.

Turning to clients, I found from my research that their ethical and cultural values were limitedly assessed by nurses, but the clients were fairly quick to identify by "trial and error" the institutional rights, standards, or rules of hospital behavior (Leininger 1983-1989). The clients' personal and cultural care beliefs and values tended to get limited attention by the hospital staff. If clients acquiesced to nurses, physicians, or institutional ethical norms, they showed some signs of being restless and dissatisfied if the norms were counter to their values. It was also difficult for the nurse and physician to fully accept and respect clients' right to choose. In the hospital context, clients often had to yield to professional staff's values and choices or to the institution norms because of fear that they would not receive any care of treatment if they asserted their own rights or choices. The client, therefore, tended to comply with health personnel's desires to get reasonable care and treatment. This is a critical ethical issue today with the extreme shortage of nurses, with many acutely ill clients in the hospital, and with short-term hospital stays, as clients may often feel that they are "at the mercy of nurses and physicians." Clients know they are not on their "home turf," able to make safe decisions or to assert their rights. Several clients told me that it was "almost impossible to refuse whatever was offered by the nurse or physician because if they did not comply they would not be able to remain in the hospital for treatment or care. Or, if they did not comply they would be treated in a non-caring way" (Leininger 1983-89). Thus the client's decision was usually to comply. Those ethical issues and other related ones merit further study and resolution by nurses and physicians.

It has also been interesting to note that in some cultures, such as the Philippine, Korean, and mainland Chinese, clients want and expect the physician and nurse to make decisions for them, especially when they are critically ill, because of their cultural value of *deference* to those in authority. However, most American clients take a different position and want to make choices and decisions as *their* ethical American right and freedom. Today many American clients are becoming more active in choosing their hospitals, therapists, treatments, and care. The "Patient's Bill of Rights" is a document often given to clients as they enter the hospital, but ethical conflicts prevail between the nurse and client as they enter the hospital, but ethical conflicts prevail between the nurse and client when their different ethical rights cannot be successfully resolved or compromised. In contrast, non-American clients are often baffled by the Anglo-Americans assertive demands for their rights and freedoms in client services. In the future, these major cultural differences in values and in ethical and moral viewpoints need to be considered in order to provide quality nursing care.

Given these differential contextual spheres that influence the nurse's ethical decisions, how does and should the nurse resolve them? What are appropriate or inappropriate ethical decisions in these different contextual spheres and with different client and nurse expectations? Is there a hierarchical ordering in which one sphere supersedes the other in different cultures? Do cultural or societal values have rights over personal, individual, or institutional rights in different cultures? What happens if the "traveling nurse" follows the Western type of utilitarian ethics in a non-Western culture? How will this nurse know what is "good for the utility," or for the assumed majority of clients in the particular cultures in which employed? Of, if the nurse makes an ethical dare decision from the *deontological* stance, how congruent is this decision for what is "best for the individual" unless the nurse knows the individual's cultural values, beliefs, and practices, let alone the societal cultural values? Do current public health policies violate cultural values? These are additional untapped ethical nursing questions that merit systematic study as important ethical and moral care issues related to ethical care.

As nurses become knowledgeable about Western and non-Western cultural philosophies, they will be able to develop comparative and new ethical theories, principles, codes, covenants, and practices. But until this body of knowledge becomes explicated, it will be difficult to provide culturally based ethical care. Most assuredly, nursing researchers using qualitative research methods such as phenomenology, ethnonursing, ethnography, grounded theory, symbolic interaction, and other methods within the qualitative paradigm will be essential because ethical and moral care values are almost impossible to measure, manipulate, experimentally control, or arrive at through the linear or positivistic logical reasoning that characterizes the quantitative paradigm (Leininger 1985b). Both subjective and objective ethical care concepts, principles, and patterns need to be sought, from the *people's* worldview, philosophical ideologies, and cultural values.

In this chapter, I took the stance that culture is the conspicuous and critically missing link to discover and understand the ethics of care and nursing, and that ethical and moral meanings and expressions are epistemologically rooted in culture. Culture, I contend, provides the broadest holistic knowledge base to build an accurate and reliable knowledge base of ethical care and to guide decisions about human care, health, death, daily life factors. It is a moral responsibility for nurses to learn about diverse ethical care practices in order to help clients retain their cultural values and ethical rights, and be cared for in therapeutic ways. The theory of culture care with focus on the worldview, social structure, and environmental context can help us discover ethical care in Western and non-Western cultures. And one of the most important discoveries in the study of ethical and moral values, norms, codes, covenants, principles, sanctions, rights, responsibilities, and obligations is to realizes that these ethical aspects are *culturally constituted and expressed* within meaningful living contexts. While some progress is being made to discover comparative ethical care, much more work lies ahead. It will be encouraging to see nurses move forward to discover the universal and diverse dimensions of ethical human care.

References

Aroskar, M. 1987. The interface of ethics and politics in nursing. Nursing Outlook 35(6): 268-72.

Beauchamp, T., and J. Childress. 1983. Principles of biomedical ethics, 2d ed. New York: Oxford University Press.

Boas, F. 1966. Race, language and culture. New York: Free Press.

Callahan, D. 1980. Autonomy: a moral good, not a moral obsession. Hastings Center Report 14(5): 40-42.

Carper, Barbara. 1979. The ethics of caring. Advances in Nursing Science 1(3): 11-19.

Curtin, L., and J. Flaherty. 1982. Nursing ethics: Theories and Pragmatics. Bowie, MD: Robert J. Brady Co.

Davis, A. J. 1981. Compassion, suffering, morality: Ethical dilemmas in caring. Nursing law and ethics 2(6): 8.

Downing, T., and G. Kushner. 1988. Human rights and anthropology. Cambridge, MA: Cultural Survival.

Fowler, M. 1986. Ethics without virtue. Heart and Lung 15(5): 528-30.

Fry, S. 1986. Moral decisions and ethical decisions in a constrained economic environment. Nursing Economics 4(4): 160-63.

Fry, S. 1988. The ethics of caring: Can it survive in nursing? Nursing Outlook 36(1): 48.

Gadow, S. 1980. Existential advocacy—philosophical foundation for nursing. San Francisco: Image Ideas Publication.

Gilligan, C. 1982. In a different voice: Psychological theory and women's development. Cambridge: Harvard University Press.

Haviland, W. A. 1987. Cultural anthropology. 5th ed. New York: Holt, Rinehart, and Winston.

Herskovits, M. 1964. Cultural dynamics. New York: Knopf.

Horn, B. 1978. Transcultural nursing and child-rearing of the Muckleshoot people. Transcultural nursing: Concepts, theories and practices, edited by M. M. Leininger, 223-39. New York: John Wiley and Sons.

Kluckhohn, C. 1970. Mirror for man. Greenwich, CT: Fawcett Press.

Lanham, Betty B. 1986. Ethics and moral precepts taught in schools of Japan and the United States. Japanese culture and behavior: Selected readings, edited by J. Libra and W. Libra, 280-96. Honolulu: University of Hawaii Press.

Leininger, M. 1970. Nursing and anthropology: Two worlds to blend. New York: John Wiley and Sons.

Leininger, M. 1974. Humanism, health and cultural values. Health care dimensions: Health care issues, 37-61. Philadelphia: F. A. Davis Co.

Leininger, M. 1978. Transcultural nursing: Concepts, theories, and practices. New York: John Wiley and Sons.

Leininger, M. 1983. Cultural care: An essential goal for nursing and health care. American Association of Nephrology Nurses and Technicians 10(5): 11-17.

Leininger, M. 1983-89. Transcultural ethnonursing and ethnographic studies in urban community contexts. Detroit: In press.

Leininger, M. 1984. Care: The essence of nursing and health. Thorofare, NJ: Charles B. Slack. Reprint 1988 by Wayne State University Press.

Leininger, M. 1985a. Transcultural care diversity and universality: A theory of nursing care. Nursing and health care 6(4): 202-12.

Leininger, M. 1985b. Ethnography and ethnonursing: Models and modes of qualitative data analysis. In Qualitative research methods in nursing, 33-73. Orlando, FL: Grune and Stratton.

Leininger, M. 1988a. Leininger's theory of nursing: Cultural care diversity and universality. Nursing Science Quarterly 1(4): 152-60.

Leininger, M. 1988b. Care: Discovery and uses in clinical and community nursing. Detroit: Wayne State University Press.

Leininger, M. 1989. The transcultural nurse specialist: Imperative in today's world. Nursing and Health Care 10(5): 251-56.

Luna, L. 1989. Care and cultural context of Lebanese Muslims in an urban US community: An ethnographic and ethnonursing study conceptualized within Leininger's theory. Ph.D. diss., Wayne State University.

MacIntyre, A. 1981. After virtue. Notre Dame, IN: University of Notre Dame Press.

Noddings, N. 1984. Caring: A feminine approach to ethics and moral education. Berkeley: University of California Press.

Ray, M. 1988. Discussion group summary: Ethical dilemmas in the clinical setting—time constraints, conflicts in interprofessional decision making. In The ethics of care and the ethics of care: Synthesis in chronicity, edited by J. Watson and D. Ray, 37-39. New York: National League for Nursing, Pub. #15-2237.

Ray, M. A. 1987. Health care economics and human caring in nursing: Why the moral conflict must be resolved. Family Community Health 10(1): 35-43.

Toulmin, S. 1987. The tyranny of principles. Hastings Center Report 11(6): 31-39.

Veach, R., and S. Fry. 1987. Case studies in nursing ethics. Philadelphia: J.B. Lyppincott.

Viens, D. 1989. A history of nursing's code of ethics. Nursing Outlook 37(1): 45-49.

Watson, J. 1985. Nursing: Human science and human care. A theory of nursing. Norwalk, CT: Appleton-Century-Crofts.

Watson, J., and M. Ray. 1988. The ethics of care and the ethics of cure: Synthesis in chronicity. New York: National League for Nursing, Pub. #15-2237.

Wenger, A. 1988. The phenomenon of care in a high context culture: The old order Amish. Ph.D. diss., Wayne State University.

Chapter 17

Elder Respect Among Young Adults: A Cross-Cultural Study of Americans and Koreans

Kyu-taik Sung

1. Introduction

The way in which older people are respected varies by culture (Holmes & Holmes, 1995 and Sokolovsky, 1990), as cultural change has a significant effect on respect for the elderly (Palmore & Maeda, 1985; Simic, 1990; Streib, 1987 and Sung, 1994). We need to understand the existence of meaningful cultural differences in the way the elderly are respected. To explore the current trends in the way, the practice must be investigated within and across cultural contexts, taking into account different cultural perspectives. (Hereafter, respect for the elderly is called elder respect. The term elder here denotes parents, elderly relatives, neighborhood elders, elders in the workplace, and older adults in general.)

It is necessary to look at younger people as a potential source of the changes occurring in attitudes toward the elderly in any given culture. In the case of college students, exposure to a liberal atmosphere on college campuses, relative lack of parental supervision, and greater peer influence affect their lives and behaviors. As a consequence, they are likely to contract new values different from their parents' and be less supportive of the traditional norms governing the manner of treating the elderly. Yet, these young adults will be an essential part of the support system for the old. How they treat elders is critical not only to the elderly, but also to society.

For older persons, food, shelter, health care, and security are all necessities. But they have another cardinal need: the need to be treated with respect. A survey of long-term care facilities found that what elderly residents needed most was in fact respect. Respect was a key factor that determined their quality of life (Cohen-Mansfield, Ejas, & Werner, 2000; Noelker & Harel, 2000). Without respect, positive attitudes toward the elderly cannot exist, nor can elders be treated with propriety. The consequences of disrespectful treatment of the elderly have been reported (Butler, 1995; Palmore, 1999 and Rowe & Kahn, 1998), and prejudice against the elderly, manifested in myths, disdain, dislike, and discriminatory practices, has been known for some time (Han, 2000; Kim, 1998; Kosberg & Torgusen, 2001; Lee, 2000; MacNeil et al., 1996 and Pillemer & Finkelhor, 1988).

The issue of elder respect has been gaining increased attention from gerontologists (Chipperfield & Havens, 1992; Ingersoll-Dayton & Saengtienchai, 1999; Mehta, 1997; Palmore & Maeda, 1985; Post, 1989; Silverman & Maxwell, 1978; Streib, 1987 and Sung, 2001a). Gerontologists hope that, by treating elderly persons with respect, the elderly can be cared for with propriety and humanity, their status can be uplifted, and they can be more fully integrated with the family and society. Therefore, elder respect remains as a critically important element in the maintenance of elderly persons' status and dignity, and in the delivery of care and services for them.

There has been, however, little research on how the young respect the elderly in the United States, let alone on the issue of cross-cultural differences in elder respect between Americans and peoples of other cultures. As a consequence, empirical data on the way the elderly are respected are extremely limited.

The present study compares two sets of data on how young adults respect the elderly. It is focused on the identification of specific forms of elder respect, as analyzed in one data set on college students in Korea and one on American college students. Reviewing the way the elderly are respected by younger Americans in Western culture, in comparison with the way non-Western young adults in East Asia respect the elderly, could reveal salient differences. Thus, we can find out what both cultures can learn from each other regarding the forms of elder respect that are, more or less, widely practiced, or are missing or undermined in the respective cultures.

The purpose of this study is to explore the forms of elder respect practiced by young Korean and American adults, and to provide a preliminary inventory of these forms for future research. The study distinguishes explicit behavioral forms of elder respect that are cross-culturally equivalent and other forms which are culture-specific, and discusses certain cultural traits associated with the forms. It is not the purpose of this paper to discuss the philosophy of respect or to conduct a causal analysis of respect-related variables, but rather, to explore the explicit forms of respect practiced in the respective cultural contexts.

2. Previous Studies

Downie and Telfer (1969: 23) and Dillon (1992) said that people respect a person by paying careful attention to that person and taking him or her seriously. Respect, however, calls for more than attention. We treat a person in a certain manner or act in a particular way to respect the person. That is, as Dillon and Gibbard (1990: 265) defined, respect for a person requires certain actions or behavioral expressions, which are deserved by the person. Such actions are intended to convey an altruistic and benevolent sense of regard. Elder respect is, hence, an open and matter-of-fact behavioral expression that can be observed and recorded (Silverman & Maxwell, 1978).

Two rare studies conducted in East Asia have introduced various behavioral expressions of elder respect. Palmore and Maeda (1985), based on their study of the status of the elderly in Japanese society, introduced descriptive expressions of the ways in which the Japanese conveyed elder respect. Ingersoll-Dayton and Saengtienchai (1999), using focus groups, distinguished similarly diverse expressions based on their extensive study of Taiwanese, Singaporeans, Thais, and Filipinos. In the two prior studies, the units of analysis were subgroups of adults and elders. Though the studies addressed the same topic—ways of respecting elders—their research methods varied. Yet, they yielded parallel results for the identification of a set of similar expressions of elder respect and their forms. The two studies distinguished altogether 13 forms, which are all important corollaries of elder respect. The forms ranged from care respect to ancestor respect. Building upon these findings, the present study distinguishes the forms of elder respect practiced by young adults in the two cultural contexts.

While the previous studies made significant contributions, neither presented quantitative data on the extent to which individual forms of elder respect were practiced and the degree to which importance was given to these forms. In addition, neither investigated the forms with regard to the age or generation of the participants in a cross-cultural context.

3. Cross-Cultural Approach

There were noticeable differences between the two comparison groups. The Koreans lived in a society influenced by the tradition of filial piety, where elder respect and parent care were stressed, whereas the Americans lived in a society which did not have such cultural influences. This finding corresponds to the finding of Streib (1987) on the differences between China and the United States in terms of traditional cultural patterns, for example, elder respect of the Chinese and low automatic respect of Americans. In addition, nearly 65% of the Korean participants lived with their parents, whereas 7% of the American participants did so. These data reflect the general cultural differences between the two societies.

A selection of study participants in different societies poses the analytical problem of how a meaningful comparison can be presented. Dogan and Pelassy (1984) proposed that, for the analysis of dissimilar systems, an abstract value and an inclusive set of comparative categories need to be adopted. Verba (1971: p. 315) indicated the need to establish the functional equivalence of items for comparison in a cross-cultural study. In line with these propositions, Streib (1987), in his cross-cultural study of China and the United States, has met the challenge by selecting an abstract scheme with an orientation to cultural values and focusing on cross-cultural subsets for limited comparability. In comparative studies, it is also important to use comparable techniques, cover the same subject matter, and apply comparable concepts for the distinct cultures (Cogwill, 1986 and Liang & Jay, 1990).

The matching of study participants is a critical issue; by doing this, at least some of the cultural and demographic characteristics of the participants can be made similar or be controlled across cultures (Van de Vijver & Leung, 1997). Liang and Jay (1990) pointed out the importance of measurement equivalence in cross-cultural contexts, for example, semantic equivalence (the variable to be compared has the same meaning) and metric equivalence (the tool for analysis has the same measurement specifications).

4. Method

The two surveys, one conducted in Korea and the other in the United States, are equivalent in their study theme—the value of elder respect. An inclusive set of behavioral expressions indicating this theme in terms of specific forms of elder respect, and their categories, was accounted for in both cultural contexts. In each context, two universities were selected purposively to obtain a subset of population of young adults, one from universities in a metropolitan area and the other from those in a local area. Both are accredited coeducational universities with undergraduate and graduate programs and have socially, economically, and religiously diverse student bodies.

Korean survey. Korean data were collected from 401 students: 211 enrolled at a university in Seoul and 190 at a university in a local city south of Seoul. These students were attending 1 of 12 classes (class sizes 9–52) in the social sciences. The classes were randomly chosen; 95% of the participants in each classroom returned completed questionnaires.

American survey. The American sample consisted of 501 students: 256 taking classes at a university in the Midwest and 245 at a university on the West Coast. In terms of ethnicity, 71% were Caucasian, 12% African-American, 12% Latino, and 5% were Asian Americans. They were more Latino and Asian Americans in the West Coast group than in the Midwest group (24.6%:9.1%). The students were attending altogether 28 randomly chosen classes (class sizes:

12–45) in social sciences. About 85% of the participants in each classroom returned completed questionnaires.

The participants at the universities in both cultural contexts were comparable in terms of average age (Koreans: 23.5 years; Americans: 23.1), gender (Koreans: male 55%, female 45%; Americans: male 51%, female 49%), and educational level (Koreans: seniors 44%, graduate students 56%; Americans: seniors 48%, graduate students 52%). Thus, the ranges of variation of the participants and the study sites were circumscribed for limited comparability. Furthermore, the study instrument (survey questions) and the measurement techniques (assessment of the "frequency," with which a form was cited, and the "rating of importance" given to the form based on a four-point scale) were equivalent in both cultural contexts.

In both surveys, the responses of the participants were elicited by the following two questions.

The first question identified the forms that the participants most often practiced. The second question assessed the levels of importance the participants assigned to the forms. These levels were rated on a four-point scale (4=*extraordinarily important* to 1=*fairly important*). Added to the questionnaire were socioeconomic items including age, gender, and ethnicity. The questionnaire was administered in classrooms, where the instructor explained the voluntary nature of participation and asked the students to complete it anonymously. In a pilot study, cultural context had no distinguishable effect on responding abilities or patterns.

The questions were phrased in simple sentences, with no idiomatic or colloquial expressions. In translating the questions, the translation-back-translation procedure was employed; the bilingual investigator prepared the questions in Korean and then had another bilingual to translate them into English. A third bilingual translated the translated questions back into Korean. The three translators compared the questions in both language versions and judged that both were culturally appropriate and linguistically equivalent.

For the analysis of the survey data, the investigator, familiar with the cultural values of both countries, collaborated with two bilingual associate investigators experienced in gerontological research. The three investigators analyzed the answered questionnaires separately; their independent testimonies regarding the interpretation and categorization of expressions of elder respect were cross checked, and discrepancies were resolved by majority rule. The categories and forms were subsequently defined and tabulated. The reason for this procedure was the belief that reliability increases validity.

5. Analysis

5.1. KOREAN DATA

Care respect was the most frequently cited form (62% of the participants). The second most frequently cited form was acquiescent respect. This is followed by consulting respect, precedential respect, salutatory respect, and linguistic respect. The rest of the forms cited by fewer participants are victual, gift, presentational, public, celebrative, spatial, ancestor, and funeral. Care respect was also rated highest in terms of importance (3.60 in the four-point scale, close to *extraordinarily important*); it is followed by consulting, acquiescent, linguistic, salutatory, precedential, and victual—all roughly *extraordinarily* to *highly important*. The rest of the forms—gift, presentational, public, celebrative, spatial, ancestor, and funeral—are roughly *highly* to *averagely important*.

Of the 14 forms, 6 (care, acquiescent, consulting, precedential, salutatory, and linguistic) were cited by over 30% of the participants and were rated *extraordinarily* to *highly important*. These forms stand out; they were practiced more often and considered more important than other the forms in the Korean context.

To examine the comparability of the findings at the two universities, the analyses were undertaken by dividing the participants into two groups. There was no statistically significant difference between the two groups in terms of frequency with which the forms were cited [χ^2 ranging from 3.23 (*P*=.07) to .65 (*P*=.45), *df*=1]. In terms of the rating of importance, no differences were found between the groups [*t* values ranging from 0.31 (*P*=.86) to 0.21 (*P*=91), *df*=400, 2-tailed). Only by age groups (20–24, 25–29, 30–34, 35+) was there any significant difference with respect to a form of acquiescent respect (*F*=1.36, *P*<.025, *df* =2, 193), which implied that older participants tended to give greater importance to this form. Overall, these results suggest that there is a similarity or consistency between the two groups in the importance ratings on the majority of the forms.

To explore the underlying dimensions of the forms, a Varimax rotated factor analysis of the forms was conducted using the data on the degree of importance. Three factors with an eigenvalue over one emerged. The first factor with five loadings is named "symbolic elder respect," as the items relate to symbolic gestures expressing respect. The second factor with three loadings is called "engaging elder respect," as the items indicate engagement in respectful actions such as caring, consulting, and serving meals. The third factor "cultural elder respect," which includes ancestor respect, has two loadings. The three factors together account for 37% of the variance. This result suggests that the forms cited by the Koreans have the three dimensions.

5.2. AMERICAN DATA

Acquiescent respect was the most frequently cited form among the Americans (50% of all the participants). Care respect was the second most frequently cited, and was followed by linguistic respect, salutatory respect, consulting respect, and precedential respect. The rest of the forms were cited by 5% or less. In terms of importance, care respect was the highest rated form (3.67, in the four-point scale), followed by consulting, acquiescent, salutatory, linguistic, and precedential. Care, acquiescent, and consulting were roughly *extraordinarily important*, and salutatory, linguistic, and precedential were *extraordinarily* to *highly important*. Although rated as important, six other forms—presentational, public, celebrative, gift, spatial, and victual—were rarely or minimally practiced by the young Americans (These forms were excluded from the subsequent analyses.) Combining the results of the analyses of frequency and importance, six forms—care, consulting, acquiescent, salutatory, linguistic, and precedential—are found outstanding; these forms were practiced more often and are rated more important than others

There was a difference between the participants in the Midwest and those on the West Coast only in acquiescent respect (χ^2=.85, df=1, P<.001). The West Coast group cited this form more often than did the Midwest group (57% vs. 46%). Next, in terms of importance, only ratings on acquiescent respect—the Midwest group with a mean score of 3.41 (S.D.=0.77) compared with the West Coast group with 3.62 (S.D.=0.61)—were suggested to be different (t=2.44, df=20, P=.09, 2-tailed). The latter cited this form slightly more often (52% vs. 50%) and gave it greater importance (3.49 vs. 3.35) than the Midwest group did, probably because of the larger number of Latino and Asian American students, who tended to give greater importance to acquiescent respect. Results of an ANOVA test suggested that, while there was no statistically significant difference in importance ratings by age groups and gender, there was a significant difference in the ratings on acquiescent respect (F=10.9, P<.004, df=3, 411) with regard to ethnicity: Latino and Asian Americans gave higher ratings (3.71) on this form than did Caucasian and African-Americans (3.54). Overall, however, the findings suggest that there is a similarity between the two groups in the ratings on the majority of the forms.

Two factors emerged in a factor analysis. The first factor, with four loadings, was titled symbolic elder respect, and the second factor, with two loadings, was named engaging elder respect. These factors are identical to the factors found in the analysis of Korean data, except for the cultural factor.

At the form level, a prominent case was ancestor respect, which was not practiced in the American cultural context. And, at the category level as well, forms, such as care, acquiescent, consulting, precedential, salutatory, linguistic, victual, presentational, and celebrative, had at least one category not directly applicable in the American context. In addition, a category of salutatory form—hugging and kissing—was minimally practiced by the Koreans.

The following categories were practiced predominantly by the Koreans: caring by living together with elders (care respect), following their advice on marriage (acquiescent respect), identifying with their values and lifestyles (acquiescent respect), consulting them over personal and family matters (consulting respect), allowing them to exit doorways and to get in and out of the car first (precedential respect), greeting them by bowing (salutatory respect), using honorifics when one speaks to or addresses them (linguistic respect), and serving drinks and foods of elders' choice (victual respect).

6. Outstanding Forms

Based on the results of the above analyses, six forms listed below can now be distinguished as outstanding forms practiced by the Koreans and the Americans. Both groups practiced these six forms more frequently than they did the other forms. The groups cited care respect and linguistic respect with similarly high frequency, while frequency sizes varied between them in other forms. Both groups rated the importance of care and linguistic respect higher than they did the other forms. The Americans rated three forms, precedential, salutatory, and linguistic, even higher than did their counterparts. Thus, variation existed by the cultural contexts. However, overall, a similar response pattern emerged: The six forms were practiced more frequently and were given greater degrees of importance than the other forms in both cultural contexts. Therefore, they can be seen as cross-cultural forms.

In addition, the following eight forms practiced predominantly by the Koreans can be considered culture specific: presentational (holding courteous manners), public (respecting elders at large), celebrative (celebrating birthdays), gift (bestowing gifts), spatial (giving honorable seats), victual (serving drinks and foods of elders' choice), ancestor (worshipping ancestors), and funeral (mourning and burying deceased elders).

These findings reflect a similarity between the two groups in terms of the six forms and a difference in terms of the eight forms specific to the Koreans.

7. Discussion

The present study provides rare insights into the specific ways the elderly are respected by younger adults in the United States, in comparison with their counterparts in East Asia. The study identified a comprehensive set of forms of elder respect, as well as a number of categories indicating these forms. Moreover, it specified the extent to which individual forms were practiced and the level of importance given to the forms in the respective cultural contexts, in addition to data on cross-cultural differences, and the similarities in the ways the elderly are respected. Previous studies lacked quantitative information on these aspects.

A typology comprised of six cross-cultural forms of elder respect has emerged, along with other forms that are culture specific. The forms are grouped into two cross-cultural types: engaging behaviors of elder respect (e.g., caring and serving, asking for advice, and serving drinks and meals) and symbolic displays of elder respect (e.g., lingual expression of respect, greeting, courtesy, demonstrating obedience, etc.). The engaging forms might be exhibited in more informal and personal ways, while symbolic displays of respect would be practiced in more formal and ritualistic contexts. Thus, the cross-cultural typology is a mix of the two types of the forms. Both types, when combined, might be seen as the embodiment of elder respect among younger adults in the two cross-cultural contexts.

7.1. DIFFERENCES AND SIMILARITIES

In terms of specific forms of elder respect, the Americans cited 6 of the 14 forms. However, if those forms cited by less than 4% of the Americans are included, the number of the forms cited by them increases to 12. In this case, the Americans and the Koreans differ only in two forms: The former did not cite ancestor respect or funeral respect. These findings provide evidence that elder respect is expressed in similar ways and for similar reasons in both cultural contexts.

With regard to the six cross-cultural forms, one might say that the basic human behavior displayed in treating the elderly is similar. We find a common thread existing between the groups. Although the Koreans practiced more of the forms in a more salient and diversified way, the Americans did practice most of the forms and gave even greater importance to them than did the Koreans. But they evidently practiced several of the forms minimally, if at all, reflecting their cultural orientation toward egalitarian and nonhierarchical interpersonal relationships. We need to consciously recognize this variation, so that it can be seen as a variation in human and cultural experience rather than serving as a source of misunderstanding or indifference. Overall, the findings imply that cross-cultural comparability is a matter of degree rather than an either–or proposition.

Although both comparison groups share the value of elder respect, the extent to which elders are respected and the kinds of forms they typically practice vary by the cultural context. For both groups, the forms had identical meanings at the form level of abstraction, but, at the category level, a degree of variation existed (Table 4). The eight forms specific to the Koreans do not appear to be emphasized or practiced in the American cultural context as much as they are in Korea.

The findings on the Korean participants are consistent with findings about other East Asians. All 13 forms of elder respect derived from the previous studies on East Asians by Ingersoll-Dayton and Saengtienchai (1999) and Palmore and Maeda (1985) are replicated in the present study (Table 1). Thus, this study and the previous studies yielded parallel results for the identification of a set of similar, if not identical, forms of elder respect, enlarging the power of the interpretation of elder respect in East Asia.

However, similarities and differences regarding the extent of elder respect between East Asians in the previous studies and the Korean participants in the present study remain empirical questions. The previous studies have not assessed the frequency with which the forms were practiced and the degree to which importance was given to the forms, as was done in the present study.

It is noteworthy that care respect is the most outstanding form in both cultural contexts. According to Dillon (1992) and Downie and Telfer (1969), respect, which involves practical concern distinguished from simple feeling, is closely interrelated with care. They also determined that care is one kind of respect. Care respect, in this sense, has special implications for human service professions. Success in human services is closely associated with a strong and growing respect between a client and the provider (Gambrill, 1983; Reichel, 1995). Thus, care respect in both cultural contexts coincides with these Western scholars' descriptions of the connectedness of care and respect, and suggests cross-cultural similarities in terms of the conception of care and respect.

It must be noted that there was some variation within the American participants. Latino and Asian Americans tended to be more acquiescent of the elderly than those of other ethnic groups were. This finding reflects the diversity of the Americans in terms of subcultural differences. The diversity means that the American society contains populations that resemble the Koreans in the way of elder respect, and that it is possible for Americans to share the respect-related values and experiences of those populations. Studies are needed to account for the methods of elder respect among the growing number of Latino and Asian Americans compared with other ethnic and cultural groups.

7.2. SHIFTING EXPRESSIONS

Some expressions appear be undergoing modification in East Asia (Sung, 2003; Ingersoll-Dayton & Saengtienchai, 1999 and Mehta, 1997). For instance, listening to elders when they talk, a category of acquiescent respect, which does not always mean obeying or following their advice, is taken as a form of respect. In the present study, Americans happened to cite this form more frequently than did the Koreans (27% vs. 15%; Table 4). This form seems to be a modification of the traditional way of being obedient. However, a traditional expression—complying with elders' directives (a category of acquiescent respect)—was practiced frequently by both groups (Koreans, 35%; Americans, 29%). Consulting elders, which involves open communication and mutually beneficial exchanges between generations, is another prevalent form, particularly among the Koreans. As more young Koreans value reciprocity between generations, consulting respect is bound to be widely practiced.

There are other noticeable changes in Korea today. For instance, juniors often shake hands with their seniors, instead of bending the body forward to greet them. Increasingly, the old and the young alike prefer separate residences to respect each other's privacy and freedom, as they do in America. As more people live longer, many families tend to postpone the celebration of parents' 60th birthday. Even ancestor worship and funeral rites are being modified: The number of days for worship tend to be reduced, and mourning rituals are simplified. Meanwhile, public respect—care and services for elders in community—is taken more seriously by individuals as well as voluntary organizations.

Looking ahead, young generations are likely to continue to alter or modify their way of elder respect. An agendum for gerontologists in the coming decades is to research to what extent the young uphold the tradition of elder respect. Will the value continue to be transmitted to future generations? This will probably depend on whether the present adult generation takes effort to instill the value in the next generation.

7.3. RESISTANCE OF THE TRADITION

On the Koreans, the Confucian values and norms appear to have had a great influence. The traditional basis for elder respect is the Confucian teachings of filial piety (Lew, 1995; Choi, 2001 and Sung, 1995). Filial piety essentially directs the young to recognize the care and aid received from elderly relatives and to, in return, respect and care for them. The tradition is deeply rooted in their family system and social structure. In the family system, respect as a benevolent and altruistic expression is heavily imbued with the sense of filial obligation, repayment of debt, and affection toward parents (Chee & Levkoff, 2001). In the social structure, consequential interpersonal relations tend to have a vertical structure that demands deference and loyalty to elders. In these relations, symbolic expressions of elder respect—linguistic, salutatory, presentational, precedential, celebratory, gift, and acquiescent—are shown more often and are more widely than in the West. A large number of Korean adults still live with their aged parents, whereby they can practice care respect—caring by staying close to them, spending time with them, providing them with hand-on care, serving them meals, etc.—more easily than do the Americans in the West where the majority of adults live separately from their aged parents.

The various forms of elder respect found among the Koreans reflect the family system and the social structure in which the young maintain familial and social relationships with elderly persons. Korea has even institutionalized its reverence for elders by celebrating Respect for Elders Day, enacting a law that mandates that elders be respected and by awarding government-sponsored filial piety prizes to persons who demonstrated exemplary filial conducts (Sung, 1990). It is still a virtue in Korea to respect the elderly. Thus, culture plays a role, as suggested by these familial and social traits of the Koreans associated with elder respect.

There seem to be marked differences between East Asian cultures and those of the countries in the West in the perspectives of care and treatment for the elderly (Holmes & Holmes, 1995 and Liu & Kendig, 2000). One of the most conspicuous social phenomena in East Asia, that is, contrasting with the West, is the way East Asians in general still respect the elderly (Kong, 1995; Palmore & Maeda, 1985 and Streib, 1987).

How long can the smaller Korean family continue to take respectful care of an increasingly larger number of elderly persons? While Western welfare states, in the face of economic difficulty, are turning to the family for help in providing eldercare that the formal bureaucracy cannot, families in Korea and other East Asian nations are facing a time when the smaller family with limited resources must turn to the state for assistance in caring for the increasing number of elderly citizens (Liu & Kendig, 2000 and Sung, 2001b).

Although there is no convincing evidence that there is an erosion of family values (Liu & Kendig, 2000 and Sung, 2001b), the family's ability to care for the elderly appears to be weakening in Korea (Choi, 2001 and Yoon & Cha, 1999). However, as long as Koreans practice elder respect, they are likely to have advantages over Americans in caring for their elderly. The values of elder respect seems to act as a driving force that minimizes or neutralizes the devastating effects of the rapid social change on the practice of family care for the aged, as well as an influence that facilitates, if not enforces, the fulfillment of filial duties by stressing the importance of respectful care for the elderly.

The cultural tradition will continue to influence the way the young Koreans treat the elderly, although today they tend to adhere to it less rigorously. As Bendix (1967) predicted, "even though industrial countries may all face similar problems, the persistence of social, cultural, and ideological differences are likely to result in different responses to these problems." The findings from the present study seem to indicate that Koreans tend to respond to the matter of elder respect differently.

Finally, the findings of the present study, based on partly randomized samples drawn from purposively selected universities, need to be carefully applied to a discussion of elder respect among young adults in the cross-cultural contexts. Further research based on more representative samples, both cross-cultural and longitudinal, are needed to develop a more comprehensive typology of the forms of elder respect and to account for shifting expression of elder respect. Knowledge of culture specifics and universals about elder respect needs to be further explored. Research needs to be extended to additional countries as well as to additional age groups including younger adults not in college.

Acknowledgements

The author is grateful to Gordon F. Streib for his comments on the draft of this paper. This study was supported by Elder-Respect.

References

Bendix, R., 1967. Preconditions of development: A comparison of Japan and Germany. In: Dore, R., Editor, , 1967. *Aspects of social change in modern Japan*, Princeton University Press, Princeton, NJ.

Butler, R., 1995. Ageism. In: Maddox, R., Editor, , 1995. *Encyclopedia of aging*, Springer, New York.

Chee, Y.K., and Levkoff, S.E., 2001. Culture and dementia: Accounts by family caregivers and health professionals for dementia-affected elders in South Korea. *Journal of Cross-Cultural Gerontology 16*, pp. 111–125. Full Text via CrossRef | View Record in Scopus | Cited By in Scopus (10)

Chipperfield, J.G., and Havens, B., 1992. A longitudinal analysis of perceived respect among elders. Changing perceptions for some ethnic groups. *Canadian Journal on Aging 11*, pp. 15–30. View Record in Scopus | Cited By in Scopus (7)

Choi, S. J. (2001). *Changing attitudes to filial piety in Asian countries.* Paper presented at 17th World Congress of International Association of Gerontology, Vancouver, Canada, July 1–6, 2001.

Cogwill, D.O., 1986. Aging around the world. , Wadworth, Belmont, CA.

Dillon, R.S., 1992. Respect and care: Toward moral integration. *Canadian Journal of Philosophy 22*, pp. 105–132.

Dogan, M., and Pelassy, D., 1984. How to compare nations. , Chatham House, Chathan, NJ.

Downie, R.S., and Telfer, E., 1969. Respect for persons. , Allen & Unwin, London.

Gibbard, A., 1990. Wise choices, apt feelings. , Harvard University Press, Cambridge, MA.

Han, J., 2000. Undergraduate students' attitude toward the elderly. *Journal of Korea Gerontological Society 20* 3, pp. 115–127.

Holmes, E.R., and Holmes, L.D., 1995. Other cultures, elder years. , Sage, Thousand Oaks, CA.

Ingersoll-Dayton, B., and Saengtienchai, C., 1999. Respect for the elderly in Asia: Stability and change. *International Journal of Aging & Human Development 48*, pp. 113–130. View Record in Scopus | Cited By in Scopus (16)

Kim, G.G., 1998. Public perceptions of elder mistreatment and its reality in Taegu. *Journal of Korea Gerontological Society 18* 1, pp. 184–197.

Kosberg, J.I., and Torgusen, B.L., 2001. Emerging issue in elder abuse: Implications for prevention and intervention. In: .

Lee, I.S., 2000. Perception of rural area college students on the aged. *Journal of Korea Gerontological Society 20* 2, pp. 129–135.

Lew, S.K., 1995. Filial piety and human society. In: Filial piety and future society (Hyo-wa Mirae-Sahoe), Academy of Korean Studies, Kyunggido, Korea.

Liang, J., and Jay, G.M., 1990. Cross-cultural comparative research on aging and health. , Institute of Gerontology and School of Public Health, The University of Michigan, Ann Arbor, MI.

Liu, W.T., and Kendig, H., 2000. Who should care for the elderly? An East–West value divide. , Singapore University, Singapore.

MacNeil, R., Ramos, C., and Magagas, A., 1996. Age stereotyping among college students: A replication and expansion. Educational Gerontology 22, pp. 229–243. Full Text via CrossRef | View Record in Scopus | Cited By in Scopus (5)

Mehta, K., 1997. Respect redefined: Focus group insights from Singapore. *International Journal of Aging & Human Development 44*, pp. 205–219. View Record in Scopus | Cited By in Scopus (5)

Noelker, L.S., and Harel, Z., 2000. Linking quality of long-term care and quality of life. , Springer, New York (Chapter 1) .

Palmore, E.B., 1999. Ageism: Negative and positive. , Springer, New York (Chapter 1) .

Palmore, E.B., and Maeda, D., 1985. The honorable elders revisited. , Duke University Press, Durham, NC.

Pillemer, K.A., and Finkelhor, D., 1988. The prevalence of elder abuse: A random sample survey. *The Gerontologist 28*, pp. 51–57. View Record in Scopus | Cited By in Scopus (250)

Post, S.G., 1989. Filial morality. *Journal of Religion and Aging 5*, pp. 15–29.

Rowe, J., and Kahn, R., 1998. Successful aging. , Pantheon Books, New York.

Silverman, P., and Maxwell, R., 1978. How do I respect thee? Let me count the ways: Deference towards elderly men and women. *Behavior Science Research 13*, pp. 91–108. Full Text via CrossRef

Simic, A., 1990. Aging, world view, and international relations in America and Yugoslavia. In: Sokolovsky, J., Editor, , 1990. The cultural context of aging: Worldwide perspectives, Bergin & Garvey, New York, pp. 17–89.

Sokolovsky, J., Editor, , 1990. The cultural context of aging, Bergen & Garvey, New York.

Streib, G.F., 1987. Old age in sociocultural context: China and the United States. *Journal of Aging Studies 1*, pp. 95–112. Abstract | Abstract + References | PDF (1542 K)

Sung, K.T., 1990. A new look at filial piety: Ideals and practices of family-centered parent care in Korea. *The Gerontologist 30*, pp. 610–617. View Record in Scopus | Cited By in Scopus (23)

Sung, K.T., 1994. A cross-cultural comparison of motivations for parent care: The case of Americans and Koreans. *Journal of Aging Studies 8*, pp. 195–209. Abstract | PDF (937 K)

Sung, K.T., 1995. Measures and dimensions of filial piety in Korea. *The Gerontologist 35*, pp. 240–247. View Record in Scopus | Cited By in Scopus (34)

Sung, K.T., 2001. Elder respect: Exploration of ideals and practicing forms in East Asia. *Journal of Aging Studies 15*, pp. 13–27.

Sung, K.T., 2001. Family support for the elderly in Korea: Continuity, change, future directions, and cross-cultural concerns. *Journal of Aging and Social Policy 12*, pp. 65–79. Full Text via CrossRef | View Record in Scopus | Cited By in Scopus (4)

Sung, K.T., 2003. Elder respect among young adults: Exploration of behavioral forms in Korea. *Ageing International 28*, pp. 279–294.

Van de Vijver, F., and Leung, K., 1997. Method and data analysis for cross-cultural research. , Sage, Thousand Oaks, CA.

Verba, S., 1971. Cross-national survey research: The problem of credibility. In: Vallier, I., Editor, , 1971. Comparative methods in sociology, University of California Press, Berkeley, CA, pp. 309–356.

Yoon, H.S., and Cha, H.B., 1999. Future issues for family care of the elderly in Korea. *Hallym International Journal of Aging 1*, pp. 78–86.

Chapter 18

A Longitudinal Analysis of Perceived Respect Among Elders: Changing Perceptions for Some Ethnic Groups

Judith G. Chipperfield and Betty Havens

Introduction

Gerontologists have become increasingly interested in the potential role of attitudinal factors in the quality of life of the elderly population. Of particular concern is the effect of devaluation of elders and what R.N. Butler (1969) has called negative "agist" attitudes. Perhaps of even greater relevance are elders' own perceptions of how they are viewed by others, because perceived devaluation may undermine independence and lead to alienation. While previous assessments have examined attitudes toward the elderly cohort as expressed by younger cohorts (Braithwaite, 1986; Brewer, Dull & Liu, 1981; Crockett & Hummert, 1987; Green, 1981), less is known about elderly individuals' perceptions of their own cohort.

The present study considered elderly individuals' own beliefs, in particular, their perceptions about the respect directed toward them by their community. The purpose was to examine patterns of perceived respect by asking two general descriptive questions. First, have there been changes in elders' levels of perceived respect over time? Second, do time-related changes in elders' levels of perceived respect vary by ethnic group? Several theoretical perspectives and methodological issues were considered in the evaluation of these questions.

While the notion of perceived respect has much in common with self-respect, a distinction between the two is necessary. Some individuals likely maintain self-respect even when they perceive that they are held in low regard by others. Moreover, other individuals probably lack self-respect even when they perceive they are held in high regard. Perceptions of community respect are surely influenced by the attitudes and treatment imposed by others in the community. On the other hand, developmental factors, associated with aging, may influence perceptions of respect, although it is not clear whether age would enhance or erode such perceptions.

Longitudinal Patterns of Perceived Respect

Because quantitative assessments of changing attitudes of respect have not been undertaken, it is unclear whether changes have occurred in elders' perceptions of community respect. To the extent that perceived community respect is akin to status, E. Palmore's (1975) notion of the "American arc of life" would suggest that, among elders, perceptions of respect should decline over time. According to the "American arc of life," status is at its highest in mid life and at its lowest at the extreme ends of the age continuum.

Historical analyses have considered long-term patterns of respect toward elderly persons. However, the conclusions that have arisen from these analyses are mixed. C. Tibbitts (1979), for example, contends that attitudes toward the elderly population have improved over time; while D.H. Fischer (1978) indicates that the status of elderly Americans has declined over the past two centuries.

Ethnic Group Differences in Perceived Respect

Just as the awarding of respect to the elderly population has fluctuated across different periods of history, it is not surprising that it should vary across different cultural groups at any given time in history. Levels of respect for elders do appear to differ cross-culturally within contemporary society. For example, China has remained a "paradise" for elders because the country's intensive agricultural society deemphasises physical strength and values thoroughness, care, and experience, qualities more prevalent in elderly persons (Ginzberg, 1981). The label "Homes of Respect" given to houses for older people without families (Cowgill, 1981) typifies the positive regard in which older people are held in China. This example suggests that the values placed on factors thought to determine respect (e.g., socioeconomic status, family structure, productivity, wisdom, religion, or magic) vary across cultures.

Ethnic groups may also differ in the values placed on such factors that determine respect. As J.D. Rempel and B. Havens (1986) point out, ethnic group differences are likely to be particularly salient within Canada's older population, and such demographic ethnic diversity has been well-documented using Canadian Census data (Driedger & Chappell, (1990). According to Rempel and Havens, the reason ethnicity influences attitudes, experience, and the behavior of elderly

Canadians may be partly due to the fact that many of these persons were socialized outside of Canadian society.

An ethnic group of particular interest in Manitoba, as well as in other parts of Canada, is the Native Canadian (Cree, Saulteau, Sioux, Chippewa, Ojibway). In a comparison of the Native and non-Native Canadians on various dependent measures, R.M. Bienvenue and B. Havens (1986) concluded that, a disadvantaged status existed for the Native population in housing conditions and availability of health services. Clearly, Native Canadians are disadvantaged on the ultimate indicator, mortality. The percentage of Native Canadians that lives to old age is substantially lower than the overall percentage for Canadians, i.e. 3.5 percent versus 9.1 percent (Driedger & Chappell, (1990).

The past decade has provided a varied literature on ethnicity, although the research has been criticized. The main criticism focuses on definitions of ethnicity which, according to K.J. Krotki and D. Odynak (1990) are "static and inflexible," and according to C.J. Rosenthal (1986), typically fail to distinguish between ethnicity and minority or inequality. The complicated connection between ethnicity and inequality is reflected in several theoretical perspectives (Rosenthal, 1986), each of which can be applied to the study of perceived respect.

Theoretical Considerations

First, from the "age as leveler" perspective, ethnic group differences that exist at younger ages should diminish over time. According to B.D. McPherson (1990, p. 241), this is so because age minimizes prior social and economic distinctions and inequalities. From this perspective, any ethnic group differences in perceptions of respect that exist for younger individuals should be weaker for older individuals.

Second, from the "multiple jeopardy" perspective, social stratification is viewed in terms of multiple hierarchies of inequality, and as such, the disadvantages associated with each of several minority groups are considered to be additive. Research suggests that certain types of disadvantages relate to ethnicity within Canadian society (Bienvenue & Havens, 1986; Havens & Chappell, 1983), and joint membership in certain ethnic and age groups is thought to produce a condition of "double jeopardy". According to this perspective then, initial ethnic group differences in perceptions of respect should be accentuated with older age.

These perspective provide a framework within which to interpret the findings of this study. For example, if ethnic-group differences. In contrast, if ethnic-group differences in perceived respect are found to be weaker initially than at follow-up, this may suggest that age combines with other disadvantages to create multiple jeopardy.

Methodological Considerations

The present study addressed two methodological concerns. First, the role of educational status, socioeconomic status, and gender were examined to minimize a concern expressed by M.C. Goldstein and C.F. Beall (1982). According to their argument, because variables like socioeconomic status or educational status overlap conceptually with notions such as respect, concepts like respect may be no more than a reflection of these other variables.

Second, this study evaluated an issue that is critical in any longitudinal analysis of change, i.e., the issue of whether participation in the study itself explains changes in the outcome variable, in this case, perceived respect. Being participant in a longitudinal study can produce serious threats to internal validity because respondents may react to their participation (Campbell & Stanley, 1966). As K.W. Schaie (1983) points out, such reactivity does not require recall of prior responses, but rather operates as a function of a reaction to a prior experience. In the present analysis, the experience of having been part of a long-term study may have inflated responses beyond what they might otherwise have been. For example, due to participation in the study, elders may have actually felt more respected or they may have simply believed that they should feel more respected. In either case, inflated responses would reflect a "participation effect," which would provide an alternative explanation for any hypotheses about change.

A test of the participation effect was possible because the design of the resent study included both a longitudinal panel of survivors who entered the study in the 1970s and a "first-time" sample of individuals who entered the study in the early 1980s. Measurements of perceived respect were taken simultaneously for the survivors of the longitudinal study and for individuals who had not previously been part of the study. To be confident that a participation effect would not explain changes in respect scores, the two groups should have similar levels of perceived respect.

Summary

Aging in Manitoba (AIM) Study Data Base

Elderly individuals' own perceptions of respect were examined using data from the longitudinal Aging in Manitoba (AIM) Studies. The AIM study began in 1971 under the auspices of the Manitoba Department of Health and Social Development, and is comprised of three independent samples of Manitoba residents, those interviewed for the first time in 1971, 1976 and 1983. The major strengths of the AIM database are its: size (nearly 9000 elderly individuals); rate of follow-up of survivors (95%); and representativeness (compared to Manitoba's overall population) on several sample characteristics such as age, gender, and marital status (Roos & Shapiro, 1981). The procedure followed is only briefly described here; however, additional details of the sampling procedures, early objectives, construction of interviews, etc., are documented elsewhere Manitoba Department of Health and Social Development, 1973; Mossey, Havens, Roos, & Shapiro, 1981; Province of Manitoba, Department of Health, 1990).

Potential participants for each of three cross-sectional samples were drawn from the Manitoba Health Services Commission registry, a registry of all Manitoba residents. For each sample, an age/gender stratified area-probability sampling technique was used to draw the potential participants. These individuals, or in some cases proxies, were then contacted and asked respondents who had originally participated in the 1971 or 1976 cross-sectional samples. Most interviewing was conducted during 1983 and 1984, however, due to tracking difficulties, reinterviewing of a small subset of survivors continued into the latter part of the 1980s. Interviews were conducted with 1518 survivors, or 31.6 percent of the original 1971 ample and 882 survivors, or 67.7 public of the 1976 sample. The majority of those not reinterviewed had died by follow-up; less than 5 percent of the survivors were lost to follow-up for other reasons, such as migration or refusal. Those who were reinterviewed, and who had begun the study in 1976, are subsequently referred to as the *7-year survivors,* and those who were reinterviewed, and had begun in 1971, are referred to as the *12-year survivors.*

Participants

The questions regarding changing perceptions of respect were addressed by examining participants who survived over time. Individuals who had to reported perceptions of respect at both times were excluded, leaving a total of 776 from the 7-year survivor sample and 1159 from the 12-year survivor sample. The main analyses were conducted on the 7-year sample, which consisted of 372 men and 404 women between the ages of 66 and 94. Most of these (approximately 78%) were under the age of 80 and living in the community (97%). Participants were of various ethnic backgrounds (North American n = 97, British = 281, French n = 37, German n = 321, Native Canadian n = 19, and Others n = 21) and had a mean level of total monthly income at follow-up of $565.11 ($SD$ = $385.98).

The evaluation of the "participation effect" involved first-time participants, i.e. those in the 1983 cross-sectional sample. Excluded from the original 2877 individuals in the 1983 cross-sectional sample, were 174 individuals for whom relevant data were missing and 806 who were younger than 65 years of age and thus had no counterparts in the survivor sample. For the present purposes, the 1983 cross-sectional sample was reduced to 1897 individuals, aged 65 and over, who had perceived respect scores.

Variables

Independent variables

The key independent variables for examining changes in perceived respect were Time of Measurement (Time 1, Time 2), Ethnicity (North American, British, French, German, Native Canadian, and Others, including European/Middle and Eastern/Asian), Age (65-69 years, 70-74 years 75-79 years, 80-84 years, 85-89 years, 90 years and older) and Education Level (0, 1-4, 9-10, 11-12, 13-16, 17+ years). In the analysis of the 12-year sample, Time 1 was 1971, while in the 7-year sample analysis, Time 1 was 1976. In both cases, Time 2 was follow-up, or 1983-84. Ethnicity was derived from responses to the question "What nationality descent do you consider yourself?" The respondent's age was provided by the Manitoba Health Services Commission registry and education, by responses to a question that asked how many years or grades of school were completed, including post high school education.

Dependent variables

The dependent variable for the analysis of changing respect in the 7-year follow-up sample was perceived respect. Ratings of perceived respect were obtained from identical items at the initial interview in 1976 ($M = 4.49$, $SD = .76$) and at follow-up ($M = 4.49$, $SD = .86$). Respondents were asked to rate, on a 5-point scale, how people of their own age are treated in the community. A score of *1* represented "with very much respect," a *2*, "with a fair amount of respect," a *3*, "with mixed respect and disrespect," a *4*, "with some disrespect," and a *5*, "with much disrespect". For conceptual clarity, responses were reversed so that a low score represented disrespect and a high score, respect.

The perceived respect measure for the analysis of the 12-year follow-up was based upon a 4-point, rather than a 5-point scale. The answer format for the perceived respect item in the initial 1971 interview was as follows: *1* represented "with very much respect," *2*, "with a fair amount of respect," *3*, "with some disrespect," and *4*, "with much disrespect". Because the scale of measurement differed across the 1971 and the follow-up interviews, the follow-up 5-point scale was converted to a 4-point scale. This was done by collapsing follow-up ratings of *3* and *4* into one category. Again, scores were reversed for conceptual clarity so that a low score indicated disrespect and a high score, respect.

Analyses

Two longitudinal analyses, consisting of repeated measures analysis of variance were conducted to explore the longitudinal patterns of perceived respect, one of the 7-year, and one for the 12-year, sample. It is important to note that, in the latter case, the minor differences across time in the measurement of perceived respect impose limitations for the interpretation of findings. Thus, the results from the 7-year survivor analyses are emphasized.

Results

Prior to constructing the model to consider the longitudinal trends in perceived respect, correlations were examined to consider whether perceived respect related to gender, socioeconomic status (total monthly income, $0-$3464), or education level (number of grades completed, 0-16+). Only education level was significantly related to perceptions of respect, r (776) = .10, $p < .005$, in 1976; r (776) = .11, $p < .005$ at follow-up. Thus, socioeconomic status and gender were not included in further analyses.

Time-related Changes in Perceived Respect

Changes for 7-year survivors

Changes in perceived respect scores for survivors who had provided respect ratings both in 1976 (time 1) and at follow-up (time 2) were assessed in a repeated measures ANOVA. Time (time 1, time 2) was entered as the within subject factor, and Ethnicity (North American, British, French, German, Native, and Others) and Age (65-69, 70-74, 75-79, 80-84, 85-89, 90+) as the between subject factors. Finally, Education (0, 1-4, 5-8, 9-10, 11-12, 13-16, 17+ years) was entered as a covariate.

Significant effects emerged for the covariate, education, the between-subject factor, ethnicity, and the within-subject factor, time. Respect scores were significantly higher with higher levels of education, $F(1,764) = 5.74$. Perceived respect also differed significantly across ethnic groups, $F(5,764) = 3.26$, and increased significantly over time, $F(1,764) = 5.45$. However, using data squared, it was determined that, in each case, the variance explained was under 3 percent.

TIME by ETHNICITY interaction

The main effects for time and ethnicity are qualified by their interaction, $F(5,764) = 2.60$. This interaction could mean that increases in perceived respect were significant for some, but not all ethnic groups, or it could mean that differences between ethnic groups were significant at time 1, but not at time 2. To explore the interaction further, the simple main effects were tested using a method described by R.E. Kirk (1982, p. 365). Because this approach involved the calculation of numerous F values, Dunns' method (c.f. Kirk, 1982, p. 369) was used to set alpha at a conservative p level (i.e. $p = .02$).

The simple main effects tests to consider whether the increase over time in perceived respect was significant for some, but not all ethnic groups revealed significant increases for the British, German, and French groups and stability for other groups. The simple main effects tests to consider whether the differences between ethnic groups were significant at each time indicated that experiencing differences in perceived respect were significant at Time 1, but not at Time 2.

Further post hoc analyses of ethnic differences were conducted to explore a specific comparison regarding a group of special interest in Manitoba, Native Canadians. From an examination of the means in Figure 1, perceived respect was lowest for Native Canadians at both measurement times. The significance of the difference between the mean ratings by Native Canadians and the mean ratings by all other groups combined was tested separately at each time period using Tukey post hoc tests and a conservative critical q value. The critical value of 4.03 was established using Cochran and Cox's (c.f. Kirk, 1982, p. 508) approach for application when error terms have been pooled. A test of the perceived respect score in 1976 revealed that the mean score for Native elders was significantly lower than the mean for others, $q(6,764) = 4.18$. Differences between Native Canadians and other ethnic groups were not however, significant at time 2, $q(6,764) = 2.83$.

Changes for 12-year survivors

Results from the analysis of perceived respect over 12 years are consistent with those found for the 7-year survivors. Again, there was a significant effect for ethnicity, F (5,1134) = 2.24, $p < .05$. Moreover, a significant interaction again emerged between ethnicity and time, F (5,1134) = 3.47, $p < .005$.

Participation Effects

To consider the possibility that the reported time-related changes in perceived respect were due to participation in the study, respect scores were compared for two groups of individuals interviewed at the same time. That is, survivors' mean Time 2 respect scores were compared to the first-time (1983) respondents' mean respect scores using ANOVAs. Because age differences between the first-time sample and the survivor sample still existed after excluding first-time respondents between 60 and 64 years of age who did to have counterparts in the survivor sample, age-specific ANOVAs were conducted in addition to an ANOVA, collapsed over age.

Three separate ANOVAs, corresponding to three age groups (i.e. 65-72, 73-79, and 80+) were run to assess differences in perceived respect between the first-time respondents and the survivors. No difference in respect scores were found in the overall ANOVA or in any of the age-specific ANOVAs. This minimizes the concern of a participation effect, i.e. the concern that inflated perceived respect scores at follow-up might explain the time-related changes in perceived respect that emerged for participants of the longitudinal study.

Discussion

Elderly individuals in Manitoba perceived a greater level of community respect in the early-to-mid 1980s relative to the level they perceived in the mid-1970s. While there are many plausible interpretations of this finding, the present results suggest that a search for the explanation must be addressed within the context of ethnic diversity. The increase in perceived respect was qualified by its significant interaction with the experiencing. That is, significant increases were found for British, French and German respondents, but not for respondents of North American descent or for Native Canadians or Others. It is particularly encouraging that, while ethnic differences did emerge, in no case were the perceptions of respect lower in the mid-1980s than they had been in the mid-1970s.

The relatively low levels of respect reported by Native Canadians are disturbing, although not unexpected. While the main analyses in this study found no significant increase over time for Native Canadians' ratings, a further comparison of Native Canadians to the rest of society (i.e. other ethnic groups combined) provided somewhat more encouraging findings. By follow-up, the significant differences in perceived respect that had occurred in 1976, had disappeared. Thus, in the mid 1980s, Native Canadians were more similar to the rest of society in their perception of respect than they had been in 1976.

In addition to experiencing and time, educational level was related to perceived respect. More highly educated elders had higher levels of perceived respect, which may imply that greater respect is given to those with higher levels of education. Furthermore, this finding is consistent with H.G. Cox's (1990) speculation that an essential factor in the attainment of status for older people in modern individual society is the "control of critical knowledge".

Theoretical Perspectives

Several concepts and theoretical perspectives can be applied to the present findings. First, the findings are inconsistent with Palmore's (1975) concept of the "American arc of life". The pattern of results over time is directly opposite to the expected patterns of declining respect that would accompany movement toward the extreme upper age limits. Moreover, the lack of differences between age groups also suggests that, among elders, the perception of respect is unrelated to age.

Second, the findings are also inconsistent with the notion that age is a "leveler." Differences between ethnic groups were significant at time 1 and not at time 2, which, on its own would be congruent with the notion that differences between ethic groups are minimized by age. However, because both age and time were assessed in this analysis, it was possible to distinguish between these effects. Age did not have a significant effect, while time did. Thus, the lack of differences between ethnic groups at time 2 appeared not to be due to the levelling effect of age, but rather the levelling effect of time. That is, something specific to this particular period (1976 to 1983-84), rather than to age per se, played a role in minimizing the differences in perceptions of respect over time.

The multiple jeopardy hypothesis could not be tested in the present study, because some of the cell sizes were too small to examine interactions between education, ethnic group, and age group. However, the findings indicated that both elders of certain ethnic groups and those with less education were less likely than others to experience increases in perceptions of respect. Thus, joint membership in both groups may create a condition of "double jeopardy" such that, relative to others, these individuals are disadvantaged in terms of their perceptions of respect. The present findings indicate that being elderly does not place one at a disadvantage for declining levels of respect. Thus, in the domain of perceived respect, age does not appear to be a factor in any "multiple jeopardy" equation.

Limitations

The present results should be considered in light of two limitations of this study. First, the findings for several ethnic groups, including Native Canadians, were based upon small numbers. Because small sample size is accompanied by a reduction in the likelihood of achieving significance, the reported non-significant increases in perceived respect for some ethnic groups may be due to a lack of statistical power. This might suggest that with larger samples, the increases in perceived respect experienced by several groups may be significant.

A second limitation in this study is the use of a single Likert-type rating scale for the measurement of perceived respect. Both more elaborate and multiple measures of perceived respect would be desirable to minimize the error in measuring such a concept. However, this study found an increase in perceived respect even with a unidimensional measure that is bound to contain error. This leads to the speculation that, with more elaborate measures of perceived respect, the magnitude of the increase in perceived respect may have been even stronger. Moreover, more reliable measures would likely lead to higher amounts of explained variance than those found in this study.

Conclusions and Summary

The low levels of variance explained by education, ethnic group membership, and time may indicate that the identified relationships have little practical significance. However, for several reasons, it may be inappropriate to dismiss these findings for that reason. First, as B.G. Tabachnick and L.S. Fidell (1983, p. 47) point out, measures of strength of association, such as eta squared suffer from several basic flaws. For example, as the number of factors and interactions in the design increases, the variance accounted for by each factor will be reduced. Second, it may be that many factors contribute jointly to one's perception of respect, and that each, on it's own, may explain only a small amount of the variance. Such complexity requires that each factor be identified, and that interactions among the variables be explored. The present findings provide a departure point for such future studies of the multiple factors that influence perceived respect.

Another research area that deserves attention is the consequences of elders' perceptions of community respect. To the extent that elders perceive they are disrespected, they may avoid participation in the community, which in turn, is likely to promote feelings of "alienation," "rolelessness," or of "being a burden" to society. Perceived disrespect may even diminish the likelihood that elders will request community assistance when needed. Ultimately then, perceptions of disrespect may undermine elders' well being and independence.

In summary, this study found that increases in perceived respect did occur over time; however, they were unrelated to age. In other words, perceptions of respect were just as likely to increase over time for 65-year olds as for 90-year olds. This finding does not support the notion that changes in perceived respect are likely to occur as a result of personal factors associated with development or aging. Alternatively, it seems more likely from these findings that societal factors, rather than personal factors, promotes changes in perceived respect. This is especially so since perceived respect was higher for those elders with more education, and the increases in perceived respect were restricted to those belonging to certain ethnic groups.

A compelling approach to understanding such findings may be to assume that there is an interplay between individual differences in psychological factors (e.g., self-concept, or self-respect) and social forces (community treatment). This interactionist approach, as outlined by E. Sherman (1985), indicates that the impact of societal forces on self-concept and self-respect, further leading to a ore generalized perception of "disrespect," while the same disrespectful behavior may have little influence on another person. The present results suggest that certain factors, such as ethnic group membership and education level may offset negative societal factors that influence perceived respect. This interactionist model, applied to changing perceptions of elderly people is a promising direction for future research.

To conclude, it is important to note that the present findings do not suggest that elderly individuals are being treated with high levels of respect or that devaluation is not occurring. Levels of respect or disrespect can only be evaluated in relative terms, since it is not possible to identify a "level" that would be preferable or acceptable. What can be concluded from this study is that *growing* devaluation is not as serious a concern in Manitoba as anticipated. That is, devaluation of Manitoba's elders has not increased over time. Framed more positively, the atmosphere for Manitoba's elderly may well be improving, or at least, elderly persons themselves seem to believe so. Regardless of whether the change is taking place within society or within the individual, the change is perceived respect for older members of certain ethnic groups is a positive one.

References

Bienvenue, R.M., & Havens, B. (1986). Structural inequalities, informal networks: A comparison of native and non-native elderly. *Canadian Journal on Aging, 5*, 241-248.

Braithwaite, V.A. (1986). Old age stereotypes: Reconciling contradictions. *Journal of Gerontology, 41*, 353-360.

Brewer, M.B., Dull, V., & Lui, L. (1981). Perceptions of the elderly: Stereotypes and prototypes. *Journal of Personality and Social Psychology, 41*, 656-670.

Butler, R.N. (1969). Agism: Another form of bigotry. *The Gerontologist, 9*, 243-246.

Campbell, D.T., & Stanley, J.C. (1966). *Experimental and quasi-experimental designs for research.* Chicago: Rand McNally.

Cowgill, D.O. (1981). Aging in comparative cultural perspective. *Mid-American Review of Sociology, 6*, 1-28.

Cox, H.G. (1990). Roles for aged individuals in post-industrial societies. *International Journal of Aging and Human Development, 30*, 55-62.

Crockett, W.H., & Hummert, M.L. (1987). Perceptions of aging and the elderly. In K.W. Schaie & C. Eisdorfer. *Annual Review of Gerontology and Geriatrics, 7*, p. 217-241. New York: Springer.

Driedger, L., & Chappell, N. (1990). Variations in aging and ethnicity. In S. Halli, F. Trovato, & L. Driedger (Eds.), *Ethnic demography: Canadian immigrant, racial and cultural variations.* Ottawa: Carleton University Press.

Fischer, D.H. (1978). *Growing old in America.* New York: Oxford University Press.

Ginzberg, R. (1981). The negative attitude toward the elderly. Paper presented at the second *International Gerontological Congress,* St. Louis, Missouri.

Goldstein, M.C., & Beall, C.F. (1982). Indirect modernization and status of the elderly in a rural third world setting. *Journal of Gerontology, 37,* 743-748.

Green, S.K. (1981). Attitudes and perceptions about the elderly: Current and future perspectives. *International Journal of Aging and Human Development, 13,* 99-119.

Havens, B., & Chappell, N. Triple jeopardy: age, sex, and ethnicity. *Canadian Ethnic Studies, 15,* 119-132.

Kirk, R.E. (1982). *Experimental deign: procedures for the behavioral sciences.* California: Brooks/Cole Publishing Co.

Krotki, K.J., & Odynak, D. (1990). The emergence of multiethnicities in the eighties. In S. Halli, F. Trovato, & L. Driedger (Eds.), *Ethnic demography: Canadian immigrant, racial and cultural variations.* Ottawa: Carleton University Press.

Manitoba Department of Health and Social Development. (1973). *Aging in Manitoba: Needs and resources, 1971, Vol 1.* Winnipeg: Department of Health & Social Development.

McPherson, B.D. (1990). Aging as a social process: An Introduction to individual and population aging, 2nd Edition. In B. McPherson (Ed.). Toronto: Butterworths.

Mossey, J.M., Havens, B., Roos, N.P., & Shapiro, E. (1981). The Manitoba longitudinal study on aging: Description and methods. *The Gerontologist, 21,* 551-558.

Palmore, E. (1975). *The honorable elders: A cross-cultural analysis of aging in Japan.* Durham, NC: Duke University Press.

Province of Manitoba, Department of Health. (1990). *Aging in Manitoba: 1983.* Winnipeg: Province of Manitoba.

Rempel, J.D., & Havens, B. (1986). Aged health experiences as interpreted through culture. Presented at the *Canadian Sociology and Anthropology Association* Meetings, Winnipeg, Manitoba.

Roos, N.P., & Shapiro, E. (1981). The Manitoba longitudinal study on aging: Preliminary findings on health care utilization by the elderly. *Medical Care, 19,* 644-657.

Rosenthal, C.J. (1986). Family supports in later life: Does ethnicity make a difference? *The Gerontologist, 26,* 19-24.

Schaie, K.W. (1983). What can we learn from the longitudinal study of adult psychological development? In W.K. Schaie (Ed.), *Longitudinal study of adult psychological development.* New York: Guildford Press.

Sherman, E. (1985). Social reconstruction variables and the morale of the aged. *International Journal of Aging and Human Development, 20,* 133-144.

Tabachnick, B.G., & Fidell, L.S. (1983). *Using multivariate statistics.* San Francisco: Harper & Row.

Tibbitts, C. (1979). Can we invalidate negative stereotypes in aging? *The Gerontologist, 19,* 10-20.

Chapter 19

Respect For the Elderly in Asia: Stability and Change[1,2]

Berit Ingersoll-Dayton
Chanpen Saengtienchai

Respect for the elderly is built into the social fabric of most Asian countries. The emphasis on social relationships among Asians (Ho, 1982) and their awareness of hierarchy within these relationships (Limanonda, 1995) has traditionally resulted in a special deference paid to the aged. The value of filial piety, which is understood as "respect and care for parents and the aged" (Sung, 1995, p. 240), has deep roots in Asian culture. This value serves as a standard by which attitudes and behaviors toward the elderly are judged (Sung, 1990).

The importance of respect for the elderly is reflected in the languages of many Asian countries. For example, the Filipino term "utang na loob" refers to a debt of gratitude that children have for their parents. This is a debt that can never be completely repaid and the failure to attempt to fulfill this obligation results in considerable shame among children (Domingo et al., 1993; Domingo, 1994; Ho, 1982). In Thailand, "bunkhun" refers to a sense of obligation, moral indebtedness and gratitude toward parents and others who have been helpful (Knodel, Saeng-tienchai & Sittirai, 1992; Pramualratana, 1992). Similarly, the Chinese word "xiao" means that children support and respect their parents and that the elderly have an important role in their families and society (Chow, 1997). These concepts reflect a traditional view of respect for the elderly based on what they have sacrificed for and provided to the younger generation. This ethic may, however, be changing over time and may differ by country. The purpose of this article is to examine the different ways in which respect for the elderly is expressed by Asians, to determine whether these expressions of respect for the elderly have changed over time, and to identify some of the factors associated with such changes.

There is a small body of cross-cultural research that has addressed the concept of respect for the elderly. To illustrate, a classic study conducted by Silverman and Maxwell (1978) examined respect for the aged within thirty-four societies drawn from Murdock and White's Standard Cross-Cultural Sample. Based on an inductive analysis of deference for the elderly across cultures, Silverman and Maxwell (1978, p. 91) identified seven different kinds of respect classified as:

> spatial (e.g., special seats for old people), victual (e.g. given choice foods), linguistic (e.g., addressed in honorifics), presentational (e.g., special posture assumed in their presence), service (e.g. housekeeping performed for them), prestative (e.g., given gifts), and celebrative (e.g., ceremonies held in their honor).

While Silverman and Maxwell made a significant contribution to the literature by distinguishing among different kinds of respect, they did not examine whether respect changed over time in these societies.

A study by Chipperfield and Havens (1992) explicitly focused on changes in perceived respect among elders in different ethnic groups. They analyzed data from a longitudinal study of older Manitobans who were interviewed in the mid 1970s and again in the early 1980s. In this study, Chipperfield and Havens focused on the differential changes in respect among six groups (i.e., North American, British, French, German, Native Indian, and Others, including Europeans and Asians). Their results indicated that some of these groups (i.e., British, French, and German) experienced increased respect over time while the others experienced stability in respect. These findings are important in that they point to ethnic differences in perceived respect over time, but they are limited by their use of a single unidimensional scale by which respect was assessed.

A third study by Mehta (1997), which is most relevant to our own research, used qualitative methods to examine respect for the elderly in Singapore. Her research was based on data from focus group interviews with the elderly and adult children, in which participants compared current and past respect for the elderly. Mehta found that the meaning of respect had changed over time. Respect connoted obedience in the past, but its meaning had now shifted to courtesy and politeness. While this shift in meaning was generally consistent across focus groups in Singapore, further research is needed to determine whether this pattern exists in other Asian countries as well.

The present study builds upon the contributions of each of these studies. Similar to the work of Silverman and Maxwell (1978), we distinguish among several different kinds of respect. We augment their work by examining changes in respect over time, as do Chipperfield and Havens (1992) and Mehta (1997). We further build on previous research on this topic by using Mehta's qualitative methodology, data from the same Singapore sample, and adding data from focus groups in three other Asian countries. In so doing, we can begin to address cross-cultural patterns of respect for the elderly in Asia.

Methodology

This study is based on information generated from focus groups conducted in the Philippines, Singapore, Taiwan, and Thailand. The data were gathered as part of the Comparative Studies of the Elderly in Asia, a comprehensive project coordinated by the University of Michigan that utilizes both quantitative and qualitative data and analytic techniques. The focus group component followed a coordinated research design that was developed collaboratively among researchers from all four countries. The seventy-nine focus groups analyzed here (21 in Singapore, 14 in Taiwan, 18 in the Philippines, and 26 in Thailand) were conducted during 1990-1991. Each focus group consisted of six to nine people. The focus groups from Singapore provided the data on which Mehta (1997) conducted her research.

Group membership was based on a number of criteria including generation, place of residence, and socioeconomic status. The two generations involved were elderly (aged 60 and over) and adult children (aged 30 to 55, who had at least one living parent aged 60 and over). For place of residence, the Philippines, Taiwan, and Thailand selected sites that were either rural or urban while in Singapore, groups were exclusively urban. Socioeconomic status was considered when selecting participants in Thailand, the Philippines and Singapore, but not for Taiwan.

In addition to these three criteria, ethnicity was considered in forming focus group discussions in Taiwan and Singapore. Similarly, after pre-testing the questions in all four countries, gender was a criteria for participating in focus groups in the Philippines and Taiwan. The focus group leaders in the Philippines were concerned that male participants would dominate the discussion, so men and women were separated. In Taiwan, men and women were separated in most of the elderly groups but not in the adult children groups. In Thailand and Singapore, men and women were included in all the groups. Finally, in Taiwan, education was used as a selection criteria such that some groups were highly educated while others had less education.

Guidelines for focus group discussions included questions concerning living arrangements and support, economic status, psychological problems, social relationships, and respect for the elderly. While many of the topics were not addressed by each country, the topic of respect for the elderly was covered in each of the four countries. For example, questions included: "How do people show respect for the elderly?" "Has respect for the elderly changed from the past to the present?" However, there was some variation in the extent to which respect was addressed within each country. That is, respect was one of the main topics for discussion in all countries, except in the Philippines where it was a sub-topic embedded within another set of questions. Therefore the discussion about respect for the elderly had significantly less depth and richness among focus groups in the Philippines as compared to the other countries.

Analysis

All of the focus groups were conducted in the native languages of the participants which, in some cases such as in Singapore, involved English mixed with the native language. Data were transcribed, translated into English, and transferred to Ethnograph (a computer software program for qualitative data analysis). The authors began by reading two randomly-selected transcript from each country to identify prevalent themes and to develop a preliminary coding scheme. The authors subsequently coded all the transcripts and had frequent discussions about their coding scheme. The authors subsequently coded all the transcripts and had frequent discussions about their coding decisions to insure reliability and minimize subjectivity.

The actual coding of the transcripts involved several steps. First, each author served as either a primary or secondary reader. The primary reader identified the portions of the transcript that were devoted to a discussion of respect for the elderly. Second, the primary reader then coded the relevant portions of the text. Third, the secondary reader re-read all the designated portions and re-coded of the text. Third, the secondary reader re-read all the designated portions of the text. Third, the secondary reader re-read all the designated portions of the text. Third, the secondary reader re-read all the designated portions and re-coded them to confirm the coding decision of the primary reader and to add any additional codes that were missing. Fourth, these coded segments were then entered into Ethnograph which facilitated our ability to locate and retrieve relevant coded segments for analysis (Seidel, Friese, & Leonard, 1995). Fifth, the results were organized and analyzed in relation to three major codes: forms of respect, changes in respect, and reasons for changes in respect. In the analysis below, a number of direct quotations from focus group members will illustrate our findings, but names of participants are omitted to protect confidentiality.

Findings

FORMS OF RESPECT

The focus group participants described different ways in which they demonstrated respect to the elderly. Data from the group discussions provided considerable detail about each of these forms of respect which we have organized into five categories: gestures and manners, tokens, customs and rituals, advice, and obedience.

Gestures and Manners

In each of the countries, participants mentioned a variety of stylized gestures and manners connoting respect. While this topic was discussed by participants in all four countries, the relative importance of specific gestures and manners differed by country.

Forms and Examples of Respect for the Elderly

Gestures and Manner
Ritualized gestures: Hands joined in front of bend head, kissing elder's hand
Respectful terms: "Third Aunty"
Helpful behaviors: Carrying heavy objects, offering a seat on the bus to an elder

Tokens
Food: Preparing special food, saving the best portion of the meal for the elder
Money: Providing for living expenses, facilitating the elder's merit making

Customs and Rituals
Celebrations focused on older people: Thai New Years, surprise gift-giving party
Celebrations involving older people: Making the marriage bed

Advice
Major purchases: Asking the elder before purchasing a television, car, or house
Auspicious dates: Asking elders about when to plan a wedding or plant rice
Consultants in family quarrels: Relying on elders as peacemakers

Obedience
Leaving home: Waiting for permission to leave the house
Marriage decisions: Following advice of elders about whom to marry

---

Many of the polite gestures described by the groups were related to ways in which younger people greet older people. Discussants addressed the importance of speaking politely when greeting older people. Many described ritualized ways of using the body during such greetings. In Thailand, for example, one of these greetings involved placing the hands together and slightly bending the head. Indeed, placing one's body lower than the elder to insure that the younger person's head was below that of the elder was a traditional form of respect mentioned by several Thai discussants. In Singapore, focus groups referred to several different ways of greeting older people: kissing their hands, bowing, and with hands joined in front of the face. These stylized greetings were described more by some ethnic groups (e.g., the Malay and Indian discussants) in Singapore than others (e.g., the Chinese). One of the Malay participants demonstrated how younger people bend their body as they passed elders. Similarly, participants in the Philippines observed that the traditional way for a young person to show respect in their country was to kiss the hand of the elder whom they were greeting.

Another form of respectful manners was displayed by the terms used in referring to older people and other family members. As one Thai respondent said, "If they are at the age of our grandma, we call them grandma. If they are at the age of our aunts, we call them so." Using appropriate names as a form of respect was discussed quite frequently by the Chinese discussants who lived in Singapore. For example, one focus group member described how important it was to her older mother that children know and accurately address older people in terms of their hierarchy within the family (e.g., "Third Aunty or Fourth Aunty" rather than simply "Aunty"). In the Philippines, focus group members described specific terms which connote respectful manners such as the way in which one said "yes." They explained that the respectful terms was "opo" while the disrespectful term was "oo." In the words of one elderly respondent, "When I hear 'oo' from small children, my ears hurt. I get really irritated."

A third form of good manners associated with respect was helpful behaviors. Several focus groups mentioned the importance of helping older people to cross the street or helping them to carry heavy objects. When discussing respectful behavior, a common concern addressed by groups in all four countries, particularly in Taiwan, was how older people were treated on buses. Some of this discussion was directed toward the behavior of the bus drivers in relation to how and when they stopped the bus for an elder. However, more of the discussion focused on the behavior of younger passengers in relation to whether or not they gave up a seat for an older person.

Tokens

Discussions in all the countries, with the exception of the Philippines, referred to material tokens of respect. These tokens were typically in the form of food or money. The provision of food to the elderly connoted respect and caring. Thai respondents described the ways in which they tried to prepare food that elderly people particularly liked and how they saved the best part of the meal for older people. In Singapore, a respondent told how he had learned from his parents to give the elders the first of any sweets that were brought home.

Similarly, the provision of money was another form of respect. Taiwanese respondents talked about giving money to their elders to provide for their living expenses. Thais described how they gave money to the elderly so they would have the ability to make merit through offerings to the temple priests. They also used money to buy material things that the older person would like.

Customs and Rituals

Discussions about customs and rituals associated with respect for the elderly occurred primarily within the Thai and Singapore focus groups. The Singapore groups focused on customs involving ways in which younger and older people socialized. Several members noted that, traditionally, children were taught to stay apart from the older guests until they were invited to join them. This custom involved children and elders socializing in separate rooms unless the children were invited to join the elders.

The Thai groups described a variety of rituals in which the elderly were an integral, respected part. For some of these rituals, older people were the focus of attention. Several of our participants described how during Thai New Years, adult children paid respect to their elders by bringing them food, presents, and pouring water over their hands. Another such occasion, described by groups in Northern Thailand, involved a surprise gift-giving party to an older, revered member of the community which was sponsored by his/her younger family members. One of the focus group participants described this celebration:

> Money is gathered from many people to buy food, things to be used, and dessert. Then we will silently go to visit to surprise an invalid old person. We'll leave those things together with some money next to that old person who is asleep. When the old person wakes up and sees those things, he will bless those who give them to him.

For other rituals described by Thai discussants, the elderly were not the focus but were central players. Such was the case for weddings when, for example, it was generally an older person who was designated to ask for the bride's hand in marriage. Group participants explained that younger people were neither sufficiently reliable nor respectable to play this role. Part of the wedding ceremony incorporated an older couple who made the marriage bed to bless the newly married couple with a long life together.

Advice

Consulting older people for their advice was a frequently-mentioned form of respect. Several adult Thai children described how they routinely asked their parents before they made big purchases (e.g., a house, a television, a car), particularly if they were still living with parents and planning to use their parents' money toward the purchase. Some explained that they asked their parents for advice about major life decisions, such as the suitability o marriage partners for their children. Others said they sought older people's advice primarily in relation to traditions. For example, a Thai participant explained the circumstances under which advice was sought, "If they are modern problems, we do not. If they are family problems, we do. Old people know nothing about modern problems." Similarly, a Singaporean respondent said, "I don't consult my mother but I would consult her on things which I'm not sure about, like customs."

In addition to asking advice on customs and major purchases, Thais consulted older people for advice in a number of ways. The Thai focus groups told about relying on elders to determine auspicious dates. They asked older people to determine auspicious dates for weddings, house constructions, festival dates, and when to plant the rice. The elderly were also consulted about quarrels within the family and village. This advice-seeking depended upon the magnitude of the problem. If the problem was relatively small, older people were consulted. For larger problems, the village headman was approached. For very serious matters, villagers would turn to the police.

Obedience

Focus groups in all four countries spoke about obedience to the directives of the elder as a crucial form of respect. In the words of one Thai respondent, respect for the elderly was when "we listen to and obey their suggestions." A Singaporean discussant described respect in terms of patiently accepting a scolding from an elder. This process involved not talking back or in any way humiliating the elder.

Focus groups in each country addressed different ways in which obedience to the elderly could be manifested. In Taiwan, there was mention of younger people following older peoples' directives as to when they could or could not leave home. In Thailand, discussants explained how grandchildren followed their grandparents' advice about whom to marry. In Singapore, a respondent described respect in relation to obediently following the advice of the elderly concerning large purchases.

CHANGES IN RESPECT

There was ample indication that these expressions of respect were changing over time. An examination of the five forms of respect described above led to the discovery that in all categories but one, themes of change were pervasive. It was only in relation to tokens of respect that the discussion did not refer to marked changes over time. Here, we will focus on the forms of respect that were associated with change.

Gestures and Manners

Focus groups described numerous ways in which traditional greetings and ritualized physical gestures had altered. In Thailand, several participants explained how younger people frequently walked by and ignored older people rather than greeting them with the traditional gestures of hands joined in front of the head. Others pointed out how few people bowed in front of elders. Referring to the younger generation's tendency not to bend low in the presence of their elders, one Thai participant observed, "The young nowadays mostly have a still waist." Similarly, a Singaporean discussant noted, "The children in the past, if they wanted to walk past an elder, they would bend their bodies. Children nowadays sweep by us as if we are grass."

In the Philippines, focus group participants decried the glib way in which younger people now greeted older people without even kissing their hands. Said one elderly Filipino, "Nowadays, kids don't know anything about respect. You'll have to offer your hand for them to kiss. Sometimes, they don't even want to kiss the elderly's hands." Another Filipino distinguished greetings between the young and the old in the city as compared to the country, young people will at least greet older people with a few words, such as 'Good morning' or 'Good afternoon.'"

Another change concerned the way in which the young addressed the old. Several discussants pointed to marked changes in the traditional attention to naming patterns. A Chinese group member in Singapore noted that the English education system had resulted in an indifference to distinctions between English education system had resulted in an indifference to distinctions between elders and juniors, "When the kid grows up, you ask him who is this person? He'll say 'uncle' but will not know how you are related—whether you're father's older or younger brother, mother's older or younger sister." In addition, younger people were portrayed as much ruder than in the past. A Taiwanese shopkeeper told how a younger person had recently asked directions by shouting, "Hey! Got a minute!"

A third change had occurred in relation to help-giving. Focus groups noted changes in the kindness previously directed toward older people using public transportation. Some noticed that bus drivers rarely waited for the elderly to be seated before moving. Others observed that young people frequently did not give up their seats to older passengers. In the words of a Filipino discussant, "Nowadays, you will often see an old man helplessly standing beside a seated teenager just looking on."

Customs and Rituals

Certain customs related to proscribed respectful behaviors toward older people appear to be in flux. Group members described changing expectations concerning how children should behave in the presence of elderly people. For example, in Singapore, young people were traditionally expected to stay apart from older visitors until they were called. They also ate separately from the older people. In the words of an older Indian participant from Singapore, "Elders don't expect young to behave in that way. The pattern is changing." Another Singaporean respondent talked about how, when in the past children did eat with their parents, it was unacceptable for children to ask for food. In contrast, children now feel quite comfortable asking to have a dish passed to them.

Among the Thai, the degree of change appeared to be related to geographical location. Those in urban areas were particularly vocal about changing expressions of respect they observed in comparison to their rural counterparts. The Bangkok participants noted that now people were asked to help in festivities based on their ability and status, rather than simply their age. One participant described the criteria for becoming president of a ceremony, "He must be an able old man or an important one to be invited. A local old man will never be invited." They also noted that, unlike the country, people in Bangkok did not wait for the elderly before beginning important ceremonies. As one women observed, "They may not even come. How can they spend time waiting for them?"

Advice

While some of our participants felt that younger people were genuinely interested in the advice of their elders, others described a form of advice-asking that was more stylized. For example, in Thailand, members of a Bangkok focus group identified a strategic form of advice-asking that was intended to enhance the elder's sense of control. These adult children described how they consulted with older people to give them the feeling that they were an important part of the decision. In so doing, the decision of the elderly was generally consistent with what the adult children wanted. Similarly, in Singapore, a participant described how whenever she bought anything, she immediately showed it to her mother or mother-in-law to help them feel that they had been consulted in the decision.

Obedience

While focus groups described obedience as a form of respect, there was considerable evidence that younger people no longer followed the dictates of the elderly. A consistent theme was that today's younger people may listen to the advice of older people but often do not follow this advice. An older participant in a Philippine focus group explained, "They still respect us, but most of the children do not obey us any more." Similarly, in Taiwan, participants described how children no longer asked their elders for permission to leave the house. An elderly Singaporean participant elaborated, "So this change of time, change of world, change of the way of accepting advice . . . they don't blindly agree."

Some discussants alluded to a new definition of respect in relation to obedience. For example, focus group participants in Singapore explained that, in the past, respect was equated with obedience and submission. Currently, however, respect is associated with seeking the opinion of elders and/or informing them after a decision has been made. Another group in the Philippines offered a variant on this theme. They observed that, in the past, respect was associated with never answering back to an elder. Now, however, it was acceptable to disagree if it was done in a nice manner and by speaking moderately. Others totally disassociated respect and obedience. These individuals felt that lack of submission to the advice and directives of older people should not be interpreted as disrespect. In the words of one older participant in Singapore, "Though they may not listen to you, they may respect you because you are the elder. But as for your advice on certain matters is concerned, they don't agree."

REASONS FOR CHANGES IN RESPECT

Discussions from focus groups in our study provided a number of reasons for why respect for the elderly had diminished over time. The major themes that emerged from this discussion pertained to changes in family structure and function, education, income, and modernization.

Changes in Family Structure and Function

Several participants alluded to the impact of changes in family organization and employment. They observed that an increased emphasis on the nuclear family had decreased respect for the elderly. In Singapore, a participant explained how older people now felt excluded from their children's families, "Presently a lot of families are pretty self-centered. I mean I a family-nucleus, I normally center my life around my family. So the parents are actually considered as outsiders." A Taiwanese discussant described a shifting pattern of loyalty within the family from the elderly to children. This participant said, "These days, familial feelings are all devoted to the children and not to parents." Another Taiwanese discussant explained that, while adult children had a "respectful mentality," it was difficult to express their respect because they no longer lived as an extended family due to the pressures of needing to leave home to make a living. Such altered living arrangements then impacted on the relationships between the elderly and their grandchildren. Several Thai respondents talked about how, in the past, parents appreciated and respected older people's discipline of their children. However, most parents now considered older people's discipline as an unwelcome interference in their child rearing responsibilities.

Participants were also vocal about the extent to which women's employment outside of the home had influenced respect for the elderly. Many associated women's employment with neglect in the teaching of values. A Filipino eloquently made this point, "In the past, all the niceties, even in eating, were taught by the mother because she was at home. Nowadays, the mother is always in a hurry. She goes to the office. In the affection, she hurriedly cooks and markets. She can no longer teach the children because she has plenty of chores." A discussant in Taiwan made an even clearer connection between women's employment and respect, "Respecting the elders was one of the four virtues. But, today there is not the same family structure. Mothers are working women. Everyone comes and goes without learning respect." Some discussants pointed out that the pressures of work and the guilt associated with not being available to their children made mothers particularly susceptible to spoiling their children, providing them with material things, and not insisting on good manners and behavior. In the words of a focus group member from Singapore, "So from here, I see that children today do not know how to respect the elders. I am also afraid that my child may treat me like that."

Education

Many focus groups held the education system responsible for lack of respect paid to the elderly. The educational system was critiqued for its lack of emphasis on teaching morals and family values. Focus groups explained that in the past, education has focused on teaching duties and morals but that these topics had little attention in current curriculums. In the words of a Thai participant, "They are taught too many subjects at school such as dancing and others but not about gratitude. In the former times, we were taught to be grateful to parents." Similarly, a discussant in Taiwan critiqued the process of learning, "Schools have put an emphasis on studying science and give morality and family relationships short shrifts. . . . Education comes up short in instilling moral thinking to the point where it makes the younger generations feel less respectful toward their elders."

Discussants also noted that education had the effect of increasing the knowledge gap between younger and older people and thereby decreasing respect. As an older Thai respondent observed, "When they finish learning, they say that the older people don't know anything because they don't even have a fourth grade education. They rarely obey us." In Singapore, an older participant spoke about how with the present emphasis on prolonged education, children frequently go to school for many years. Due to this focus on education, they often postpone entering the family business and thus have much less contact with older family members. Others described how the focus on English language training resulted in poorer communication between the young and the old, who did not speak English. One Singaporean group members spoke poignantly about this communication gap, "When the children come, they learn only English. How are the old to talk to the children? You can only say, 'I don't know.' You can't communicate. We want to talk and the children don't understand. He wants to talk and we don't know what he's saying."

Changes in Income

According to some of the focus group participants, changes in the earning power of young people made them less reliant on and therefore less respectful toward their elders. In the words of an old Taiwanese man, "Before, they were respectful. No matter what sort of older person one was, he was always revered. Now young people all think the elderly can't work any more and only eat. I think it's because the standard of living is higher. With industry and commerce in full boom, everybody can earn more money and they don't need to rely on parents." A participant in Singapore identified a connection between income and respect by saying, "If you have to ask your parents for money, then probably you have to be more obedient to get the money from them." An older Thai discussant elaborated on this connection when he remarked, "If they are students or going to find jobs, they will listen to us a little, but if they are employed and earn their incomes, they won't listen to us anymore."

Modernization

Many of the focus groups described how changes in the broader world, including moving from an agrarian way of life and adopting Western ways, had negatively influenced respect for the elderly. In the words of a participant in Taiwan, "People who live in cities, and who are involved in the industrial society, tend to be fully occupied with their work. They don't have as much time to spend with others. People in rural areas are rich in genuine human warmth and have more time to show their respect to the elderly." A participant in a Thai focus group observed that the trend among adult children in villages was to move to the city to earn money. In so doing they "surpassed the footprints of their fathers." By moving beyond the experiences of the village elders, they became more immune to their advice and criticism.

Several groups spoke about how this pressure to succeed among adult children had resulted in an overly permissive environment for the succeeding generation. A Singaporean discussant noted a direct correlation between such parental permissiveness and a decrease in respect for the older generation, "Another reason why children are losing respect is that they are given much freedom by their parents. These parents resort to just giving them money in order not to be distracted from their other activities."

This emphasis on materialism and individuality was frequently attributed to the West. Numerous respondents referred to the effect of Western values which had been transmitted by television, films, and advertisements. A Singaporean discussant described this impact, "I think it's the Western influence. You'll see from American films, children who rebel against their parents. . . . The Western system invariably affects us."

DISCUSSION

By examining focus group data from four Asian countries, this study addresses various forms of respect for the elderly. Group participants identified a number of different ways in which respect could be expressed: gestures and manners, tokens, customs and rituals, advice, and obedience. While specific expressions of respect and their relative importance differed by country, the general categories of respect were described by focus groups in all four Asian countries. With a few significant exceptions, the categories of respect that emerged from our study overlap with those identified by Silverman and Maxwell (1978) based upon their analysis of thirty-four societies. However, Silverman and Maxwell did not categorize either asking for advice or obedience as forms of respect. Our work and that of Mehta's (1997) suggests that obedience to the dictates of the elderly may be a form of respect that is changing most pervasively. Mehta observed this change in Singapore, and we observed this change in the three additional countries added to her sample.

Unlike Chipperfield and Havens (1992), who found that respect for the elderly increased or remained stable, participants in our study perceived that tradi-

tional expressions of respect for the elderly were changing. The difference between the results of these two studies may be partially attributable to their contrasting methodological approaches. Our study used a qualitative approach asking
participants for their views of how respect for the elderly was expressed while
Chipperfield and Havens used a unidimensional Likert scale to measure perceived
respect for the elderly.

The present study identified factors associated with changing forms of respect for the elderly: family structure and function, education, income, and
modernization. These attributions are supported by researchers who have examined changes in the status of the elderly in other Asian countries. For example,
Baginda (1987) noted that in Malaysia the loss of stature among the elderly is
related to several phenomenon including: a shift toward a nuclear family form, the
differences in educational levels between young and old, and the migration of
young families to the city such that older people are left behind. Similarly,
Goldstein, Schuler, and Ross (1983) discussed the complex changes in authority
relationships in Nepal as sons work for the government or business and are no
longer dependent upon their fathers' land. These studies, in combination with our
own, identify ways in which changes in authority and status among the elderly are
associated with changes in respect for the elderly.

Our study suggests that while expressions of respect for the elderly are
changing in these four Asian countries, respect remains a central value. The degree of concern expressed about how respect for the elderly is changing is an
indication of its vital importance to the value system of Asians. Respondents were
actively engaged in the process of redefining the meaning of respect. Mehta
(1997) noted that respect was redefined, among her Singaporean sample, from
obedience to courteous behavior. Similarly, in a study of youth and elders in Hong
Kong, Chow (1997) determined that young people are still willing to provide
financial support and personal care but are less willing to consult older people for
their opinions. Wee observed this same process of redefinition occurring among
the Singapore, Thai, Taiwanese, and Filipino focus groups. Participants in all four
countries indicated that respect for the elderly could no longer be equated with
obedience. However, they redefined respect to encompass a number of other
kinds of acceptable respectful behavior. They augmented their definition of respect to include being polite, asking for the advice of elders, and informing the
elders of their decisions. Our study suggests that while traditional expressions of
respect for the elderly are changing, the value of respect remains stable. Asians
are actively engaged in the process of searching for alternative definitions of
respect for the elderly.

These findings must be consider within the context of the limitations of this
study. First, while the topic of respect was addressed in focus groups in all four
Asian countries, the specific questions varied by country. In particular, the focus
groups in the Philippines devoted less attention to the topic of respect. While the
Filipino groups discussed forms of respect for the elderly and changes in respect
over time, there was less richness and detail in these data than for the other

countries. Further research which makes such cross-cultural comparisons should insure more similarity among the questions asked.

Second, this research is limited in its generalizability by our sampling techniques and our cross-sectional data. The sample was purposively drawn to include people who represented a variety of pre-determined characteristics (e.g., generation, gender, and socioeconomic status) and change in respect was ascertained by asking each group to compare the present with the past. While our sampling techniques resulted in findings that were remarkably consistent across the four countries, it is important that future research on the topic of changes in respect use representative, longitudinal samples. It would be particularly interesting to examine changes in respect for the elderly among the younger generation of Asians who are now adolescents and young adults.

Third, our study represents a broad-brush approach to examining respect across four Asian countries. In so doing, we did not look at specific factors that differentially affect respect for the elderly within each country. For example, it may be that respect for the elderly is more influenced by their socioeconomic status in some countries than in others. Examining the affect of such variables as gender, ethnicity, socioeconomic status, and urbanicity on respect would be a fruitful direction for future cross-cultural research on this topic.

Our research suggests that Asians are concerned about changes in respect for older people. Others have documented ways in which Asian countries are taking steps to address these changes. In Japan, for example, older people are included in school functions as a way of enhancing the contact and good will between children and elders. Elders are invited into the classroom to share folk tales, traditional games, and skills (Nakamura, 1994; Yamazaki, 1994). In Korea, a Filial Piety Prize is awarded to individuals who long-standing service demonstrates exemplary respect and care for the elderly (Sung, 1990). In Singapore, the government is using the media to emphasize the importance of filial duty and is using legislative initiatives to induce three generational families to live together by offering such families more desirable housing units (Mukerjee, 1982).

Respect for the elderly has deep roots in traditional Asian cultures. These roots retain their stability but also evidence change. Our study indicates that, within a sample of four Asian countries, the value of respect for the elderly continues to be important. However, the expression and meaning of respect are changing. Asians are concerned about these changes and are developing creative strategies to renew expressions of respect for the elderly. Westerners can learn by carefully observing these attempts to retain deeply rooted values in a changing world.

Acknowledgements

The authors wish to thank John Knodel and David Morgan for their advice and encouragement.

Notes

1. This research was supported by grants from the Michigan Exploratory Center on the Demography of Aging, the Office of the Vice Provost for Academic and Multicultural Affairs, and the International Institute at the University of Michigan. The focus group data were obtained from an archive that is part of the "Rapid Demographic Change and the Welfare of the Elderly," funded by the National Institute on Aging (R37AGO7637) for which Al Hermalin is the Principal Investigator.

2. Portions of this article were presented at the 16th World Congress of the International Association of Gerontology in Singapore, August 1997.

References

Baginda, A. M. (1987). The emerging issues of the aging population: Malaysia. In *Population aging: Review of emerging issues* (pp. 33-43). Bangkok, Thailand: Economic and Social Commission for Asia and the Pacific, Asian Population Studies Series.

Chipperfield, J. G., & Havens, B. (1992). A longitudinal analysis of perceived respect among elders: Changing perceptions for some ethnic groups. *Canadian Journal on Aging, 11* (1), 15-30.

Chow, N. (1997). *The policy implications of the changing role and status of the elderly in Hong Kong.* The University of Hong Kong: Monograph Series Number 28.

Domingo, L. J. (1994). Governmental and non-governmental response to the issue of aging in the Philippines. In Department for Economic and Social Information and Policy Analysis (Ed.), *The aging of Asian populations* (pp. 104-111). New York: United Nations.

Domingo, L. J., Asis, M. M. B., Jose, M. C. P., & Kabamalan, M. M. M. (1993). Living arrangements of the elderly in the Philippines: Qualitative evidence. *Comparative Study of the Elderly in Asia.* Ann Arbor, MI: Population Studies Center, The University of Michigan.

Goldstein, M. C., Schuler, S., & Ross, J. L. (1983). Social and economic forces affecting intergenerational relations in extended families in a third world country: A cautionary tale from South Asia. *Journal of Gerontology, 38*(6), 716-724.

Ho, D. Y. (1982). Asian concepts in behavioral science. *Psychologia, 25*(4), 328-335.

Limanonda, B. (1995). Families in Thailand: Beliefs and realities. *Journal of Comparative Studies, 26*(1), 67-82.

Knodel, J., Saengtienchai, C., & Sittitrai, W. (1992). The living arrangements of elderly in Thailand: Views of the populace. *Comparative Study of the Elderly in Asia,* Report No. 92-90. Ann Arbor, MI: Population Studies Center, University of Michigan.

Mehta, K. (1997). Respect redefined: Focus group insights from Singapore. *International Journal of Aging and Human Development, 44*(3), 205-219.

Mukerjee, D. (1982). Singapore: Reviving filial duty. *People, 9*(4), 21-22.

Nakamura, K. (1994). Education for understanding aged people and the aged society in Japan. *Educational Gerontology, 20*(5), 521-531.

Pramualratana, A. (1992). The impact of societal change and role of the old in a rural community in Thailand. In B. Yoddumnem-Attig, K. Richter, A. Soonthomdhada, C. Sethaput, and A. Pramualratana (Eds.), *Changing roles and statuses of women in Thailand* (pp. 44-54). Salaya, Thailand: Mahidol University.

Seidel, J., Friese, & Leonard, D. C. (1995). *The ethnograph v 4.0: A users guide.* Amherst, MA: Qualis Research Associates.

Silverman, P., & Maxwell, R. (1978). How do I respect thee? Let me count the ways: Deference towards elderly men and women. *Behavior Science Research, 13*(2), 91-108.

Sung, K. T. (1990). A new look at filial piety: Ideals and practices of family centered parent care in Korea. *The Gerontologist, 30*(5), 610-617.

Sung, K. T. (1995). Measures and dimensions of filial piety in Korea. *The Gerontologist, 35*(2),240-247.

Yamazaki, T. (1994). Intergenerational interaction outside the family. *Educational Gerontology, 20*(5), 453-462.

Chapter 20

Filial Piety in Asian Chinese Communities

Nelson Chow

Introduction

For thousands of years, the Chinese culture has been described as one of respecting the old, or xiao, as known in the old classic (Liang, 1987). Though some people have found this value too oppressive and inapplicable in modern society, it is still upheld as sacrosanct in all Chinese communities in Asia. Even in socialist China, article 42 of the Constitution of the People's Republic of China states that the old "have the right to material assistance from and be supported by their sons in their old age." An Advisory Council on the Aged, set up by the Singapore, recommended in a report in 1989 that "Filial piety and respect for the aged should be fostered and preserved. The family has the foremost role in this. Family members can transmit such values to children by example" (Advisory Council on the Aged, 1989, p. 3). The Singapore government has also recently introduced a legislation to make it an offence for children refusing to support their elderly parents. Filial piety, rather than being a dying value, is still very much treasured in Asia, especially among the Chinese. My following presentation will try to explain, first, the meaning of filial piety and, secondly, how the notion has, in practice, influenced the making of policies on the aged in Asian Chinese communities.

The Meaning of Filial Piety

To understand the meaning of filial piety, it is important to realize first the significant position of the family system in Chinese societies. The importance of the family system in traditional China arose not only because of the many functions it performed for its members, but also from the many roles it undertook on behalf of the wider society (Freedman, 1979). Mencius, an old Chinese sage, once taught that "The root of the world is the nation and the root of the nation is the family." In the Chinese conception, an orderly family system formed the starting point of a harmonious cosmos and a family could only be orderly when members within it learned to behave properly towards each other.

Furthermore, it should be realized that in traditional China, the meaning of filial piety is much broader than simply showing respect. It was recorded in the Book of Rites that the highest level that children should aim to attain in xiao was to bring honour to their parents, next was not to bring them disgrace and the least that they could do was to provide them with a decent living. Other than ordering the proper behavior of the children towards their parents, xiao has another function in preparing the young for the adult world. C.K. Yang wrote: "While the functioning of filial piety was limited to relationship between parents and children, their veneration of age was traditionally a means of inspiring respect and obedience by the young toward all the other senior members of the family and society as a whole" (Yang, 1959).

Hence, in making the family the most fundamental unit in society and using xiao as the regulator of proper behavior both within the family and in the wider society, a simple yet complex social order was formed in traditional China. It was a simple one because it was largely constructed upon the relationship that children maintained with their parents and once a person learned how to behave within the family, he then knew how to go about in the wider society. In other words, based on the notion of xiao, a network of relationships was established with distinct entitlements and obligations.

In modern times, the significance of xiao as well as the family system has no doubt gradually been watered down (Fei, 1985). However, filial piety is still perceived in most Chinese communities as an important value for it is often emphasized as the guiding principle for the formulation of policies for the aged in Asian societies.

Filial Piety in Practice

So far, I have touched only on the meaning of filial piety. How was the notion practiced in the past and has it still an influence on the behavior of people today? Briefly, there are few records on the practice of filial piety in both traditional and modern Chinese societies as discussions on the subject are mostly didactic in nature. What is known is that pressures on children to take care of their elderly parents in traditional China were so strong that deviation from the norm would not only result in rejection by one's family but also by the wider society. Thus, elderly persons who could truly command the respect of their children were honored by the state through the bestowal of certain privileges, such as the leading positions in communal ceremonies. Children known for their pious deeds would also be given preferential treatment in civil service examinations. The picture that was often portrayed was one in which "parents enjoyed a serene old age, honored by all, with their descendants about them, and tenderly cared for as declining years brought physical weakness" (Latourette, 1964, p. 572).

What actually happened in traditional China as far as respecting the old is concerned is unfortunately not as rosy as that described above; incidents of elderly persons being deserted by their children were not unheard of in old times. But it would be unacceptable for children not to support their parents even if they had great difficulty in doing so. State measures to provide for the elderly were largely unknown in traditional China as children were expected to take up this responsibility. What was required of the state was to teach the children about their duties and to ensure their observance. Under certain exceptional circumstances when the elderly person did not have the support of a family, help would still not come from the state but from the individual's kinsmen and the clans to which the person belonged. In addition to the material assistance provided by their kin and clan, a small number of the lonely elderly could also enter institutions specially set up for them. Such institutions were usually established by philanthropists and religious orders, most were run by village communities using the proceeds from properties held in common.

What was practiced in traditional Chinese societies under the mandate of xiao had once been described as follows:

(1) The elderly should be helped as far as possible outside of the institution which should only be regarded as a last resort.
(2) The elderly should continue to make their contribution towards their families.
(3) The elderly who are admitted into institutions should be put in different categories according to their health conditions.
(4) The support of the elderly should rely on the combined efforts of the entire community (Ke, 1944, p. 124).

The above principles are still largely observed in modern Chinese communities. It has ben mentioned that the Chinese Constitution required children to support their elderly parents and even after the period of the Cultural Revolution, this mandate had remained unchanged. Deborah Davis-Friedmann described the situation in the early 1980s as follows: "The general patterns of interaction between elderly parents and their adult children continue to show high levels of solidarity between the different generations and a pronounced preference for parent-son interdependence" (Davis-Friedmann, 1983, p. 103). The interdependence appears to be more so in the villages as William Parish and Martin Whyte wrote in the mid-1970s that "Parents still expect to live with and be supported by their sons in their old age" (Parish & Whyte, 1978, p. 154).

Other than China, the notion of filial piety in its various forms appears also to be exerting an influence on the making of policies regarding the elderly in other Asian societies. Taiwan, Hong Kong and Singapore, all with a predominant Chinese population, have emphasized in various ways the importance of respecting one's elderly parents. While both Taiwan and Singapore have made support for one's elderly parents a duty of the children, the Hong Kong government has taken a less punitive approach and provided, instead, the children with the necessary incentives to fulfill their obligations. These incentives include tax allowances and a shortening of the waiting period for public housing when children are prepared to live with their elderly parents. As for other Asian countries, similarly influenced by the Chinese cultures, like Japan and the Republic of Korea, the notion of filial piety has also been regarded as an important value influencing the way in which the elderly are being treated both within the family and in the wider society. There is no denying that the family system in these countries has been diminishing in its functions in providing support for its elderly members, but it would certainly be a grave mistake to assume that filial piety is no longer relevant in the formulation of policies on the aged (Chow, 1991).

In summary, an examination of the meaning of filial piety and its application in today's Asian Chinese communities reveals the following:

(1) That despite the fact that the notion itself is no longer treasured as in the past, it is still the most important value in regulating the behavior of the younger generations towards the old.

(2) Based on the assumption that it is the responsibility of the children to take care of their elderly parents, state measures to support the old have slow been coming into existence and are perceived as playing a supplementary role to the family system.

(3) In order to enable the elderly to remain as long as possible in the community and close to their families, an explicit or implicit "community care" approach has often been adopted as the guiding principle for the development of state social services for the aged.

(4) Efforts are made to inculcate among the young the notion of respecting the old and legislations are enforced in some societies to make it an offence for children not to support their elderly parents.

(5) The notion of filial piety has made the support of the elderly a responsibility shared between the family system and the state, rather than one falling entirely on the government.

The above sums up what currently exists in Asian Chinese communities, as far as the support of the elderly is concerned. Filial piety is certainly not a dying notion and it is a value, and in many ways an asset, that societies in Asia must strive to keep as they formulate their policies for their aged members.

References

Advisory Council on the Aged, Government of Singapore. (1989). *Report of the advisory council of the aged.* Singapore, Government Press.

Chow, N.W.S. (1991). Does filial piety exist under Chinese communism? *Journal of Aging & Social Policy, 3*(1/2): 209-225.

Davis-Friedmann, D. (1983). *Long lives, Chinese elderly and the communist revolution.* Cambridge, MA: Harvard University Press.

Fei, X.T. (1985). The caring of the old in families undergoing structural changes. In C. Chia (Ed.), *Proceedings of the conference on modernization and Chinese culture* (pp. 121-132). Hong Kong: Faculty of Social Sciences and Institute of Social Studies, The Chinese University of Hong Kong.

Freedman, M. (1979). *The study of Chinese society.* Essays selected by G.W. Skinner, Palo Alto, CA: Stanford University Press.

Ke, X.F. (1944). *Shehui jiuji (Social relief).* Chongqing: Zhenzhong Press.

Latourette, K.S. (1964). *The Chinese, their history and culture.* New York: Macmillan.

Liang, S.M. (1987). *Zhongguo chengshi jiating (Families in Chinese cities).* Jinan: Shendong People's Press.

Presented at:
Symposium on Filial Piety,
5th Asia/Oceania Regional Congress of Gerontology
20 November 1995

PART V

Religious Perspectives

In the final part, we will explore ethical and religious issues that affect the practice of respect for elderly persons. Part V consists of four chapters. Chapter 21 presents an essay that takes up the issue of filial morality in an aging society, focusing on the Judeo-Christian ethical and theological perspective. This perspective stresses that the elderly must be cared for and respected in any moral society which refuses to sanction abandonment or senicide. It concludes that Judeo-Christianity offers an aging society the concept of caretaking as a religious-ethical vocation or calling. Chapter 22 discusses the Jewish way of providing respectful service for ill parents as efforts to fulfill their filial obligations as indicated by their religious commitments. Chapter 23 presents the Buddhist way of respecting parents, particularly the mother. Buddhist teaching directs the followers to recognize the kindness of their parents and in return to respect and care for them. Thus repayment of the debt to parents is an important filial obligation. The chapter introduces a Sutra which enables the followers to understand the importance of repaying parents' kindness, enlightens them about the parents' boundless and fathomless kindness, and teaches them to repay the kindness in the Buddhist way. In Chapter 24, we review the Muslim way of respecting elderly persons. Islamic teachings stress the importance of respecting elders, particularly parents. Respectful behavior and devoted service to parents is a must in Islam. Worship of Allah is always a necessity. Similarly, service to parents is always necessary during their lifetimes and by prayer after their death. Teachings prescribed in the Qur'an are introduced, with regard to good behaviors towards parents, e.g., giving mothers gratitude and respect, serving parents in old age with kindness, and paying respect for all elderly persons.

All four chapters evidence that all religions teach that children must respect and care for their elders. Judeo-Christianity is clear as to the moral importance of respect for parents and elders, which is rooted in its theological ethical heritage. Buddhism stresses respect and care for elders, especially for the mother whose kindness could not be fully reciprocated by even the most filial of children. Recognizing and practicing respect and care for parents and elders is taken even more emphatically in Islam teaching. Allah's commands in the Holy Qur'an repeatedly alert followers to conduct respectful and caring behaviors with parents and elders. Thus, Judeo-Christian and Muslim teachings on respect for parents and elders fit in with the Buddhist teachings.

Chapter 21

Filial Morality in an Aging Society

Stephen G. Post

Currently we are in the midst of a demographic revolution of monumental proportions—ours is an aging society. Science and medical technology have advanced to the point at which the human life span has been extended far beyond what, in previous centuries, was allowed by the balance of nature. The traditional demographic triangle, with the young at its base and the elderly at its apex, has been replaced by a rectangle. As the number of elderly increases relative to other age groups, greater caretaking responsibilities will be placed on the shoulders of the young and middle-aged. Striking a moral balance between the needs of the elderly and those of younger generations is no easy task. As philosopher Leon Kass comments with the goals of current research to delay the aging process in mind, "If people lived healthily to 100 or 120, if institutions were altered to meet their needs, we would likely have traded our problems of the aged for problems of youth."[1] No society can expect younger age groups to sacrifice their opportunities for adequate careers and families of their own by any total or even radical policy of self-abnegation. This is because no society can have a healthy future without investing in the young, and because the young themselves have a right to realize their human potential just as the now elderly did in their youth. On the other hand, the elderly must be cared for and respected in any moral society which refuses to sanction abandonment or senicide. Thus the imposing moral dilemma of inter-generational justice.

This essay takes up the question of the basis and nature of filial morality in an aging society. What do adult children owe their elderly parents, assuming that their parents fulfilled ordinary child rearing obligations? Parental obligations vary from culture to culture, of course, but I assume here that parents who fail to meet the fundamental welfare needs of their children (food, drink, shelter, clothing, health, education, affirmation, and so forth) can expect relatively little from other than supererogatory offspring. With certain qualifications, what follows here is largely a defense of filial obligations and of the Judeo-Christian moral heritage in which these obligations are grounded. While it is extremely difficult to reach any empirical conclusions, it can be surmised that as the demographic revolution continues, adult children will find themselves with obligations beyond what they might have anticipated. Such heavy burdens can sap limited resources and sympathies, resulting in a temptation to unravel the traditional arguments affirming filial obligations. One pollster, Daniel Yankelovich, has written that one of the most far-reaching changes in current moral norms is the view that parents today cannot and should not make the demands on their children that their parents made on them.[2] If there is a trend away from filial obligations, it is one which must, as far as possible, be reversed, or so I shall argue. The old and frail are particularly vulnerable to the vicissitudes of moral consciousness, and they must be firmly ensconced in the moral domain. And yet, as will be shown, there are a good many philosophical revisionists who claim that adult children owe their parents absolutely nothing.

Moral Philosophy: An Hiatus and a Recent Dispute

Before turning to the Judeo-Christian ethical perspective on filial morality, some assessment of recent moral philosophy will underscore the extent to which several revisionists have tried to undercut the notion that elderly parents are owed anything by their adult children. There has been an effort to retrieve the grounds for filial obligations made by some philosophers in response to the revisionists. In addition to examining this effort, I will make some comments on the lack of interest in familial relationships characteristic of moral philosophy as a whole.

What is modern philosophical ethics able to tell us regarding filial morality? In short, very little indeed. As Roger Wertheimer points out, "Probably the least discussed and most badly treated matter in the literature of moral philosophy is the one that matters most in most people's lives: filial relationships.[3] Given that so much of day-to-day moral experience occurs in the context of family relationships, this hiatus is quite astounding and merits some explanation.

According to Alisdair MacIntyre, this hiatus in moral philosophy derives from the view of the human self characteristic of the Enlightenment. Specifically, the Enlightenment philosophy of the self ignores the social-biological embeddedness of human existence. Atomistic "rational" beings, virtually unconnected with one another in any essential manner, have little or no need for a theory of filial morality. As MacIntyre says, "The self thus conceived, utterly distinct on the one hand from its own social embodiments and lacking on the other any rational history of its own, may seem to have a certain abstract and ghostly character."[4] MacIntyre is critical of the Enlightenment tendency to strip the self of essential membership in family, household, and friendship groupings because these memberships "are part of my substance, defining partially at least and sometimes wholly my obligations and duties."[5] What parents owe children or children owe parents can at best be a very marginal concern for moralists steeped in the Enlightenment tradition.

Whether Kantian or utilitarian, post-Enlightenment moral thought has adopted an impersonal standpoint which overlooks the obligation "to treat preferentially people to whom we are related by special ties of affection, such as parents, children, spouses, friends, and lovers."[6] The "moral point of view" has gone too far in the direction of impartiality, so that "special relations" are lost sight of. These relations are merely irrational sympathies from the perspective of strict universal impartiality. As Stanley Hauerwas has noted, current moral philosophy is preoccupied with "what we owe one another as strangers rather than friends or kin. Indeed, all so-called 'special relations' such as husband-wife, father-daughter, brother-sister are seen as ethically anomalous."[7] The moral field is one in which all persons, no matter how distant, have absolutely equal claim on the moral agent, so that morality becomes a matter of transcending the familial.

The hiatus is post-Enlightenment moral philosophy is best identified in the recent literature by Christina Hoff Sommers' distinction between "equal pull" and "differential pull" images of the moral domain. The first of these images, descriptive of post-Enlightenment thought, is described with the help of an analogy: "Then it is as if we have a gravitational field in which the force of gravitation is not affected by distance and all pairs of objects have the same attraction to one another."[8] In contrast, the second of these images is a more adequate one because in any gravitational field, the proximity of objects determines the "pull" between them. If one conceives of the moral domain with the gravitational analogy in mind, then "equal pull" theories appear odd. Sommers concludes that in fact the moral domain is not constituted by "beings whose ethical pull is equal on all moral agents."[9] There are, she allows, universal obligations which include even the most distant beings, but these obligations only partially define moral existence.

The views of MacIntyre and Sommers I can add nothing except a comment on the thought of feminist Carol Gilligan. If we hold with Gilligan that women "define themselves in a context of human relationship,"[10] and that by and large women judge their moral behavior in reference to familial and other "special relations" involving considerable caretaking and nurturing, then the tendency of Enlightenment and post-Enlightenment moralists to overlook the various spheres of "differential pull" may finally be reversed by increased numbers of women in the field of philosophy. If Gilligan is correct in saying that men stress autonomy, detachment, and universal rules of "the game," then the abstract character of current moral thought which Sommers highlights may reflect the values of a largely male profession. Gilligan does not, incidentally, make this contrast between male and female voices as an absolute generalization about the sexes, but rather underscores "a distinction between two modes of thought."[11] As it happens, both men and women are contributing to the recent debate over filial morality, and no defined feminine perspective has emerged. Nonetheless, Gilligan's thesis may indeed have some explanatory value with regard to the hiatus in Kantian and utilitarian thought.

Turning now to the dispute over filial morality, no revisionist has been more extreme that Michael Slote nor more vehemently critical of Judeo-Christian ethics. Slote argues that filial obedience and submission to parental authority are grounded in the illusion of divine authority. After an extensive critique of religious dependence on God, Slote writes that "What we have just said about submission to divine authority carries over, in great part, to the authority of parents."[12] It is precisely this authority which Slote rejects on the grounds that it violates child authority. If the "noble lies" of religion and parental authority can be exposed, young and adult children can be liberated from the yoke of oppression. Clearly Slote's argument, while focused on questions of submission and autonomy, contains implications that filial obligations can be outgrown.

The value of Slote's position is that it highlights the moral ambiguity of parental authority. It is common knowledge that in some cultures adult children are harmed by aging parents who demand too much. Lydia Bronte reports that in rural Arkansas, as a young girl growing up after the Second World War, she observed something resembling a form of familial slavery, in which the child is viewed by parents as "property" and by virtue of her gender is forced to live at home as caregiver while being denied the right to marry. While many women resigned themselves to this custom, some rebelled and either escaped to a different area or married against their parents' wishes; some of these were driven to emotional breakdowns "by the resulting anger and vindictiveness of the disappointed parents." [Based on the author's correspondence with Lydia Bronte, Staff Director of the Carnegie Corporation of New York Aging Society Project.] Doubtless filial obligations and be carried to such morally unsavory extremes. Slote's suspicions, then, have some merit.

Another moral revisionist is the late philosopher Jane English. She asks, "What do grown children owe their parents?" and responds that "the answer is 'nothing.'"[13] English is willing to affirm that adult children who are friendly with their parents should aid the latter on the basis of an affectional bond; but in the absence of friendship and love, parents have no claim on their children. Daniel Callahan writes that while the views of English have some "plausibility," they are "ultimately unsatisfying" because when friendship wanes, filial obligations continue to exist.[14] There is, it seems, more to filial obligations than the vicissitudes of human emotion can capture.

In response to the moral revisionists who would either dismiss filial obligation as illusion or place it on the thin ice of duty-free sentiment, I have two responses. First, filial morality and obligations do in fact have a major place in the moral experience of many persons. I would like to be able to marshal clear empirical data that in fact *most* persons do fulfill obligations to aging parents based on the duty of gratitude, and that the revisionists are out of touch with "common morality." Then the revisionist position could be dismissed because, as Everett W. Hall writes, our knowledge of values must "find its test in the main forms of everyday thought about everyday matters in so far as these reveal commitment in some tacit way."[15] Revisionism would then fail to correlate with moral experience. However, there is too much abuse of the elderly, and too much data indicating that in certain other cultures senicide is the norm, for me to make large claims about either "common morality" or "natural moral law." Nevertheless, *many* of the people we encounter in our families and neighborhoods do take filial obligations and duties very seriously, so that something can be said for Henry Sidgwick's claim that "filial duty" based on the ethics of gratitude is not open to doubt "except of the sweeping and abstract kind with which we have not here to deal."[16] However, if pollster Yankelovich is correct in stating that in recent years the moral consensus on filial morality has deteriorated to some extent, then we can no longer rely on Sidgwick's assessment in any sanguine manner.

A second critical response to the revisionists is one that appeals to moral tradition. Sommers, in her effort to reestablish filial obligations, writes as follows: "Before this century there was no question that a filial relationship defined a natural obligation; philosophers might argue about the nature of filial obligation, but not about its reality."[17] Today, adds Sommers, "not a few moralists dismiss it as an illusion, or give it secondary derivative status."[18] In addition to Slote and English, she lists Jeffrey Blustein's argument that parents who have done no more than their duty may be owed nothing by their children.[19] These thinkers, and several others, display a "modern hostility to tradition" which "encourages a hasty style of playing fast and loose with practices and institutions that define the traditional ties binding the members of a family or country."[20] I agree with Sommers' criticisms, and will carry the suspicion of a modern hostility to tradition further by making a case for the Judeo-Christian moral vision in which the Western ethic of filial obligation is thoroughly embedded, albeit now stripped of its religious trappings. Moreover, I will argue that in an aging society, the pressures to unravel filial obligation are so severe as to require a purposeful retrieval of a specifically religious ethic. Strictly philosophical and secular appeals to tradition are certainly valuable, as is the case in Sommers' writings, but the tradition itself is a religious one and can only be properly appreciated or understood as such.

Filial Morality in Theological Perspective

Historian Philippe Aries suggests that modern men and women must regain "the naive confidence in Destiny which had for so long been shown by simple men when dying."[21] In a death-denying culture such as our own, the bio-medical vanguard leads the technological assault on death, the ultimate enemy. Researchers promise a life span of 120 years if only "scavenger cells" that feed on "free radical" molecules which clog the cell machinery can be better understood. However, as philosopher Leon Kass has written, the human aspiration for the infinite cannot be satisfied by a few more years of prolonged earthly life.[22] At least in part the assault on death is the culmination of that loss of confidence in the

Judeo-Christian image of immortality which began with the Renaissance. Judeo-Christianity teaches that bodily life is finite, and in this finitude it sees the
wisdom of nature and nature's Author. As the Book of Ecclesiastes says, "nothing
is new under the sun," and life anyway is only "labor and toil." There is "a time to
be born and a time to die," and death is in fact a liberation from vanity and emp-
tiness. One discerns a similar pessimism about earthly existence in the writings of
Augustine, who tells us that our brief stay in the earthly city is but a pilgrimage far
from heaven. There is much in Judeo-Christian teaching to suggest that death is
friend rather than enemy, and so it has generally been viewed prior to modernity.
I mention this tension between Judeo-Christianity and the assault on death as a
contextual prelude to the assessment of filial morality.

Though Judaism and Christianity are not sufficiently continuous so as to
constitute a coherent "Judeo-Christian tradition" with regard to a great many
theological and ethical ideas, on the question of filial morality both faiths agree.
On this particular point, then, Judeo-Christianity as a whole has bequeathed to the
West a religious and ethical affirmation of filial obligation. Granted, Judeo-Christianity can benefit from the criticisms of Slote and others who suspect
that the tradition affords too little a role for child autonomy. While there is reason,
then, to avoid any naive credulousness regarding the tradition, what Judeo-Christianity says about filial morality can be retrieved critically. My view is
that this retrieval is in fact important if our aging society is to elude the "conve-
niences" of a utilitarian ethic which abandons the very old because they no longer
contribute to either the greatest happiness of the greatest number of to the emotional and economic well-being of their families. Because the "common morality"
of which Sidgwick wrote is no longer quite so common, there is the possibility
that the demographic revolution will finally place before us a choice between the
"two ways" of which early Christian ethicists spoke. To shun the path of infanti-
cide and senicide, they proclaimed, is to follow the true way of respecting even
the most helpless of persons on the basis of their being nothing less than fully
dignified images of God. It is not clear that anything other than a theological ethic
such as this has the power to guide our "nation of believers" through the demographic quagmire. True, ours is not entirely a believing nation—the Gallop Report indicates that Judeo-Christian religion is "very important" for 56% of
Americans and "fairly important" for another 30%.[23] For the vast numbers of
people for whom religiously grounded morality holds sway, some clarification of
Judeo-Christianity may be of use.

Judaism is clear as to the moral importance of filial obligation. The first
commandment in the Decalogue dealing with interpersonal relationships is this:
"Honor thy father and thy mother that your days may be long" (Exod. 20:12).
That this moral prescription precedes those against murder, adultery, theft and so
forth is evidence of its high status. The word "honor" means to hold in high regard
or esteem, and the commandment uses it rather than the word "love"; without
suggesting that love for parents is less than ideal, the injunction places filial
morality beyond wavering sentiments. Here Judaism casts doubt on the proposi-

tion that friendship, however much it may characterize parent-child relations, catches the "fullness of the moral bond," to use Daniel Callahan's phrase.[24]

Where the language of Judaism goes too far is in this passage: "Each person shall revere his mother and his father" (Lev. 19:3). "Revere" seems to go beyond "honor" in so far as it nearly deifies parents. In a passage which follows, the child is to "rise up and respect the presence of an old man" just as one would be in awe before God (Lev. 19:32). Slote's suspicions of Judeo-Christianity might be substantiated by this language, although my own inclination is to view it as hyperbole in the light of Judaism's relentless denunciation of idolatry.

Rabbinic scholar Asher Finkel has addressed the question of how filial honor translates into practice. According to the rabbinic codes, filial honor "begins with maintenance and personal service."[25] While rabbinic tradition encourages love as the motivating attitude in this service, when love is lacking the sense of awe "must guide the filial response."[26] Even when parents are not present, the rabbinic codes require an attitude of respect.[27] Moreover, Finkel states that filial morality is grounded in the metaphysical concept that "the person created in the image of God" is a being of dignity and worth.[28] To shed the blood of any person "was reckoned as if one destroyed God's image,"[29] and those who "face suffering and death, namely, the infirm and the elderly"[30] are to be especially protected. Finally, Finkel states that according to Jewish scripture and tradition, life is a "gift" which God gives and God takes.[31] Adult children are stewards of their parents until God brings an end to filial obligations with the cessation of life.

These Jewish principles and prescriptions, together with the image of the elderly as sages and pillars of the country to be respected by all, provide the framework for filial obligations in so far as Judaism has contributed to the wider history of Western thought. In addition, this framework lies at the foundation of that Christian affirmation of the duties of filial morality which has permeated Western culture and to which attention now will turn.

The continuity between the commandment to honor parents central to Judaism and the moral teaching of Christianity is evidenced by Jesus of Nazareth's heated argument against a group of Pharisees who had compromised the traditional prescription. Jesus cites the commandment, and sharply condemns those who would make exception to it (Matt. 15:4-6). This continuity is again evidenced by Jesus' reaffirmation of the injunction to honor parents as he responded to the question of a man seeking salvation (Matt. 19:19). As the prolific historian of Christian social thought, Cecil John Cadoux, writes, "Jesus displayed the greatest reverence for the institution and laws of family life. The command to honor father and mother had, he said, been given by God Himself, and carried with it the obligation of supporting them in their old age."[32]

It is true enough that this Nazarean Jew placed a proviso on filial morality as he affirmed it. "No man is worthy of me," he proclaimed, "who cares more for father or mother than for me" (Matt. 10:37). At one point, Jesus told a would-be disciple who asked to be allowed to bury his dead father before following his new path to "let the dead bury their own dead" (Matt. 7:21). From these passages, it might appear that Christians have scriptural basis for the abolition of filial obligations. Taken in context, however, these passages must be understood as indicating a temporary suspension of the ethical for the purposes of building the Kingdom. Again, to cite Cadoux: "He does not contradict what he has said elsewhere concerning the duties owed to parents. . . . He simply puts these duties resolutely on a lower level than those concerned with the spreading of the Kingdom of God."[33] Ultimately, as Jesus stated, his task was not to abolish but to fulfill the Jewish law.

The most influential passages on the Western heritage respecting filial morality are those of St. Paul, himself trained in Jewish law. "Children, obey your parents for it is right that you should," states Paul, who immediately cites the commandment to honor parents (Ephesians 6:1). Paul adds that no children should rebuke an older man but rather must "appeal to him as if he were your father" (I Tim. 5:1). Finally, the passages which proved to have immeasurable impact on Western thought are these: "But if a widow has children or grandchildren, then they should learn as their first duty to show loyalty to the family and to repay what they owe to their parents and grandparents" (I Tim. 5:4). Not to make provision for parents and other members of one's household "is to be worse than an unbeliever" (I Tim. 5:8). All of these Pauline passages may be the inventions of particular children communities some decades after Paul's death; thus biblical scholarship doubts the authenticity of these materials. However, for centuries these injunctions were taken at face value as the work of Paul himself and thus morally authoritative. Moreover, they clearly indicate that early on filial morality was understood by the Christian movement as an absolute canonized requirement of moral behavior.

Thus Augustine writes that the Christian is to care for parents and those in the immediate household, not only because "the law of nature" requires it, but because I Timothy 5:8 demands it."[34] Thomas Aquinas follows suit, citing both Augustine and I Timothy in addition to Ambrose.[35] Bishop Butler, writing in the early eighteenth century, merely continues the Christian moral tradition when he states that neighbor-love requires the care of particular persons "committed to our charge by nature and Providence" including children and family members generally.[36] Thus the "common morality" of which Sidgwick speaks at the close of the last century is really nothing other than common Christian morality, though no longer in identifiable religious language. Like so many moral values, filial obligation is rooted in the theological ethical heritage.

Having identified in reasonable detail what the thrust of Judeo-Christian morality is, the question remains as to its significance for our aging society. What positive contribution can Judeo-Christianity make as adult children experience the often unanticipated degree of care that elderly parents require in an age of technologically extended life?

The Technological Expansion of Care for the Aged

One of the ironies of our times is that the very technology which myth suggests should free us from burdens in fact creates responsibilities for caretaking far beyond those that existed in a previous era when the human life span was still determined by the balance of nature. The technological expansion of care for aging parents who in earlier times would have died younger poses a monumental dilemma for many middle-aged children, and especially for women who do so much of the caretaking.

Judeo-Christianity's moral affirmation of filial obligation can serve to mitigate any trends toward abandonment or even senicide that might emerge as the physical and emotional pressures of caretaking multiply. In an aging society the elderly can make "an easy target."[37] Judeo-Christianity resolutely defends the frail and socially marginal whose value according to a utilitarian calculus is minimal. Furthermore, Judeo-Christianity offers an aging society the concept of caretaking as a religious-ethical *vocation* or calling. Moral idealism in the form of beneficence and even supererogation certainly exists outside of a religious framework; and certainly some persons within the Judeo-Christian fold are morally minimalistic in so far as they fail to go beyond the bottom line of nonmaleficence or "do no harm." However, Judeo-Christianity at its best can provide a worldview with gift-love at its theological center. One thing is certain—the demographic revolution is already pressing many caretakers to muster all the idealism they can. Some would say that ours is essentially a contractarian society based on mutual self-interest so that significant self-denial is a contradiction in terms. Robert Bellah et al. have concluded that Americans, largely confined to the language of individualism, have lost the moral vocabulary to make sense of commitment and sacrifice for others.[38] However pessimistic one might be with regard to the moral resources of our society, there is room for optimism if the caretaking covenant between adjacent generations can be fairly sustained in communities that view generosity towards the elderly as virtuous and even as fulfilling a religious image of the good life.

In affirming the continued importance of Judeo-Christian moral thought in an aging society, I do not want to oversimplify matters. While, as Callahan writes, "The venerable idea of piety toward the elderly, however strange its sound to modern ears, is still pertinent," this idea does not solve all our moral dilemmas.[39] Callahan goes on to comment that adult children and their families cannot be expected to totally sacrifice themselves on behalf of aging parents.[40] Moreover, it is not the case that "persons in a middle generation have an obligation to deprive their own dependent children of necessary financial support in order to support their elderly parents."[41] The Judeo-Christian notion of filial obligation must be placed in the context of competing obligations to other dependents, particularly the young, for they have not had the opportunity to achieve fulfillment. In short, filial obligations do not necessarily hold a blank check.

Furthermore, I fully realize that some parents fail to provide for their children, and even subject them to abuse. In such cases—and I think it i with such cases in mind that many of the philosophical suspicions of filial obligations arise—one can argue persuasively that children owe parents little or nothing. However, I do not want to see these suspicions extended very far, for most parents love and care for their children. In an aging society, with those over the age of 85 constituting the fastest-growing age group, we must struggle to preserve at least the basics of that religious-ethical affirmation of parents, for without it the abuses of the elderly will no doubt mushroom.

In sum, it is far from clear that filial morality can be sustained in an aging society without the insights of Jewish and Christian ethics. It may well be that such insights are both necessary and morally appropriate: to play fast and loose with the assumption that grown children have serious obligations toward their parents may be of some abstract interest, but one would hope that such revisionism will remain the agenda of only a few.

Notes

1. Leon R. Kass, "Mortality," in Powers That Make Us Human, ed. Kenneth Vaux (Urbana, Illinois: University of Illinois Press, 1985), pp. 7-27, p. 12.

2. Daniel Yankelovich, New Rules: Searching for Self-Fulfillment in a World Turned Upside Down (New York: Random House, 1981), p. 104.

3. Roger Wertheimer, "Philosophy on Humanity," in Abortion: New Directions for Policy Studies, ed. Liu and Solomon Manier (Notre Dame: University of Notre Dame Press), pp. 128-149, p. 136.

4. Alasdair MacIntyre, After Virtue (Notre Dame: University of Notre Dame Press, 1981), p. 31.

5. Ibid., p. 32.

6. Jeffrey Blustein, Parents and Children: The Ethics of the Family (New York: Oxford University Press, 1982), p. 174.

7. Stanley Hauerwas, A Community of Character (Notre Dame: University of Notre Dame Press, 1981), p. 171.

8. Christina Hoff Sommers, "Filial Morality," The Journal of Philosophy 83/8 (1986): 439-456, p. 443.

9. Ibid., p. 443.

10. Carol Gilligan, In a Different Voice: Psychological Theory and Women's Development (Cambridge, Massachusetts: Harvard University Press), p. 17.

11. Ibid., p. 2.

12. Michael A. Slote, "Obedience and Illusion," in Having Children: Philosophical and Legal Reflections on Parenthood, ed. Onora O'Neill and William Ruddick (New York: Oxford University Press, 1979), pp. 319-326, p. 322.

13. Jane English, "What Do Grown Children Owe Their Parents?" In Having Children: Philosophical and Legal Reflections on Parenthood, pp. 351-356, p. 351.

14. Daniel Callahan, Setting Limits: Medical Goals in an Aging Society (New York: Simon & Schuster, 1987), p. 90.

15. W. Everett Hall, Our Knowledge of Fact and Values (Chapel Hill, North Carolina: University of North Carolina Press, 1961), p. 6.

16. Henry Sidgwick, The Methods of Ethics (Indianapolis: Hackett, 1981), pp. 259-260.

17. Sommers, op. cit., p. 439.

18. Ibid., p. 439.

19. Ibid., p. 439.

20. Ibid., p. 455.

21. Philippe Aries, Western Attitudes Toward Death: From the Middle Ages to the Present, trans. Patricia M. Ranum (Baltimore: Johns Hopkins University Press, 1974), p. 89.

22. Kass, op. cit., p. 22.

23. George Gallop, Jr., The Gallop Report, No. 236 May 1985, p. 22.

24. Callahan, op. cit., p. 34.

25. Asher Finkel, "Aging in Jewish Perspective," in Aging: Spiritual Perspectives, ed. Francis V. Tiso (Lake Worth, Florida: Opera Pia International/Sunday Publications, 1982), pp. 108-132, p. 122.

26. Ibid., p. 122.

27. Ibid., p. 123.

28. Ibid., p. 127.

29. Ibid., p. 128.

30. Ibid., p. 129.

31. Ibid., p. 129.

32. Cecil John Cadoux, The Early Church and the World: A History of the Christian Attitude to Pagan Society and the State Down to the Time of Constantinus (Edinburgh: T&F Clark, 1925), p. 58.

33. Ibid., p. 60.

34. Augustine, The City of God, trans. Marcus Dods (New York: Modern Library, 1950), p. 693.

35. Thomas Aquinas, The Summa Theologica (Chicago: Encyclopedia Britannica, 1950), p. 549.

36. Joseph Butler, "Fifteen Sermons," in The British Moralists: 1650-1800, ed. D. D. Raphael (Oxford: Clarendon Press, 1969), pp. 325-377, p. 374.

37. Nancy Foner, "Old and Everywhere Unequal," The Hastings Center Report 15/2 (1985); 27-31, p. 29.

38. Robert Bellah et al., Habits of the Heart: Individualism and Commitment in American Life (San Francisco: Perennial Library, 1985), p. 8.

39. Callahan, op. cit., p. 111.

40. Ibid., p. 113.

41. Ibid., p. 94.

Chapter 22

Respectful Service and Reverent Obedience

A Jewish View on Making Decisions for Incompetent Parents

Benjamin Freedman

Too often, caregivers and ethicists misunderstand the motivations of adult children who are involved in the care of their parents. They sometimes fail to appreciate the ways in which adult children may be trying to carry out their filial obligations toward a parent, obligations dictated by their religious commitments. Exploring these obligations within the Jewish tradition can help to illuminate these issues and provide an alternative to a rights-based framework in which to reason about them.

Conflicts between staff and family regarding the care of elderly and incompetent patients have dominated my own involvement in clinical ethics consultations, and that of many of my colleagues. These conflicts are framed in categories that have become canonical in bioethics: the best interests of the patient, advance directives and substituted judgment, death with dignity, and the family's right to privacy, among many others. There are of course a range of issues—about tube-feeding, or resuscitation, or pain control, or restrains—and a range of conditions causing incompetence—dementia, stroke, psychosis, acute metabolic instability. Yet the major themes underlying the diversity of appearance are conflicts: over the goals of treatment, over the aggressiveness with which these should be pursued, and over who should decide.

I had been involved in these discussions—often long, sometimes heated—many times before realizing that I had been failing to identify what the underlying issue is, from the family's point of view. The failure was not mine alone. It was shared by nursing and medical colleagues. In retrospect, I believe the problem to have been one of perception, a substitution of ground for figure, as the

Gestalt psychologists would put it. And bringing bioethical categories to bear was obscuring the family's point of view, rather than clarifying it.

The family members with whom I dealt were most commonly the patient's adult children rather than the patient's spouse, who was deceased, or incompetent, or overwhelmed. The children dreaded, rather than welcomed, their involvement in this task; there was, in their assumption of this role, no prideful claiming of a right. And while they might, in the course of discussion, claim superior knowledge of the patient's wishes and values and judgment of his or her best interests, these claims too did not exhaust the reasons why they demanded decisionmaking authority.

At its heart, the claim of these adult children was simple: for them, the duty of rendering medical decisions was continuous with, or an extension of, a general duty upon the family to care for its members who cannot care for themselves. As an ethicist and as a Jew, that claim should have been clear to me. Reaching sound decisions about medical care was, for these children, the last chance they would have to fulfill the Fifth Commandment: to honor their fathers and mothers.

In what follows, I want to explore the dimensions of this filial obligation, and how it may apply within typical clinical settings. The sources that I will bring to bear come from my own tradition, but I think they are (to coin a phrase) "small-j Jewish." Unlike many realms of Jewish reflection, the law and norms of the duty of children to their parents is not dominated by ritual or parochial concerns. The issues raised, and the ways they may be resolved, may be shared by persons of whatever background, as in this case.

Ethics Consultation: Mother, Daughter, Home Gare Services. A ninety-two-year-old woman had been cared for at home by her daughter for the past eight years; the daughter is said to have made a deathbed promise to her father to tend the woman. The patient was admitted with an infection (probably pneumonia), which has now been cleared. She is ready for discharge, scheduled for tomorrow. However, she is not mobile and discharge evaluation has confirmed she is not "rehabilitable." In all respects, however, she has regained the same level of ability she had prior to admission.

Her daughter was described to me as "pathologically devoted." She has been by the mother's bedside day and night throughout this hospitalization, leaving only to nap for a few hours while someone else stays with her. This daughter refuses to sign high-care, long-term care nursing home papers for her mother; she wants to bring her back home. The physician agrees that with maximal community and home care support this could be attempted safely. However, the government agency that provides community and home nursing services, acting on the discharge evaluation of one of their social workers, refuses to provide this support. The agency has found that by their norms the mother is not functional enough to remain at home, and insists that she must rather be placed in a skilled nursing facility. The patient herself is competent and wants to go home.

This case is one among many raising issues about the discharge of frail elderly patients on which I have been consulted. One factor the system fails adequately to consider is the nature of the daughter's involvement and claim. She is not claiming a "right," and there is no need to weigh her "rights" to be with her mother against her mother's "right" to safety. She wishes rather to fulfill a vow made at her father's deathbed; a duty, moreover, to which she is bound "by an oath made at Mount Sinai," in the rabbinic phrase: the duty of kibud, respectful service, to parents. Sometimes this duty is implicated directly, as in decisions about discharge of a parent. But it is equally implicated indirectly, when a son or daughter demands a role in determining the nature of care that a parent will receive in the hospital. By helping to ensure that an institution adequately attends to a parent's needs, the child's involvement in the care of a parent makes the institution act as the child's agent in fulfilling this duty. The daughter in this case has perhaps taken her obligation to saintly extremes, but certainly to describe her actions as "pathological devotion" says more about the speaker's values than about this daughter's.

First Category of Filial Obligation: The Claims of *Kibud*

How are we to understand the daughter's stance in this case? From the point of view of Jewish law, the most natural starting point is the Bible:

> Honor your father and your mother; so that your days may be lengthened upon the land that G-d your L-rd gives to you. (Exodus 20:12)[1]

The Jewish (and, especially, talmudic) manner of describing and prescribing duty typically involves the furnishing of specific, concrete instantiations of the duties in question. These paradigm cases are then further analyzed by examining their distinctive normative characteristics. The talmudic definition of the Fifth Commandment is exemplary in this regard:

> What is "honoring?" Causes to eat and to drink, clothes and covers, brings in and brings out (ma'akhil aumashke, malbish um'khase, makhnis umotzi)." (Talmud Bavli Kidushin 31b)

This particular concretization of the obligation subsumes the following points: The duty must be manifest through behavior, and not—or, not only—through attitude or emotional attachment. The child is commanded, inter alia, to serve the parent personally, to provide the parent's basic physical needs: food, water, clothing, transportation. In this way, everyday filial interaction is invested with dutiful solemnity (and so, in Judaism's religious world view, sanctified).

These instantiations share a characteristic form of talmudic ambiguity. How, precisely, does one cause a parent to eat? The answer will depend upon the condition and need of the parent, and will vary as the parent's circumstances of life change; yet while the expression of the duty will vary, its essential content will remain unchanged.

Think of a child and parent through the years. The young son accompanies his mother shopping and "helps": he has caused her to eat. In early adulthood, flush with his first paycheck, he takes her out for a restaurant meal. The years pass, she is widowed and grows frail: he arranges for a homemaker to visit. She suffers a stroke, and needs to be fed carefully by hand. Finally, she loses the ability to swallow, and he is faced with a decision to have her fed by tube. "Causes to eat": The duty to honor parents is the red thread running through, and binding together, these events and circumstances; it is that which explains the role the son seeks to fulfill in medical decisionmaking concerning his incompetent parent.

The term found in the Bible that we translate as "honor" admits of no fully satisfactory English translation. Kibud in its origins relates to the Hebrew root KBD, meaning weighty, heavy, considerable. To provide kibud to parents therefore implies recognizing their importance, treating them as "weighty," avoiding behavior that takes them "lightly." At the same time, this form of honor is expressed by personal attention to the needs of the other; to grant kibud is in fact one Hebrew phrase for serving a meal to a guest. The single Hebrew concept of kibud, then, instantiates respectful and fitting service to the parent.

A language reflects a culture and its norms and crafts terms accordingly. The stilted, artificial, awkward quality of the English translation I have of-feted is itself testimony to our culture's discomfort with the associated norm. Yet such a phrase is peculiarly appropriate to the above case. The decision by the patient's daughter to take her mother back home was not just a medical decision about discharge. It was the means by which this daughter would fulfill her obligation to her mother, to "cause to eat and to drink, clothe and cover, bring in and bring out." It was motivated by her desire to render to her mother respectful service.

Second Category of Filial Obligation: *Morah*

There was, however, an additional element to the daughter's determination to bring her mother home. She had sworn to her father at his deathbed that she would care for her mother after his passing. By taking her mother home, then, she would both render respectful service to her mother and fulfill a duty of reverent obedience to her father. This second aspect of filial duty may be called, in Hebrew, *morah,* commonly translated in English as "fear":

Each of you shall fear his mother and father, and guard my Sabbaths, I am God. (Leviticus 19:3)

The same talmudic passage cited above about honor defines fear in this way:

What constitutes "fear"? He does not sit in his [parent's] place and does not speak in his stead and he does not contradict his statements.

The Talmud connected these signs of formal respect and obedience to the injunction to fear the parent, an expression that signifies subjugation of the will. The verse compelling this attitude toward parents, and that behavior which is appropriate to fear, appears a the beginning of a biblical section known in Jewish sources as the "Chapter of Holiness" describing the solemn obligations imposed by a transcendent G-d. The term, its concept, and the context in which it appears all point in the same direction: the child's reverence of a parent as of a master, a ruler—and even, a Ruler. Indeed, the rabbis had said that in this verse God equated the fear owing to a parent to that fear owing to God Himself."[2]

The behavior appropriate to that attitude of ear is reverent obedience. Within Jewish law's usual classification of duties, *kibud* is often taken as a portmanteau term that encompasses all forms of filial obligation, including obedience. But for heuristic purposes, it may be more useful to distinguish service from obedience, *kibud* from *morah*.

In fulfilling her deathbed promise, the daughter fulfilled this second norm for honoring parents, *morah*, reverent obedience. But the most common bioethical context within which *morah* would arise is in connection with the fulfillment of any prior instructions on medical care an incompetent parent had provided, including so-called "living wills." When such instructions are available, family members are often relieved that the burden of decision making has been lifted from them. Within Jewish terms, we would say, their duty of *morah* is clear.

ETHICS CONSULTATION: COMA OR LOCKED IN

Mr. L is an Ashkenazic Jewish man, about eight years old, with a variety of pre-existing medical conditions. In January of this year he was treated for a stroke and released. Other indications are that he has had a series of mild strokes. Last month, he had another major stroke.

The CT scan has confirmed a stroke in the brain stem that has conserved his ability to breathe. His current status is grim. On a couple of occasions he may have been volitionally moving his eyes or eyelids. He is now either in a coma (that is, permanently unconscious) or in a profound locked-in state (that is, totally paralyzed). If he improves any further, it would be to a definite locked-in state with an irreversible etiology. He has to date been treated quite aggressively.

The discussion of his treatment was held with three sons and one daughter; a second daughter lives elsewhere. The issues raised about prognosis, and the resolution—that the only criterion for treatment decisions should be Mr. L's comfort—were not remarkable. Mr. L could not in any event be heroically maintained for any prolonged period, and the best medical outcome would be the worst personal one: initiation into a stable locked-in life for some shorter period.

Mr. L had prepared a living will assigning one son to render medical decisions on his father's behalf in the event that his father should become incompetent. The directive included instructions that in the event of permanent incapacity heroic life-prolonging measures are to be avoided, but all comfort measures, including those that may result in reduced lifespan, are to be adopted.

Did these instructions reflect Mr. L's true wishes? The document had been prepared by a lawyer who apparently used a standard form. All of the children were certain that their father would not have had any input into the drafting and would not have attended when the document was read to him before signing. He never had any patience for legal documents of any sort. Nonetheless, it is plausible that Mr. L, in engaging legal assistance to prepare such a document, dreaded most precisely the situation in which he now finds himself (if he is locked in rather than comatose and insensate)—helpless in bed, unable to communicate, the victim of medical perpetrations.

Following a parent's instructions on treatment contained in a living will is a means of fulfilling the duty of reverent obedience, morah. But there are limits to morah itself: a parent's instructions are not to be obeyed if they conflict with one's obligations to others or to God. The source verse itself indicates this: "Each of you shall fear his mother and father, and guard my Sabbaths; I am God." Important as parental obedience is, it does not justify violations of the To-rah's commandments. And those commandments themselves restrict the autonomy of patients when making medical decisions.[3]

These sources specifically derive from Jewish law and tradition; yet underlying them is a principle that might garner general assent, namely, that even filial obligation must yield when in conflict with some fundamental moral demands. I discuss elsewhere, but will not pursue here, the difficult question of whether Mr. L's instructions involved such a conflict in Jewish law, as well as associated questions regarding Jewish law and end-of-life decisions.[4] That question is irrelevant for our present purposes. What is important is that while some values supercede filial duty, until that point is reached, a child is obliged to adhere to a parent's advance directive for reasons of morah.

Dying in the Hospital: Pain and the Anatomy of Shame

In addition to *kibud* and *morah*, which place the child under positive obligations toward the parent, Jewish sources discuss negative aspects of filial duty: refraining from those actions that cause the patient pain or indignity. As was said before, many authorities subsume all aspects of filial obligation, negative and positive, under *kibud*; but as before, the relevance of these sources to contemporary bioethical issues becomes clearer when distinctions are drawn.

Sadly, the hospital experience of a patient with a terminal illness regularly seems to include liberal doses of harm and pain, and, most particularly, indignity. A family member who speaks for the voiceless patient by approving or denying medical treatment must inevitably decide when, on balance, the advantages that some treatments offer are outweighed by their associated harms of pain and indignity. A final case and some discussion will help set the context for considering these last elements of family obligation.

ETHICS CONSULTATION: "SAINT JAMES INFIRMARY"5

Ms. C is a sixty-one-year-old woman with a complicated form of Alzheimer disease with additional physical disability due to fontal impairment of the brain, as well as confirmed brain damage caused by a series of small strokes. The course of her disease had begun three years past with tics in the left arm and shoulder, and progressed one year ago to trouble with walking. However, she was living alone at home until her hospital admission, she had seizures and was found to have low blood glucose levels. Since that time, she has gotten progressively worse despite tests and treatment. Communicative at first, she has become increasingly less oriented and less communicative. At this time, her only child, a forty-year-old businessman, claims that she no longer can recognize him. She cannot respond in any meaningful way to questions asked of her.

The question this case raises concerns continuing nutrition and hydration of this woman. She has had restraints placed to prevent her from pulling out the intravenous line. She has been fairly vigorous at pulling out tubes, including, on at least two occasions, success in pulling out a Foley catheter after the balloon had been inflated.

Her son brought up the question of feeding, saying that he did not want her to be fed any longer. In his view, he said "She's not a human being any more." In addition, to him, "having a life by means of these tubes is not living." The attending physician mentioned that the son brought up this request after it had become clear that there was nothing reversible in Ms. C's condition.

With nutrition, the current downhill course would be expected to continue. The consulting geriatrician estimates that Ms. C would survive perhaps another two months on a nourishing regimen. The only safe means of providing her with food would be by surgical insertion of a tube into her stomach, which would require close restraint during a healing period of about ten days.

One would need a heart of stone not to sympathize with this family member's plight. His mother lies in a hospital. Her mental deterioration has robbed her of even the slim comfort of a familiar face now that she no longer recognizes her child. Beyond the reach of pleasure, she is, sadly, not beyond the reach of pain. The cost of briefly prolonging this sad existence is a surgical procedure to feed her by tube. She would need to be tied down until her surgical incision has healed. Some demented patients become agitated when placed in restraints, struggling against them to the point of exhaustion. If that would happen, she will need to be sedated.

While he did not express it in these terms, Mr. C's plea is likely to be construed as a wish that his mother be allowed to die with dignity. Yet to say that may be to go too far. His plea may have been the simpler, and more precise, wish that she be spared pain and indignity—shame—in her last moments of living.

Although much has been written about the patient's right to die with dignity, little is offered in the way of describing what a dignified death or dying process is like. This is not in itself surprising. We do not, after all, share any common idea of what constitutes living with dignity; why should we agree about dying with dignity? Perhaps the problem is in presuming that there is one single valued way to die, "death with dignity."

There is, though, a smaller and more manageable task of describing ways in which dying has been made shameful and humiliating. Persons are as a rule more likely to share aversions than preferences, and so it is often easier to describe wrongs, harms, things that we hate about dying, than positive aspects of the process that we all value and wish to experience. Having done that, we need to face the further issue of how Jewish sources might respond to such concerns. At any rate, I believe that Mr. C, like many relatives of the dying, may have quite a clear concept of what is wrong about dying without necessarily having any vision of the ideal death.

What is likely to make us see shame and humiliation in a hospital death? Rather than a single answer, many different aspects of a patient's experience conspire in this direction. There is, first of all, that shame which is unavoidably connected with any dying. As Carl Schneider writes, "Shame and death are close-linked. The ties are many. Death, along with suffering, deep grief, pain, and violence, belongs to those human experiences that are appropriately veiled from public view. They are deeply vulnerable to shameful public intrusion and profaning violation."[6] Death shames one by making one an object for others to view, by robbing one of one's ability to control how one will be perceived; and dying shames one by leading to death. But that is no more than a sad fact, and does not distinguish what is specifically felt to be undignified and humiliating about dying in hospital.

A common focus for that specific shame is the tubes going in and out of a patient. Those tubes going in are for feeding, and those going out are for excretion: this is both a truth about reality and about symbolism, about fact and about perception. Both eating and excretion have been, throughout history and in many different cultures, focal experiences for shame.[7] Being tied to those tubes denies the patient the ability to control the involvement of others in these private activities. The tubes are, moreover, transparent, laying bare for all to see the patient's private needs.

A second and related focus for that shame is helplessness. For many patients, their greatest humiliation occurs when they lost control over excretion, "lying there and being cleaned up like a baby." Many would, and some do, choose death over that embarrassment. But loss of control in itself, without regard to the function in question, is a powerful source of shame; in the same way retaining control, however it be used, preserves one's dignity. As the rabbis state:, "There is no comparison between one who treats himself without dignity, *mitbaze mei'atzmo*, to one who is treated by another without dignity" (*Talmud Yerushalmi Ta'anit* 2). Death is of course the ultimate loss of control, and so shameful; but dying in a hospital, subject to the intrusions and schedules of others, is not far behind.

Perhaps the ultimate source of shame for a patient in a hospital is the exposure that he or she experiences, the uncovering, exemplified but not exhausted by the hospital gown open in back, by the physical examination conducted without closing the door or drawing the curtain. The association between shame and being uncovered is one that reaches well back into history and is ingrained within the very language we use:

> Our words for shame drive from two Indo-European roots, both with the same meaning. One cluster of words includes our establish words custody, hide (both as a noun meaning "skin" and as a verb meaning "conceal"), house, hut, shoe, and sky. In terms of meaning, the common thread in these otherwise disparate words is their relation to covering. In terms of derivation, each of these words derives from an Indo-European root *(s)que-, *(s)qewa-, which means "to cover." From this same root comes the Lithuanian word kuvetis meaning "to be ashamed." A second Indo-European root *(s)kem-; *(s)kam-, also meaning "to cover," gives us both our English word shame as well as the English camera, the French chemise, and the German Hemd. Shame, then, is intimately linked to the need to cover—in particular, to cover that which is exposed.[1]

Etymologically, then, "shame" derives from "uncovered." But behind that literal truth stands an even more important recognition of their symbolic connection; and it is fascinating to observe some such recognition emerging from a convergence between English etymology and a parallel talmudic folk etymology. The Talmud describes a conversation R Ze'ira had with R Yehuda when he saw the latter was in a playful mood (chazya d'have b'dicha da'atei). R Ze'ira asked why garments are called by the term l'vusha. R Yehuda responded that the source of the word l'vusha is lo bush: No shame (Talmud Bavli Shabbat 77b).

Pain, Shame, and Dying in Jewish Sources

From the point of view of Jewish law, what relevance do pain and indignity possess? How can we parse the ethical obligations of children under these circumstances?

Some connections are clear from what has been said already. A child will be concerned that a parent be well attended to from a physical standpoint as a result of the obligation of kibud, respectful service. In addition, if the parent has prepared a living will that deals with these matters, the failure to implement those instructions may be a violation of reverent obedience, morah. In addition to these positive commandments, however, I believe that a child's involvement in securing appropriate care in dying for a parent has an even stronger basis. Failure to ensure that a parent is spared pain and indignity represents a violation of the scriptural prohibitions against striking or cursing a parent:

One who strikes his father and mother shall surely die. One who curses his father and mother shall surely die. (Exodus 21:15, 21:17)

The relevance of the first of these verses is straightforward. As a child is compelled not to strike a parent, Jewish law finds that a child is culpable as well for the pain that the parent experiences if the child was in a position to spare the parent that pain and failed to do so.[9] It is true that pain in the dying process can be a complicated thing, comprising an amalgam of psychological factors—anguish—as well as physical pain. But there is a long tradition within Judaism for treating anguish at least as seriously as physical pain. A good example of this is found in Sefer Chasidim, dealing with the case of a son who, in an attempt to spare his parents pain, threatens that he will initiate a fast unless they agree not to fast themselves. This is prohibited, the author writes, "since his father and mother have more pain from his fast than from their own" (section 340). One constant theme in ethical consultations around the dying process is that of pain management. The prohibition against allowing a parent to suffer pain compels the children of patients to satisfy themselves that pain management is an active medical priority.

My claim that the second verse prohibiting a child from cursing his parents also prohibits his causing them indignity, shame, or humiliation is on its face puzzling. What does the antique concern with cursing a parent have to do with a dignified death? In fact, the concepts of cursing and that of indignity are etymologically identical in Hebrew. The term for cursing, whose root is *KLL*, is a verbal form deriving from *KL*. *KL* itself means, literally, "light" in the sense of "lacking in weight." To *KLL* someone therefor means to treat that person "lightly," without dignity—the precise linguistic and conceptual antonym to *KBD*, "honor."[10]

There is of course a close connection between the desire to spare a parent pain (including psychological anguish) and to ensure that the parent not experience indignity. For most practical purposes, therefore, each of these two verses will serve the same purpose.[11] There is one potential difference between them, though, which looms large within our bioethical context.

I have argued that the adult child's responsibility to care for an incompetent parent requires close attention to shame and indignity. It is, however, often true in these cases that the patient is, or seems to be, oblivious to his or her social situation, for example, being disrobed. If the parent is unaware of being treated in a shameful or undignified way, has the child violated his responsibility by failing to rectify such treatment? Or, as the staff of a geriatric unit will sometimes argue, does his scrupulousness under these circumstances indicate that he is more concerned about his own perception of the proprieties than about his obligation to his parents?

To respond to these questions, it is necessary to distinguish between anguish on the one hand and shame or indignity on the other. The patient's own perceptions are the only possible measure of anguish or any other forms of pain. Because the anguish associated with the experience of shame requires a considerable degree of self-awareness and abstract thought, patients with brain damage may well lose the capacity for that form of social pain we call shame before they lose the capacity to experience physical pain. I take this to express a logical truth about the concept: "I was in pain, but felt nothing," if meant literally, is a logical contradiction.

But indignity or shame is different. A person need not be aware of having been humiliated to be in fact humiliated; and a person need not experience the harm of being shamed in order to be shamed. Unlike pain, therefore, which is a truth about the patient's own perceptions, humiliation at least incorporates (without necessarily being restricted to) a truth about the perceptions others have of the patient. A deeply demented patient who is left bare before the sigh of every hospital passerby feels no pain at this fact, but the person who that patient is has nonetheless been shamed by it. The child who is that parent's caretaker but fails to address this indignity has not violate the prohibition against causing the parent pain, but has violated the injunction against "cursing" the parent, that is, treating the parent "lightly."

What then is the measure of shame, if not solely the person's own reaction to treatment; and, what is its connection, if any, to pain? Several sources can be brought to bear. It is clear that a child is required to demonstrate honor of the parent formally even following the parent's death, in spite of the fact that the parent is (from the mundane point of view) insensible of that fact. By strict logic, it follows that a child is required to refrain from humiliating a parent even if the parent is unaware of the act. As the Jewish mystical classic the *Zohar* writes, "'Honor your father and your mother': This *mitza* obligates him [the child] during life; after their death, should we say perhaps that he is free of it? It is not so, for even after death he is obligated to honor them, and even more so than during their lifetimes" (*B'chukotai* 115b).

The voluntary reaction of the competent parent toward a child's actions determines whether that action constitutes honor or humiliation. A good example of this principle, which has been accepted as authoritative law,[12] is found in the Talmud's lengthiest sustained discussion of filial obligation,[13] in which tales are told of the extent of the obligation of kibud and different ways in which it is fulfilled. One of the stories told is of the mother of Rabbi Yishma'el. In her pride at his scholarly accomplishments, she claims the "honor" of washing the feet of her son when he returns daily from the Study Hall. (A possible contemporary analogy: the mother of a Nobelist physicist launders her child's clothes when he returns from a professional conference.) Rabbi Yishma'el, out of concern for his mother's dignity, has refused to permit this. She approaches the rabbinic council, asking them to rebuke her son, for he fails to accord her appropriate honor! And the council agrees, stating that insofar as this act is her desire, it is her honor as well.[14]

The reaction of a parent can only be decisive, however, if that person is in full possession of his or her faculties. On behalf of incompetent persons, the measure of humiliation depends upon an estimation of how a member of that person's group would ordinarily react to the situation at hand. For example, in general, the guardian of the estate of orphans who are incompetent (for instance, because they are minors) is not permitted to use their funds for charity.[15] An exception to that rule: if the father of the orphans had provided financially for impoverished relatives, the guardian may continue these charitable disbursements. Failure to continue these provisions, to satisfy this familial duty, is considered a cause of shame to both the (deceased) father and to the orphans, both of whom are objectively shamed by this failure to carry out a familial duty.

There remain, however, conceptual as well as empirical difficulties in describing the class to which a patient belongs, and what may follow from that determination. The Talmud states, for example, that "A man's pain is greater than a woman's" (Talmud Yerushalmi K'tubot 5.8); by contrast, "The embarrassment (bushata) of a woman is greater than that of a man" (Talmud Bavli K'tubot 67). Are these statements descriptively accurate? Does it follow from them, for example, that a child needs to be relatively more concerned about a mother's physical modesty than that of a father? Jewish sources may or may not dictate a particular answer to these questions. They do, however, challenge us to struggle with them when we face difficult moral dilemmas arising from our obligations to our parents.

Alternative Visions

No easy resolution of the dilemmas of caring for an incompetent patient will necessarily emerge from these sources. For one thing, filial obligations may work at cross-purposes: sparing a parent pain may cause indignity; service may conflict with obedience.[16] There may be several children, each with a different estimation of what their parent is owed in the current extremity. And, of course, I have not dealt at all with the moral stance of the medical and nursing team. Rather than supply answers, I have tried to supply a language, an alternative conceptual framework that family members may use to reason about some common bioethical issues, and that we outsiders may use to understand their positions.

At the same time, this article may suggest how some Jewish sources can be mobilized in the current search for alternative perspectives on bioethical issues. Enough may have been said to suggest how distinctive a Jewish approach to bioethics, grounded in notions of duty and obligation, may be from a right-based approach. The contrast is deep and pervasive. Within society's current rights-based framework, for example, to be a legal person is to possess rights. When persons come of age, they gain rights: to vote, to drive, to make medical decisions, and so forth. To come of age in Judaism is to be a *ben* or *bat mitzva*, literally, "a child of commandments"—to have arrived at an age in which one may be subject to duties.[17] Within our society, a person is competent if he or she can claim exercise rights. Within the Jewish perspective, by contrast, I would argue that competency is judged relative to duties rather than to rights. In the context of bioethics, the preeminent right that has preoccupied scholars is the right to informed consent. In my view, the idea of consent should play a similarly important role within Jewish thought, but as a duty, rather than a right. Within Judaism, persons are charged to be thoughtful and prudent caretakers (or stewards) of their own physical, psychological, and social well-being, a duty that must be expressed in all areas of choice that life presents. By working through one case, that of family involvement in medical decision making. I hope to have opened up one alternative vision of bioethical issues.[18]

Benjamin Freedman, "Respectful Service and Reverent Obedience: A Jewish View on Making Decisions for Incompetent Parents," *Hastings Center Report 26,* no. 4 (1996): 31-37. This article is adapted from one section of my *Duty and Healing: Foundations of a Jewish Bioethic.* This book-length manuscript is available in its entirety on the World Wide Web, at http://www.mcgill.ca/CTRG/bfreed/.

Acknowledgments

I am grateful for comments and suggestions provided by the editors of the Report, and by one anonymous reviewer.

Notes

1. Here and elsewhere in this text all translations used are my own. Because some Hebrew terms have no exact English translation, and because some of the translations I have supplied are arguable, I have included within the text some Hebrew words and phrases in transliteration.

2. *Torat Kohanim* on Leviticus 19:3.

3. For example, *Sefer Chasidim* (at 234) rules accordingly that a father who asked his son to provide him with food or drink against medical instructions need not be obeyed. *Birkei Yosef* (*Yore Dei'ah* 240.15, s.v. *im haya*) qualifies this by saying that this is only true if the food or drink is dangerous, *sakana*; if it is only going to harm him, but not endanger him, the son should obey. For a discussion of this and related citations see *Sefer Kibud Av V'em,* R Ya'akov Pinchas Feldman, privately printed, Jerusalem 1990, p. 17.

4. See my *Duty and Healing,* Sec 4 (Risk).

5. Critical changes to this case have been made at the editor's request for the sake of clarification.

6. Carl D. Schneider, *Shame, Exposure and Privacy* (Boston: Beacon Press, 1977), p. 77.

7. See Schneider, *Shame,* Ch. 7: "Eating and Elimination." Compare the statement, "The bride turns aside and eats because of embarrassment," *TB P'sachim* 82.

8. Schneider, *Shame,* pp. 29-30.

9. Responsa *Meishiv Davar* part 2 Sec 50.

10. See further to this the discussion in Sefer Hachinuch 260 on the prohibition against cursing a parent. In describing the details of the law, the author mentions that this includes bizayon, humiliation or indignity, of any sort.

11. Thus the responsa literature often treats psychological pain and humiliation in common. See for example Responsa Zichron Yehuda section 78 s.v. ken ira: "And so we found that a person cares more about his humiliation than his physical suffering"; also in R Moshe Feinstein, Igrot Moshe, Yore Dei'a vol. 2, section 63, s.v. Al kol panim kevan: Dealing with the question of whether honoring a parent must be done with a parent's money or the child's own money, and with paying a parent's debts following his/her death, he writes: "Perhaps Ri reasons that regarding pain (tza'ar) it is different, for that [must be avoided even by using the resources] of the son, and indignity (bizayon) is similar to suffering, and perhaps even more serious than suffering."

12. R Tzvi Hershel Schechter, "Regarding Laws of Death and a 'Dead Man'" (B'dinei meit v'gavra k'tila) in Sefer Assia, ed. Mordechai Halperin, vol. 7 (Jerusalem: Falk-Schlesinger Institute, 1993), pp. 188206 at 203, who quotes Responsa Maharam Schick (Yore Dei'a section 218).

13. Talmud Yerushalmi Pei'a, chapter 1, Halakha 1.

14. The principle that a parent's reaction to a child's deed helps determine whether that deed was one of honor, of humiliation, or neither, appears to conflict with sources that state that a parent cannot absolve a child of the prohibition against causing pain or shame. Cf. Tzitz Eli'ezer part 7 section 49, Kuntres Even Ya'akov (on saying of kaddish while the father lives); Responsa Yabia Omerpart 5 Yore Dei'a section 21 (on naming a child after a relative of the mother rather than the father); Responsa Meishiv Davar part 2 section 50 (on a son's marriage plans that cause the father pain and embarrassment). I have seen no discussion of this serious contradiction, but believe it may be resolved in accordance with rabbinic skepticism over whether a person who purports to absolve another for causing him pain does so in reality; see the discussion in my Duty and Healing in the final appendix to section 2: "Consent: The 'Reasonable Caretaker' and the Obligation to Consent."

15. Babylonian Talmud Gitin, chapter Hanizahin.

16. I am grateful to Professor Karen Lebacqz for suggesting that I note this point.

17. See Robert Cover, "Obligation: A Jewish Jurisprudence of the Social Order," Journal of Law and Religion 5 (1988): 65-74.

18. For further discussion, see my Duty and Healing especially sections 2 ("Consent: The 'Reasonable Caretaker'"), 3 ("Competency: Jewish Sources and the General Theory of Competency"), and 4 ("Risk: Principles of Judgment in Health Care Decisions").

Chapter 23

Repayment for Parents' Kindness: Buddhist Way

Kyu-taik Sung

Introduction

Filial piety has long dominated the cultures of East Asia and laid the ideological foundation for elder respect and elder care (Lang 1946; Silberman 1962; Park 1983).

The moral ideal underlying filial piety is that parents should be respected and cared for, as they suffered to raise and care for a new generation. Thus, an important concept of filial piety is repaying the parents' kindness.

In Buddhism, repaying parents' kindness is filial piety (Michihata 1994; Ch'en 1973). The importance of repaying parents' kindness is prescribed in "*The Sutra about the Deep Kindness of Parents and the Difficulty of Repaying It*" (Nicholson 2000). This Sutra makes people understand the importance of parents' kindness, enlightens them about their boundless and fathomless kindness, and teaches them how to practice the Buddhist way of filial piety.

The purpose of this paper is to introduce the Sutra, which has been recited, upheld, and is endeared by peoples of East Asia—the Chinese along with Koreans and the Japanese—for centuries. The paper discusses the assimilation of Buddhist filial piety with Chinese filial piety in the Confucian cultural setting, and introduces excerpts of the Sutra including discourses on the ten types of the mother's kindness and Buddhist ways of repaying the kindness. The emphasis given to the kindness of the mother and certain similarities and differences between Confucian filial piety and Buddhist filial piety are discussed.

Assimilation with the Confucian Culture

After a long period of assimilation, Buddhism from India established itself as a major system of religious practice in China (Ch'en 1973: 1-13; Singhal 1984; de Bary and Bloom 1999: 415-420). In the early stage of assimilation, however, Buddhism was confronted with formidable obstacles in a civilization dominated by Confucianism and other religious and philosophical systems (Ch'en 1973: 14-18; Zuerucher 1987; Banerjee 1977). In particular, the dominant ideal of Confucianism—filial piety—was not consistent with some of the fundamental notions of Buddhism. In the Han dynasty (202—220 B.C.), during the very beginning of the religion, there was already criticism of Buddhism as being unfilial. In succeeding centuries, this charge of unfilial conduct against the Buddhists was emphasized (Ch'en 1973: 15-18).

The traditional Chinese social system was based on the family, and to preserve the family, Confucian ideology insisted that filial piety be the foundation of its ethics. Therefore, the key factor in filial piety was the family. The family was the foundation for the practice of filial piety in terms of the provision of practical forms of parent care, affective as well as instrumental. Hence, the maintenance of supportive, stable, and continuous family relations was of utmost importance.

Meanwhile, Buddhism aimed at individual salvation in nirvana, a goal attainable by leaving the household life and entering the houseless stage, which means the life of celibacy and mendicancy (Thursby 1992). Upon assuming the monastic role, the Buddhist monk terminated his ties with family and society (Nakasone 1990).

The great conflict ensued between Buddhists and Confucians. As Nakasone (2000) described, "The Indian practice of celibate monastic life and beliefs in karma, transmigration, and rebirth into another life form came into immediate conflict with the Confucian society that venerated ancestors, valued family, and desired descendents."

This practice caused a number of obstacles for Buddhists which hindered their assimilation with the Chinese society. The following are examples of the obstacles.

The primary obstacle was that a monk had to sever his relationship with his family. To become a monk, a person left his or her family behind and joined a monastery based in temples located in the forests outside the village.

The purpose of the isolation was neither to seek physical ease, such as enjoying physical comfort, eating sumptuous foods, or dressing luxuriously, nor to seek fame and property. This was done to avoid the cycle of birth and death and rebirth, and to sever worldly passions.

Buddhist monks were subjected to harsh criticism for this practice from Confucians. The family was the foundation of the traditional Chinese social, political, and ideological systems. It was the arena where filial piety was practiced. Without the existence of the family, nothing else was conceivable in the Confucian society. Therefore, Chu Hsi (1130-1200), a prominent Neo-Confucian scholar, harshly criticized Buddhist monks. "The mere fact that they discard the Three Bonds (between ruler and minister, father and son, and husband and wife) and the Five Constant Virtues (righteousness on the part of the father, deep love on the part of the mother, friendliness on the part of the elder brother, respect on the part of younger brother, and filial piety on the part of the son) is already a crime of the greatest magnitude. Nothing more need to be said about the rest" (Chung 1988).

Another considerable obstacle the Buddhists encountered was clerical celibacy (de Bary and Bloom 1999: 424). The renunciation of marriage and family life was a serious matter, for being without descendents was a grave offense to filial piety. One of the most important features of Chinese filial piety was a devotion to ancestors. The monks, however, forsook wife and children and rejected property and wealth. This conduct was the antithesis to filial piety and felicity. If there are no descendants to make the offerings, then there will be no sacrifices for the ancestors. In addition, monks rejected the natural desire for progeny; there could be no greater tragedy for a Chinese than childlessness (Chan 1963: 426).

Still another weighty obstacle was the aversion of Chinese society to the shaving of the head, which was required of all members of the Buddhist clergy. The Confucians held that the body is the gift of one's parents and that to harm it is to be disrespectful toward them. Confucius said, "Our body, limbs, hair, and skin are all received from our fathers and mothers. We dare not injure them" (Teaching of Filial Piety, Ch. 1). But the monks shaved their heads. This violated Confucius' saying and was against the tradition of filial piety (de Bary and Bloom 1999: 423)

Finally, one more impediment that hindered assimilation was not showing respect for secular potentates. When a person entered the Buddhist clergy, he left his clan, his caste, and all his worldly possessions. As one removed from ordinary society, a monk paid no outward signs of veneration to the potentates. Buddhists knelt in their religious ceremonies, but displayed no signs of respect to laymen in positions of authority, not even to the emperor (de Bary and Bloom 1999: 424). This became a serious problem. In traditional Confucian society, showing one's reverence to the ruler and the sovereign was the duty of the subjects.

Such religious practices of Buddhists turned out to be discordant with, if not contrary to, the ideals and practice of Confucian filial piety. Hence, filial piety became a weapon used by the Confucians to criticize the Buddhist monks who had left their parents for the monastic life, did not marry to ensure a family's posterity, did harm their body given by their parents, and so forth (Chung 1988).

In the Confucian tradition, filial duty was the fundamental principle of morality. For Confucius, filial piety was the foundation of all virtues and the root of civilization (Teachings of Filial Piety, Ch. 1). When Teng Tzu, his disciple, asked what surpassed filial piety as the virtue of a sage, Confucius replied, "Man excels all the beings in Heaven and Earth. Of man's acts none is greater than filial piety. In the practice of filial piety, nothing is greater than to revere one's parent (Teachings of Filial Piety, Ch. 10).

Confucians maintained that the ideals of human existence were to be realized in this life and in the secular world, and that doctrines must be appreciated according to their practical applicability and sociopolitical effectiveness rather than for their metaphysical qualities (Zuercher 1987; de Bary and Bloom 1999). These attitudes also characterized the major non-Confucian tradition of thoughts of Taoism in China. Buddhism was bound to meet with the disapproval of the Confucians and Taoists (Zuercher 1987).

These evidences indicate that Buddhists were heavily pressured by the Chinese orientation toward filial piety. The pressure to conform to cultural standards of filial piety continued for Chinese Buddhists in the later period of Buddhist history (de Bary and Bloom 1999; Ch'en 1973).

In the face of the pressures, Buddhists were compelled to adapt to the indigenous cultural values to win over the hearts of the elite as well as the common people in China. They laid down a new course of religious practice that was congruent with the indigenous culture and ideals. Consequently, they developed a way of conducting its religious practice in the secular world and in the household (de Bary and Bloom 1999: 427; Michihata 1994; Chung 1988). Those who revered the Buddhist laws but remained in their homes were seen as followers whose course of conduct conformed to the secular world. This way of life included the affection of natural kinship and the proprieties of obedience to authority. They also decided that Buddhists should not hide themselves deep in a mountain valley for monks to follow (Chung 1988). As a necessary first step toward this goal, temples and monasteries were erected in urban and rural areas (Chan 1963).

Buddhists adapted also to the Chinese practice of ancestor worship. Specific ways in which ancestors are honored by Buddhists in East Asia have been described by Ch'en (1973) and Nakasone (2000).

Along with this change, as an important vehicle to counter Confucian attack, Buddhists developed "*The Sutra about The Deep Kindness of Parents and The Difficulty of Repaying It*"—commonly called "*Sutra about the Importance of Parental Love*" (*Fu-mu en-chung ching*) or "*Filial Piety Sutra*" (Michihata 1994: 82; Ch'en 1973: 36-37; Jan 1991).

The adaptation to the family orientation of Confucianism contrasts the earlier characterization of the Buddhist religious vocation as 'leaving home'. As a major concession to Chinese values, this new view of Buddhism as fulfilling the ends of filial piety became a marked feature of East Asian Buddhism (Ch'en 1973: 14-60; de Bary and Bloom 1999: 439).

The Sutra about Filial Piety

The composition of the Sutra helped to establish deep Buddhist roots into Chinese society and facilitated the integration of Buddhist ideals into the national life of Chinese people.

The Sutra had existed since the Sui and T'ang dynasties (589-906) in China (Zuerucher 1987). Over many eras in Chinese history, the Sutra has been developed and revised (Michihata 1994: 85; Ch'en 1973). It has been treasured in much of the Far East, including Korea and Japan, with an obvious emphasis on the importance of filial piety.

This Sutra is unique in that it teaches the importance of parents' kindness. It describes the hardships and labor experienced by parents in bringing up their children. The efforts of a mother are depicted with special vividness.

The Sutra prescribes in detail ten types of kindness and ways in which the mother bestows the kindness upon her children. The kindness is explained in terms of the mother's undergoing physical and mental sufferings (fear and anxiety while the child is in her womb and pain and exhaustion during and after the delivery on the child's behalf), joy of having the baby, deep and indescribable love and affection toward the baby, incessantly wanting the child to feel full and to be healthy, concern over the child's safety and well-being from dawn to dusk, and a kindness that does not even begin to dissipate until her life is over. The ten types of kindness reflect the boundless, unconditional, and selfless love a mother has for her child. The Sutra presents probably the most touching descriptions of the mother's kindness that one can find in literature.

The background of the discourses reflects the life of a common, poor mother of a farming family. One might say that the Sutra was designed to appeal especially to the hard-working farming masses, not the well-to-do upper classes (Ch'en 1973: 41). It depicts clearly the maternal kindness that is universal and unchanging regardless of the mother's social status or walk of life.

The Sutra is made up of five parts: the first explains the kindness of a mother; the second describes the difficulty of repaying the kindness; the third is a discourse on unfilial children, the fourth explains the hell into which they are to fall, and the fifth teaches the Buddhist way of repaying the kindness.

The Sutra about the Deep Kindness of Parents and the Difficulty of Repaying It

(Excerpts)

Ananda said to the World Honored One,
"How can one repay one's mother's kindness and virtue?"

The Buddha told Ananda,

"Listen well, for I will explain it to you in detail. The fetus grows in its mother's womb for ten months. What difficulties she goes through while it dwells there! In the first month of pregnancy, the life of the fetus is as precarious as a dewdrop on grass: It might not last from morning to evening, but drip off or evaporate by midday! During the second lunar month, the embryo congeals like curds. In the third month it is like coagulated blood. During the fourth month of pregnancy the fetus begins to assume a lightly human form. During the fifth month in the womb, the child's five limbs—two legs, two arms, and a head—start to take shape. In the sixth month of pregnancy, the child begins to develop the essences of the six sense faculties: the eyes, ears, nose, tongue, body and mind. During the seventh month, the three hundred sixty bones and joints are formed, and the eighty-four thousand hair pores are also complete. In the eighth month of pregnancy the intellect and the nine apertures are formed. By the ninth month the fetus has learned to assimilate the different nutrients of the foods it eats. During the tenth month of pregnancy, the body of the fetus is completed and ready to be born . . . The birth will feel like the slices of a thousand knives or like ten thousand sharp swords stabbing her heart."

"To explain more clearly, there are ten types of kindness bestowed by the mother on the child:

The First Kindness is providing protection and care while the child is in the womb.

"The human birth is not easy to attain in the many countless lives of rebirth. It is easy that the child ends up in its mother's womb, with karmic connection with its parents. As the months pass, the five vital organs gradually develop. Within seven weeks, the six sense organs start to grow. The mother's burden becomes greater as the child grows. The movements of the fetus are like frightening earthquakes and hurricanes in the mother. With her mind only on her child, the mother is too tired to make up. Her fine clothes are left untouched while her mirror gathers dust."

The Second Kindness is bearing suffering during birth.

"The pregnancy lasts for ten months, and culminates in difficult labor at the approach of the birth. Meanwhile every morning, the mother feels ill, and she is constantly drowsy and sluggish. Her fear and anxiety are beyond description. Grief and tears fill her heart. She painfully tells her family that she is only afraid that death will befall her baby."

The Third Kindness is forgetting all the pain once the child has been born.

"The day of the birth, the mother's five organs all open wide, leaving her totally exhausted both physically and mentally. She faints several times and bleeds profusely, like a slaughtered lamb. Yet, after the ordeal, upon regaining consciousness, her first concern is the well-being of the child. Upon knowing the child's well-being, she is overcome by redoubling joy. But after the initial joy, the physical pain returns and the agony wrenches her very insides."

The Fourth Kindness is eating the bitter herself and saving the sweet for the child.

"The kindness of parents is the most profound, deeper than the sea. Their care and devotion never cease. Never resting or complaining, parental love is indeed deep and indescribable. As long as their children get their fill, parents will rather go cold and hungry. As long as they are happy, parents are satisfied."

The Fifth Kindness is moving the child to a dry place and lying in the wet herself.

"Only wanting the child to feel full, the mother doesn't speak of her own hunger. The mother is willing to be wet, so that the child can be dry. With her two breasts she satisfies the child's hunger and thirst, bringing it health. Covering the baby with her sleeve, she protects it from the wind and cold. So long as the child is comfortable and happy, the kind mother seeks no solace for herself."

The Sixth Kindness is suckling the child at her breast and nourishing and bringing up the child.

"The mother is like the great earth, supporting and nourishing the child's life. The stern father is like the encompassing heaven that covers from above, while the mother supports from below. The kindness of all parents is the same, which despises no offspring even when it is born ugly. It knows no hatred or anger. And they are not displeased, even if the child is born crippled. The parents care for and protect their children together until the end of their days, simply because they are their offspring. Such is the greatest of parental love."

The Seventh Kindness is washing away the unclean.

"Originally, she had a pretty face and a beautiful body. Her spirit was strong and vibrant. Her eyebrows were like fresh green willows. And her complexion would have put a red rose to shame. But her kindness is so deep she will forgo her beauty. Although constant washing away the filth of her children and taking care of them injures her constitution. The kind mother acts solely for the sake of her sons and daughters without conditions, and willingly allows her beauty to fade."

The Eighth Kindness is always thinking of the child when it has traveled afar.

"The death of loved ones is difficult to endure. But separation is painful as well, like when the child travels afar. The mother worries at home. From dawn till dusk, her heart is always with her child, praying for an early return. Some children leave for years without a message while their aged parents wait day and night, shedding a thousand tears. Like an old monkey weeping silently in love for her child. Bit by bit her heart is broken."

The Ninth Kindness is deep care and devotion.

> "How heavy are parental kindness and their emotional concern! Their kindness is deep and difficult to repay just a fraction. Willingly, they wish to undergo suffering on their children's behalf. If the child toils, the parents feel uncomfortable. If they hear that he has traveled afar, they worry that at night he might have to lie in the cold. Even a moment's pain suffered by the children, will cause the parents sustained distress."

The Tenth Kindness is ultimate pity and sympathy.

> "The kindness of parents is profound and important. Their tender concern never ceases. From the moment they wake up each day, their thoughts are with their children. Even if a mother has lived for a hundred years, she will still worry about her eighty-year-old child! Do you wish to know when such kindness and love ends? It doesn't even begin to dissipate until her life is over."

The Buddha told Ananda:

> "When I contemplate living beings, I see that although they are born as human beings, nonetheless, they are stupid and dull in their thoughts and actions. They don't consider their parents' kindness and virtue. They are disrespectful and turn their backs on kindness and what is right. They lack humanness and are neither filial nor compliant."

> "The virtue of one's parents' kindness is boundless and limitless. If one has made the mistake of being unfilial, how difficult it is to repay that kindness!"

The Buddha told Ananda:

> "If a person is not filial, when his life ends and his body decays, he will fall into the Spaceless Avici Hell. This great hell is eight thousand yojanas in circumference and is surrounded by iron walls. Above, it is covered over by nets and the ground is made of iron. A mass of fire burns fiercely, while thunder roars and bright bolts of lightning set things afire. Molten brass and iron are poured over the offenders' bodies. Brass dogs and iron snakes constantly spew out fire and smoke which burns the offenders and broils their flesh and fat to a pulp."

The Buddha said:

> "Disciples of the Buddha, if you wish to repay the kindness, then for the sake of your parents print this sutra and distribute widely to benefit others. This is truly repaying their kindness. If one can print one copy, then one will get to see one Buddha. If one can print one hundred copies, then one will get to see one hundred Buddhas. If one can print ten thousand copies, then one will get to see ten thousand Buddhas. This is the power derived when good people print sutras. All Buddhas will forever protect such people with their kindness and can immediately cause the parents of such people to be reborn in the heavens, to enjoy all kinds of happiness, and to leave behind the sufferings of the hells."

At that time, Ananda, with a dignity and a sense of peace, rose from his seat and asked the Buddha, "World Honored One, what name shall this sutra have when we accord with it and uphold it?"

The Buddha told Ananda, "This sutra is called *THE SUTRA ABOUT THE DEEP KINDNESS OF PARENTS AND THE DIFFICULTY OF REPAYING IT.* Use this name when you accord with it and uphold it."

Note: **The World Honored One**: The Buddha
Ananda: One of the Buddha's chief disciples
Avici Hell: Hell where tortures are suffered by climbing up mountains of sharp knives, having molten bronze poured into their mouths, and swallowing red hot iron balls while being scorched all over by fire.

The Parents' Boundless Kindness

The Sutra extolled parents' kindness, particularly the mother's. It describes the sacrifices the mother makes for a child. This portrayal of a mother's kindness and selflessness was so touching, that on hearing the Sutra, the Buddha's disciples were moved to deep grief and remorse, thinking of the kindness they never appreciated before.

A mother is most helpful and beneficial to her child. She breast-feeds and nurtures the child at all times to help him grow. The following discourse in a sutra about parent love explains this aspect of mother's kindness (Ch'en 1973: 38-39). The Buddha said:

"In this world our parents are closest to us. Without parents, we would not be born . . . When the child is hungry and needs food, only the mother will feed him. She allows the baby to sleep on the dry place while she herself occupies the wet spot . . . Vast and boundless indeed is the love of a mother for her child."

"At times, a mother might go to a neighboring village to draw water or gather kindle wood and would not return on time. On such occasions, the child at home would cry and think about his mother. When she returns home, the child in the cradle would see her coming from the distance, and at this sight, he would shake his head back and forth, or crawl toward his mother to welcome her. The mother would bend down, stretch out her hands to wipe away the dust from his face, and kiss him. The mother is happy upon seeing the child and the child is likewise glad upon seeing the mother. There is really nothing that can surpass such mutual expressions of loving care and compassion."

"Again, the mother might go to a party elsewhere, where she might obtain some sweet meats and cakes; instead of eating them herself, she would take them home to give to her child. In nine cases out of ten, she would return with something, and everybody would be happy."

The above discourse teaches us the boundless, vast love and kindness that a mother bestows on her child.

In Buddhism, mother needs to be understood in relation to the place accorded to women in that religion. The Brahman Vaisista shows the regard a woman could achieve as a mother: "The teacher is ten times more venerable than the assistant teacher, the father is a hundred times more than the teacher, and the mother a thousand times more than the father" (Murcott 1991: 74). The mother is characterized by archetypal traits such as devotion, compassion, and self-sacrifice. She is the symbol of life, generation, and fertility. And, she is treated with the status of wisdom and practice (Tsomo 1988). Motherhood remained the most honored phase of a woman's life in Buddhist culture (Murcott 1991: 76). The Sutra about the kindness of the mother evidences the symbol, the status, and the honor accorded to the mother and motherhood in Buddhism.

Repayment in the Buddhist Way

The Sutra teaches us that we have the kindness of our parents to be grateful for. After becoming aware of the kindness of one's own parents, one extends to all other parents and all other sentient beings the feelings of love and gratitude that this awareness generates. Here, the awareness of the kindness of parent is treated as one facet of the awareness of the greater Buddha's grace.

This practice is based on the Buddhist understanding of karma (Nakasone 2000; Curtin and Curtin 1994), according to which each person has been reborn an infinite number of times, and each lifetime has been determined and conditioned by past actions—good deeds are rewarded with meritorious rebirths and evil deeds with rebirth in one of the evil modes of existence. Because past rebirths are numberless and because future rebirths are also numberless, a Buddhist can conclude that he/she has been in every possible relationship with every other sentient being, and that every sentient being has been his/her mother, father, best friend, etc. In this ceaseless cycle, all existences are mutually related and mutually dependent. The next step is to realize that one owes each sentient being a great debt of gratitude for past kindness. Thinking in this way, one resolves to repay not only his/her parents but also all other parents.

The requital of the kindness of parents is filial piety. The Buddha incisively prescribed in the Sutra that it is only right that children should provide aging parents with food and drink of delicious flavors. Thus, the issue of support for parent is frontally addressed. Furthermore, as part of the requital of the parents' kindness, one has to protect the helpless parents of others as well.

Buddhists' conception of filial piety extended further (Ch'en 1973: 45). In the Confucian ideology, severing all ties with parents and siblings, and terminating the family line in order to become a monk, was a condemnable unfilial conduct. However, Buddhists viewed this conduct differently; by joining the monastic order, the monk was able to convert his parents to Buddhism, so that they would attain salvation and avoid the endless cycle of transmigration. This was the greatest filiality that a monk could confer on his parents. The Chinese Buddhists further contended that the monk would be fulfilling even greater filial piety that is far superior to the Confucian filial piety, which is confined to one family and limited to serving only one's parents, whereas the Buddhist filial piety is all-inclusive, embraces all living creatures, and is universal (Ch'en 1973: 45; Nakasone 1990; Lancaster 1995).

The Sutra on parents' kindness became an important teaching for common people to practice filial piety and the teaching on parents' kindness, particularly the mother's kindness, is deeply engrained in the hearts of East Asian people.

Discussion

During the long history of China, Buddhism became more and more acceptable to the Chinese. What the traditional Chinese philosophers did was to secularize Buddhist ideas and, by so doing spread them beyond the Buddhist monasteries to the whole Chinese population (C'hen 1973). The Sutra was a very influential and remarkable vehicle, which facilitated this historical process.

The Sutra extols the mother's profound and boundless kindness and stresses the obligation of adult children to repay her kindness. The kindness of a father is mentioned, too. The Sutra states (in the discourse of the sixth kindness) that the kindness of all parents—mother and father—is the same; they care for and protect their children together until the end of their day.

The discourse in the Sutra proceeds in the form of the dyadic communication between the Buddha and Ananda. The Buddha explains to the disciple sufferings, agonies, and sacrifices that the mother endures in the course of her pregnancy, delivery, and raising a child. Her kindness ranges from providing the baby in her womb with protection and care to deep devotion and ultimate pity and sympathy for the child until her life ends. The Buddha said that the virtue of parents' kindness is boundless and limitless. A profound feeling of gratitude lies at the very heart of the Sutra.

The Sutra explains how difficult it is to repay the kindness by saying "If a person were to circumambulate Mount Sumeru for a hundred thousand cycles, that person would still not have repaid the kindness of his parents" (Nicholson 2000). Asians very often quote this saying when they talk about the parent's kindness.

In Confucian teachings, unfiliality is the worst crime children could commit. In the Sutra, the gravity and severity of the consequences of unfiliality are prescribed even more sternly in terms of hell wherein unfilial children would face torture, sufferings and the eventual karma in which they would be transformed to beasts. This version of unfiliality corresponds well with the Confucian ideal of filial piety.

And then the Buddha said, "If you wish to repay your parents' kindness, write out this Sutra on their behalf. Repent of transgressions and offenses on their behalf . . . For the sake of your parents, practice giving and cultivate blessings. If you are able to do these things, you are a filial child" (Nicholson 2000).

Writing out the Sutra means reading or reciting the Sutra, thereby having a better understanding of the kindness and repayment. So, by writing the Sutra one can be a filial person. The Buddha furthermore prescribed that if one can print many copies of the Sutra, that is, by spreading the teachings to many people, he will see to it that many Buddhas protect such a person for their kindness and can cause the parents of such person to be reborn in the heavens, to enjoy all kinds of happiness, and to leave behind the sufferings of hell. The grace of a mother for her child and the child's repayment are the paradigms for cultivating an attitude of cherishing all other beings (Curtin and Curtin 1994: 4). Care for parents is treated as one facet of the larger issue of universal liberation.

The Sutra does not prescribe how to repay the kindness on a one to one basis, i.e., a child to a parent. This is in contrast to the Confucian way. In the Confucian writings, specific ways of caring and serving a parent by a child are prescribed. For example, "In caring for a parent, a child should make the parent feel happy, not act against his/her will, let the parent see and hear pleasurable things, provide him/her with comfortable places to sleep . . . The parent should be served foods of his/her choice and the foods should be tasty, fresh, soft, and flagrant" (Book of Rites, Bk. 1, Ch. 2; Bk. 2, Ch. 12).

In Buddhism, the ways are oriented toward awakening persons to understand parents' kindness and teaching to practice Dharma (the Buddha's knowledge) (Rinpoche 1993). Can we repay our parents by giving our possessions? The things will benefit them for a short time in this life only. Besides, wealth does not bring them real joy and happiness. With things, we cannot afford to repay our parents and all sentient beings. We need to practice Dharma and meditate. Then we attain the enlightened state and are able to help all of them.

The family is the arena where Confucian filial piety is practiced. The traditional Confucian practice tends to be overly, if not staunchly, family-centered. Filial piety was confined by a kinship structure. This fact prevented the Chinese and other East Asians from strong and enduring alliances outside of the structure. The fixity of the kinship-centered culture stands in contrast to the situation we find in Buddhism. In Buddhism, the awareness extends far beyond the boundary of the family. It is to be done not only for relatives but also for all other parents and all sentient beings in this life and the next life (Lancaster 1995; Nakasone 1990).

The Sutra depicts the life of a common and working mother. This is in contrast to Confucian writings, which are predominantly descriptions of filial piety toward an authoritarian, educated, or aristocratic person, usually a male figure; whereas the mother in the Sutra is an ordinary, working mother with minimal possessions for her daily living.

Although these differences exist between the two tenets of the ideals and practices of filial piety, Buddhist filial piety complements Confucian filial piety by stressing the importance of understanding the kindness of parents, by incorporating filial piety for women and poor people, by prescribing the grave consequences of unfilialty, and by extending filial piety for all sentient beings in this life and the next life. Buddhists made these contributions. They adapted to the filial piety tradition of China and fulfilled the ends of filial piety in the Buddhist way.

Finally, it must be noted that the Sutra is the Buddha's prescription of how to repay the kindness of elderly parents—a religious and ethical tenet. The prescription has been secularized in the Chinese cultural setting and bolstered the ideal and practice of elder care throughout East Asia for many generations. The prescription is still pertinent. In an aging society, we need to struggle to preserve the basics of religious and ethical affirmation of care and support for parents and elderly persons. In recent years, a social concern over the disrespectful treatment of older people has been voiced by gerontologists in different societies. Without such reaffirmation, the mistreatment of the elderly may increase. The Sutra of Buddhism—one of the world's great religions—provides insights of religious ethics with which an aging society can mitigate any trend toward elder mistreatment and sustain filial morality.

References

De Bury, W. T.,& Bloom, I. (1999). *Sources of Chinese Tradition.* (2nd Ed.). New York: Columbia University Press. Chap. 15, 415-35.

Ch'en, K. K. S. (1973). *The Chinese transformation of Buddhism.* Princeton, NJ: Princeton University Press.

Curtin, P., & Curtin, D. (1994). Mothering: Moral cultivation in Buddhist and feminist Ethics. *Philosophy East and West, 44,* 1-18.

Lancaster, L. R. (1995). The role of filial piety in Buddhism: A study of religious spread and adaptation. Pp. 786-796, In *Filial Piety and Future Society.* Kyunggido, South Korea: The Academy of Korean Studies.

Michihata, R. (Mok, J. B., Trans.). (1994). *Confucian filial piety and Buddhist filial piety: Comparative study of filial piety in Confucianism and Buddhism (Bulkyo-ae HyoYukyo-ae Hyo: Yu-Bul-ae Hyoron Bikyo-Yunku).* Seoul: Bulkyo Sidae Sa.

Murcott, S. (1991). *The first Buddhist women.* Berkeley, CA: Parallax Press.

Nakasone, R. Y. (1990). *Ethics of enlightenment: Essays & sermons in search for a Buddhist ethic.* Fremont: Dharma Cloud Publishers.

Nicholson, U. T. (Trans. from Chinese); Tao, B. H. (Reviewed); Ch'ih, B. H., and Rounds, U. S. (Ed.); Venerable Abbot Hua and Tao, B. H. (Certified). (2000). *Sutra about the deep*

kindness of parents and the difficulty of repaying it.
[http://www.sinc.sunysb.edu/Clubs/buddhism/fmeznbj.html]

Rinpoche, S. (1993). *The Tibetan book of living and dying.* P. Gaffney and A. Harvey (Ed.). San Francisco: Harper San Francisco.

Scovill, N. B. (1995). *The liberation of women: Religious sources.* Milwaukee, WI: Religious Consultation on Population, Reproductive Health and Ethics.

Schumann, H. W. (1989). *The historical Buddha: The times, life and teachings of the founder of Buddhism* (M. O'c. Walshe, Trans.). London: Arkana.

De Silva, Swana (1988). *The place of women in Buddhism* (A talk given to the Midlands Buddhist Society (UK) on Sanghamitta Day 1988.) June 1994.

Singhal, D. P. (1984). *Buddhism in East Asia.* New Delhi: Books & Books.

Tsomo, K. L. (Ed.)(1988). *Sakyadhita: Daughters of the Buddha.* New York: Snow Lion Publications.

Chapter 24

Islamic Teachings and Elder Respect

This chapter is comprised of excerpts from the following three sources.

Respecting Parents: The Muslim Way. Ahmad H. Sakr. 2007. Walnut, California: The Islamic Education Center.

The Family Structure in Islam. Hammudah Abdalati. 1977. Indianapolis, Indiana: Islamic Book Service.

The Dignity of Parents. Maulana Qazi Syed Shah Azam Ali Soofi (Compiled); Syed Mohammed Ghouse & Mohammed Iftakharuddin Siddiqui (Translated). 1998. Hydrabad, India: Syed US Soofia Academy.

Islamic teachings include an ideal way to respect elders, particularly the parents. Respectful behavior and affectionate devoted service to the parents is a must in Islam. Next to Allah and Prophet comes the respect and dignity of parents in Holy Quran. Father is declared as Main Gateway of Heaven where as Heaven lies beneath the feet of Mother as per Hadith, where much importance is given to fulfill the rights of the parents in general and at their old age in particular.

Allah is original Creator of children while parents are apparent and worldly source for their birth.

Allah favors and fosters every human being neither for any compensation nor any greed. Similarly parents too foster their children neither for any compensation nor for any greed.

Worship of Allah is always a necessity; similarly service of parents is always necessary during their life times and by prayer after their death.

The good behavior with parents can be classified into three:

1. Acts and talks of children shall not cause physical harm or hurt the feelings of parents.
2. If parents are in need of anything, to which children can afford to do it, they are bound to do it either by rendering services or by spending money without fail.

Allah has cautioned His Commands in Holy Quran repeatedly for good behavior with parents.

Parents in Qur'an

A Muslim child should respect and appreciate his or her parents every day throughout the year. Allah asked human beings to recognize their parents after recognition Allah Himself. Throughout the Qur'an, we notice that parents are mentioned with appreciation and with respect, even if they are senile. In Surah Al-Isra' (Children of Israel) there is a very beautiful description of how parents are to be treated. Allah (swt) says:

"Your Lord had decreed, that you worship none save Him, and (that you show) kindness to parents. If one of them or both of them attain old age with you, say not "Fie" unto them nor repulse them, but speak unto them a gracious word. And lower unto them the wing of submission through mercy, and say: My Lord! Have mercy on them both, as they did care for me when I was young." [17:23-24]

The recognition and respect of parents is mentioned in the Qur'an eleven times; in every instance, Allah remind children to recognize and to appreciate the care and love they have received from their parents. In one aspect, Allah demands that children recognize their parents by saying to them:

"We have enjoined on man kindness to parents." [29:8/46:15]

1. The demand for recognizing parents is made ore emphatic when Allah says in the Qur'an Surah Al-Baqarah (The Cow) the following.

   "And (remember) when We made a covenant with the children of Israel, (saying): worship none save Allah (only), and be god to parents." [2:83]

2. In Surah Al-Nisaa' (The Women) Allah (swt) emphasized again that children should be kind to their parents.

   "And service Allah. Ascribe nothing as partner unto Him. (Show) Kindness unto parents." [4:36]

3. In Surah Al An'Am (The Cattle), Allah (swt) reemphasized that people should be kind to their parents.

"Say: Come, I will recite unto you that which your Lord has made a sacred duty for you; that you ascribe nothing as partner unto Him and that you do good to parents." [6:151]

Islam teaches us that respect for parents comes immediately after praying to Allah and before Jihad (struggle and striving in the way of Allah). In this respect, the Prophet (pbuh) said the following:

Narrated by Abi Abder Rahman Abdullah bin Massoud (May Allah be pleased with him) saying: I asked the Prophet (pbuh), *"which deed is more liked by Allah?"* He replied, *"Prayers on time."* Then I asked, *"Then which one is next?"* He said, *"Jihad in the way of Allah."* (Agreed)

In Islam, respect for parents is so great that the child and his wealth are considered to be the property of the parents. In this regard, the Prophet (pbuh) said:

Narrated by Aisha (May Allah be pleased with her) that a person came to the Prophet (pbuh) to resolve his dispute with his father regarding a loan given to the father. The Prophet (pbuh) said to the person, *"You and your wealth are to your father."*

Mothers

Although Islam recognize both parents, mothers are given particular gratitude and respect. This attitude of Islam is understood if we realize the hardships and the suffering that mothers experience in their lives. In this regard, Prophet Muhammad—Muhammad (pbuh) said:

It was narrated by Abu Hurairah (R) that a man came to the Prophet (pbuh) and asked him, 'Who is to be close to my friendship?' The Prophet (pbuh) answered:

Your mother, your mother, your mother, then your father, then the one closest to the one closest to your kinship, and the one after.

Hardship of mother during pregnancy:

The mother carries the weight for months together and suffers from continued weakness. Because she fosters her blood to the child: in addition to this she gets lost of exertion of body and pains at the birth of the child. After the birth she feeds her blood in the shape of milk for two years to foster the child. The favors of mother's obligations cannot be compensated at all in any respect, similarly to the favors of Allah there cannot be any compensation. But to the extent possible, it is commanded to thank the favors of Allah as well as parents.

Command to serve parents in old age with kindness:

> If one of them or both of them to attain old age with you say not "fie" unto them
> nor repulse them, but speak unto them a gracious word. And lower unto them the
> wing of submission through mercy, and say: My Lord! Have Mercy on them
> both as they did care for me when I was little. (Q17:23, 24)

Whether parents are either young or aged, it is necessary for the children to serve them. But especially when they attain old age their condition is liable to deserve sympathy. Because of old age and weakness the strength and energy to walk and work or to earn is extinguished. The vision and hearing become weak and they experience difficulty. . . . Give good treatment in their period of pains and sickness so that they may get relief and rest as far as possible by sacrificing services and money. Because during the period of disability of children they had already taken every care and fostered them, therefore it becomes necessary for the children to look after them and take every care during the period of helplessness of parents and serve them in a perfect manner.

> Be kind with your mother, and then be kind with your father and then with those
> who are very close to you.

One person appeared and stated before Rasoolullah (SAS) that Ya Rasoolullah (SAS) under this hot sun I have carried my mother on my neck up to two "Farsak" distance, when even meat will be fried like 'Kahab'. Whether I have thus offered my thanks. Then He(Sas) replied, "Perhaps this may be equivalent to one jerk of her labor pains" (Tibrani).

Good behavior with parents is that after their death, pray for their pardon with Allah (Ibne-Al-Najjar).

The Child's Duties; the Parents' Rights

The parent-child relationship is structurally complementary. Parent and child in Islam are bound together by mutual obligations and reciprocal arrangements. But the age differential is sometimes so wide that parents have grown physically weak and mentally feeble. This condition is often characterized by impatience, degeneration of energy, heightened sensitivity, and perhaps misjudgment. It may also result in abuses of parental authority or intergenerational estrangement and uneasiness. It was probably with a view to these considerations that Islam has taken cognizance of certain facts and made basic provisions to govern the individual's relationship to his parents.

The demarcation line between the rights of God and those of the parents must be guardedly maintained. Basically, however, these two sets of rights are mutually complementary and reinforce one another. They seem to be designed in such a way as to reduce to a minimum the possibility of conflict. This is probably best indicated by the fact that the parental rights come second only to the highest value in Islam, namely faith in God and exclusive worship of Him. The same idea is reiterated in the Prophet's statement that was pleases one's parents is also pleasing to God, and what annoys them likewise annoys Him. Nevertheless conflict does arise, and accommodation may be difficult to obtain. In such situations, the rights of God must be rendered supreme.

Ihsan

One of these rights is to provide the parents with certain basic securities, irrespective even of their religious preferences. Parents may disagree with or differ from their children with respect to religious values and moral standards. But this does not affect the parents' basic rights upon their children, so long as the former do not engage in or contemplate active conflict with the latter. The Qur'an sums up the whole matter in a master concept called *ihsan* which denotes what is right, good, and beautiful. It means in the Islamic context, among other things, kindness, compassion, charity, reverence, conscientiousness, and sound performance. It is the Muslim's religious duty as well as virtue to show *ihsan* to his parents, be they Muslims like himself or otherwise. Concrete behavioral manifestations of this Divine Ordinance of *ihsan* to the parents include active empathy or "role taking" compassionate gratitude, patience, prayer for them after their demise, honoring their commitments on their behalf when they can no longer do so, sincere counsel, and veneration.

Deference

It is also implied in the concept of *ihsan* that the parents have the right to expect obedience or deference from their children, if only in partial return for their investments and authority. But parents, like any other persons, may not expect such obedience if they demand the wrong or ask for the improper; if they do, disobedience becomes not only justifiable but imperative. Obey or disobey, the children's attitude may not be allowed to become one of indiscriminate submissiveness or irresponsible defiance.

Support and Maintenance

An integral part of the children's absolute religious duty is to provide for their parents in case of need and help them to be as comfortable as possible. Jurists disagree on some details and as usual, their differences at times appear highly complex. However, they agree on several general principles. First every individual is responsible for his own maintenance and should try to be self-supporting, especially as far as subsistence is concerned. To this rule there is one exception, namely the wife, whose maintenance is the husband's responsibility whether she is poor or wealthy. Secondly, no individual in particular is held responsible for the maintenance of any other individual of a different religion. To this rule also there are some exceptions, namely one's wife, immediate parents, and children. These categories are entitled to maintenance irrespective of their private beliefs. Thirdly, parents are entitled to maintenance by their children when the former are in need and the latter capable of supporting them. Fourthly, a poor man is not responsible for anyone else's support except his wife, parent and child. In this case, whatever is spent on their maintenance by other relatives or by the Muslim community will be considered a free community service, according to one school of law, or a debt to be paid when possible, according to one school of law, or a debt to be paid when possible, according to another. Fifthly, maintenance includes adequate provisions for food, lodging, clothing, and general comfort for the parents and their dependents, even though these may not be directly related to the providing children, who are required, for example, to provide for the father's wife and maid, and to help him to remarry if this is needed for his comfort. The parents' need-level, the children's capacity for support, the constituents of comfort, and other variables shall be determined in accordance with the standards of the time, but with a view to equity, kindness, and moderation—*ihsan*. Finally, support for poor parents shall be shared by their children equally without regard to the children's sex, according to one interpretation, or in proportion to their shares of inheritance, according to another.

Support for parents was apparently so taken for granted that a certain pioneering savant, al Sha'bi (d. ca. 105/723), thought it improper to speak of it in terms of legal rulings. It was built into the religio-moral system of Islam to be kind to and thoughtful of parents. So much was this natural and internalized that it needed neither coding nor any specific emphasis. But this position was abandoned by the succeeding jurists who elaborated the intergenerational duties of mutual support and care. These jurists did not subscribe to al Sha'bi's interpretation of the child-parent relationship for some interesting sociological reasons. Ibn al Qayyim insightfully observed that al Sha'bi's doctrine was conceived at and practicable or appropriate for a time when Muslims were highly conscientious, leading a simple life, and freshly infused with religious enthusiasm. As those conditions changed, there arose a need to formulate in specific legal terms the duties of children to parents, as well as other mutual obligations of siblings and collaterals.

Brother-Sister Relationships

A general review of the relationship between brothers and sisters in the heart of the Muslim world of both ancient and modern times reveals some interesting patterns and contrasts. From the very early days of life in that part of the world, that relationship was sometimes marked with rivalry, jealousy, and hostility. Sibling rivalry often involved the parents as favoring one child, almost invariably the youngest, to other children. This was further aggravated by the practice of polygamy as well as other social considerations. For example, there are indications that even among contemporary Middle Easterners sibling rivalry is conscious, deliberate, and contemplated by some families so that the child may, in Patai's words, "stand up to its rivals upon becoming an adult."

However, the sibling relationship, especially between brothers and sisters, was more often than not profoundly amicable. There are indications that brothers were allies, helpmates, and reliable supporters of one another. So commonly it seems, was this the case that their solidarity, compassion, and natural fealty became proverbial or set apart as lofty ideals whose implementation is both desired and desirable. The Qur'an, for example, speaks of the Believers as constituting one brotherhood and refers to the Muslim individual as the brother of every other Muslim.

The very concept of brotherhood was broadened to include the entire body of the Believers. Brotherhood in faith transcended brotherhood in blood, although it did not necessarily replace it completely. The principle of *ihsan*, with all its denotations, was to be implemented in and applied to the brothers' relationships. It is the religio-moral duty of the Muslim to support his needy brother or sister adequately. Failure to discharge this kinship duty is not only indicative of ingratitude and disrespect for blood ties, but also punishable here and now as well as on the Day of Judgment. Other schools interpret *ihsan* among brothers and sisters to mean a general sentiment of compassion and consideration that does not necessarily amount to any specific compulsory pattern of aid and, above all, does not involve recourse to litigation. Needy individuals accordingly, are the collective responsibility of the whole community, not only of their blood brothers and sisters.

Respect for All Elderly

Our beloved Prophet (pbuh) instructed us to respect all those who are old and at the same time we are to have mercy on the young. In one Hadith, it is said:

I advise you to be good to the elderly, and to have mercy on the youth. [El Dailami]

It was reported by Aisha that Prophet (pbuh) instructed us to respect people according to their position. The Arabic text is as follows:

We are informed that any young person who respects the elderly, is to be respected when he becomes old. In one Hadith, the following is reported:

Narrated by Anas (May Allah be pleased with him) saying that the Prophet (pbuh) said:

Any young person who is kind to an elderly because of his age, Allah will send him someone who will be kind to him when he becomes old. [Tarmazi]

In another place, our beloved Prophet (pbuh) denounces the young if they don't respect the elderly in as much as the elderly are denounced if they don't have mercy on the young. The Hadith is as follows:

Narrated by 'Amr Ibn Shu'aib through his father and from his grandfather (May Allah be pleased with them), saying that the Messenger of Allah said: He is not of us, the one who does not have mercy on our young ones, and the one who does not know the respect of our old ones. [Dawood & Tarmazi]

The respect that the Prophet (pbuh) instructed us to give to the elderly is also in the field of prayer itself. We are to feel sympathy and concern for the elderly while we are performing the prayer. We should not extend or prolong the congregation prayer especially if there are elderly among the faithful. In one Hadith the Prophet (pbuh) said:

Narrated by Abu Hurairah (May Allah be pleased with him) that the Prophet (pbuh) said:

When a person leads a congregation prayer, let him make it short, as there may be around the weak, the sick and the elderly. However, when a person prays by himself, he may extend his prayer as much as he wishes. [Agreed]

I wish to mention here that Allah Himself gives, among other things, respect to the elderly Muslims. The Prophet (pbuh) says in this regards:

Narrated by Abu Musa (May Allah be pleased with him) saying that the Messenger of Allah said:

Among the respect that Allah bestows is to the one who is elderly, gray-haired Muslim, the one who memorized the Qur'an without bragging or deserting it, and the respect to the just ruler. [Abu Dawood]

Index

acquiescent respect, 64, 131, 136, 138, 149, 153~156, 159, 187, 191, 194, 198~204, 207, 225~229, 251, 269~271, 274

affective qualities, 149, 223

Agape, 14~20, 109

American arc of life, 280, 287

Asian families, 237

attention, 1, 17, 25~29, 31~37, 40, 42, 46, 52, 63, 70, 76, 85, 88, 101, 115, 120, 132, 137, 139, 147, 152, 155, 158, 161, 167, 185, 200, 207, 221, 239, 255, 258, 266, 288, 297, 301, 304, 321, 330, 336

behavioral expressions of elder respect, 149, 205, 267

Belmont principles, 65, 66

beneficence, 63, 66, 70, 78, 92, 96, 106, 323

bioethics movement, 68, 73

care respect, 1, 30~40, 47, 64, 131, 136, 149, 153~155, 159, 161, 183, 187, 191, 192, 197~200, 202, 204, 206, 225, 229~232, 251, 267, 270~273, 275

caretaking responsibilities, 315

categorical imperative as the principle of respect, 24

celebrative respect, 133, 136, 139, 140, 141, 149, 157, 191, 203, 224

changing expressions, 1, 47, 299

child rearing obligations, 315

Chinese communities, vi, xviii, 56, 59, 175, 204, 209, 251, 307~310

Chinese cultural norms, 258

collective societal good, 258

commandments, 332, 335, 338

commonality among all persons, 32

concern and love, 105

Confucian filial piety, 59, 209, 234, 341, 343, 350, 352

Confucian teachings, xiv, 1, 45, 47, 48, 58, 182, 185, 202, 221, 229, 230, 274, 351

connection between care and respect, 40

consulting respect, 139, 149, 153, 154, 156, 159, 161, 191, 225, 228, 229, 269~271, 274

cross-cultural forms, 47, 182, 272

cross-cultural study of Americans and Koreans, 61, 211

cultural change, 265

cultural contexts, 45, 134, 145, 165, 168, 221, 224, 237, 259, 265~268, 271~ 273, 276

culture-based ethical care values, 255

customs and rituals, 50, 149, 294, 296, 303

debt of gratitude, 291, 350

deference, 16, 58, 116, 166~173, 194, 195, 198, 202, 203, 213, 216, 227, 231, 232, 237, 254, 258, 260, 275, 291, 292, 359

demographic revolution, 315, 316, 320, 323

demographic triangle, 315

dignity and respect, 115, 126

dignity of parents, 355

disrespectful treatment, 266, 352

doctor-patient relationship, 85, 86, 88

economic theory to medicine, 77

empathy, 11, 12, 77, 81, 82, 87, 108, 132, 359

ethical and moral care values, 251, 260

ethical role of nursing, 101

ethical values of respect and deference, 254

ethnic group differences, 118, 280, 281

European American, 120

evaluative respect, 27, 33, 35, 42

expressions of elder respect, 47, 48, 56, 58, 133, 159, 182, 185~ 187, 191, 197, 200, 205, 208, 225, 231, 267, 269, 275

family orientation of Confucianism, 344

filial obligation, 58, 177, 202, 231, 232, 274, 313, 316, 318~323, 327, 328, 331, 332, 337, 338

filial piety, 45~48, 52, 58~62, 123, 164, 175~182, 185, 196, 198, 206~211, 221, 231~235, 251, 267, 274,~278, 291, 306~310, 341~344, 350~353, 367
filial respect and obedience, 256
Filipinos, 149, 223, 267
Five Constant Virtues, 343
forms of elder respect, 47, 55~58, 64, 133~135, 140, 141, 149~151, 154~159, 182, 186~190, 198, 200, 204, 207, 209, 222~224, 228~233, 266~268, 272, 273, 275, 276
funeral respect, 56, 225, 229, 272
gestures and manners, 56, 149, 294, 303
gift respect, 47, 133, 136, 139, 140, 141, 149, 157, 182, 191, 204, 224, 225
harmonious moral relationship, 35
health care ethics, 93, 97
honorable status, 165
honorific language, 152, 213, 219, 225
human emotion, 318
humanistic traits, 82
Ihsan, 358
injunction to honor parents, 321
institutional respect, 27, 28, 42
intergenerational relations, 196, 229, 233, 237, 238, 242, 248, 306
Islamic teachings, xviii, 313, 355
Japanese American, 121, 122, 129
Jewish principles, 321
Judaism, 118, 320, 321, 329, 335, 338
Judeo-Christian moral heritage, 316
Kantian ethics, 91, 92
Kantian respect, 1, 33~37, 40
Kibud, 329, 330, 339
Korean elders, 122
language of individualism, 323
linguistic respect, 47, 48, 64, 131, 133, 136, 149, 153, 182, 183, 187, 191, 197, 201, 204, 224, 225, 229, 251, 269, 270, 271
love and concern, 106, 245, 248
love and respect, 23, 24, 217
malpractice, 89
medical education, v, 63, 66, 68
medical ethics, 69, 72, 77
medical norms, 77
medical obligations, 74
medical practice, (clinical practice), 66, 67, 73~76, 82~89
medical profession, 70, 88
medical school, 82, 83
medicine in the social context, 67
Mexican American, 119, 120, 128, 162
minority elders, 123
mistreatment of the elderly, 161, 352
Morah, 330
moral principle, 5, 15, 18, 19, 101, 106
moral worth, 30, 31, 33
multiple jeopardy, 281, 287
Muslim way, vii, 313
nonmaleficence, 63, 92, 96, 97, 323
nursing, codes for , 108
nursing, moral art of, 107
nursing, primary obligation of, 92
nursing education, 106
nursing ethic, 63, 91, 101, 106, 107, 109, 256, 263
nursing practice, 97, 99, 103, 107
nursing profession, values of, 111
nursing scholars, 101,
nursing students, 108
obedience, 56, 149, 159, 203, 206, 216, 228, 241, 242, 246, 247, 256, 258, 272, 292, 294, 298, 300, 303, 304, 308, 318, 330~332, 335, 338, 344, 359
optimal health care, 84
parent-child relationship, 175, 358
passive deference, 171
patient autonomy, 73, 90, 92, 96
perceived respect, 106, 160, 162, 251, 276, 279, 281~289, 292, 303, 305
precedential respect, 48, 136, 140, 183, 191, 197, 202, 225, 229, 251, 269, 270, 271
presentational respect, 47, 48, 64, 131, 133, 136, 138, 149, 153, 182, 183, 191, 197, 201, 224, 225
principle of justice, 63
professional ethics, 103, 113
professional values, 103, 104, 106, 109, 258
public respect, 57, 135, 149, 158, 191, 195, 198~200, 204, 217, 219, 225, 227, 274
quality of life, 6, 61, 143, 210, 266, 277, 279
quantitative assessment, 280

rational will, 1, 8~11, 14, 18, 20, 21
recognition respect, 27~31, 43
religious ethics, xv, 352
respect and care, 1, 23, 24, 45, 63, 175,
    178, 179, 181, 205, 230, 274, 291,
    304, 313
respect for authority, 69
respect for autonomy, 63, 96
Respect for Elders Day, 218, 220, 227,
    231, 232, 275
respect for persons, 1, 5, 6, 7, 10~12,
    16~20, 23~32, 35, 36, 42, 43, 63, 66,
    67, 71~75, 94, 96~99, 102
Respect for the Aged Day, 214
respect for the patient, 63
salutatory respect, 48, 64, 131, 136, 138,
    149, 153, 183, 191, 197, 202, 225,
    229, 251, 269, 270, 271
self-respect, 104, 109, 116, 117, 257,
    279, 288
senicide, 46, 313, 315, 318, 320, 323
service deference, 170, 172
Singaporean, 238, 240, 248, 297, 298,
    299, 300, 302, 303
social work setting, 133, 135, 141
social workers' ethnic and cultural
    differences, 140, 141
social workers, 87, 131~141
social workers in public agencies, 134
social workers' attitudes and behaviors,
    133

social workers' views, 141
spatial respect, 47, 131, 133, 136, 138,
    149, 157, 182, 191, 197, 202, 224,
    225
supreme attitude of morality, 12
Sutra about the Deep Kindness of
    Parents, 341, 345
Taiwanese, 149, 223, 267, 296, 299,
    300, 302, 304
ten types of kindness, 345, 346
Thai, 295, 296, 297, 298, 299, 301, 302,
    304
theological perspective, 313
time-related changes in perceived
    respect, 286
tokens, 56, 294, 296, 298, 303
universal moral obligation, 255
universal respect for all persons, 92
value of persons, 34, 43
vertical relationship, 215
victual respect, 47, 133, 136, 139, 140,
    141, 149, 157, 182, 187, 191, 197,
    224, 225, 271
Western culture, xiv, 92, 247, 253, 257,
    260, 261, 266, 321
Western ethic, 319
Western heritage respecting filial
    morality, 322
younger generations, 147, 237, 238,
    246, 247, 248, 249, 301, 310, 315

About the Editors

Kyu-taik Sung graduated from the University of Michigan (M.S.W. & Ph.D.) and Seoul National University (B.A., M.A.). He was professor at Yonsei University, Michigan State University, and the University of Wisconsin-Madison. At the University of Southern California, he was the Frances Wu Chair Professor in the cross-cultural study of aging. He has written extensively on East Asian culture and aging. A large number of his articles have been published in major journals in the United States. Prof. Sung has also presented several keynote speeches at international conferences on aging. As visiting professor at the University of Michigan, he is involved in the study of elder respect in the human services setting, while exploring the ideological foundation for social interventions relevant to East Asian culture. He has received several awards for his research and writings on the modern way of filial piety. He has served as the president of The Korea Gerontological Society and Korean Academy of Social Welfare. He directs Elder Respect, Inc., which advocates the enhancement of respect for the elderly.

Bum Jung Kim serves as the associate director of the Center for Policy Research on Aging (CPRA) in the School of Public Affairs at the University of California at Los Angeles. He has directed several research projects, including "Social Security in the Latino Communities" and "Baby-boom Generation and its Aging" in collaboration with Dr. Fernando Torres-Gil, the director of CPRA and the acting dean of the School of Public Affairs, UCLA. His research covers topics such as long-term care, aging networks, immigration, the baby-boom generation, social security in minority communities, and elder care and respect. His writings have focused on cross-cultural differences in care for the aged. He explores changes taking place in elder care in different cultures based on his extensive knowledge of cross-cultural aspects of aging. His study extends to long-term care service delivery in South Korea and the United States. He served public agencies before joining UCLA. Mr. Kim graduated from Chung-Ang University (B.A.) and the University of Michigan (M.S.W.).